PREHISTORIC MESOAMERICA

PREHISTORIC MESOAMERICA

Richard E. W. Adams
THE UNIVERSITY OF TEXAS AT SAN ANTONIO

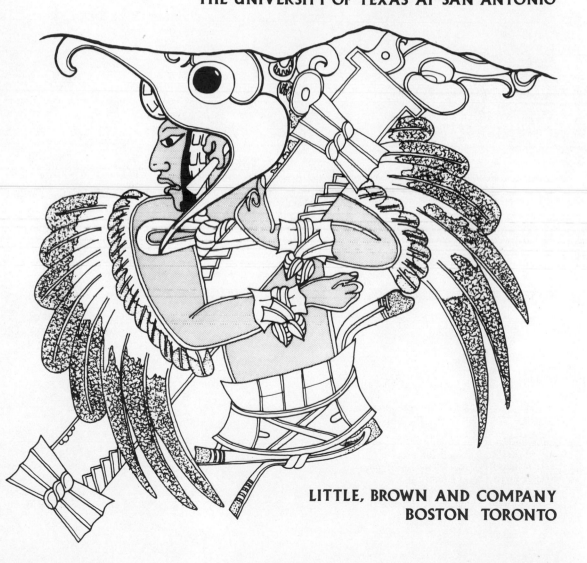

LITTLE, BROWN AND COMPANY
BOSTON TORONTO

For Joey 1966-1975

LIBRARY OF CONGRESS CATALOG CARD NO. 76-41615

ISBN 0-316-00890-7

10 9 8 7 6 5 4

HAL

Published simultaneously in Canada
by Little, Brown & Company (Canada) Limited

PRINTED IN THE UNITED STATES OF AMERICA

Book design: Clint Anglin
Art editor: Tonia Noell-Roberts
Art: Nancy Reid and Olivia Rodriguez
Master map: David Lindroth
Cover art: Olivia Rodriguez
Cover design: Tonia Noell-Roberts

Illustration Acknowledgments

R. Abascal, Davila, Schmidt, and de Davila from "La Arqueologia del Sur-Oeste de Tlaxcala," (primera parte) Supplemento, cover; VI 29

Richard E. W. Adams, pp. 2–3; I 2, 3, 5, 6, 8, 9, 10; II 3; IV 13; V 9, 11, 14, 21, 31, 32, 33, 47, 51, 56, 59, 61, 63, 64, 65, 74; pp. 188–189; VI 7, 8, 31, 43, 44

Courtesy of the American Museum of Natural History/Frank C. Graham, III 17; IV 16, 17, 19; V 7

Reprinted from *Archaeology*, Vol. 28, No. 2 © 1975, Archaeological Institute of America, VI 6

Betty Bell and Sociedad de Estudios Avanzados del Occidente de Mexico, III 2, 9

Margaret Bond I 15; II 12, 13, 20, 24; III 10, 11, 12, 20; pp. 78–79, 108–109; V 3, 10, 12, 16–19, 27, 28, 35, 52; VI 37, 38, 46, 48, 49

Brigham Young University Press, IV 21

Mary R. Bullard, V 29

Edward Calnek, II 6, 10

Courtesy of the Carnegie Institution of Washington, IV 24; V 45, 62; VI 23, 32

William R. Coe, IV 26; V 34

Benjamin N. Colby, I 4

T. Patrick Culbert (ed.) after figures 1 and 2, *The Classic Maya Collapse*, University of New Mexico Press, 1973, V 2

Jack D. Eaton, V 30

Permission of The Fine Arts Museums of San Francisco/Frank C. Graham, IV 14

Fondo de Cultura Economica after Codex Borgia, *Comentarios al Codice Borgia* by Eduardo Seler, II 9

By permission of Gebr. Mann Verlag from Nowotny, *Tlacuilolli*, II 15

Charles Gibson, after map 3 in *Aztecs Under Spanish Rule*, Stanford University Press, II 2

Frank C. Graham, I 7; pp. 22–23; II 4, 5, 7, 8, 14, 16–19, 21–23, 25–30; pp. 56–57; III 1, 3–8, 13–16, 17, 19, 21; IV 7, 9, 11, 12; pp. 136–137; V 5, 6, 8, 13, 22–26, 36–44, 46, 48–50, 53–58, 66–73; pp. 216–217; VI 4–6, 9–11, 14–22, 25–28, 30, 33–36, 39, 40; pp. 258–259, 296–297

Ford Green, II 11; V 4

David Grove, courtesy of Dumbarton Oaks Library, IV 20

Wynn Hammer, courtesy of Hasso von Winning, III 18

Dan Healan from *Studies of Ancient Tollan* by Richard A. Diehl, University of Missouri Press, VI 3

Robert F. Heizer, IV 2, 3, 4, 5, 6, 8, 10

Thomas R. Hester, VI 12

INAH Departamento de Promocion, II 3; VI 45

Ricardo Mata, by permission of the Peabody Museum, Harvard University, I 12

Arthur Miller, black and white print prepared from color, 1973, figure 167, V 10

Rene Millon, from Map 1, Millon, Drewitt, and Cowgill, *Urbanization at Teotihuacan, Mexico*, Vol. 1, 1973. © 1972 by Rene Millon. All rights reserved.

Museo Nacional de Antropologia, Mexico City, II 3, 4, 5, 8, 12, 13, 14, 16, 17–19, 21–30; III 1, 3, 4–8, 10–12, 15, 19–21; IV 9, 11, 12; V 5, 8, 12, 13; VI 37–40 (See also Richard E. W. Adams, Margaret Bond, Frank C. Graham)

Museum of the American Indian, Heye Foundation/Frank C. Graham, IV 27

Courtesy of New World Archaeological Foundation, Brigham Young University, IV 22, 23

John Paddock, reprinted from *Ancient Oaxaca: Discoveries in Mexican Archaeology and History*, John Paddock (ed.), with permission of the publishers, Stanford University Press. © 1966 by the Board of Trustees of the Leland Stanford Junior University, V 20

Courtesy of the Robert S. Peabody Foundation for Archaeology, Andover, Massachusetts, I 13, 14

Courtesy of the Peabody Museum, Harvard University, I 12/Ricardo Mata; IV 18; VI 13, 41

The University Museum, University of Pennsylvania, IV 25

Reproduced by permission of the Society of American Archaeology, *American Antiquity*, 24 (3), 1960, V 31; 27 (4), 1962, V 34; 37 (1), 1972, II 6, 10

Photo by Richard Stewart © National Geographic Society, IV 28

Antonio Tejeda, courtesy of Richard E. W. Adams, V 60, 62

Robert Wauchope(ed), *Handbook of the Middle American Indians*, by permission of the University of Texas Press, after map 1, page 461, Vol. 11 from article 19, "The Peoples of Central America and their Historical Traditions" by Pedro Carrasco, VI 1; after figure 36, page 757, Vol. 3, 1965 from the article "The Olmec Style and Its Distributions" by Michael D. Coe, IV 15; after figure 2, page 327, Vol. 10 from "Writing in Central Mexico" by Charles Dibble, VI 42; after map 1, page 660, Vol. 3, from article 26, "Lowland Maya Native Society at Spanish Contact" by Ralph Roys, VI 2

Douglas Schwartz, VI 24

Preface

IN EACH AGE MAN TRIES TO UNDERSTAND HIS past. In our own, as we accept the universality of man's cultural experience, we must also attempt to understand the past of cultures other than ours. This book is a synthesis of archaeological findings from Mexico and Guatemala and an interpretation of them. It is built on the work of predecessors who worked in the prehistoric past, 16th century chroniclers, and several generations of more contemporary scholars. It is up to the reader to judge how well I have succeeded in bringing together the findings of the past, and the success of my interpretation of these findings. My colleagues and predecessors have my gratitude, but I accept responsibility for any shortcomings of this book.

Thanks are due to Donald Brockington, Ronald Spores, David Grove, K. V. Flannery, Wigberto Jimenez-Moreno, Jacinto Quirarte, and all my colleagues not mentioned in the seminars on the origins and collapse of Maya civilization, sponsored by the School of American Research. I am deeply grateful to Douglas Schwartz, director of the School of American Research, for the exciting opportunities afforded to examine these questions. An intellectual debt is owed to G. R. Willey and W. T. Sanders, and the exchange of ideas with John Ingham benefited me greatly.

Critical appraisals made by Barbara Price, George Cowgill, Margaret Bond, and George Stuart have been very useful and stimulating, and all went beyond the call of duty in pointing out systemic and factual errors, as well as new information that should be added. If, at times, I have not taken their advice, the decision has not been lightly made. I am most grateful to them all. John Paddock carefully read Chapter 9 and wrote a detailed commentary on it. David Kelley performed the same valuable service for Chapter 10, and I thank them both. Of course, all the above share in any credit this book may receive.

Robert Heizer furnished badly needed photographs, Joseph Campbell kindly aided with the pronunciation guide, Clemency Coggins with a problem in hieroglyphs, and Frank Saul with a problem in physical anthropology. I thank them all. Special thanks go to Nancy Reid and Olivia Rodriguez, who prepared the finely drawn art, and to my excellent typist, Elizabeth Branch. Franklin Graham most generously provided many slides, and I am grateful.

As with any such book, this is the expression of an intellectual adventure. For me, the adventure has spanned thirty years, and perhaps will continue for as long again. Dr. Eduardo Noguera introduced me to field work in Mesoamerican archaeology, and to him I tender fond thanks. To E. M. Shook, Linton Satterthwaite, and W. R. Coe, who gave me my first Maya field experience, I am deeply obliged. E. A. Hoebel, R. S. Spencer, and Eldon Johnson at the University of Minnesota encouraged me in the beginning stages of this project, and I hope that the result does not disappoint them.

Finally, my wife and children sustained me in this, as in much else.

Contents

List of Illustrations

PREHISTORIC MESOAMERICA

CHAPTER 1

INTRODUCTION

There were writers from each branch of knowledge. Some composed the historical annals, setting in order the events that took place every year, stating the day, month, and hour. Others recorded the genealogies and descendants of the kings, lords, and personages of high lineage; they would make note of those who were born and cancel the dead. Others painted the limits, boundaries and border stones of the cities, provinces and villages, and of the fields and plantations, indicating their owners. Yet others made records of the laws, and the rites and ceremonies performed in pagan times. The priests made records regarding the temples of the idols, of their idolatrous doctrines and the feasts of their false gods and their calendars. And finally, there were philosophers and wise men among them who recorded in picture writing the sciences they were versed in.
—Ixtlilxochitl in Bernal, 1964: xxv.

These writings would have enlightened us considerably had not ignorant zeal destroyed them. Ignorant men ordered them burned, believing them idols, while actually they were history books worthy of being preserved instead of being buried in oblivion as was to occur.
—Duran, 1971: 396.

TEOPISCA ZONE, Maya house, Teopisca Zone, Chiapas; a Tzeltal Maya house, with cornfield in the foreground. The traveller driving in Southern Mexico and Guatemala can observe farming practices that resemble those of a thousand years ago.

THIS BOOK WAS WRITTEN TO FILL THE VOID created by the unfortunate loss of native records, but it also deals with matters that presumably were never thought of by native historians and philosophers of Mesoamerica. The goal is simple: to present an up-to-date, interpretative synthesis of Mesoamerican prehistory. It is intended for the student as well as for the curious person who has somehow become intrigued with the past native civilizations of Mexico, Guatemala, Belize, Honduras, and El Salvador.

This book has been organized to aid the reader in understanding those alien and destroyed cultures which form part of the New World's heritage. The people of the Valley of Mexico, usually and inaccurately grouped together as the Aztecs, were the Mesoamericans who claimed the attention of the Spaniards most forcefully. We shall thus begin with the Aztecs (or properly, the Mexica) to present a native civilization as it was seen in full tide and also to introduce in this more familiar context some of the archaeological and anthropological concepts on which presentation of the later material depends. In Chapter 3 we shall revert to more standard procedure and begin a sequential survey of development from earliest times up through the time of the Aztecs. The presentation is aimed not just at dusting off the ancient pots and pans, but at reconstructing ways of life and making functional interpretations based on archaeology. The reader should thus have an impression of the earlier cultures which will be akin to that given for the Aztecs, even if lacking in the wealth of historical events and personality.

This book, then, is an interpretation of the technical archaeological data. It is an interpretation which can be documented, however; it is not made of whole cloth. When there are theoretical alternatives, these will usually be indicated and discussed.

An appendix deals with technical matters of chronology, spatial divisions within Mesoamerica, and definitions of sociopolitical organization. These matters have been placed in a separate section in order not to disturb the flow of the book, but the student and professional will probably want to know, for example, the bases on which I have categorized the Early Classic Maya and the Preclassic Olmec as "pristine states."

Several themes run through the book: (1) The native civilizations of Mesoamerica are worth knowing about not just because they are exotic examples of human behavior, but because their historical and cultural experiences are worth considering. They faced universal problems of human existence and either solved them or failed. We can learn from their successes and failures, if we will. (2) Mesoamerica was a sphere of cultural interaction. Part of what made civilization possible was the interaction among the diverse cultures that flourished there. The varieties of culture and their interrelationships through time and space are fascinating, and involve not only economics and militarism, but also religion and ideology; interaction took place along all of these lines. Occasionally personality and character break through the flow of historical process, especially where we can read some of the texts left us in native writing systems. (3) Civilization, in the sense of complexity and sophistication of development, was in the main an elite-class phenomenon. (4) There are continuities between the deep past and the Indian cultures of the colonial and modern worlds. Much that we see in Mexico and Guatemala today is related to the historic past, although the ties are usually unrecognized. The richness and diversity of the native cultures of Mesoamerica are attractive to us of the West, if only because they document the endless variety of forms in which man's behavior, society, and artifacts occur. I hope that the reader can gain an understanding of some of the native cultural experience and thereby also better understand that of our own tradition.

A BRIEF HISTORY OF MESOAMERICAN STUDIES

As varied as is the subject matter of this book, the sources of information are, if anything, even more various and colorful. The history of Mesoamerican studies might be formally divided into five periods.

The first period is that of the Spanish conquest and immediate aftermath of approximately fifty years, 1519–1570. Hernan Cortes himself wrote five famous and lengthy letters to Charles V reporting on the progress of the exploration and conquest of Mexico (Cortes, 1963), and many others did the same over the next forty years or so. Francisco de Montejo, conqueror of Yucatan, wrote official reports and documents, for example (in Chamberlin, 1948). Several conquerors wrote memoirs, the most famous being Bernal Diaz del Castillo's account (1968). Cortes evidently dictated his autobiography and story of the conquest to his chaplain, Francisco Lopez de Gomara (1964). Even the "Anonymous Conqueror" left us his tale (1917). All of these personal and eyewitness stories have substantial quantities of information on native life and civilization in them, although they are often frustratingly vague and are also frustratingly spotty in distribution.

Formal compilations of information were begun shortly after the conquest by Father Andres Olmos, who set the standards for the later chroniclers. Olmos developed the system of collecting all of the native books available to him, having them translated, and supplementing them by systematic interviews of persons of high and low estate who had lived before the conquest. Unfortunately, Olmos' account is lost, but Father Bernardino de Sahagun followed the same research methods as did many other illustrious writers, including Landa, Duran, Burgoa, Ixtlilxochitl, Tezozomoc, and, much later, Boturini. In a sense, all of these men were doing ethnology and ethnohistory, using participant observation when possible and documents where they existed. Diego Duran grew up in Texcoco across the lake from Aztec Tenochtitlan, and in the days of his youth there were many Aztec buildings still in use or at least visible. All of these priests wrote to provide guides to aid in the conversion and further instruction of the Indians, and to guard against unrecognized heresy. The Spanish bureaucracy provided much information on the working of native society, especially that of the Aztecs, since they found these data to be of practical administrative use. The first viceroy of New Spain (Mexico), Antonio de Mendoza, had the *Codex Mendoza* compiled as a guide to the amounts of tribute that the Aztecs had received from their conquered vassals and what the Spaniards therefore might reasonably expect.

A series of documents that fall into this and later periods are those written by natives, or *mestizos,* who, having taken an interest in their own origins and illustrious pasts, gathered as much information as they could. Many of these documents are written in native languages. Some of them are frankly attempts to save knowledge and information that the Spanish would not have approved of, being ritually important and definitely non-Christian. The *Popol Vuh* (1971), *Rabinal Achi* (Carmack, 1973), and the books of *Chilam Balam* (1967) are all examples of this category. Many are also self-serving in the sense that they are attempts at bolstering the social and economic statuses of survivors of the native elites. Withal, and despite the chaotic nature of the material and the difficulties, these documents make up an immense treasurehouse of information which grows in value each year as it is confirmed, elucidated, or amplified by further historical and archaeological work.

A second period might be defined as from 1570 to 1790. The documentary data from this period include not only some from the above categories, but also more formal administrative questionnaires. These questionnaires are known generally as the *Relaciones Geograficas* (reviewed in HMAI, 12). There are two main sets, the best being the earliest and dating from 1578 to 1580. The second set dates from the dying days of the Spanish Empire, 1742–1792, and is much less complete. Supplemented with accounts of ecclesiastical visits by bishops to native towns (for example, Father Cortes y Larraz of Guatemala), native lawsuit records (for example, the Mapa de Teozacoalco from Oaxaca), and miscellaneous papers, the last 200 years of Spanish colonial rule produced a remarkable amount of information, in spite of being further removed in time from the native cultures with which they deal.

Toward the end of the Spanish colonial era, the third period of Mesoamerican studies began — that of exploration, broad scholarly participation from several fields and individuals, and awakened national interest in the various former colonies. Antonio del Rio and Guillelmo Dupaix were Spanish army officers commissioned to investigate the reports of ruins in Mexico. Del Rio went to the newly discovered ruins of Palenque in 1787 and his report was published in 1822, stimulating further exploration. Dupaix, a retired Royal Dragoons officer, made a good first survey of some of the major archaeological sites in Mexico. By roundabout circumstances, his report was published in the Kingsborough volumes, which appeared from 1830 to 1848 (Brunhouse, 1974).

As the Spanish empire crumbled, and as the former colonies achieved independent national status, they came more and more into contact with the outside world. After centuries of purposeful isolation from non-Spanish Europe, suddenly the remarkable features of the Americas became available. The first activity stimulated by these curiosities created collections of documents. An Englishman, Lord Kingsborough, beggared himself in collecting and publishing many of these materials in a hand-colored edition.

Scarcely a generation after the achievement of independence came the fourth period of scholarship, led by a remarkable group of historians (Cline, 1973). They revived the tradition of document collection and comparative studies which had lapsed after the sixteenth century. Jose Ramirez, Joaquin Icazbalceta, Alfredo Chavero, and Francisco Paso y Troncoso all made collections of immense historical value during the nineteenth century. Manuel Orozco y Berra, however, was the principal person to attempt to apply the newly developed sophistication in historiography to these collections, and his *Historia Antigua* is a noteworthy achievement. He attempted a first synthesis of what was known about the pre-Columbian cultures as part of this magnum opus. These collections, explorations, and the resultant studies of the natural and cultural wonders of the Americas stimulated a series of more systematic explorations which led directly to the development of present-day Mesoamerican archaeology.

The first great explorers were John Lloyd Stephens, a New York lawyer, and his colleague, Frederick Catherwood, an English architect. These men explored the Maya lowlands and, with Catherwood's superb drawings, presented an extraordinarily accurate picture of a largely unrecorded ancient civilization. They published their travels in four volumes which were best-sellers for their day — 1841 and 1843 (Stephens, 1949, 1963).

Teobert Maler worked in Guatemala and Yucatan for the Peabody Museum of Harvard University in the late nineteenth century, recording ruins and texts by photography and producing a series of excellently illustrated volumes (Wauchope, 1965). A. P. Maudslay's monumental archaeological supplement to a giant English work on the biology of Central America concentrated again on the Maya area. Brasseur de Bourbourg discovered many native language texts, including the *Popol Vuh* (Mace, 1973). W. W. Holmes, an American anthropologist, traveled through most of Mexico and northern Yucatan in the 1890s making accurate drawings and descriptions of the ruins. Leopoldo Batres, an official in charge of antiquities under Diaz, did the first excavation at Teotihuacan in preparation for the celebration of the Mexican centennial of independence from Spain. However, the quality of his work is better left uncommented on, especially when compared with others of the period. Desire Charnay traveled extensively and dug occasionally into such places as Tula and Teotihuacan in the 1870s and 1880s and also produced a well-illustrated book.

None of the above explorers were trained archaeologists; indeed, there was hardly such a profession as archaeology yet in existence. Certainly none of them had available the kinds of historical and ethnohistorical information which are routinely consulted today. Most of that data lay undiscovered and untranslated in archives, in private collections scattered over Europe, in obscure Latin American parish churches, and in other places equally difficult of access. The Mexican historians had started to publish some of the documents, and Kingsborough earlier had put a great deal (somewhat inaccurately, alas) into print. It remained for the great Eduard Seler to begin the systematic comparative studies of chronicles, native documents, and archaeological remains. Stephens had made a start in this direction, but Seler, with his intense and profound scholarship, was able to produce a magnificent series of commentaries on the religious picture manuscripts of the Borgia group from central Mexico. He ex-

plained the divinatory purposes of the native calendars and other complexities of native civilizations (Nicholson, 1973). At about the same time (late nineteenth and early twentieth centuries) Ernst Förstemann, J. T. Goodman, and Charles Bowditch were independently working out the basic features of the Maya arithmetical and calendrical system (Thompson, 1950). Indeed, much of the exploration done during the early twentieth century was directly stimulated by the need to record more texts and sculptures in aid of this decipherment work.

Archaeology, developed as part of the physical and natural sciences in Europe and as part of anthropology in the United States, became a field of study in its own right. At the point during the early twentieth century when all of these traditions began to combine into a coherent focus on native cultures, both prehistoric and ethnographic, Mesoamerican studies as such came into being. If one has to pick a date at which archaeology began to assume its modern form as a part of this intellectual development, 1910 is a likely selection. Seler, together with Alfred Tozzer of Harvard and Franz Boas of Columbia University, founded the School of American Studies in Mexico City in 1908, with Seler as its first director. Boas, the great founder of modern anthropology, became director in 1910, and recruited Manuel Gamio as his associate.

Gamio had already done extensive excavation in the sites around the Valley of Mexico, but, in the style of the time, it was more in the nature of digging for things rather than for information. In 1910, probably under Boas' influence, he suddenly began to dig by metric stratigraphy, thus introducing a fundamental field method into New World archaeology and also setting up a ceramic sequence for the Valley of Mexico. Gamio already had intellectual ties with the Mexican historical tradition through his chief, Nicolas Leon,

Director of the National Museum, who had been a member of the group of nineteenth-century Mexican historians mentioned above. He continued to prepare himself through graduate studies at Columbia, and then returned to Mexico to put into practice one of the most far-reaching plans for integrated anthropological research ever conceived. He proposed to study every aspect of several major regions of Mexico.

The Teotihuacan Valley was the first region to be selected, and a government project began in 1917 with Gamio as director. The project's breadth of conception is amazing for its time, and comprehended ethnographic studies of the modern populations, historical studies of the colonial period, and archaeological studies of the prehistoric past. These were supplemented with geological and geographical projects. Gamio's work was interrupted by personal political troubles, and after he returned to Mexico in 1929 his interest was concentrated on problems of integration of modern Indian populations into the national fabric, and remained so until the end of his life. He had shown the way, however, in prehistoric studies.

In the Maya area, about the same time (from about 1908 until 1914), S. G. Morley was working under various auspices, recording Maya glyphs. In 1914, Morley persuaded the Carnegie Institution of Washington to undertake a long-term program of intensive research that would deal with selected sites from all known periods. From 1914 until 1958, when the program was abruptly abolished, the Carnegie group, led by A. V. Kidder, Sr., worked at many Maya lowland and highland sites in Guatemala, Mexico, and Honduras, establishing the basic outlines of Maya prehistory and providing the critical mass of data needed to begin to attack the most sophisticated questions (Adams, 1969). The Carnegie group produced a monumental series of publications, packed with data and with excellent illustrations. Their standards of scholarship and of field techniques were very high.

Kidder was by then perhaps the preeminent person in archaeology and an innovator in field excavation techniques developed in his work at Pecos in the United States Southwest. He carried these methods into the Maya area and developed them further. His ability to synthesize and to carefully, if conservatively, theorize on the meanings of the data were a great part of his scholarly strength (Willey, 1967).

Alfonso Caso began his remarkable professional life in 1927 and continued his active scholarship until his death in 1970. His amazing luck, combined with a powerful intellect and a gift for lucid analysis and writing, made him outstanding in his field. Caso focused early on the Valley of Oaxaca, and began work at Monte Alban near Oaxaca City early in the 1930s. His concurrent studies in calendrical matters carried on the momentum built up by Seler in the decipherment of writing systems. To round off his career, he produced a remarkable series of commentaries on the historical-genealogical books of the Mixtec. Caso and Gamio were the founders of modern anthropology in Mexico, and their intellectual descendants carry on today. Likewise, the Carnegie group in the Maya area formed a tradition which has influenced workers coming afterward in that field.

The work of George Vaillant in the Maya lowlands and later in the Valley of Mexico was of great importance in establishing basic chronologies. Indeed, during the 1930s and 1940s, the major issues of Mesoamerican archaeology were largely tied up with time-space relationships. Vaillant, however, was somewhat ahead of his time: he was willing to wring data for more implications than most of his contemporaries. His gift for large-scale synthesis and his almost poetic feeling for the ancient cultures of Mexico are nowhere better shown than in his book, *Aztecs of Mexico* (1941). Vaillant, with Matthew W. Stirling, Alfonso Caso, and Miguel Covarrubias, was one of the first to recognize the importance of the series of finds on the Gulf Coast and in the central highlands which ultimately were shown to be traces of the earliest civilization in Mesoamerica, that of the Olmec. His tragic death in 1945 cut short what would have undoubtedly been further contributions.

In the fifth and most recent period of Mesoamerican studies, integration of the various fields seems finally to be taking form. Since about 1960 it has become evident that the new generations of field workers are not satisfied with simply sorting things out in terms of time and space, but also demand that data be collected and interpreted to deal with whole societies. Culture process — the study of cultural change — has become the major objective of research in this area. More sophisticated theory derived from cultural ecology, general systems theory, comparative history, and general anthropology has stimulated interpretations which are testable in the scientific sense. A certain daring and willingness to hypothesize from data is more evident in this younger group.

Present-day Mesoamericanists are perhaps a much more heterogeneous group than before. From a field largely dominated by Mexican and United States scholars from a few institutions, the effort has become one enlisting many researchers from United States state universities as well as from Ivy League schools. Further, the Mexican national effort has deepened in numbers of people involved and the sophistication of their training. French, German, and English research groups have appeared and are making significant contributions. Theoretical systems such as cultural ecology, and field techniques such as settle-

ment pattern studies, have taken hold of the whole field. The Selerian tradition continues, as does the Mexican ethnohistorical school of studies, but these are now much more integrated into other branches of scholarship.

As will be seen, we have not yet, and likely never will, achieve a completely satisfactory understanding of Mesoamerican prehistory. The work of our illustrious predecessors who pioneered in the field has made it possible for us to set up and test complex models of social, historical, and ecological dynamics by amassing the vast amounts of requisite information. The field continues to develop in a quantum manner. Partly by necessity, as much work has been done in the past thirty years as was done in the preceding hundred. Archaeological data is unique and limited and is being rapidly destroyed by the "ignorant zeal," not of religious enthusiasts this time, but of zealots of development and aesthetic admirers. The archaeologist today engages in a desperate race with bulldozer, dam-builder, and antiquity hunter to retrieve and record the ever-shrinking data which will aid in understanding the unique civilizations that developed in Mesoamerica.

GEOGRAPHY

One of the most formidable barriers to understanding the Mesoamerican past is the names, which at first glance may seem bizarre and unintelligible, let alone forgettable. Frequent reference to the maps can help. Many centers or regions had similar or identical names. Some of this confusion comes from the fact that many names are descriptive. For example, Chapultepec means "Grasshopper Hill." A very important late Mixtec center in coastal Oaxaca was named Tututepec. But there was also the Huastec center of Tututepec far to the north in Hidalgo. Both names mean "Hill of the Bird." To further complicate matters, during the sixteenth century many non-Aztec place names were translated into Nahuatl, creating a more apparent uniformity than was really the case. Tututepec's Mixtec name was originally *Yucu dzaa,* which means the same thing: Hill of the Bird. Historical charisma was another reason for duplication of names. The great Toltec center of Tula was commemorated by having its name applied to a number of smaller and usually less important places. The matter is more than a technicality. The cultural differences among places of the same name were often as great as those which exist between Paris, France, and Paris, Texas.

The geographical features of each major cultural area will be discussed as we explore each area in the text. However, there are some general features that are important aids to understanding the ecological stage on which the Mesoamerican drama was played out. The modern nation-states of Mexico, Guatemala, Honduras and El Salvador, and the commonwealth country of Belize occupy the space once controlled by various native high cultures. Mesoamerica is thus a culturally defined area; its distinctive features are outlined below. The northern border is roughly at the Sinaloa River in the northwest and the Soto la Marina River in the northeast, with a dip in the middle to exclude the central deserts of Chihuahua, Nuevo Leon, and Coahuila. This desert zone was known to ancient Mesoamericans as the Gran Chichimeca, and civilized life existed only fitfully and fragilely in it. The southern frontier runs from the mouth of the Ulua River in Honduras, angling south in Salvador, to end at the Gulf of Fonseca on the Pacific Coast. These borders between them frame an area of about 1,015,280 square kilometers or 392,000 square miles. The borders fluctuated through time, and the frontiers given here represent the maximum extensions of Mesoamerican culture.

Extraordinary diversity compressed into a relatively small space characterizes Mesoamerica. The surface configuration is broken up by the great mountain ranges which are part of the circum-Pacific volcanic ranges. The resulting compartmentalization of ecology has caused complex patterns of climate, vegetation, and animal life. Robert West notes that rainfall and altitude are the most crucial factors in determining the kind of climate of any single region (1964). All of this diversity, both ecological and cultural, can generally be organized into two polarities — highland and lowland. However, as Sanders and Price have pointed out, zones from both of these categories were often economically combined into what can be called symbiotic regions (1968). The compressed ecological diversity of Mesoamerica allowed cultural evolution to take place, but cultural forms were needed to organize Mesoamerica in order to realize the maximum potential achieved. Interaction among cultures adapted to very different ecological areas is a constant and recurring phenomenon in Mesoamerican prehistory.

The following are the major cultural areas of Mesoamerica; they are both major physiographic zones and the centers of development of major cultural patterns.

1. The Northeast: the Huasteca.
2. The Northwest Frontier.
3. Western Mexico.
4. Mesa Central: the Basin of Mexico, and the surrounding Valleys of Morelos, Puebla, and Toluca.
5. Puebla-Oaxaca Highlands.
6. Oaxaca, Central Valley, and Pacific Coast.
7. The Isthmian zone: Gulf Coast Veracruz, Tehuantepec Isthmus, and the Guatemalan Pacific Plain.
8. The Maya lowlands.
9. The Maya highlands: Chiapas and Guatemala.

MESOAMERICA AS A CULTURAL CONCEPT

Walter Lehmann in the 1920s and Paul Kirchhoff in 1943 developed the concept of Mesoamerica as a large area of interaction with a basic cultural unity. These scholars depended heavily on historical and ethnographic traits in their definitions. Later, Gordon R. Willey, Rene Millon, and Gordon Ekholm reworked their concept to make it operational for archaeology (1964). In turn, I have made adjustments in definition to take account of the latest research.

Basic agricultural technologies tended to be extensive in the tropical lowlands and intensive in the highlands. This distinction blurred in periods of high population density, however, when intensive agriculture was practiced in both sorts of zones. Regional crop lists always included varieties of corn (maize), squashes, and beans, but varied wildly in regional plants such as cacao, avocados, tropical fruits, and many sorts of vegetables. Settlement patterns tended to conform to these differing subsistence systems — dispersed in the lowlands and nucleated in the highlands — but, again, this distinction was a matter of degree, as will be seen in the discussion of varieties of urbanism in the final chapter.

Stone Age technologies were common to all Mesoamerican cultures. New World cultures lacked the wheel and many useful domesticated animals, and did not use the true arch. Metal was not ordinarily used for utilitarian purposes. Movement of goods and people was largely by canoe or by foot.

Organization of society and economy centered on the agricultural village. Aristocratic leadership controlled all affairs of import through civil servants. Merchants, warriors, and artisans formed special social classes ranking above the main class of farmer-laborers. Temple centers in both highlands and lowlands functioned as headquarters for the elite and bureaucratic classes, both initially and later when the centers had been transformed into varieties of urban communities. Market systems were integrated with the various population centers and furnished the sinews binding together the symbiotic regions. The dispersed and nucleated towns, cities, and metropolises all were built of stone, plaster, and mortar. A variety of architectonic forms were expressed in these materials, and they were decorated with art styles which were intimately connected with the elite classes. Other manifestations of hieratic art appeared in elaborate pottery, murals, sculpture, and jewelry. After the establishment of state-level organizations, the city-state was the basic and stable unit, combinations of which made up the larger political structures of kingdom and empire.

Intellectually, there were certain cross-cutting philosophical and religious principles. One set was bound up with the fatalistic cosmologies of the Mesoamericans. Man lived in a hostile world with capricious gods. Mathematics, hieroglyphic writing systems, astronomy, and calendrical systems were all tied up with these philosophical tenets. Two ritual games were widely played, the ball game and the *volador* ceremony. Both still survive in isolated regions.

Regional diversities existed within these and other characteristics which bound Mesoamerica together. Willey has characterized Mesoamerica as a vast diffusion sphere. That is to say, whatever happened of importance in one area sooner or later had some effect on most of the rest of the areas.

PREHISTORIC DEVELOPMENT. Let us now quickly survey the main features of Mesoamerican prehistory by stages of development. These stages will be used in organizing the material in each of the following chapters. Again, we refer to Willey, Millon, and Ekholm's synthesis (1964).

Lithic.   Man filtered into the New World as an immigrant in an Upper Paleolithic state of culture and gradually developed a radically distinctive set of New World variations. The earliest certain settlers in Mesoamerica date about 11,000 B.C., but possibly there were people there as early as 40,000 years ago.

Incipient Agriculture (7000–1500 B.C.).   Transitions from hunting and gathering life took place during this stage, and agricultural village societies were established all over Mesoamerica by 1500 B.C. The major events were the beginning of sedentary life based on agriculture and all of the consequences of that shift.

Preclassic (1500 B.C.–A.D. 300).   Development of most of the early civilizations is based on cultural elaboration that took place during these 1800 years. The Olmec seem to have been the earliest florescence and appear near the beginning of the period. By A.D. 300 most of the features defining Mesoamerica and distinguishing it from North and Central American cultural areas were in existence.

Protoclassic (ca. A.D. 1–A.D. 300).   In certain selected regions of Mesoamerica precocious developments lead to what is called the Protoclassic. In most ways these cultures are distinguished from the following Classic cultures in only three ways: (1) in their artistic styles, obviously transitional between late Preclassic and Classic cultures; (2) in their appearance earlier than most Classic cultures; and (3) in

their contemporaneity with late Preclassic cultures. Generally, the concept of the Protoclassic has only been used in the Maya area, but it might also be useful in areas such as the Valley of Mexico.

Classic (A.D. 300 to A.D. 650/900).   Rise in populations and development of elaborate social organizations led to the highly developed culture of the Classic stage. The ending date is strictly dependent on the area with which one deals. Tendencies started in Preclassic cultures came to fruition in exotic variety during the Classic stage.

Postclassic (A.D. 650/900 to A.D. 1250).   The reformulation of regional cultures after the collapse of most Classic cultures in Mesoamerica was the major feature. More standardized and secularized forms of states seem to appear.

Protohistoric (A.D. 1250–A.D. 1519).   Essentially, this is the stage of culmination of the reformulated cultures put together in the preceding period. For this period we also have historical and native documents as well as eyewitness reports.

The above schema frame the subject matter in terms of time, space, and content. We shall now turn to the Aztecs as they were seen at the time of the Spanish conquest, as an example of developed Mesoamerican civilization in full tide.

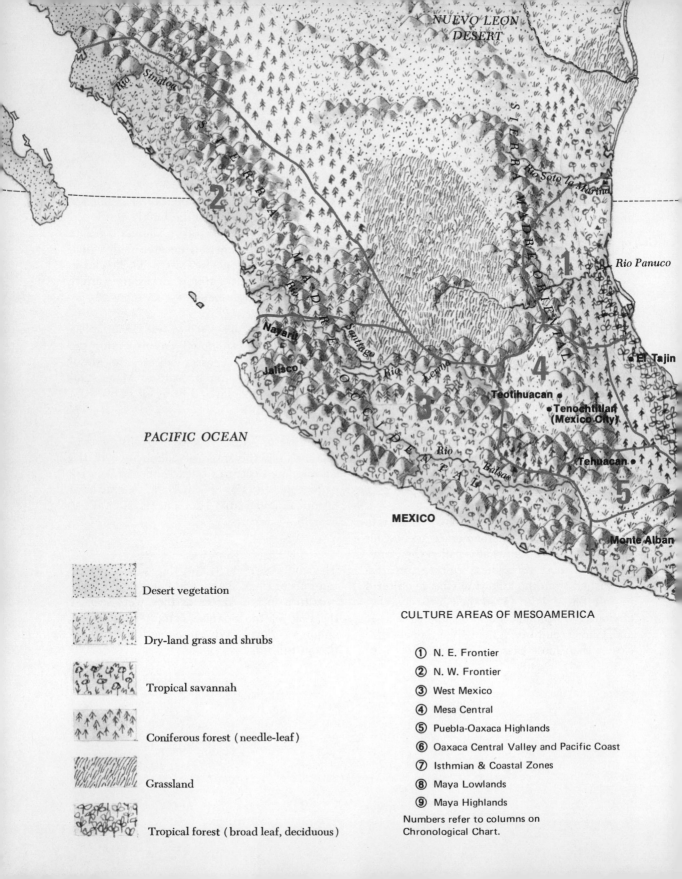

NUEVO LEON
DESERT

Rio Sinaloa

SIERRA MADRE OCCIDENTAL

2

SIERRA MADRE ORIENTAL

Rio Soto la Marina

1

Rio Panuco

Rio Santiago

Nayarit

Rio Lerma

4

• El Tajin

Jalisco

3

Teotihuacan •

• Tenochtitlan
(Mexico City)

PACIFIC OCEAN

Rio Balsas

Tehuacan •

5

MEXICO

Monte Alban

Desert vegetation

Dry-land grass and shrubs

Tropical savannah

Coniferous forest (needle-leaf)

Grassland

Tropical forest (broad leaf, deciduous)

CULTURE AREAS OF MESOAMERICA

① N. E. Frontier

② N. W. Frontier

③ West Mexico

④ Mesa Central

⑤ Puebla-Oaxaca Highlands

⑥ Oaxaca Central Valley and Pacific Coast

⑦ Isthmian & Coastal Zones

⑧ Maya Lowlands

⑨ Maya Highlands

Numbers refer to columns on
Chronological Chart.

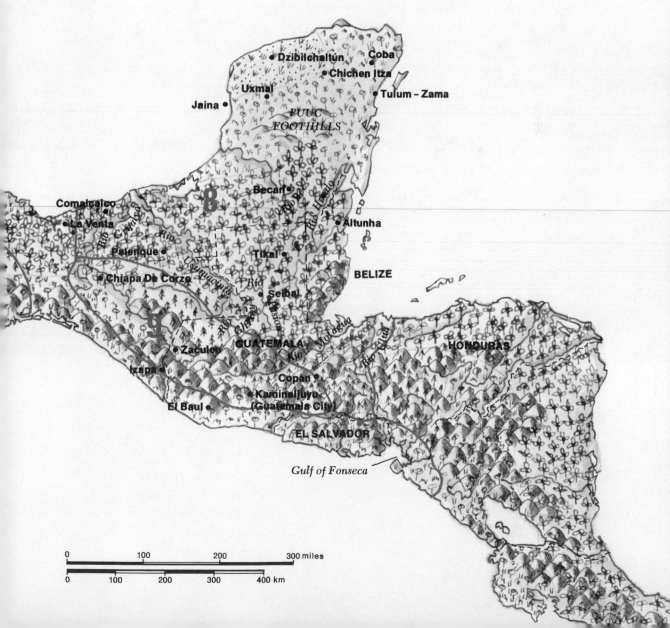

Geography and the Past in Mesoamerica. *The intimate relationship between man and the diverse ecological environments in Mesoamerica gave rise to diverse cultures. Great ecological differences are reflections of distinctive rainfall patterns, growing seasons, soil conditions, and crops. Continuous interaction between these geographical compartments (1) is a theme central to the area's prehistory.*

Gulf of Mexico

Dzibilchaltún

Coba

Chichen Itza

Uxmal

Tulum – Zama

Jaina

PUUC
FOOTHILLS

Becan

Comalcalco

Río Hondo

Altunha

La Venta

Río Candela

Río

Palenque

Usumacinta

Tikal

BELIZE

Chiapa De Corze

Río

Río de la Pasion

Seibal

GUATEMALA

Río Chixoy

Río Motagua

Zaculeu

Río

Río Ulúa

HONDURAS

Izapa

Copan

Kaminaljuyu
(Guatemala City)

El Baul

EL SALVADOR

Gulf of Fonseca

0		100		200		300 miles

0	100	200	300	400 km

2 △

▽ 3

The Valley of Oaxaca (2) is one of many fertile highland basins in Mesoamerica. Intensely cultivated since 1500 B.C. or earlier, the Maya highlands show the geographic variation within one region. The Sacatepequez fault zone (3) contrasts with the haystack hills of Alta Verapaz (5) and the volcano rimmed lake of Atitlan (7). People have adapted to their environment in agriculture (4) as well as in housing (6).

4 △

▽ 5

▽ 7

6 ▽

8△

9△   ▽ 10

In the highlands, rich volcanic soil and plentiful water made high-density population possible from early times. The lowlands, however, presented different problems for agriculture-based societies. Lowlands such as those surrounding Altar de Sacrificios (11) and Kohunlich (9) were rich in forest products but difficult to cultivate intensively, partly because of poor soils and high rainfall. Where rivers were absent, as in northern Yucatan, water was, and still is, obtained from cenotes. This sinkhole at Chichen Itza (10), however, was apparently too steep-sided and consequently was used for ritual purposes only.

Throughout this patchwork of environments, archaeologists daily encounter the inheritors of the land in such places as highland Mexican corn fields (7, 8) and unearth the past in excavations such as that of Altar de Sacrificios (12).

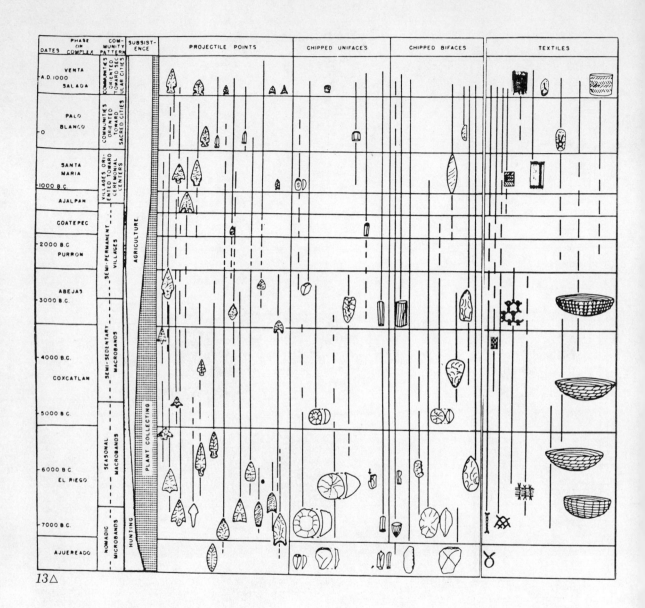

DATES	PHASE OR COMPLEX	COM-MUNITY PATTERN	SUBSIST-ENCE	PROJECTILE POINTS	CHIPPED UNIFACES	CHIPPED BIFACES	TEXTILES

13△

Richard MacNeish's reconstruction of the changing material technology of the Tehuacan · Valley (13) dramatically illustrates the evolution from hunting and gathering cultures to agricultural village societies. This happened in Mesoamerica many times with many variations. The biological evolution of maize, its increase in size and quality through human intervention (14), was a process many plants underwent. Mesoamerican culture ultimately rested upon a richly diverse food complex of domesticated plants. Many of these plants were processed by grinding on a metate with a mano (15). Wherever an archaeologist encounters a site, these basic food preparation tools are almost certain to be found.

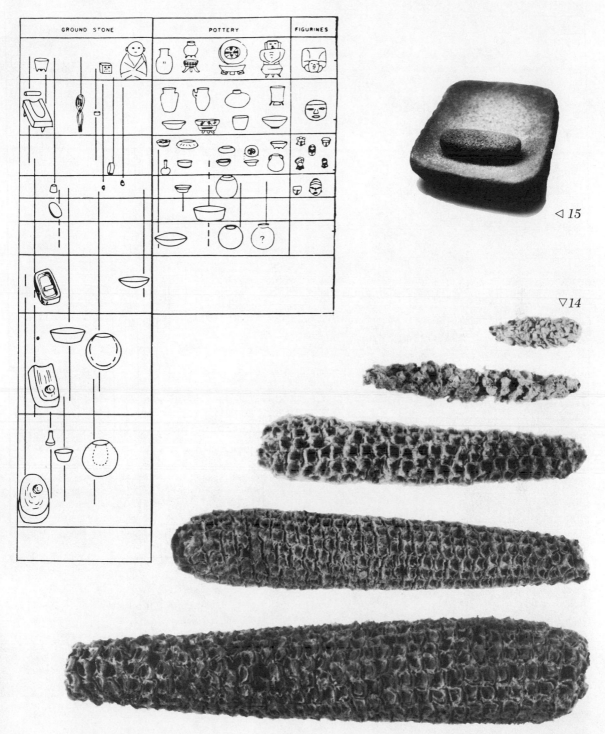

GROUND STONE			POTTERY				FIGURINES

◁ 15

▽ 14

CHAPTER 2

THE AZTEC

We welcome you
To this city of Mexico Tenochtitlan
Which is in the great pool of water,
Where the eagle sang and the snake hissed!
Where the fishes fly,
Where the blue waters came out to join
  the red waters!
—Priests' address to captives of Tepeaca being led
  into the city of Mexico, in Duran, 1964: 101.

Coming to what all of us saw in this country, a
thing that amazed us was the number of people
found here. This was observed by the Spaniards
who came early to this country, before the great
plague.
—Duran, 1964: 4.

Then Montezuma took Cortés by the hand and
told him to look at his great city and all the other
cities that were standing in the water and the
many other towns and the land around the lake.
. . . So we stood looking about us, for that huge
and cursed temple stood so high that from it one
could see over every thing very well, and we
saw the three causeways which led into Mexico
. . . and we saw the [acqueduct of] fresh water
that comes from Chapultepec, which supplies
the city and we saw the bridges on the three
causeways which were built at certain distances
apart . . . and we beheld on the lake a great
multitude of canoes, some coming with supplies
of food, others returning loaded with cargoes of
merchandise, and we saw that from every house
of that great city and of all the other cities that
were built in the water it was impossible to pass
from house to house except by drawbridges,
which were made of wood, or in canoes; and we
saw in those cities Cues [temples] and oratories
like towers and fortresses and all gleaming white,
and it was a wonderful thing to behold!
—Bernal Diaz del Castillo, 1968: 218.

MITLA, Valley of Oaxaca. The Zapotec-Mixtec ceremonial center is a reminder of the fate of native religious centers under Spanish rule. Like Tenochtitlan, now obliterated beneath the streets of Mexico City, Mitla also was occupied by the Spanish who built their religious edifices directly on top of the earlier architecture. In this way, Catholic ritual melded with that of the native cultures, even to the extent of capitalizing upon the native belief that the ground of certain places was holy and sacred.

THE WONDERFUL CAPITAL CITY OF THE Aztecs is gone. It disappeared in 1521 in an agonizingly brutal Spanish siege of ninety-one days during which the canals were filled up with the demolished remains of its inhabitants' houses. This was done to open large areas for cavalry operations and fields of fire for the artillery. At the end of the siege the city was a scorched, battered zone with some areas of low one-story houses left and the fire-marred remains of the larger public buildings. Even these were not allowed to remain, but disappeared rapidly after the conquest to be used in building the new colonial capital.

The inhabitants of the city were much reduced in number. Many were buried in the ruins of the old city, and the few who remained and the many more Indians from other cities of the valley were impressed into building a new colonial capital. In so doing, they were forced to systematically dismantle the remains of Tenochtitlan. The public buildings of the Aztecs were not only unsuitable for the new social structure and administration, but were looked on as positively demonic in their associations with the pagan religion. The Spaniards had no interest in preserving the ruins, certainly not the hated remains of the great temple and other buildings where so many of them had died in combat or had been sacrificed to the Aztec deities after capture. Although the city itself is gone, there are two means by which we can reconstruct a picture of the Aztec capital and Aztec culture. One way is through documents written in the early sixteenth century.

The sixteenth century was one of rebuilding of the city of Mexico, but it also was one in which the Church saved and converted thousands of souls daily. At the same time there were, among these early churchmen, individuals who wished, for various reasons, to record information about the old native culture they were supplanting. One motivation was to be able to avoid the evils of concealed survivals of Aztec religion and its practices. Father Diego Duran wrote two of the best accounts from this motivation with his *History* (1964) and *The Book of the Gods and Rites,* and *The Ancient Calendar* (1971). Bernardino de Sahagun was another priest who worked at this task of salvage. Both men talked with many Indians who had lived and been important before the conquest. A crown official, Judge Alonso Zorita, in his *Life and Labor in Ancient Mexico* (1963), wrote one of the best accounts of Mexican social structure and economics in answer to a government questionnaire! Numerous others wrote documents which preserve the Aztecs in both description and illustration. Duran and Sahagun each employed a team of scribes and artists.

The conquerors also wrote documents, either in self-justification or as memoirs or bureaucratic reports. Cortes' five letters to Charles V (1963) written during the conquest, Bernal Diaz del Castillo's memoirs (1968) written in his old age, Francisco Lopez de Gomara's *Life of Cortes* (1964), and others are all examples. Paradoxically, then, these men who destroyed and rooted out the civilization of the Aztecs, also furnish us the means for reconstruction of that same culture and give us eyewitness accounts of Tenochtitlan–Mexico City at its height.

There are frustrations and dead ends in such material, inasmuch as none of the chroniclers answers all of the questions which we would like answered. For example, none gives an exact figure for the population of the Aztec capital. Possibly the Aztecs themselves had no precise idea, although this is unlikely. Possibly the census records mainly perished in the holocaust of the conquest, and the knowledgeable native scribes and bureaucrats were probably never consulted even if they did survive. We are not even certain of the exact arrangement of the buildings or even of the number of buildings in the central square of

Tenochtitlan. We can come to a fair approximation of an answer to both these questions by comparing the accounts and factoring out errors and weighing the evidence, but, in the end, we will still be left with a substantial residue of doubt and probable error. This being so, it is well that we have another source of information to which we can turn — archaeology.

Unfortunately, archaeological research in Mexico City proper has been mainly opportunistic salvage work, without the orientation and systematics that would indicate some of the answers to our many questions. The recent Metro construction has produced an enormous amount of material and some problem-oriented information. The plaza of the three cultures at Tlatelolco gives us still more data; and the general sequence established for the Basin of Mexico aids us in reconstructing the ancient city.

NATURAL SETTING

The closed Basin of Mexico before 1519 was physically occupied by a chain of interconnected shallow lakes: three or six, depending on how one splits them up. The Aztecs themselves seem to have spoken mainly of three lakes — Chalco, Texcoco, and Xaltocan, proceeding from south to north. The basin is at about 7200 feet above sea level and has an area of about 3024 square miles (7833 square kilometers). Of this total, about 15 percent was occupied by water. These bodies of water profoundly influenced climate, agricultural systems, population size, and even the social forms developed in the basin. William Sanders, based on a recent careful study (1970), estimates the population of the basin in 1519 as between 1 and 1.2 million. He estimates the population of the city of Tenochtitlan as between 122,000 and 200,000, depend-

ing on how many tributaries the city called on. The Spaniards have left records indicating that about fifty small city-states existed in 1519, and Sanders estimates that most of these domains had between 14,000 and 16,000 people. There were also a few large cities besides the Aztec capital. These figures seem well-reasoned, although Sherburne F. Cook and Woodrow Borah have made higher estimates totaling 2.5 million for the basin (1960).

Whatever demographic estimates one accepts, it is clear that there were substantial numbers of people involved; and the next question is, How were they all fed? This was also a continual question in the minds of the rulers of these vast numbers. The ancient chronicles mention a number of famines brought on by natural disasters — plagues of locusts, drought, storms, and floods. In 1454 there was a particularly bad harvest, and people sold themselves and their children into slavery in order to survive. One answer, then, is that they were not all fed all of the time (Kovar, 1970). Another, as Sanders has pointed out, is that the living standard for many of the lower-class people was even lower than it is for the rural population of central Mexico today. Zorita (1963) mentions the extreme poverty of the lower classes, and Duran (1971) says that one of the tasty feast-day dishes was a bean and corn stew (*etzalli*) which was considered costly enough that not all could afford it. He further says that no people were capable of eating better at their neighbors' expense and more frugally at their own expense; food, because of its scarcity, was too valuable. Confirmation of this picture of subsistence-level existence for the masses comes from the nearby Tehuacan Valley in which extensive use of cactus fruits (*opuntia*) and grass seeds was made in the local diet. A Spanish questionnaire of the sixteenth century from the Teotihuacan Valley indicates the same use of wild plant seeds and fruits as staples for poor people. The implication, then, is of a density of population which at times exceeded its food supply.

AGRICULTURE AND THE CHINAMPAS. The Basin of Mexico was one of the most intensely exploited agricultural zones of Mesoamerica. Nearly every agricultural system was used in some ecological zone of the basin. A highland slash-and-burn system was used on the upper slopes of the surrounding mountains. Dry farming was practiced widely. Irrigation systems of both the flood-water and the canal types were in use. Further, the famous *chinampa* or floating garden technique was extensively used.

At the time of the entry of the Spaniards into the basin, there were over 25,000 acres (10,000 hectares) of chinampas in the southern basin alone (Chalco). The system is one of the most productive and intensive ever devised. Because of studies by Pedro Armillas, Benjamin West, and Elizabeth Schilling on both archaeological and present-day chinampa gardening, we know quite a bit about it (Armillas, 1971; Schilling, 1939; West and Armillas, 1950). Any tourist who has floated around Xochimilco on a Sunday afternoon in the pleasantly decorated flower boats has seen the system in operation although he may not have realized it.

The system is essentially one of land reclamation or swamp drainage, akin, as M. D. Coe points out, to the drainage of the fens in England or the polders in the Netherlands (1964). These so-called floating gardens never actually floated, but were created by making efficient use of the standing water, rich alluvium, and the marsh grasses and other vegetation in the swamps. Mats of floating water plants growing on the deeper and open ponds in the basin were used to build up the marshy areas for chinampas. These mats, long, rectangular strips of vegetation, were towed to suitable sites in the marshes and dragged onto the selected spot for the new chinampa. The mats were then anchored by stakes from the native cypress, which would take root and eventually become trees, like those which one sees at Xochimilco today. Successive layers of vegetation were dragged into place until the chinampa site was raised above water. The sites usually measured about 30 feet by 330 feet, and canals were dug on three or four sides of them. They were laid out in a grid pattern which allowed for continual percolation of nutrient-rich water through the entire chinampa. The next stage of construction was to pile on lake mud from the canal bottom. This mud was periodically renewed and was also rejuvenated by the use of night soil. Special canoe-latrines collected human waste in Tenochtitlan for this purpose.

One of the most efficient aspects of the chinampa system was in the use of the farm land thus created. A small section might be set aside in a corner for germination purposes and all crops planted there first. Tomatoes, corn, squashes, and other vegetables would be planted in small squares of mud and the resultant plants transplanted to crop plots elsewhere on the chinampa. Thus, germination losses were taken on a relatively small amount of ground and the transplanted crops were made up of those plants which already had a good start, presumably being the hardiest. The main part of the chinampa was devoted to either a variety of truck crops or a main food crop such as corn. Another form of seedbed indeed floated, and it is from these that the legend of the floating gardens no doubt comes. Floating nurseries of reeds, cattails, and other water plants supported the germinating seedlings which were then towed to the appropriate chinampa for transplanting.

Several chinampas made up the farm land for one family. This is clear from various maps and documents. The variety of crops indicates that throughout the year there were a number of different foods coming into harvest stage. At Xochimilco, modern *chinamperos* expect about seven crops a year from a plot. Once a crop is harvested another set of newly germinated plants replaces it in the fertilized soil. In other words, the chinampa system allows a year-round productivity of amazing amounts and variety of roots, vegetables, cereals, and fruits. The 25,000 acres of chinampas in 1519 in the Chalco zone, Armillas estimates, supported about 100,000 people. However, each family of chinamperos did not nearly consume their yearly produce, and over half would be available to feed nonfarming people: the ruling elite, artisans, soldiers, and bureaucrats of the Aztec Empire. Sanders estimates that 25,000 acres would support 180,000 (1971: 9). In other words, production is estimated at a carrying capacity of 10 to 18 persons per hectare (25 to 45 per acre). Some of the production, however, was of flowers, as at Xochimilco today. Duran says that one of the greatest pleasures of the senses among the Aztecs was in smelling flowers: "They find gladness and joy in spending the entire day smelling a little flower or bouquet made of different kinds of flowers; their gifts are accompanied by them; they relieve the tediousness of journeys with flowers" (Duran, 1971: 238).

Xochimilco, incidentally, counted among its principal gods two which were associated with the chinampas and canals, Amimitl and Atlahuac, aspects of the general water god complex.

The use of the marshes for crops did not discourage waterfowl and aquatic animals, both of which were desirable items of diet. The *axolotl,* a large salamander (*Ambystoma mexicanum*) was and is esteemed for its meat in the chinampa zones. Sahagun's informants said that they are "good, fine, edible, savory: what one deserves" (Sahagun, Book 11:64, 1963).

The start of the chinampa system is possibly in the Preclassic period, dating to the last centuries before Christ. Armillas' work (1971)

seems to show a sort of regression in chinampa activity from about A.D. 1 to A.D. 1200, and he thinks that this is due to the rise in the lake level for that period. Such rises are historically known, and if such a rise did occur it would flood out much of the marshy areas and coalesce the deeper ponds into still larger lakes. About A.D. 1200, however, it is thought that the lake level dropped; and beginning about A.D. 1400, because of the pressures of population, the chinampa system was spread into the new marshes under planned guidance. The chinampa grids, feeder, and main canals are too well integrated to allow for individual initiative as the prime mover in this expansion.

Small islets dotted the lakes or were created in the marshes by filling cribbing of posts and wickerwork with mud and vegetation. These supported households or even communities, and the Aztecs began their city of Tenochtitlan-Tlatelolco in this way. Even today, these small sites of Aztec culture can be seen in the form of low mounds as one drives across the former lake bed near Chalco. They are locally called *tlateles.*

In the sense that the chinampa system uses a drainage technique, it resembles the "drained-field" techniques that are found in the lowlands of the New World, usually in a tropical forest environment. The chinampa system seems to have been more widespread in Central Mexico than is generally allowed. Long strips of formerly cultivated fields have been found in Puebla, while the old name of Cuautla in Morelos, Cuautla Amilpas, is suggestive. Amilpas(n) means watery fields in Nahuatl.

The famous "Maguey Map" possibly shows a section of the northwest corner of Tenochtitlan, and a series of household heads are illustrated sitting on their chinampas. Calnek believes that this map belongs to another of the many island "suburbs" in the western embayment (1972). Chinampas were definitely part of the main city, in any case, as Calnek demonstrates from legal documents of the colonial period. A striking aspect of this study is that chinampa land associated with each household is only enough to produce from 1 to 15 percent of the needs of the estimated population. In other words, the city was heavily dependent on the surrounding chinampa and other agricultural areas for support. Indeed, Sanders estimates that from 40,000 to 120,000 of the possible 122,000 to 200,000 population of the city were tributary farmers from outside the city. The core city had a probable nonfarmer population of about 82,000.

The Chalco zone is apparently where the chinampa system got its start. The southern basin has fewer killing frosts and is generally better for agriculture because of greater rainfall. These circumstances would lead to intensification of cropping as population grew. The southern lake was fresh water, and the system requires constant fresh water circulation. Texcoco, the central lake and the location of Tenochtitlan, was more turbulent, deeper, and, most crucial, brackish or saline. A heavy charge of minerals was picked up by the rivers draining into the eastern edge, the deepest section of the lake. The other lakes also overflowed into Texcoco. The ever-accumulating saline waters would usually lie in the eastern, deeper edge of the lake with the fresh water riding on top. The western edge of the lake was shallow, mostly fresh water, and marshy, a likely spot for chinampas. However, prior to the Aztec arrival in the basin in the thirteenth century this area had never been extensively used for this purpose in spite of population pressures. This was because of periodic floods which drove the saline waters from the eastern side of the lake to the west, penetrating the chinampas located there and ruining them for a substantial period until they could be flushed out with fresh water. The western embankment where Tenochtitlan

was located was unsuitable for extensive chinampa development until this problem of saline penetration was overcome. This was done after the Aztecs rose to power, with the help of the allied city of Texcoco. Civil engineers under the direction of the Texcocan king, Nezahualcoyotl, built a long dike closing off the western embayment. This effectively controlled most of the flooding problems, but also impeded circulation in the embayment. The aqueduct from Chapultepec where there were fresh water springs was built to the center of Tenochtitlan to bring fresh water not only for household use but probably also for the chinampas. The chronicles record that it took thirteen years to build the aqueduct and that it was completed in 1466 (Chimalpahin, 1965). A later Aztec emperor undertook to bring still more fresh water from Coyoacan against the advice of the king of Coyoacan. The latter was posthumously vindicated when the flow proved so strong that the Aztec capital suffered severe flooding.

Lake Texcoco was a formidable place with hot springs, volcanic activity, whirlpools and geysers. Many of the problems of the Aztecs, living on an island in this lake, were hydraulic, and the dikes, aqueducts, canals, and other developments were all responses to these problems. The chinampas, located mainly in the more peaceful southern lake and marshes, provided a great deal of the subsistence base for these later local large-scale efforts at hydraulic engineering. The manpower to carry out such projects and, indeed, the population pressures motivating them were in part fed by the chinampas.

ECONOMICS, THE MARKET SYSTEM, AND TRIBUTE

The agricultural system sketched above may seem complicated and sophisticated, but it was only a part of a vastly more complex interrelated system. Distinct ecological zones produced, naturally, distinctive products by different means of cultivation. These products passed into a highly organized marketing system which redistributed them. Agricultural products were also an important part of the tribute system, which was the other major means of redistribution in the area dominated by the Mexica. Although the present-day tourist is impressed with the diversity and size of the traditional markets of Indian Mexico and Guatemala, these are much simplified remnants of the pre-Hispanic markets.

To begin with, the Valley of Mexico was part of an economically interrelated set of regions which consisted of the surrounding valleys of Morelos to the south, Puebla to the east, the Mezquital to the north, and Toluca to the west. Sanders calls this the Central Mexican Symbiotic Region (1956). Although many of the food crops produced in any of these areas were the same as those grown elsewhere, each zone had its specialty crops, which it supplied to the others. Thus, in the market of Mexico, there was available not only maize, peppers, beans, and tomatoes grown in the valley, but also tropical fruits, cotton, and cacao, from the Morelos and Guerrero zones, beans and *chian* from the Puebla area (Atotonilco), and maize and beans from Toluca. Maize surpluses were more common in the far eastern reaches of the Aztec Empire, near the gulf in Veracruz, and these were imported by the state in times of need.

Markets were held religiously (literally and figuratively) at stated periods: usually once each five days — four times each month according to the native calendar. Every community of any size held markets. These markets, some specialized but all with enormous variety of selection, reflect community craft specialization in the basin as well as imports from outside it. It is known that many small towns, villages, and hamlets combined agricul-ture with the manufacture of items such as pottery, salt, mat-weaving, adobe and cotton cloth. Slaves were especially to be found at Azcapotzalco and Itzocan, and tasty dogs for eating were sold in the market at Acolman. Duran reports over 400 for sale on a slow day (1971). Craft speciality markets were apparently to be found only in the larger towns. Texcoco, across the lake from Tenochtitlan, was noted for cloth, fine gourds, and exquisitely worked ceramics. Cholula, east of the valley, was renowned for jewelry, precious stones, and fine featherwork.

Bernal Diaz del Castillo says of the market at Tlatelolco, after spending a good deal of ink listing items sold there, "But why do I waste so many words in recounting what they sell in that great market? — for I shall never finish if I tell it all in detail" (1972: 197–198). Fortunately for us, he did continue, and tells us that paper, tobacco, yellow ointments, skins of animals, cooked foods, honey, pottery in a thousand different forms, and all of the other items had special places assigned to them in the marketplace. This market was open daily. Tlatelolco itself was a most-favored city within the Aztec domain since the principal men of the city were long-distance merchants who belonged to a special class. These were the *pochteca*, a group which will be discussed further in considering social organization. The market system was deliberately fostered and protected by the state; no one could transact business outside the market. Order and quality control were kept by special officials, and three judges were in attendance to decide any dispute. Commodities and goods were exchanged in a barter relationship and there was only a skeletal monetary system based on blankets, cacao beans, and gold dust. It was fully as rational a system as our own international monetary arrangements. The Valley of Mexico actually was an economic unit before it was politically unified. Another aspect of this unity was that craft guilds in the valley included Mexicans from several city-states.

As noted, the tribute system was the other means of redistribution in this nonmonetary economy. The system was based on the kinship, social, and political units, with the various units assigned specified amounts and kinds of tribute. Zorita mentions maize, peppers, beans, and cotton as tribute. Water, fuel, and domestic service were other forms of tribute. The magnificent *Codex Mendoza* was made for the first viceroy of New Spain in the 1540s in order that the Spaniards might know how much had been exacted from each community before the conquest. It was a copy of an Aztec bureaucratic document made in about 1512, called the *Matricula de Tributos*. The tribute was onerous. Sahagun sympathetically cites the dilemma of the commoner overwhelmed by the burden of the religious tribute. The amounts and variety of stuffs, manufactured items, slaves for sacrifice, food, raw materials, and other things demanded by the Aztecs of their conquered vassals were truly staggering. Based on a study of the quantities of tribute recorded in the *Codex Mendoza*, it seems that Tenochtitlan received enormous amounts of foodstuffs alone. One year's yields of grains and cereals were approximately as follows: corn, 6000 metric tons; beans, 4000 metric tons; chian, 4000 metric tons; and *huauhtli* (amaranth or "careless weed"), a total of 18,000 metric tons or 19,841 short tons (Barlow, 1949).

PHYSICAL PLAN AND ORGANIZATION OF TENOCHTITLAN-TLATELOLCO

Calnek's recent and very important study of Tenochtitlan (1971) gives for the first time some idea of the physical arrangements of urban life in the city outside of the ceremonial precincts. Tenochtitlan shared its artificially created island with Tlatelolco. The island had

been in part built up by chinampa construction and by use of small islets and landfill operations around them. However, the main city was only the largest of at least nineteen island communities in the western embayment of Lake Texcoco. As such, it measured at least 12 square kilometers (about 4.5 square miles). All of the other island communities were smaller, and most were agriculture-craft specialist towns. Whereas the interior chinampa districts of Tenochtitlan had households that measured about 400 square meters (4320 square feet) at most, those on the outskirts and presumably of the outer islands averaged about ten times that extent. High-density urban buildup was probably largely confined to the main island.

The heart of Tenochtitlan-Tlatelolco consisted of the two main ceremonial precincts, and in Tlatelolco included the large market. The precincts were actually a series of adjacent plazas around which were arranged the major temples, administrative structures, palaces, and other pieces of monumental architecture. Sahagun lists for Tenochtitlan's center alone, some twenty-five pyramid temples, nine attached priests' quarters, seven skullracks, two ball courts, arsenals, shops, and many other features (Marquina, 1960). Calnek shows that the residential areas around these central zones were house-to-house concentrations with no chinampas. Farther away from the precincts were the smaller chinampa-household plots in which extended families lived. In addition to the gardens, household lots included a low one- or two-story residence surrounded by a wall which defined a large open space next to the house. Several generations and related families lived in these buildings, which meant that from ten to thirty people of both sexes and all ages might be found in one household.

Six major canals ran through the city from north to south with many smaller canals feeding in. At least two major canals ran east-west through the city. Three major causeway systems connected the city with the mainland and with other island communities, but the best way of getting about was by canoe. Gomara reports that there were about 200,000 small boats on the lakes, carrying people and supplies (1964: 160–163). This was an enormous advantage in a land where the alternative to water transport was carrying things on one's back.

The city was divided into sixty or seventy wards, which corresponded to the *calpulli* kinship units discussed below. Each of these had its own set of communally constructed and maintained buildings including a temple, a school, and an administrative structure. Judging from this, the numbers of large and formal buildings in Tenochtitlan must have numbered in the hundreds, and the city was probably dotted with smaller plazas around which these calpulli buildings were grouped.

Aztec architecture has flowing lines, and since most of the buildings were one or two stories, the temples impressively raised their gleaming white bulks above the general mass. The green trees and crops of the chinampas lightened the masonry mass of the city, as did the surrounding water of the canals and lake. The huge causeways stretched into the distance across the lake. With the mountain walls and snow-capped volcanoes crowding the horizon in the clear air and the intense blue sky above, it is no wonder that the Spaniards thought themselves marching into an enchanted land like those described in their medieval romances.

SOCIAL ORGANIZATION

Although the smallest social group in Aztec society was the nuclear family, a man and wife and their children, it was around the *calpulli* (big house) that social, political, and religious life revolved for most people. The calpulli was the unit that controlled land. Indeed, this communal land-holding function still is a characteristic of most traditional Indian communities in Mesoamerica today. Membership in the calpulli was by birth, and generally the calpulli was the rural community, or in the city, a ward. Mexica families who traced their descent through the male line to a common ancestor considered themselves in a lineage. A group of lineages made up a calpulli, and the ordinary members married within the calpulli. One of the lineages traditionally furnished the leader of the calpulli — the *calpule*. One of his most important functions was as custodian of a set of land maps showing the distribution of the calpulli lands. The calpule (*calpuleque* pl.) was assisted by a council of heads of households. These men enforced the rules of land distribution and redistribution. Land-holding by the individual family was only in usufruct and the amount was enlarged or diminished according to its needs. Therefore, as a family added more children its allotment was increased, and when the couple was alone and the children had married and left, the land allotment was decreased. If the couple were infirm or disabled, or if a man left a widow and orphans, the calpulli arranged for the cultivation of the man's land for the benefit of those persons. Social security was thus provided. Other economic functions were that the men of the calpulli worked as a unit on large-scale construction, such as building temples, or maintenance of large-scale irrigation works. Taxes to the city-state ruler were paid in labor and produce by the calpulli, and thus the calpule acted as the intermediary for the individual with the state. Traditional crafts were carried on by the calpulli. In time of war the calpulli went into battle as a unit and was about the size of our modern rifle companies, 200 to 400 men. Young men of commoner class (*macehualtin*) were educated in a school called the *telpochcalli* which was established and maintained by the calpulli in a special building. Each calpulli had its patron deity, which was worshipped in a small temple set on a high platform.

From the above, it can be seen that the calpulli was a fundamental unit of Aztec society. On it all of the larger social organizations — religious, political, economic and military — were based. These functions were reflected in the architectural assemblage which would make up the typical Aztec small community center. All the structures would be made of stone and oriented around an open square. The house of the calpule would be a low, one-story structure with a few rooms and probably a patio. The calpule both resided there and used the house as an administrative building. He kept the land maps in his house. Another side of the square would be the location of the pyramid-temple, probably with quarters nearby for a resident priest. The young men's school, would be both that and a residence until marriage. The building would be found on the main square. The plaza would act as a marketplace if the community were large enough. "The markets in this land were all enclosed by walls and stood either in front of temples to the gods or to one side" (Duran, 1971: 275).

SOCIAL STRATIFICATION.   Although the calpulli was the basic unit, and most Mexica belonged to one, apparently not all lineages within the calpulli were equal. As noted, the calpulli head was elected from a specific lineage. Similarly, calpulli were ranked in terms of social importance. Yopico was a calpulli of importance in Tenochtitlan, for example, and seems to have furnished some of the leadership of the Mexica. Duran mentions (1971) that some of the most prestigious religious duties in the main temple at Tenochtitlan were performed by young men and women who came on an annual basis from six favored wards, which were probably calpulli.

Social stratification was also very important and modified the effects of the calpulli organization. There were four principal social categories. At the top were the ruler of the city state and his relatives. These, with the descendants of the preceding rulers made up the class called the *pipiltin.* Moteczoma II (the Aztec ruler at the time of Spanish conquest) was a member of this class and had been selected as ruler of Tenochtitlan from a specific lineage, but outside a calpulli organization. Pipiltin attended separate schools called *Calmecac.* The great mass of the population were *macehualtin* or free men; but as noted above these were organized on kinship lines into calpulli. These free men could move either way in social rank. Upward mobility was through achievement and service to the state, usually in war, religion, or trade. In this case, the city-state ruler would ennoble the macehualtin, who became what the Spaniards called "gray knights." These men were nobles with rights and privileges for their lifetimes only. They were awarded small private estates with resident serfs, but these reverted to the state at their deaths, in contrast to the pipiltin estates, which were passed on to their descendants. Private ownership of land thus distinguished aristocrat and temporary aristocrat from commoner. It is interesting that the estates of nobles bear a great resemblance to the later haciendas of colonial and republican Mexico.

Mayeques were the serfs working the landed estates of nobility and presumably were also outside of the calpulli system, being landless peasants with no rights to either usufruct or inherited lands. It may be that calpulli were in some manner or other assigned to a *pilli* (singular of pipiltin) as serf labor and thus lost their independent status. How or why this might have happened to a specific group, however, is not clear. Mayeques could not leave the land and were obliged to render menial service.

The bottom of the social scale was occupied by slaves, who were not only landless, but who had lost their individual rights. One might become a slave by selling oneself or one's children. This happened not infrequently when famines occurred. Gambling could lead to slavery, the ultimate wager being one's freedom. Many porters who made the cross-country trips with merchants were slaves. Captives taken in war were occasionally enslaved, but usually they were dedicated to sacrifice and did not last long. Slavery was a reversible status: one could purchase one's way free, and a slave's children were born free. There were other specified circumstances under which one could regain freedom.

As noted above, one of the distinctions of social ranking was in the disposal of land, private land ownership being restricted to the nobility. Much of the rest of the land was held by the individual calpulli. However, a significant amount of land was attached to high public offices, the salaries for which were in the form of produce from this entailed real estate. Other land was set aside for support of temples and schools. Specific towns, devotees of gods, or students from the community schools worked these lands. Some land was also set aside for the defense budget. Especially in conquered communities, the Mexica would thus provide for the support of a resident garrison.

Caso points out that the so-called military and religious classes of the Aztecs did not really exist independently (1963). Instead, one had access to these offices by belonging to a specific calpulli, lineage, or class, and also through individual qualifications. Thus, though a man might have qualified through birth to fill an office, he was not necessarily elected or selected for it. There is an inherent tendency toward incompetence in rigidly aristocratic societies if birth is coupled to a right to specific social functions. This can lead to certain dilemmas such as occurred in the seventeenth-century armies of Europe when military leadership was aristocratic. Thus one was not merely promoted to one's level of incompetence, but was born into it. However, specification of a certain lineage or set of lineages as the social pool from which one draws the candidate for a certain office means that the best man can be chosen. One hopes that the best man will be competent to deal with the job. Moteczoma II was the nephew of the preceding ruler and not the son. Unfortunately, he did not possess the necessary qualities to deal with the unforeseen event of a Spanish invasion, but he was felt to be the most suitable of the candidates for the leadership of the Aztec state at the time.

On a lesser level, the possibility of distinguishing oneself in war or administration left a door open to talent from lower social levels (war was the most important means in the later stages of the Aztec empire). In addition there was the opportunity of trade, and members of the merchant class, the *pochteca*, might be either aristocrats or plebians. In either case, it was a further chance for individual distinction, especially if one dealt with long-distance trade. Military intelligence activity was often combined with foreign business dealings, a practice not unknown in our own day. Middle-class occupations also were in terms of the lower specialty jobs in religion, administration, and certain craft specialties, such as jewelry-making. Thus, social mobility was based on personal achievement in the several areas open to distinction.

To summarize, Mexica society was organized, to a great degree, around the calpulli. This group had land-holding, social security, military, religious, and educational functions. However, this kinship-based unit was truly only fully in operation in the middle ranks of society. Social strata above and below the macehualtin level lacked calpulli organization, as did individuals who had fallen into evil circumstance. Thus it was most important to be born a member of a specific aristocratic lineage at the upper levels, in which case one was considered for certain offices and at least had the perquisites such as holding private lands. At the lower levels of society it was of little importance to a serf attached to a ruler's estate how adjacent calpulli operated. Such a serf had left or been born outside the calpulli system and lacked the rights inherent in calpulli membership. Slaves, of course, had dropped out of the calpulli system altogether and, in addition, had forfeited individual rights.

Aztec society seems to have been moving more and more toward a rigid aristocratic principle, however, especially under the last Moteczoma, who made it a crime for a commoner to enter the same waiting room in the palace as nobility. There were other moves toward despotism and establishment of caste. Each member of the state apparatus had a special dress and badges of rank to set him apart. Warriors were given decorations and different uniforms according to the number of enemies they had captured. The warrior societies of Eagles and Jaguars, and Otomis all had special uniforms, and fought as units in time of war. At the same time, there was a rapid expansion in sheer numbers of the pipiltin owing to the fact that they were taking large numbers of concubines. These were often of lower-class (macehualtin) origin, but their children assumed their father's rank. On the other hand, a pilli could not be assured of distinction simply because of birth, and might wind up with a very pedestrian administrative job whereas one of the "gray knights" could well be placed above him.

Other social categories of people who were at least implicitly recognized were gamblers, thieves, and prostitutes. Gamblers played at the game of *patolli*, a kind of parchesi which invoked numerological symbolism tied up with the sacred calendar. Bets were also placed on the outcomes of ball games played with rubber balls in special courts. Thieves are mentioned as being a certain problem, with sometimes a gang of thieves terrorizing a household, taking it over and stripping it of its goods. Prostitutes were at least common enough that those young men who had distinguished themselves in war had the privilege of consorting with them for a short period. Porters, innkeepers, barbers, and beggars fill out the social scene and confirm Tenochtitlan's fully urban status.

POLITICAL ORGANIZATION

In the Basin of Mexico, the ultimate unit of political stability was the city-state. Kingdoms and empires were all extant at various times, but these nearly always reduced down to the city-state, or sometimes were completely destroyed. The fifty city-states in the basin in 1519 were each ruled by a petty king with all the trappings of royalty. A member of the pipiltin, he dwelt in a stone palace with a harem, bodyguard, and court ritual. Such a ruler was known as the *tlatoque*. As was the case with the calpule, the tlatoque was supported by cultivation of designated communal lands, and also received tribute in the form of labor and services. Being a member of the pipiltin, he also had landed estates with serfs and the production was his to dispose of in support of his household, or as reward for services. The small estates reverting to the state by the deaths of the temporary nobles and the acquisition of new lands by war gave him immense power to bind the allegiance of talented men to him. However, religious sanctions also bolstered his position, since most of the tlatoque-rulers of the basin claimed descent from the divine Quetzalcoatl through the *Toltecs*. For this reason, as Sanders has pointed out, the upper classes of the various communities in the basin formed an endogamous caste (1965). One could not marry beneath one's social class. Women of suitable rank were scarce within any community, considering the incest taboo. The common practice was to exchange women among the ruling lineages. These marriages had political implications and remind one of the dynastic marriages of Europe. Nezahualpilli, king of Texcoco, for example, was married to Moteczoma II's sister. Such an alliance did not preclude hostilities. Nezahualpilli, indeed, executed his wife for adulterous conduct, although this was partly motivated by a desire for revenge on Moteczoma who had betrayed the Texcocan army into an ambush. Compare this system with the circumstances in Europe in 1914: the heads of state of England, Germany, and Russia were then all cousins.

The social and political structure outlined above was the ideal. The reality of the situation depended, as always, on historical circumstance, personality, and the run of fortune. Rules were to be obeyed; they ordered the social universe and, in a sense, reflected the divine order. Larger or smaller units accommodated themselves to special natural circumstances as they did also to the historical circumstances that made them more or less important in the eyes of men. The Aztecs had come from very humble beginnings in their rise to domination of the central plateau of Mexico, and the empire was a relatively late political structure, built on already existing patterns found when they came into the basin. It seems clear that they followed the historically recorded pattern in building their empire. There had been the Toltec empire of the golden age. There had also been another, greater state earlier, whose name and history had been lost but whose institutions had passed into the tradition of the people of central Mesoamerica. This had been the empire of Teotihuacan. Taking this legacy of organizational tools and concepts, the Aztecs developed their own features of governance.

An empire, by simplest definition, is a state that includes, under one administrative umbrella, a diversity of peoples in language and culture. Generally, this means that a vast area is dominated, and thus natural diversity is also usually characteristic. The empires before that of the Aztecs had penetrated northward into the barbarian lands of the Gran Chichimeca, where the hunting and gathering peoples of the deserts and mountains lived. Both preceding empires had at least briefly established enclaves of control in the exotic Maya country, both lowlands and highlands. Toltecs and Teotihuacanos had established garrisons and routes of access to far-flung outposts instead of physically controlling all of the intervening country. The Aztecs followed this pattern as they expanded outside of the central plateau. The Aztecs eventually ruled over an area of 200,000 square kilometers and from 5 to 6 million people. To govern this vast area there was an elaborate political apparatus built on the kinship, social, and political principles discussed above.

At the top of the Mexica state was a dual leadership, religious and military. This reflected the dual hierarchy of offices. Since the state was nearly continuously at war throughout its later history, the military segment became dominant. The supreme leader was chosen from a special lineage by a set of important men who were members of the pipiltin and also heads of state or high officials. Duran says in his *History* that all of the civil officials attended the election proceedings, but it is quite evident that only the most important had a voice. Brother succeeded brother in the normal order of things. For example, the three sons of Moteczoma I served in succession; Axayacatl, Tizoc, and Ahuitzotl. These four were, in turn, related to the other two great expansionist rulers of the Aztec state. Moteczoma II was the grandson of Axayacatl. Itzcoatl, who preceded Axayacatl, was the latter's cousin.

The ruler was assisted by a royal court

structure which consisted of advisors and administrative heads of the various segments of the Aztec state. The state was divided into functionally distinct departments: church, military, justice, treasury, and commerce. These were controlled by the court, which acted as the executive branch. The departments were organized internally in a hierarchical manner with various classes of officials in each. Such a civil service also had its paperwork. "The nation has a special official for every activity, small though it were. Everything was so well recorded that no detail was left out of the accounts. There were even officials in charge of sweeping. . . . And so the officials of the Republic were innumerable" (Duran, 1967: 183).

Below the supreme level of government, there was a division of the empire into provinces which represented groups of conquered city-states. There were some thirty-eight of these provinces, but also some so-called independent kingdoms. C. N. Byam Davies, in his study of these independent pockets within the empire (1968), came to the conclusion that the Aztecs controlled their empire much as the British had India. That is, the Aztecs controlled key points with garrisons, secured the routes of access through territories, and arranged for tribute to be paid, but usually made no effort to otherwise assimilate conquered peoples. The provinces had governors appointed over them, members of the pipiltin caste, with garrisons to assist them, and civil servants, most of whom were tax collectors. The native ruler was often maintained in power as long as he collaborated. Some "independent kingdoms" were actually less crucial polities and in reality were "protectorates" of the Aztecs, with varying degrees of independence. Those on the frontiers of the empire tended to be the most independent. An example of this type of buffer state was that of the trading state of Xicalango, on the Gulf Coast, between Maya country and Nahua

speakers. Others, Tlaxcala and Tututepec, were well placed to menace the Aztec lines of communication and were truly independent. However, most, except for Tlaxcala, had been militarily neutralized. The Tlaxcalans became the original and most constant allies of the Spaniards. At the time of Spanish contact, the Aztecs were constantly nibbling away at the territories of the independent kingdoms, in an obvious attempt to absorb them into the empire-tribute system.

Tribute was regulated by the calendar, and payments were made quarterly, semiannually, and annually. Provinces farthest away from Tenochtitlan made payments less often. However, tribute was always given on certain religious festival days, whatever the frequency.

JUDICIAL BRANCH. The judicial branch is a good example of the graded bureaucracy. Both princes (pipiltin) and commoners were chosen for judgeships, mainly according to their accomplishments and qualities. They were supported by the state.

Such as these the ruler gave office and chose as his judges — the wise, the able, the sage; who listened and spoke well; who were of good memory; who spoke not vainly nor lightly; who did not make friends without forethought nor were drunkards; who guarded their lineage with honor; who slept not overmuch (but rather), arose early; who did nothing for friendship's or kinship's sake, nor for enmity; who would not hear nor judge a case for a fee. The ruler might condemn them to death; hence they performed their offices as judges righteously" (Sahagun, 1954, Bk. 8: 54).

Inasmuch as society was rigidly graded and since there was a caste system in effect, a two-level system of courts was necessary to take care of justice at all social levels. The Aztec judiciary seems to have functioned something like the modern European continental system with its pretrial review, magistrates, and higher courts. Common folk were able to use the lower courts, the *teccalli,* to lodge complaints. The judges acted as magistrates on this level. They decided matters of lesser importance, arrested offenders, and did the preliminary work on complex cases. A careful record of the proceedings of the lower courts was made in hieroglyphic writing by a secretary, which record was then forwarded to the higher court for disposition. Appeals from the lower courts were also sent up for review. The higher court (*tlacxitlan*) consisted of twelve distinguished judges and the city-state ruler, and met each twelve days. This higher court was responsible for review of cases and decisions on complex cases; it called witnesses and examined testimony; and it was expected to detect miscarriages of justice. Princes and great lords were tried by the tlacxitlan. The final decisions and appeals were handled by the ruler. Offenses were social and ideological, the latter including religious offenses. Sacrilegious people who stole items from temples were tried, and if condemned, were dragged by the throat with a rope and thrown into the lake. Three of the titles of the superior court are also those of religious officials, indicating that the higher officers of the church participated in the judicial system (Sahagun, 1954, Bk. 8:54). Judges were also found in the marketplaces and immediately acted on such matters as false weights or the sale of stolen goods. Since sale of items outside the marketplaces was forbidden, these men acted as economic controllers.

Of the ordinary judges, Zorita says: "The Indian judges of whom I spoke would seat themselves at daybreak on their mat dais, and immediately begin to hear pleas. The judges' meals were brought to them at an early hour from the royal palace. After eating they rested for a while, then returned to hear the remaining suitors, staying until two hours before sundown" (1963: 126). Zorita also states that

each province was represented in the capital city of the empire by two judges.

Police were appointed by the wards or calpulli. Persons accused of a crime and waiting to come to trial were confined in jails which were wooden cages, and there they received little or no food and water. When a person was found guilty and condemned, execution was carried out by special personnel appointed by the ruler. Lesser sentences were jailing, mutilation, and slavery.

The previously mentioned case which involved the sister of Moteczoma II occurred not long before the arrival of the Spaniards. This woman was married to Nezahualpilli, the ruler of the important allied state of Texcoco. However, her extramarital affairs became notorious, and her husband had her tried in 1498, presumably by the tlacxitlan, and she and her current lovers were condemned and executed.

RELIGION AND COSMOLOGY. The people of central Mexico generally believed that there had been several worlds before: four "suns," each with different types of inhabitants. Each of these preceding worlds had perished through its own imperfections, and the fifth sun or world in which man now dwelt would also perish — through a series of devastating earthquakes. It was not known when this end would come, but it was known that the ultimate catastrophe would occur at the end of a particular calendrical cycle, the fifty-two-year cycle. The famous Aztec calendar stone depicts the four suns that have preceded the present sun, which is in the center of the stone.

The earth was visualized as a crocodile-like monster floating in the primeval sea, the edges of which turned up to support the sky. The heavens were arranged in a pyramidal manner with either nine or thirteen layers. There were also nine underworlds.

A jostling, busy, and generally malevolent

crowd of deities made up the Aztec pantheon. Nicholson has analyzed them in terms of fundamental characteristics, cult themes, and deity clusters, bringing some order out of this supernatural chaos. Most deities were invisible and made manifest only in dreams and visions and by other special means. Most gods were in human form, at least in part, and dwelt in the celestial sphere. There were specific underworld deities, and occasionally some others went to the underworld temporarily. The rain gods, the *tlaloque*, resided in particular mountains which generated the rain clouds. A basic conception was that of the gods having multiple aspects. Creator deities came in pairs and in both sexes. Most gods had four or five aspects which related directly with the four directions and the zenith (the fifth direction). All world directions were associated with different colors. These associations between directions, colors, and aspects of divinities led to such conceptions as the Red Tezcatlipoca of the West, who also took the name of Xipe. The White Tezcatlipoca of the East also was Quetzalcoatl. History and a protean philosophy combined to make special patron relationships with certain sociopolitical units such as city-states, craft groups, or calpulli. Huitzilopochtli, the patron god of the Aztecs, became extremely important with the rise of the Aztecs to power.

Three major cult themes pervaded Aztec religion according to Nicholson. The first had to do with celestial creativity and divine paternalism, and was the most abstract, poetic, and philosophical segment of the whole body of religious thought. It is to this cult theme that such relatively well known material as the writings of Nezahualcoyotl, the philosopher-king of Texcoco, belong. The fierce, capricious Tezcatlipoca also belongs in this category. This deity was a supernatural magician, and associated with the things of the night and darkness. "No deity better expressed the pessimistic, fatalistic *weltan-schauung* which prevailed in pre-Hispanic Central Mexico. . . . It can be argued that this god, true to his name (smoking mirror), mirrors in his supernatural personality the essential ethos of the whole culture" (Nicholson, 1971a: 231).

The second major cult theme had to do with rain, moisture, and agricultural fertility. This cult undoubtedly had deep roots in the past, being so tied to fundamental affairs of life-giving plants, rain, soil, and water. The rain god complex, Tlaloc and all his helpers, is especially important. Another group of deities clustered about the maguey plant and the fermented cactus juice it produced, one bunch being known as "400 rabbits," which may have been how one felt after sufficient pulque. A whole roster of female deities is also present, many of whom are aspects of rain and water, or personifications of the various stages of growth of the maize plant. The dreadful Xipe-Totec complex, dreadful in its sacrificial aspect of flaying the skin of the sacrificial victim, was clearly an expression of the idea of death and rebirth, rest and growing seasons. It is thought to have been introduced from the Guerrero area. Many of the female deities of these complexes were represented by the multitudinous small clay figurines made and used in home worship. It might be noted that this practice of figure making continued into early colonial times, except that instead of Coatlicue, the mother of the gods, the Virgin Mary was depicted.

The third cult theme was that of the state-fostered war-sacrifice-blood nourishment of the sun and earth. Here the justification of human sacrifice was worked out in the following terms. The very existence of the universe depended on the sun being kept nourished by the blood of victims or else the end of the world, the fifth sun, would come about. Incessant war was necessary to gain such quantities and constant supply of victims. The death god complex was of course an important deity cluster, but so also was Tonatiuh, the sun god complex. Tonatiuh was the patron of the warrior societies, the eagle and jaguar "knights."

Quetzalcoatl, the great patron deity of the Toltecs, is a unique deity because he crosses many of the lines drawn above. He is a creator deity, associated with the war-and-blood nourishment cult, and also was conceived of as being a great culture hero. There seems little doubt that we are here dealing with the mythological apotheosis of an historical personage. The story of Quetzalcoatl will be taken up in the consideration of the Toltecs.

There was a basic ritual pattern to nearly all of Aztec religious life. It was mainly an elitist religion: most of the many and continuous ceremonies involved only a few members of the state-supported church, or at most, were attended by upper-class members. A ceremony usually started with a preparation by fasting, and other abstentions. The main business of the ceremony varied but usually involved offerings, processions, deity-impersonations, dancing, singing, mock combats, and human sacrifice. Feasts usually followed, and more secular dancing and singing was featured at this time.

Ceremonies were both calendrical and noncalendrical. The calendrical ceremonies of the 365-day calendar were called "fixed" ceremonies by the early Spaniards, and occurred in each of the eighteen months of the year. There was also a 260-day calendar with "movable feasts" which rotated in relation to those of the 365-day year. Movable feasts were somewhat like the Christian Easter, which shifts in the 365-day calendar according to a lunar calendar. Noncalendrical ceremonies were usually tied up with the individual life cycle, crises, homecoming ceremonies, domestic ritual, curing ceremonies, and so forth. Again, many of the small clay figurines so common in the Basin of Mexico were made for curing ceremonies, according to Sahagun. They were also strung over the fields for fertility purposes, according to Duran.

The major ceremonies were, of course, held in the temple precincts, with and under direction of special personnel, and were patronized by the state and elite leadership. The Spanish friars concentrated upon this religion when they engaged in the first generation's massive conversion efforts. Several aspects of Aztec religion seemed especially remarkable to them because of similarities to Christianity. One such feature was the use of confession of sins among the Aztecs, although this was done infrequently. Another parallel was the use of a sacred dough which was often made into an image of a god and ultimately eaten by the participants. The similarity of the concepts of the mother of the gods, Coatlicue, and of the Virgin Mary has been remarked. Indeed the shrine to the Virgin of Guadalupe presently occupies the site of the old center of worship of Tonantzin, an aspect of Coatlicue.

The Aztecs felt themselves surrounded by and acted on by the supernatural. Religion permeated every aspect of life. The gods were in this world and unknowable and capricious, and man was at the mercy of their whims. The future was perhaps divinable if one knew enough to detect the cycles of time, events, and ritual. Life might be controlled to some degree, or at least foreseen if one had such knowledge. The small town of Malinalco was noted for its sorcerers and fortune-tellers, some of whom used the device of staring into tubs of water. The calendars were inextricably bound up with life, and one's whole life pattern to a large degree was bound up with one's birthday and its lucky or unlucky aspects. Small shrines dotted the countryside, much in the manner in which Catholic shrines are still found in profusion around Mesoamerica today. Mountain shrine worship was especially dedicated to the rain gods, the tlaloque. Even the emperor and his court repaired at a certain time of the year to a remote and gloomy forest on Mount Tlaloc for a ceremony dedicated to the rain god. Long-distance merchants on a trip worshipped their Pinocchio-nosed god, Yacatecuhtli, asked his protection from the dangers of the trip, and made a temporary shrine to the god each evening with their staves and clay images of the god's face. One still finds these small clay masks as far south as the highlands of Guatemala. The agriculturalist of course felt the wrath or beneficence of the gods in all of his activities. The chinampero had his own patron deities. The breath of cooling air which preceded the rain squall was Quetzalcoatl in his guise as the wind god sweeping the road before the moisture of the rain god Tlaloc. The world was mysterious and awful in many ways, but there was an explanation for nearly everything. The universe was in order and man was meant to help keep that order by proper worship and sacrifices. The regularity and pageantry and drama of Aztec religion went far to allay anxieties about the essential hostility and unpredictability of the world about him and served also to bind the commoner's allegiance to the state.

HISTORICAL SUMMARY

Like many imperial peoples rather suddenly reaching gloriously improved circumstances, the Aztec-Mexica looked back on the past and found it lacking. In fact, at one point, they went so far as to burn as many of the older history books as were available and then rewrote their own history. Therefore much of what comes down to us is in the form of the official history of the Aztecs and is as they themselves wished to be seen. Fortunately, there are histories which have survived from other city-state archives, Chalco and Texcoco, for example, and which give us a chance to balance off other more realistic versions against the chest-beating tone of the official record.

The Aztecs considered themselves as part of a group of seven Chichimec tribes which left a semimythical place, to the west of Mexico, Aztlan. It is from the latter place name that "Aztec" is derived. The Aztec were also called Mexicas after a famous leader named Meci. All seven tribes arrived in the basin, but the Aztecs were the last to do so. After several generations of wandering and adventuring, following their tribal deity, Huitzilopochtli, they arrived in the Basin of Mexico about 1193. It is difficult to say exactly what the political status of the Aztecs was, but there seems little doubt that it was of a politically weak, militarily aggressive, and probably tributary group. Until about 1427 the Aztecs barely maintained themselves in this precarious and politically fragmented condition. One group is stated to have settled with the civilized people of the city-state of Colhuacan. Another group settled on a rocky group of islets in the western embayment of Lake Texcoco and founded what became the city of Tlatelolco, Tenochtitlan's sister city. The "Plaza of the Three Cultures" in Mexico City today reveals the remnants of this ancient town.

Tenochtitlan was founded on land that belonged to three powerful city-states, Azcapotzalco, Texcoco, and Colhuacan. The Aztecs had located the place after many vicissitudes, largely of their own making, when they found the promised sign of the eagle nesting on the prickly pear cactus in the swamp. They built their initial shrine to Huitzilopochtli, who had led them through all of these years. "Although the wood and stone were not sufficient, the Aztecs began to build their temple. Little by little they filled in and consolidated the site for the city. They built foundations in the water by driving in stakes and throwing dirt and stone between the stakes" (Duran, 1967: 23). The city was divided into four districts according to the four world quarters; each district was made up of several calpulli.

At this point, having established and developed their town somewhat, the Aztecs requested a king from Colhuacan. It seems clear that they needed someone of the necessary distinguished genealogy, that is, who could claim descent from the Toltecs, to lend status to their ruling class. Acamapichtli became king in about 1364 and ruled until 1404. During this time, the Aztecs were tributaries of Azcapotzalco, and paying heavy tribute to that city-state. Huitzilhuitl, Acamapichtli's successor, married a daughter of the ruler of Azcapotzalco and thereby gained a means of reducing the tribute to the Azcapotzalcans. The daughter begged her father to remit the taxes and he agreed to do so.

The Aztecs during these years made a distinct effort to live in peace with their more powerful neighbors, establishing relationships with them by inviting people from the other city-states to settle in Mexico City. Commerce was also encouraged, with much coming and going among the various regional markets of the basin, and that of Tlatelolco-Mexico City became more important. About 1417 the third king, Chimalpopoca (Smoking Shield), took office upon his father's death and continued the peaceful development of the city.

After about ten years, a crisis took place which threatened the very existence of the Aztecs as a separate state. More water was needed for the increasingly large *chinampa* zone and the growing population of the city, and an aqueduct-causeway was planned and attempted. However, the Aztecs needed help and requested it of Azcapotzalco. Whether or not the request was insolently phrased, it was said to be, and Azcapotzalco took this as a good chance to destroy a growing rival. They sent assassins who killed Chimalpopoca and his son, and Azcapotzalco instituted an economic blockade. At this point, the first of the great conqueror-kings ascends the throne, and

the ferocious personality of Tlacaelel makes its appearance. The new king, Itzcoatl, aided by his nephew, Tlacaelel, first resisted and then conquered Azcapotzalco. For the first time the Aztecs were an independent city-state, free of tributary obligations. Itzcoatl is the first of the six rulers who presided over the imperial expansion of the Aztec state. Tlacaelel was first general and then chief counselor to all but Moteczoma II, the last pre-Hispanic ruler. In point of fact, Tlacaelel was emperor-ruler in all but name for most of his life time. As such, the Aztec state and its ultimate form, ideology, social structure, and accomplishments are very much the achievement of this extraordinary personality. It was Tlacaelel who planned and, at first, largely carried out the military campaigns which subjugated the basin for the Aztecs, and who then spread the empire beyond the basin. Tlacaelel, according to R. C. Padden's interpretation, was also responsible for the psychopathic emphasis on human sacrifice as an instrument of terror and political and social control (1967). The use of the lands of the conquered city-states by the Aztecs relieved their hunger, and the tribute exacted from the same conquered places provided the economic support for the rapidly expanding aristocracy (pipiltin), bureaucracy, and church. Much of the expenditure of the state was in the form of extravagant building: glorious architectural monuments which embellished the capital city and which provided the physical stage upon which the pageantry of social and religious activities were acted out.

The above reconstruction of Aztec history is almost wholly derived from the official version. However, according to other city-state chronicles, the initial struggle with Azcapotzalco was successful only because of an alliance with two other city states, Texcoco, and Tacuba. Texcoco was the home of another extraordinary personality, the ruler Nezahualcoyotl, who was also an accomplished engineer and warrior. Much of the initial domination of the Basin and the Central Plateau of Mexico was due to this man's achievements, it appears. However, it also appears that the Aztecs expurgated the history books to omit both the historical and cultural accomplishments of the rival city of Texcoco. Unfortunately, the great library of Texcoco was destroyed in the course of the Spanish conquest.

It seems quite clear that shifting power balances took place within the century of Aztec expansion, 1427–1519, among the allies of the basin and that although Texcoco retained its reputation and eminence in cultural achievements, it had become politically and economically subordinated to Tenochtitlan by the late fifteenth century.

Padden argues that the Aztec state by this time had also become a mad world of bloody terrorism based on the cynical, psychopathic policies of the high imperial rulers. Coronation ceremonies of later kings were accompanied by the offering of fantastic quantities of human victims to the gods. These victims were both purchased slaves from Aztec society itself, coerced members of a society who played the parts of god impersonators, and the collected captives from the constant foreign campaigns of the Aztec armies. Some 80,000 captives are said to have been sacrificed at the dedication of the enlarged great temple housing Huitzilopochtli in 1487. Incredibly, the Aztec elite invited the rulers of other hostile city-states to view the spectacle as honored guests — "enemies of the house." The consumption of human flesh by the pipiltin was massive, and it is said that one reason that pork was so popular after human flesh became unavailable in 1521, was its similarity in taste to human meat. The expansion of the pipiltin class, the increasing tribute loads on the macehualtin, the increasing strain of ever more far-reaching military campaigns and the increasing hostilities of the conquered provinces all produced internal and external strains

on the empire that set the stage for its fall in 1521.

Tlacaelel died in 1496, and Moteczoma II came to power in 1503. The latter moved almost immediately to deify himself. Duran records that he asked an old man what the emperor Moteczoma looked like, and the old one replied that he in truth did not know, not having dared to look on Moteczoma's face (1964). Much of the later majesty, elaborate protocol, and almost Byzantine procedure were Moteczoma's creation. He arranged for the assassination of most of the court officials who had served his predecessor, Ahuitzotl. Those men knew too much to accept his divinity.

The king of Texcoco, Nezahualpilli, became an enemy — covert, but powerful. He made dire predictions, moreover, about the end of the Aztec hegemony; it would come within a few years, he said, although he himself would not see it. Whether or not this was psychological warfare, it certainly upset Moteczoma. Many other upsetting events occurred in the years shortly before the appearance of the Spaniards. A bird with a mirror in its head was brought to the emperor who gazed into it and saw first a starry constellation and then men on horses. A fire broke out in a temple dedicated to Huitzilopochtli and it burned to the ground. A great comet was seen in the sky. These and other omens reminded Moteczoma of the now-dead Nezahualpilli's prophecy and also of the ancient traditions that the god Quetzalcoatl would one day return or send his sons back to reclaim his patrimony. The appearance of Spanish exploring vessels in the period 1507–1510 greatly alarmed the empire's rulers.

The extraordinary story of the conquest of Mexico by Cortes and how it was aided by the psychological preparation mentioned above, and by the internal stresses of the Aztec system are well known. It took Cortes only two years to reduce the Aztecs to slaves and their marvellous city to malodorous rubble. As much as cultural and political destruction figured in the conquest, there was the horrific population loss during the conquest period and for the next 160 years of the colonial era. It is estimated that the Indian population of the basin was reduced from about 1.2 million in 1519 to some 70,000 by 1680. This was accomplished by all causes: war, slavery, diseases, overwork, malnutrition, and famine. The basin was not alone in suffering this process. It is estimated on good grounds that the total population loss in Mesoamerica during the same period was on the order of 85 to 95 percent, in some areas.

The Spaniards retained the collaborating native elites for the first part of the colonial period, but the increased tribute, and the reduced populations and depressed economic conditions rapidly reduced these descendants of the pipiltin to poverty-stricken remnants hardly distinguishable from their former vassals and serfs. One wonders if the sadness and bitterness of the world view of much of Indian culture today in the highlands is not the legacy of this disastrous past which has not yet been fully redeemed.

They have been destroyed by the great and excessive tribute they have had to pay, for in their great fear of the Spaniards they have given all they had. Since the tribute was excessive and continually demanded, to make payment they sold their lands at a low price, and their children as slaves. When they had nothing left with which to pay, many died for this in prison; if they managed to get out, they emerged in such sorry state that they died in a few days. Others died from being tortured to tell where there was gold or where they had hidden it. They have been treated bestially and unreasonably in all respects (Zorita, 1963: 207).

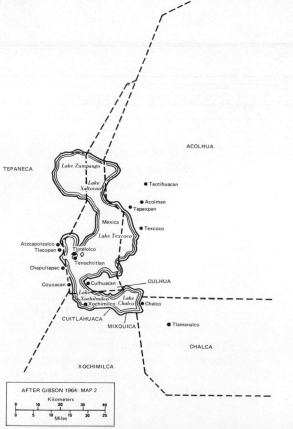

1 △

2 ▷

The Aztec. *By 1519 the Aztecs had complete control of the Basin of Mexico and less secure control over a vast territory outside the basin (1, 2). The series of lakes in the basin influenced the main political divisions of the region (2). Supported by intensive agriculture and by extensive tribute systems, the valley population may have reached 11 million people.*

AFTER GIBSON 1964: MAP 2

3 △

4 ▽

A reconstruction of Tenochtitlan's central civic precinct (3) features twin temples dedicated to the gods Tlaloc and Huitzilopochtli. Other temples were dedicated to Tezcatlipoca and Quetzalcoatl. This zone, including rulers' palaces, formed the administrative heart of the empire.

The emperor Tizoc ruled from 1481 to 1486. The basalt sculpture known as the Stone of Tizoc (4) shows fifteen scenes of Tizoc with defeated opponents. In reality, Tizoc was a failure as a militarist and may have been poisoned by his colleagues, clearing the way for Ahuitzotl, a much more successful ruler.

Ahuitzotl (1486-1502) came to power at a time when work on the Great Temple was being completed. A sculpture (8) commemorates this ruler by depicting his name glyph.

The splendid raiment of Aztec rulers is only hinted at by the reconstructed replica of Moteczoma II's headdress made of quetzal feathers in gold armatures (5).

5 ▽

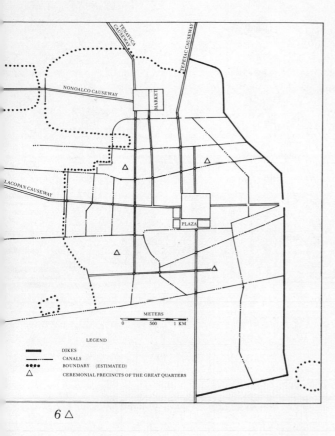

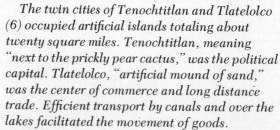

The twin cities of Tenochtitlan and Tlatelolco (6) occupied artificial islands totaling about twenty square miles. Tenochtitlan, meaning "next to the prickly pear cactus," was the political capital. Tlatelolco, "artificial mound of sand," was the center of commerce and long distance trade. Efficient transport by canals and over the lakes facilitated the movement of goods.

Examples of materials traded in the urban markets are the fine ceramics shown here (7, right and bottom). Craftsmen residing in the cities produced these items and stone ceremonial vessels (7, upper left). Surviving codices of the period, such as the Codex Borgia, attest to the inheritance by the Aztecs and their neighbors of the Mixtec-Puebla art style.

6 △

8 ▽

7 △

47

9 △

10 ▽

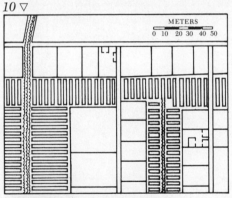

The Codex Borgia is a screen fold document painted on deer skin and probably made at Cholula. Among the supernatural events depicted, the rain god Tlaloc here (9) tends his growing corn in a chinampa.

The chinampa system was one of the most productive gardening systems in the world. Large areas of the shallow lakes were occupied by fields built of layers of water plants and lake mud. Tenochtitlan and Tlatelolco were chinampa cities, as can be seen in Calnek's reconstruction of a chinampa zone (10) in what is now downtown Mexico City. Xochimilco (11) represents a beautiful fragment of a chinampa area that once occupied more than 25,000 acres.

11 ▽

12 △

13 △

14 △

Aztec cosmology and religion were preoccupied with cycles of time and deities, such as Tonatiuh, the sun god, depicted on the giant disc known as the calendar stone (12). Coyolxauhqui, the moon goddess, is usually shown dead (14), having been decapitated by her brother, the great Huitzilopochtli, patron of the Aztecs. On earth, the mother of the gods, Coatlicue (13), influenced both life and death. Her shoulders support a head made up of two serpents, signifying the life-death dualism of nature. Her hands, belt, and skirt are stylized serpents. The necklace is made of human hearts and hands, and the central pendant is a skull. Filled with religious meaning, such Aztec sculptures both explained and probed the universe.

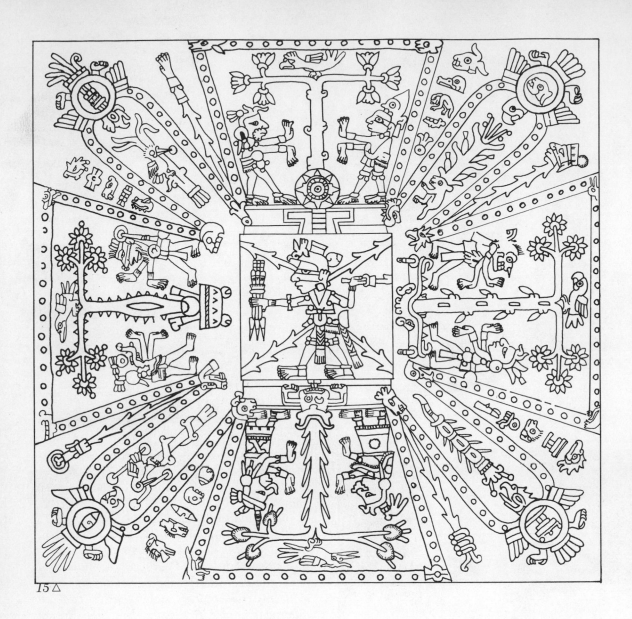

15 △

Gods of the five directions—including the zenith—are shown in the Codex Fejervary-Mayer (15), demonstrating a fundamental connection with religions of Indian North America, where gods are similarly identified with the directions. Success or failure of crops was controlled by the gods. There were a multitude to be placated by sacrifice, such as the three corn deities. One of these was Centeocihuatl, goddess of mature maize (17). The fire god is one of the most ancient and widespread in Mesoamerica and is here shown as Xiuhtecuhtli, the fire serpent (16). Ocelocuahxicalli, shown by the large stone jaguar effigy, was a god connected with sacrifice (18).

50

16 △

△ 17

18▽

51

19 △

△ 20 ▽

◁ 21

22 △

23 ▽

Sacrifice was a constant and onerous burden, but the Aztecs practiced it with dedication. Hearts of human victims were extracted with flint-bladed knives (20), often decorated with mosaic inlay on the handles. The hearts, offered to the gods, may have been deposited on the Chacmuls (19), or in other suitable receptacles, such as the stone jaguar effigy heart bowl (18).

Stone tzompantli (22, 23), or skull racks, supported wooden frames with the skulls of victims. A sculptured "year bundle" indicates the concern for the cyclical nature of time and its renewal through human sacrifice. Tezcatlipoca, a god of death, night, and evil events, shown here being born (24), was a principal deity among Central Mexican groups. War was the principal source of sacrificial victims and the gods' faces were used as decoration on shields (21) and other implements of war.

24 ▷

25 △

26 ▽

The following examples of small scale Aztec art offer insights into the culture not afforded by the monumental art. Clay figurines (25, 27) were used in curing and fertility rites. A stone mask from Teayo in Veracruz (26) was probably attached to a god's image. Small clay replicas of temples (28) perhaps were architectural models. Humble but useful items of daily life were a nicely polished clay pitcher (29) and a molcajete bowl (30) scored on the bottom for grinding chilies, tomatoes and other foods.

27 ▽

28 △

29 ▽

△30

CHAPTER 3

FIRST IMMIGRANTS
AND THE ESTABLISHMENT
OF SETTLED LIFE

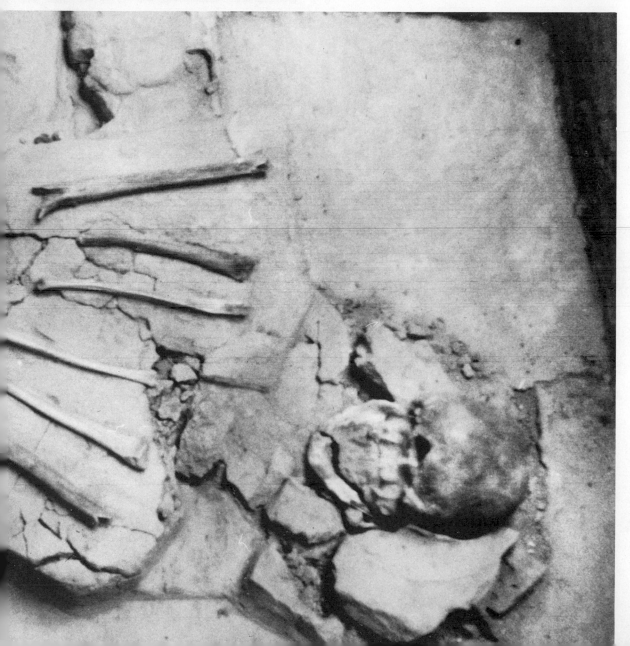

O protector of all, O giver of life, O Titlacauan [Tezcatlipoca], pity me, give me what is necessary for my life and for my strength—of thy gentleness and sweet essence. For now there is want; there is fatigue in gaining one's needs. . . . Take pity upon me.
—Sahagun, Book 3, 1963: 11.

If one looks closely he will find that everything [these indians] did and talked about had to do

with maize; in truth, they fell little short of making a god of it. And so much is the delight and gratification they got and still get out of their corn fields, that because of them they forget wife and children and every other pleasure, as if their corn fields were their final goal and ultimate happiness.
—Cronica de la Santa Provincia del Santissimo Nombre de Jesus de Guattemala, in Morley, 1946: 2.

TEPEXPAN. Excavations along the former shoreline of northeastern Lake Texcoco led to the discovery of human fossils perhaps dating as long ago as 10,000 B.P. The remains, actually those of a woman, help to prove that paleo-indians occupied this part of Mexico during the Late Pleistocene.

POSSIBLE EARLIEST FINDS. It is nearly an article of faith among archaeologists that the earliest inhabitants of the New World came from northeast Asia, crossing at the Bering Strait. It is also unfortunately true that the earliest surely dated material found in the New World is in South America dated at about 22,000 B.C. Most of the certain evidence for man's appearance in North America, where geography would dictate that the earliest remains should occur, are in the 16,000 to 11,000 B.C. range. Mesoamerica is no different from the rest of the northern continent, in that the earliest secure evidence of man's presence is placed at about 11,000 B.C. The areas closest to Asia — Alaska and Canada — have not produced any significantly earlier material. Thus, we immediately run into difficulties of the first magnitude when attempting to outline the first migration and the nature of the first cultures appearing in the area. We are not sure, within 40,000 years, when man actually arrived, nor do we even have a certain idea as to the stone tool kit that he carried with him.

No evidence for morphologically primitive man has yet been found in the Americas. All skeletal material falls well within the range of variation of native groups as they are known from the five hundred years of European contact. There are few and uncertainly dated skeletal remains recently discovered in Minnesota and Texas which are possibly earlier than 13,000 B.C. and more "primitive," but these are incompletely published or not at all.

Taken together, the above indications suggest that man was a relatively late arrival from Asia, perhaps as late as 35,000 years ago, and that later arrivals may have brought with them a set of ideas about stone tools which included the punched blade technique and the lanceolate point. Nearly all of the securely dated material from North America includes some sort of lance-like projectile point de-signed to be attached to shafts to form darts or spears.

However, there is a body of material, nearly all uncertainly dated, which is scattered through dozens of sites over all of the Americas, and which consistently lacks the projectile point in the inventory of stone tools. These sites also fairly consistently show an emphasis on the cruder means of manufacturing tools, by percussion or direct blows of one stone on another. Thus, most of the forms produced are flakes and choppers, or generalized scraping, digging, and gouging tools. It is claimed that this material represents the real beginning of man's habitation of the New World and that it may go back in time to around 100,000 years ago. This claim seems exaggerated to many. This is not the place to discuss in detail the various aspects of arguments except as they apply to Middle America. However, it might be noted that the earliest stone tool, or *lithic* complex in MacNeish's recently excavated Peruvian sequence, the Paccaicasa, tentatively dated at 22,000 B.C., displays the general characteristics noted above for the pre–projectile point sites. Considering the distances involved between the Bering Strait and Peru, and the necessarily halting and random nature of the earliest migrant movements, MacNeish thinks that 100,000 years is not an unreasonable estimate for the entry into the Americas of men and tools ancestral to Paccaicasa (1971). However, as Cowgill points out, this estimate would assume that early man was extraordinarily infertile and that there were only tiny groups in the New World for 85,000 years, after which population growth took off. The other alternative is that man did not get here until 12,000 to 15,000 years ago.

Pre–projectile point material in Middle America is best represented by Irwin and Juan Armenta's sites in Puebla. Valsequillo is a well-known locality, and its stone tool complex lacks projectile points but includes some interesting pictures of Ice Age mammoths incised on elephant bone. The depictions were found with the tools in gravels which seem clearly to be of Wisconsin glaciation age. (The Wisconsin is the last of the four major glacial stages in North America and ended about 7000 B.C.) However, there is considerable difficulty in dating the Puebla materials, because dates before 200,000 B.P. have been produced by uranium series techniques on some bone. An initial estimate of 600,000 years of age on the Valsequillo gravels on a geological basis also conflicts with the archaeological evidence. Again the associated artifacts are a rather nondescript group of flakes, chips, choppers, and other generalized stone items. Other dating estimates have indicated that the Valsequillo material may be between 40,000 and 20,000 years old. In this case, as in the case of most of the pre–projectile point material, one aspect that worries cautious archaeologists is that the forms of the stone tools are such that they could date from any period up to and including Aztec times. The pictures of mammoths certainly indicate some antiquity, but do not necessarily date the material before 11,000 B.C., which is the date of securely documented kill finds of these animals in the Basin of Mexico. Perhaps the best that can be said is that Valsequillo, Hueyatlaco, and other Puebla finds give us intriguing possibilities which may yet be proven true.

Another possibly very ancient find is that of a carved sacrum of a Pleistocene cameloid, related to such present-day animals as the llama, and vicuña. The carving seems to be that of a dog's, wolf's, or coyote's face. The find was made in 1870 at Tequixquiac in the Basin of Mexico. Later reevaluation of the site has indicated that the find was made at the bottom of the Pleistocene lake deposits known as the Becerra formation. Simple stone scrapers and splinters of mammoth bone have been found at the same site, perhaps evidence

of early man's animal-killing and -processing activities. The splinters would represent butchering and perhaps marrow-extraction, and the scrapers could have been used as general cutting tools, and also to scrape pieces of hide. Dating is again insecure, but the bottom of the Becerra deposits are thought to have been laid down beginning around 40,000 years ago.

Again, the best we can say is that if MacNeish's finds in South America are dated correctly, then there should be finds of the age suggested by Valsequillo and Tequixquiac in Middle America. However, so far these finds have been sparse, anomalous, and unconvincing to most archaeologists.

ELEPHANT HUNTERS OR DARING PLANT GATHERERS? Really solid evidence for man's presence in Mesoamerica at an early date has been found by Luis Aveleyra Arroyo de Anda at two kill sites near the small town of Santa Izabel Iztapan in the northern Basin of Mexico (1964). The sites have similar stratigraphy and represent similar situations.

A couple of layers of recently deposited soil overlie a level candidly called the "green muck" which is part of the upper Becerra. The mammoth skeletons are mired in the green muck and are the remains of animals chased into the marshy edges of the Pleistocene lake, stabbed and irritated with javelins and spears, and literally "worried to death." Six stone tools were found with mammoth no. 1 and three other artifacts with mammoth no. 2. There are some difficulties with the dating of these items because some of them resemble stone points (Scottsbluff, for example) from elsewhere in North America which are pretty securely dated as in use from 7000 to 5000 B.C. However, the carbon 14 dates on the mammoth remains and upper Becerra fall between 9000 and 14,000 B.C. The difficulty has been resolved by the fact that the typological resemblances are not exact and that therefore the dating of the Mexican points need not be exactly that of the somewhat similar points from the Great Plains area. This being so, it seems best to accept the median dates on the upper Becerra and the mammoth bones, which is about 11,000 B.C. and which nicely overlaps with the earliest securely dated material in the rest of North America — Clovis points and their associated tool types. West Mexico has produced some finds of early projectile points, for example, at Zacoalco, Jalisco.

Cave sites in the Tehuacan Valley to the southeast of the Basin of Mexico and in Tamaulipas, far to the north, have produced approximately contemporary remains in the form of somewhat nondescript collections of scrapers, flakes, and chips. Inasmuch as the rest of the Tehuacan and Tamaulipas sequences show definite and increasing reliance on small animals and plant gathering, Mac-Neish suggested that big game hunting as a way of life never was the great thing that it was on the North American Great Plains. Indeed, MacNeish has made the statement that in central Mexico, if a man killed a mammoth he probably never stopped talking about it. The view of Mesoamerican Lithic stage peoples as engaging in plant gathering and small animal hunting and only occasionally and opportunistically hunting big game accords with the geographical and faunal evidence. As ecologically favorable as it was for many purposes, Mesoamerica did not have the vast and grassy plains to support large numbers of Pleistocene megafauna. Mammoths and other large game animals did occur, of course, but their numbers were small, and the kinds of specializations in meat eating and hunting which parallel the European Ice Age cultures were simply not possible.

An argument over the role of man in the extinction of large Ice Age game has become quite heated in recent years. Some authorities think that the changing climatic conditions after the retreat of the glaciers are the prime factor in the extinction of the large herd animals such as the mammoth. Paul S. Martin has argued, persuasively, that man, in combination with natural factors, played an important role (1965). However this argument may eventually be resolved in regard to the North American plains, in the restricted environmental zones of Mesoamerica, where the populations of large animals were relatively thin, this certainly seems a reasonable explanation of their extinction.

The physical remains of early human life in Mesoamerica were ingeniously found by Helmut de Terra in 1948 in the Basin of Mexico near the small town of Tepexpan. Unfortunately, the excavation technique and circumstances of discovery left much to be desired, and for some time there was grave doubt as to whether Tepexpan "man" was really a Pleistocene individual. The skeleton was found by means of a mine detector, which also detected a number of water pockets in the former lake bed. Finally, after many false alarms, the bones came to light and apparently were in association with the upper Becerra formation. However, the association was not certain, and proof had to wait for the later discoveries of the mammoths at nearby Santa Izabel Iztapan. Fluorine content of the mammoth bones is the same as that of the human bones, indicating that the human is indeed about the same age as the elephants. The individual was female and between twenty-five and thirty years old. It is interesting that the skeleton is morphologically modern and well within the normal range of variation of present-day Indian populations of central Mexico. Tepexpan woman, if resurrected and dressed correctly, could lose herself in present-day Mexico City crowds without comment. These characteristics fit with most other data from North America and again are possible indications of a relatively late human migration to the New World. However, this late migration could have been as much as 100,000 years ago, and so we again come against the difficulty of dating the initial migrations.

PLANT COLLECTORS AND INCIPIENT CULTIVATION, 7000–1500 B.C.

The record is not continuous between the first glimpse of the earliest cultures at the Iztapan and Tepexpan sites to the earliest remains in the dry cave sites of Tehuacan and Tamaulipas. As noted, there are hints that plant collecting and small animal hunting and trapping were always very important for the diet of early man. Indeed, the pattern of life developed during these periods never entirely died out. Even as late as Aztec times there were people called Chichimeca living near the Valley of Mexico. Duran says of these people:

They lived among the peaks and in the harshest places of the mountain where they lived a bestial existence. They had no human organization, but hunted food like beasts of the same mountain, and went stark naked without any covering on their private parts. They hunted all day for rabbits, deer, hares, weasels, moles, wildcats, birds, snakes, lizards, mice and they also collected locusts, worms, herbs, and roots. *Their whole life was reduced to a quest for food. . . .* These people slept in the hills inside caves, or under bushes, without any heed for sowing, cultivating or gathering. They did not worry about the morrow, but ate what they had hunted each day" (Duran, 1964: 12).

These statements are a fair match for the archaeological reconstruction of life during the long buildup toward village communities based on cultivation. However, it should be noted that the Aztecs and Duran are speaking of the survivors of this way of life in the sixteenth century, who had been relegated to only the least desirable zones. From 7000 to 1500 B.C. most people lived on wild foods and had access to the best and most fruitful zones. The Aztecs' views are also tempered by the prejudice of civilized people toward "more primitive" peoples. On the other hand, it is clear that most of human existence in these early times revolved around getting the next meal, even if the task was easier than in the sixteenth century.

SOCIAL AND ECOLOGICAL FACTORS. Social organization during the late Ice Age and early Postpleistocene epoch is reconstructed as having been family-centered with, at most, "band"-type organization. Apparently, at certain favorable times, these blood-related groups came together temporarily to form larger social groups. This type of society was necessary when population was thin and the way of life nomadic. MacNeish has characterized the smaller family groups as "microbands" and the larger, multifamily groups as "macrobands" (1964). The yearly economic rounds involved continual fissioning and regrouping between these two types of society. It is crucial that the same type of society is the one that developed Mesoamerican agriculture and that it formed the basis for the later village farming societies.

With the advantage of knowing the principal food plants that were important among later peoples, we can trace some of the ancestry of these plants through the archaeological sequences. Wild corn pollen has been detected from a core taken beneath the Palace of Fine Arts in downtown Mexico City, and dated as about 80,000 B.P. This and distributional evidence indicates that the central highlands of Mexico was one of the zones where wild corn (*Zea Maize*) grew. The Oaxacan and Mayan highlands also seem to have been areas which contained many of the wild ancestors of maize and others of the eventually cultivated plants.

The wild plant inventory for any single region of Mesoamerica, even if all of the plants were developed to the point of being productive when cultivated, would not be sufficient to support village life. The plants would be neither diverse nor productive enough. About fifty food plants of New World origin are for sale at present in Tehuacan's market, and most of these certainly did not originate or occur as wild plants in the valley at 7000 B.C. when plant domestication began there. However, the already-noted compressed ecological diversity within Mesoamerica, along with easy communication between the diverse zones, meant that a necessary condition was present: the possibility of trading both wild and "improved" (semidomesticated or domesticated) plants from zone to zone. That this necessary condition was taken advantage of in central Mexico is self-evident; we do have the rise of village life based on agriculture there. However, we apparently do not have the sufficient conditions, whatever those may have been, in the Maya highlands, to lead to the establishment of village farming life in that area. This is to say that just because the ecological conditions exist for something to happen, there is no inherent necessity for that event — the move to agricultural sedentism in this case — to occur. Ecological or environmental determinism does not explain all, then. Historical and other factors must be brought into the explanation. We will consider some of these factors after a review of the archaeological evidence. In the meantime, the environmental stage is set with the existence of the vast diversity of topography and associated diverse plant and animal communities crammed into a relatively small geographical area.

THE ARCHAEOLOGICAL EVIDENCE. The two major sequences which reflect the development of highland agriculture have both been developed by R. S. MacNeish. In an extraordinary and sustained effort, beginning in 1948 and continuing until the present (1975), the major features of this botanical, and social evolution have been recovered from a series of dry, dusty caves in the mountains of northeastern and central Mexico.

The Tehuacan Sequence. To the southeast of Mexico City, the modern provincial resort town of Tehuacan is located in a semiarid highland valley, about 5500 feet (1676 meters) above sea level. The valley rises toward the south and is delimited by mountainous terrain on the east and west. Better-watered zones occur on the margins and in the canyons of the area, and it was in these favored environments that the wild ancestors of corn grew. Porous rock formations in these mountains allowed the development of shelters and caves. These were favored habitation sites by early human populations. Families and groups of families visited these caves frequently, carrying their gathered plants, and the animals they trapped and hunted, with them for processing and eating. Wild plant seeds were ground on convenient stones, the animals skinned (or sometimes not) and cooked and eaten. Seeds, fragments of animal bones, the grinding stones, pieces of gourd rind, fireplaces, human feces, bits of basketry and netting, chipped stone tools, and other debris littered these caves when in use. These discarded and lost items gradually built up in layers over time, and preserved the record of man's activities, and his increasingly successful manipulation and utilization of plants. As usual, archaeologists have divided up the long period of time involved into convenient segments or phases, each of which is defined by a certain group of stone tools, plants, and, later, pottery. The chronology chart of the Tehuacan phases and other phases from about 7000 to 1500 B.C. in Mesoamerica shows how these fit together from one region to another. The longest, most continuous, and most informative of these sequences is from the Tehuacan

Valley. The accompanying illustrations also show the changes in food sources, in food gathering activities and in food preparation through time, all based on the Tehuacan data. About 10,000 pieces of plant remains, more than 11,000 zoological specimens, and over 100 pieces of human feces were recovered. The latter are very important for dietary information, representing as they do, complete meals and direct evidence of human consumption. A scientist named Callen has ingeniously devised a way in which to restore these feces to their pristine condition. Although this procedure has its disadvantages, it also results in such information as the proportion of meat in a diet. Hair and bone fragments even allow identification of animal species consumed.

The earliest phase, *Ajuereado*, is clearly one of a society already adapted to small animal hunting and wild plant collecting at around 7200 B.C. Over 40 percent of the diet was derived from wild plants and some 54 percent from meat. These trends continue into the better known *El Riego phase,* which begins about 7000 B.C. At least nineteen kinds of wild plants were used, but already three plants show evidence of domestication, the most important of which is a type of squash (*Cucurbita mixta*). Chili peppers and avocados are also probably early domesticates, but all three contribute less than 5 percent to the diet. Many uncultivated cactuses, grass seeds (especially *Setaria*), and mesquite beans were eaten. *Amaranth,* important among the later Aztecs as a cereal, is also important as a gathered plant. Callen's basic data tells us that meat was eaten but he cannot identify it. Population of the valley is estimated to have been three family groups, twelve to twenty-four people.

The *Coxcatlan phase* (5500–4500 B.C.) is one of the most significant in the sequence because of the initial appearance of maize. It appears in an economy which is still heavily plant-collecting and is wild or semidomesticated. Human population is still thin. How-

ever, the amounts of food from gardening activities have risen to 14 percent and include primitive corn, chilis, squash, and amaranth. For both El Riego and Coxcatlan times, the principal subsistence activities were rabbit drives, stalking game with darts, and collecting fruits and pods and seeds, all of which were more important than gardening. These mainly wild foods were eaten after having been boiled (vegetables and fruits), milled (grass seeds), and steamed or boiled (meat). Marrow was extracted from the bones. Meat and plant products were also eaten raw. Life was still somewhat nomadic although gardening and gathering allowed staying in one spot from spring to fall. Nearly all of the stone technology was devoted to exploitation of natural resources. Chipped flint points tipped the darts used for hunting; game was skinned with flint flakes, and hides were prepared by scraping with special stone tools. Hide preparation was aided by bone awls for punching holes. Large choppers represent general digging tools which could be used for digging into rodent burrows, and for grubbing up roots. For both El Riego and Coxcatlan phases, there are stone bowls, which are probably mortars. A certain amount of ritual in the lives of these people revolved around the burial of the dead. Some offerings accompanied the bodies — probably blankets, baskets, and perhaps food. No permanent housing or special buildings of any sort are known.

The next two phases of the sequence, *Abejas* and *Purron,* are the last Tehuacan phases that we shall consider, although the sequence continues into the sixteenth century. Abejas and Purron represent a block of time from about 3500 to 1500 B.C. During these phases, agricultural output provided first 21 percent and later 35 percent of the diet with a continuous increase in productivity until, about A.D. 600, a peak of 75 percent of all foodstuffs is reached. On the other hand, meat diminishes steadily throughout the sequence, falling from nearly 70 percent of the diet in Ajuereado (7200 B.C.) to 17 percent about A.D. 600. Major factors in these changes are plant improvement through various genetic modifications, and continual addition of plants which are not native to the Tehuacan Valley, such as various races of beans. An excellent example of genetic change is the history of corn, which has been reconstructed by Paul Mangelsdorf of Harvard University (Mangelsdorf, 1974, esp. 45–52 and 180–185).

Wild corn was a primitive and unpromising plant, and one wonders why it was selected at all for development. It was both a pod and pop corn, with the individual tiny kernels wrapped each in their own glume. The cobs are only about the length of a one-cent piece. Quids from the 7000 B.C. material show that ancient people ate corn by simply chewing it up for the juices and then spat out the remainder. Early corn might have had a dispersal problem because of the kernel wrappings, but in compensation, the ear was placed high on the plant. There might also have been a fertilization problem for the same reason — the kernel wrappings — but this was not the case, since each ear had its own tassel carrying pollen. Mangelsdorf and his associates, through a series of genetic experiments, tried to reproduce the primitive ancestor of corn (Mangelsdorf et al., 1967). They did not precisely succeed, but as Mangelsdorf says, they did succeed in developing the world's most unproductive corn.

To reach the productivity and characteristics of modern corn, one of the world's great cereal crops, an incredibly complex series of genetic changes and crosses had to take place. Mangelsdorf and his colleagues have worked these out through experimentation and theoretical genetics, and their reconstructions have been partially confirmed by archaeology. Corn was domesticated not only in Mesoamerica, but also in the South American west coast area of Peru and Ecuador where races of wild maize occurred. The primitive domesticate from Mesoamerica almost certainly crossed with the equally primitive domesticate in South America. This dropped certain genetic barriers and another crossing took place between the improved corn and *Tripsacum,* a grass that grows in Bolivia and other parts of the Andean area. The second crossing resulted in explosive evolution with changes in ear and kernel sizes and in other characteristics. For example, the tassel moved to the top of the plant and the ears lost their individual tassels. The improved corn was traded back to Mesoamerica, and there crossed with another native grass, *teosinte.* Teosinte has its own complicated history, and seems to have been an offspring of primitive corn and Tripsacum. Improved South American corn crossed with teosinte, leading to a second explosive evolution and resulting in the modern races of maize. This was still not the extraordinary series of races of modern hybridized corn with which we are familiar, but more resembled North American dent corn.

The long quiescent controversy about the origins of corn and the place of teosinte in its evolution has proved to be only dormant and not dead. George Beadle, former provost of the University of Chicago, has retired to his teosinte patch and has been building a case for teosinte as the direct ancestor of corn (Beadle, 1972).

Beadle's arguments revolve around the fact that teosinte is the closest relative of corn, with a genetic difference on the order of only four or five genes. In Beadle's view this renders acceptable the hypothesis that teosinte might be ancestral to corn, especially since Mangelsdorf now suggests that wild corn is probably the ancestor of both maize and teosinte. If one accepts the latter, Beadle argues, then why not consider the reverse: that is, that teosinte is the ancestor of corn and modern teosinte? Teosinte is the more successful wild plant and therefore a more likely candidate. Further, teosinte can be rendered into a good food by either popping or grinding it. Beadle argues that the earliest archaeological corn, as found in the Tehuacan sequence, represents a transitional form from teosinte to maize and not an ancestral wild maize. He is forced to speculate, however, that domestication began much earlier than we have evidence for.

Mangelsdorf has replied in his magnum opus entitled (what else?) *Corn* (1974). He accepts the fact that teosinte is the closest relative of maize, and that it can be eaten if popped or ground. His main refutation rests on the fact that Beadle's possibilities are not probable, and, indeed, go against all the factual evidence now in hand. No evidence has ever been found for the extensive use of teosinte as food, in either ancient or modern times. Ground teosinte is over half kernel shell which, if eaten, would show up in prehistoric feces. None of the Tehuacan coprolites had teosinte kernel fragments in them. Further, although Beadle once consumed 150 grams of ground teosinte a day, Mangelsdorf points out that this yields only one-sixth of an adult's average daily caloric needs. Also, a meal does not make a diet. Mangelsdorf also says that teosinte's characteristics are much more specialized than those of maize and that the transition from teosinte to maize would therefore be more difficult than the reverse process. The large part of the rebuttal rests on the massive archaeological evidence which is compatible with Mangelsdorf's theory and incompatible with the teosinte theory.

The Tamaulipas Sequence.   It is now time to turn to the other major sequence showing a series of phases of domestication; that from Tamaulipas. The northeastern corner of modern Mexico is mountainous and much of it is semiarid mesquite country, and it is thus drier than the Tehuacan zone. An indication of the hotter climate might be noted in MacNeish's phase names for the sequence (1958), one of which is *Infiernillo* (Inferno). Again there is a long developmental buildup through phases beginning about 7200 B.C. and culminating with the establishment of full-time agriculture and village communities about 1500 B.C. The sequence and timing of appearance of plants is different from that of Tehuacan. In Tamaulipas, squashes are the first domesticate, but they are of a different species (*Cucurbita pepo*) than, and presumably represent the domesticated version of, the local wild plant. The same intensification of gathering and gardening activities takes place with the same social changes from nomadic bands to semi-nomadic groups, and finally, to semipermanent villages. Early Tehuacan squash (*Cucurbita mixta*) does not occur at the Tamaulipas sites until well after A.D. 1. The greatest difference is in the appearance of corn, which shows up first at Tamaulipas sites about 3000 B.C., nearly 2000 years after its first appearance at Tehuacan. It also is an improved variety, in its first appearance, albeit not greatly so. There are other contrasts in appearances of crucial food plants: species and varieties of beans, for example. However, enough has been said to make the point that domestication and development of food plants was a process in which all of Mesoamerica was involved, and at times, even areas outside Mesoamerica made their contributions. By 1500 B.C. nearly every major region of the cotradition area had achieved a village farming level.

It is noteworthy that there are no domesticated animals of great food importance. Dogs show up as domesticates about 3000 B.C. and certainly were eaten as well as being used as aids in hunting, but dogs are no substitute for cattle, sheep, goats, or pigs, all of which were lacking in the New World.

There is no direct evidence from the tropical lowlands for domestication of food plants, but there are important plants which are certainly of lowland origin, such as vanilla, cacao, various squash-like vegetables such as *huisquil,* and many fruits. MacNeish has considered this data as well as the highland evidence and has suggested a comprehensive explanation for the establishment of village life in both major altitude zones and one which also explains certain later events (1966).

Possible Early Lowland Villages.   Large shell mound sites exist both on the Gulf and Pacific coasts of Mesoamerica, but few have even been cursorily examined. Exceptions to this are the Sanja and Puerto Marquez sites located on lagoons on the Pacific coast of Guerrero. A date on material from the shell middens has been read as about 2900 B.C., and is preceramic. Another date, 2400 B.C., is associated with the earliest appearance of pottery in Mesoamerica. The mounds are large enough to suggest semipermanent village life. Other hints of early communities come from some shell heaps on the Veracruz coast where James Ford and Alfonso Medellin-Zenil have found masses of chipped stone and fire-cracked rocks in large sites located on top of fossil sand dunes. No pottery was found on these sites, indicating a date possibly earlier than 2400 B.C. The chipped stone tools from the Veracruz sites are roughly similar to those from the general period of 5000–3000 B.C. in the Tehuacan Valley. Not many grinding stones are present, indicating a reliance on food sources other than seeds. The locations of these sites suggest that shell fishing, fishing in the lagoons and off shore, and small animal hunting supported these semipermanent early lowland villages. MacNeish (1966) suggests that this pattern of life and its subsistence base developed between 7000 and 5000 B.C. when the highland groups were taking their first halting steps toward cultivation and settled life. Certainly, MacNeish thinks, perma-

nent, sedentary villages were in existence on the coasts between 5000 and 3000 B.C., and thus a longer tradition of sedentism belongs in the lowlands. These early villages were in favored ecological situations with the resources of the sea, lagoons, estuaries, swamps, and several transitional types of microzones available to them. This localized compression of resource zones led to a stable pattern of village life. After 3000 B.C. it is clear that lowland societies begin to acquire domesticated plants and techniques of cultivation from the highlands, and this meant instant food surpluses. The major centers of initial lowland cultivation were probably along the rivers, where the most fertile land was located. Lowe has suggested that population growth associated with the possibilities of agriculture, and the anxieties that an agricultural way of life brings, led to the establishment of more formal religious concepts (1971). The food surpluses, the longer tradition of sedentism in the lowlands, the motivation of religious assuagement of anxieties over crops and hazards to the crops, may well have combined to lead to the establishment of formal ceremonial architecture dedicated to ritual. We shall return to this argument when the origin of Olmec civilization is discussed.

There are indications of early regional specializations in cultivated plants in the lowlands as well as in the highlands. The Altamira site on the coast of Chiapas, Lowe has suggested, is in a zone that is more suitable for the cultivation of the tropical root crop, *manioc,* than maize. Although this site dates about 1500 B.C., it may well reflect a continuation of long-established tradition.

All of the above is rather unsatisfactory in terms of hard facts and evidence, but there is at least one thing in its favor. It fits the pattern of large-scale and intense interaction among the various parts of Mesoamerica which characterized it in later periods of prehistory. The symbiotic patterns of Aztec times seem prefigured in the simpler, but no less significant trading of early domesticates among the regions of the highlands. There is nothing to hinder the participation of the lowlands in this kind of interaction, and all of the hints in the archaeological record point toward it. It is clear that much more work is indicated in this problem, and especially in the unglamorous but crucial matter of shell midden excavation. At this time MacNeish's model seems the best explanation of domestication of plants, establishment of village life, and the basis for later, more sophisticated communities.

COMPARISON WITH OLD WORLD DOMESTICATION. In going over the sequences of New World plant domestication one is struck by the inordinate length of time that it took to achieve a viable food plant complex — over 5000 years. When we look at the record of this process in the Old World we find that things moved much faster. In the Greater Middle East, the development of agriculture and animal domestication took place from about 8500 to 6000 B.C., about half the time of that of the New World. K. V. Flannery has suggested that this could be due to three main factors (1973). The first is the nature of the differences between the New World and Old World cereal crops. Wheat is nearly as productive in the wild as it is under cultivation and needs little modification to bring into domestication. Second, the larger numbers of animals available for domestication in the Old World apparently took up the slack when the first plant domesticates were being developed. Goats and sheep were domesticated first, and then cattle and pigs, all of which carry considerably more meat per animal than dogs and turkeys, the principal Mesoamerican domesticates. The third factor is the nature of the societies involved. Flannery suggests that due to the general lack of larger animals available in the New World, and the general

emphasis on gathering, there was not the specialization of labor by sex that one found in Old World hunting and gathering communities. Even a child can hit a lizard on the head, but it takes a man in full strength to deal with hunting and attempts at domestication of wild cattle. In the Old World men and women in Pleistocene societies had distinct task roles, which preadapted them for agricultural life, in which women also stay around the village or base camp and the men are out cultivating. In the New World hunting and gathering societies, apparently everyone did everything, and it took time for social organization to change and develop the greater efficiency conferred by work specialization according to sex.

THE PROBLEM OF THE ORIGINS OF MESOAMERICAN POTTERY

The earliest Mesoamerican pottery, found at Puerto Marquez on the Pacific coast of Mexico, was apparently fiber-tempered. Tempering (or grog), as any potter knows, is material added to the clay to encourage more uniform expansion of the clay during firing. Otherwise, uneven expansion causes spalling, breakage, and other kinds of disappointment. The initial tempering material used in much of early pottery in the New World was chopped grass or other organic material. This material burns out or carbonizes during firing, leaving characteristically porous and lightweight ceramics. The earliest pottery in the Tehuacan sequence is similar to that found at Puerto Marquez, but dates about 2200 B.C. It has been suggested that the stone bowls of the same form found in the sequence are prototypes from which the ceramic forms were developed. However, the dating of these bowls is not certain, and it may be the other way around; the stone bowls are imitations of ceramic forms.

Fiber-tempered pottery is also the first pottery of any kind to occur in the New World and is found at a site called Puerto Hormiga on the northern, Caribbean, coast of Colombia at about 3000 B.C. Such pottery also shows up on the Atlantic coasts of Georgia and Florida around 2500 B.C. The late James Ford argued that the first ideas about pottery were developed in South America, possibly from concepts introduced from Japan, and thence spread north and south over the North American continent (1969). Whether or not we want to stamp all of this earliest pottery as "made in Japan," the similarity in form and tempering among all of the earliest ceramics and their dating sequence make it plausible to derive these ceramics from South America. A newly found site, on the northern tip of Yucatan, is a shell midden which contains fiber-tempered pottery, and may well be a way-station in Ford's theoretical pottery diffusion from south to north.

In any case, there is clearly a horizon of large, round-sided, neckless jars, and flat-bottomed, open pans, tempered with organic material, found in a wide area around 2400 to 2000 B.C. in Mesoamerica. From this basic horizon all the later regional, diverse, and very sophisticated ceramic traditions apparently stem.

There is no inherent quality in pottery, however, that means that any great cultural change is taking place. Pottery is simply an easily replaceable container material which has certain advantages over basketry; it can be used for cooking, for example, and water does not leak out of it so easily. It may reflect a greater sedentism in village life with consequent accumulation of more storable material, although this is not necessarily so. It is certainly large in the consciousness of archaeologists, but this is mainly because of its utility as an analytical device for defining cultural regions, and marking phase boundaries.

THE ESTABLISHMENT OF REGIONAL VARIETIES OF VILLAGE LIFE

The *Barra phase,* is associated with mound building and manioc cultivation at the site of Altamira. It is located in the low, swampy coastal zone of Chiapas and dates to around 1650 B.C. or so. Nothing so far found ties it up with the earlier Puerto Marquez "pox" pottery. Barra pottery is sophisticated in decorative techniques compared to either pox ceramics or Purron pottery in Tehuacan. At Altamira, the ceramic forms are those of squashes or gourds complete with the fluting and undulating surface which imitates the segmented surfaces of pumpkins or squashes. Obsidian chips were found which may have been used in the scraping of manioc in preparation for eating. Lowe has suggested that this pottery developed when a preceramic group which had previously used gourds as containers adopted pottery from a South American source (Green and Lowe, 1967). They simply imitated the forms of their older containers.

About 1500 B.C., another early ceramic complex appears in the Pacific coast of Guatemala which is also apparently South American in origin: the Ocos complex. This is the first detectable period of cultural uniformity for a large area of Mesoamerica. The area is the Isthmus of Tehuantepec and the coastal regions of Veracruz-Tabasco on the north side and the Chiapas-Guatemalan-Salvadorean Pacific coast on the south. The Grijalva River trench seems included in this area. The use of very similar pottery and settlements soon spread over the isthmian area and are presently known from at least twenty sites. Most of these are in a coastal, lagoon-estuary environmental setting, but some are on inland rivers at favored locations. Subsistence activities clearly are lagoon fishing, farming the piedmont zones, and the annually flooded river levee zones. The ceramics are again very sophisticated and distinctive, with large, globular jars (*tecomate* forms) and flat pans decorated typically with stamped designs of various sorts including rocker stamping, zoned dentate stamping, shell-back stamping, as well as cord marking and fabric impression. Color occurs in iridescent stripes and in specular hematite red bands around the mouths of the jars. The type site of La Victoria is located on a former lagoon and is even today not far from the Pacific. Its excavator, M. D. Coe, has pointed out striking similarities between Ocos pottery and Chorrera phase (around 1500 B.C.) ceramics in the Guayaquil coastal zone of Ecuador (1960). Among the similarities and near identities is the use of the open pan form, rocker stamping, and iridescent banding. The coast of western South America was noted in the sixteenth century for the development of seamanship and varying sorts of crafts, which include sailing rafts of the sort made famous by the Kon-Tiki expedition. Coe has shown how currents and seasonal winds would aid and make possible voyages between the regions involved.

At this point then, several things come together in a possible explanation. South American contacts have been indicated several times already — the earliest mention was in the genetic reconstruction of maize's domestication history. Pottery-using communities may have intruded onto the Mesoamerican coasts several times and at several places, both on the Gulf and Pacific sides. Manioc use is possible in the Barra phase, and the emphasis on this plant is definitely more South American than Mesoamerican. The mechanism of contact would have been voyages across the Caribbean and Pacific, mainly coastal voyages or even inside the lagoons which stretch for miles and which provide protected waters. However, there is every evidence that early sailors in the New World did not hesitate to leave the sight of land, at least for short distances. Recent work indicates that the West Indies were initially colonized by island-hopping sea-travelers at least by 5000 B.C., again coming from South America.

Although ceramics were introduced several times from outside Mesoamerica, directly from South America or from intermediate Central American regions, the Ocos horizon is the first which really took hold and spread the idea across a broad area. Almost certainly the ideas were not carried by South American populations, but accepted by already sedentary Mesoamerican populations.

Coe and Gareth Lowe suggest that Ocos pottery is so sophisticated that some people must have spent almost all of their time producing it. If so, there must have been a new kind of society, one in which there are non-food producers and in which there are specialists of other sorts. If a group can support a potter at least part-time, it certainly can support a religious specialist, a shaman, equally well. Little information is available on religious concepts of this time, but female figurines appear and perhaps indicate the sort of fertility ideas with which they were associated in later Aztec times. Lowe also suggests that family possession of the crucial agricultural and orchard crop resources might lead to high-status lineages and social stratification based on relative wealth.

Although the highlands of central and southern Mexico were clearly occupied during this period by village agriculturists, and many of the lowland areas were being utilized by pioneer farmers using Ocos horizon pottery, it seems equally clear that large areas of Mesoamerica were essentially vacant. Although a negative case is difficult to prove, it appears that much of the Maya highlands and the tropical forest zone of the interior of the peninsula of Yucatan were empty zones which were used only by hunting and gathering groups. In much of the Guatemalan highlands there is only very weak evidence or no evidence at all of village agriculturists, and in the Guatemalan lowlands the first colonists appear only about 800 B.C. or at the outside, 1000 B.C. However, human population was rapidly expanding and there are a significantly greater number of sites known for the period 1350 to 1100 B.C.

As will be seen, the relatively low Salvadorean mountain valleys, and even the Caribbean coastal lowlands of Honduras, were occupied by Ocos horizon cultures. The Cuyamel Caves of Honduras have yielded bottle forms which are very similar to those found at San Lorenzo in the Bajio phase (1350–1250 B.C.).

Ocos horizon sites are found in the wetlands of the Veracruz coast and underlie at least two of the later great ceremonial centers of Olmec civilization, San Lorenzo and probably La Venta. Ojochi, Bajio, and Chicharras phases are clearly developments from an Ocos base, and it is upon this base that the first, and in some ways most spectacular, civilization of Mesoamerica rests.

1 △

2 ▽

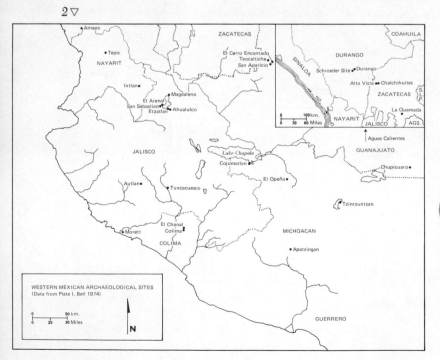

WESTERN MEXICAN ARCHAEOLOGICAL SITES
(Data from Plate I, Bell 1974)

▽ 3 △

4 ▷

5 △

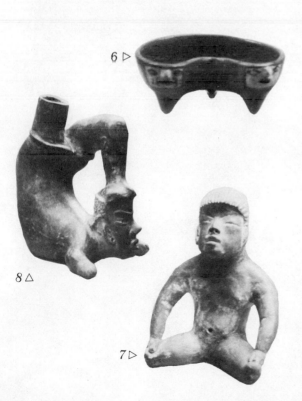

6 ▷

8 △

7 ▷

Cultures of Central and Western Mexico (2).
*Our knowledge of the long period of the western
and central Preclassic cultures is dominated by
ceramics from burials. These items should be
seen in the context of the village societies
that made them and whose lifeways they reflect.*

*Special burial vessels such as those from
Tlatilco (3) show evidence of linkages with Western Mexico and other regions. Clay female
figurines (1) indicate that the curing and fertility
rites of Aztec days came from deep in the past.*

*Large hollow "babies" imported from the Gulf
Coast Olmec culture (4, 7) indicate trade and
perhaps closer connections for Tlapacoya and
other basin centers. Unique clay figures of acrobats, this one from Tlatilco (8), may represent a
style native to the basin.*

*A Late Preclassic culture Chupicuaro, cen-
tered on the Lerma River, is known principally
from the excavation of over 400 burials (5).
Spider-legged tripods (5) and kidney-shaped
bowls (6) are typical ceramic forms.*

73

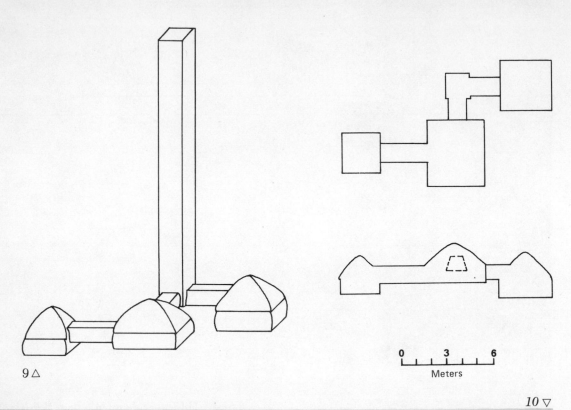

9 △

10 ▽

The rich western tradition of ceramic figurines began in the Preclassic and lasted long into the Classic. Shaft tombs such as the one from El Opeño (9) have produced thousands of lively figures which reflect everyday life. Large, seated figures from Jalisco (11, 15) suggest that tattooing, body painting and scarification were all practiced.

Cranial deformation may be represented in the Chinesca style, such as this example (12) from Nayarit. Ball game players (13) are frequent and indicate the popularity of the game. Certain styles such as the "gingerbread" types from Jalisco (10) do seem to have been ritual in function. What were probably village temples (14) show up as models. Western Mexico was Mesoamerican in rural patterns, even if it lagged behind in the development of civic centers.

11 ▷

12 ▽

13 ▷

14 ▷

15 ▷

16 △

*Nowhere does the reality of ancient life appear
more strongly than in the models of village scenes
from Nayarit. This example shows a group of
people and three houses (18). The people who
lived in such villages are portrayed in the figures
of women gesturing and nursing babies (16, 20)
and a man holding a ball and paddle (17), along
with their dogs (19) and parrots (21).*

18 ▽

17 ▷

76

19 △

20 ▷

21 ▽

CHAPTER 4

THE EXTRAORDINARY OLMEC

In 1862 I was in the region of San Andres Tuxtla, a town of the state of Veracruz, in Mexico. During my excursions, I learned that a Colossal Head had been unearthed a few years before in the following manner. Some one and a half leagues from a sugarcane hacienda, on the western slopes of the Sierra of San Martin, a laborer of this hacienda, while cutting the forest for his field, discovered on the surface of the ground what looked like the bottom of a great iron kettle turned upside down. He notified the owner of the hacienda, who ordered its excavation. And in place of the kettle was discovered the above-mentioned head. It was left in the excavation as one would not think to move it, being of granite and measuring two yards in height with corresponding proportions. . . . We went, and I was struck with surprise: as a work of art, it is without exaggeration a magnificent sculpture.
—Melgar, vol. 1, 1869: 292.

Emerald green Jade. . . . its appearance is like a green quetzal feather. And its body is as transparent and as dense as obsidian. It is precious, esteemed, valuable. . . . It is one's lot, the lot of rulers, of the old ones.
—Sahagun, Book 11, 1963: 222.

LA VENTA, Altar No. 4. La Venta has been called the first truly great ceremonial complex of Mesoamerica, dating from the Middle Preclassic. The art forms, such as this altar, continued well into the Classic period and influenced Maya and Mexican cultures long after La Venta was abandoned.

OLMEC CIVILIZATION DEVELOPED WITHIN a very limited geographical zone of around 7000 square miles (18,130 square kilometers) lying along the Gulf Coast and centering on the volcanic uplift called Los Tuxtlas Mountains. These mountains are primarily composed of extinct cinder cones and larger volcanoes, perhaps the largest caldera of which today contains Lake Catemaco. Two major drainage basins flank the mountains and make up the rest of what Bernal calls the "metropolitan Olmec area" (1971). The area is watery, swampy, and drowned by heavy rainfall and the annual flooding of the great rivers which flow off in marshes, estuaries, and lagoons on the edge of the sea. From 80 to 125 inches of rain per year fall in a period of six months (June to November). Rivers form the most important means of communication. Exuberant and flourishing vegetation covers the drier land between watercourses. As in most of the coastal tropical zones of Mesoamerica, there are rich plant and animal communities in the varied natural zones.

This area was probably occupied by MacNeish's early and primitive coastal villages living on wild resources, and certainly was occupied by around 1400 B.C. by early pottery-using cultures of the Ocos horizon. These were farming cultures, using slash-and-burn techniques to master the thick jungle, but they did not abandon the intensive hunting, gathering, and collecting techniques and schedules that had led to sedentary life in the first place. These communities were not Olmec, however; they lack the defining features of that culture which are discussed at length below.

CHRONOLOGY

Olmec culture lasted a long time, and in order to look more closely at the trends and events during this period, Ignacio Bernal (1971) has broken it up into three stages, which we shall follow here. Based on rounded off carbon 14 dating, and stratigraphic and stylistic phasings, the following chronology includes all of the major events of Olmec culture history.

Olmec I	1500–1200 B.C.
Olmec II	1200–400 B.C.
Olmec III	400–100 B.C.

In accepting this scheme, however, we should note that Olmec I may not be the earliest period of Olmec culture. M. D. Coe (1968a) and R. Heizer (1968) have suggested that still earlier phases may lie hidden in the Tuxtlas Mountain area. Olmec III may be a figment of carbon 14–fevered imagination, although there seems to be hard stratigraphic evidence for such a construction phase at the site of La Venta. Finally, we should note that Olmec II represents the development of high culture; Olmec I is the local expression of Ocos horizon culture.

These large blocks of developmental time are still not sufficient for understanding some of the events of Olmec culture history. On the basis of work both in the highlands (Tolstoy and Paradis, 1970) and in the lowlands (Coe, 1976), it is now possible to break down Olmec II into at least two phases which correspond to Mesoamerican-wide horizons. These phases are based on the shifting importance of two of the four major lowland Olmec sites. The first is the San Lorenzo horizon (1200–900 B.C.), which is the period of apogee of the San Lorenzo and possibly the Laguna de los Cerros sites. Outside of the heartland, this horizon is marked by the appearance of the hollow, white-slipped, ceramic "babies," and bowls, dishes, and bottles all decorated with specific Olmec motifs, such as the jaguar paw–wing motif. Coe thinks that the highland sites of Tlatilco and Tlapacoya in the Basin of Mexico, Las Bocas in Puebla, and the San Jose phase in Oaxaca belong to this horizon (1976). The Juxtla-huaca cave paintings and the Pijijiapan petroglyphs on the Chiapas coast also pertain to this period.

The second phase of Olmec II is the La Venta horizon (900–400 B.C.), and is signaled in the heartland by the destruction of San Lorenzo and the rise to power of La Venta. A different set of exported items marks this horizon in other parts of Mesoamerica. Hard white pottery decorated with double-line breaks and other decorative abstractions appears. Coe notes the first appearance of jade among the Olmecs, and the export of finished carvings to places outside the heartland (1976). Chalcatzingo's Period B in Morelos and the Oxtotitlan murals in Guerrero date from this horizon; and Olmec culture was most widely distributed.

OVERVIEW OF THE OLMEC

Before plunging into the mass of detail on the Olmecs it seems appropriate to give an overall view of the culture as we now know it. Briefly, the culture is made up of two components: a "civilized" elite; and the older, simpler "folk" component. The Olmecs were apparently the first in Mesoamerica to bring forth an elite cultural component, and it was the elite who determined such matters as art style, complex political and economic affairs, and religious movements.

The elite component centered on clusters of civic architecture in the Gulf Coast zone. These ceremonial centers were made up of large earthen pyramids and platforms which probably supported perishable structures in some of which lived an upper class. The leadership class and the centers were supported by the folk component, the mass of the population, who, because of their slash-and-burn style of agriculture, were unable to live in true towns and cities, but instead lived dispersed through the lowland area in hamlet- and village-sized communities.

Olmec leadership was handled by dynastic lineages of rulers who seem to have been identified with the basic deities of Olmec religion, especially the jaguar–rain god. A magnificent art style expressed in sculpture and lapidary products depicted the Olmec gods and elite. The elite also developed a dynamic religious and social organization, which brought more people from throughout Mesoamerica into the Olmec orbit through either religious conversion or military activity. Exotic goods, both sumptuous and religious, were either demanded by the elite class from various parts of Mesoamerica as tribute, or obtained through trade. Outposts of Olmec culture obtained obsidian, jade, cacao, iron ores, and other items. These outposts were in some cases actual colonies, and in other cases non-Olmec Mesoamerican communities heavily influenced by the Olmec. Political and religious power seem to have shifted among the various centers of the Olmec heartland, but by around 500 B.C., the Olmecs became victims of their own precocity. Other, more sophisticated, and demographically more powerful centers were arising elsewhere in Mesoamerica at least partly under the stimulus of the Olmec, and these later cultures finally overshadowed them.

OLMEC CULTURE

COMMUNITIES AND POPULATION. At least three food-producing systems were available in the Olmec zone. One was the early intensive gathering and hunting system which had led to settled life in the first place. There were also two major farming possibilities based on the kind of land used. The most favorable lands for cultivation were and are those of the river levees which are annually flooded and enriched by deposits of silt. This Nile-like situation allows two or more crops per year, using slash-and-burn techniques. Away from the rivers, and on the slopes of the Tuxtlas Mountains or the edges of the highlands, one crop per year is more usual. Coe suggests that the families who initially controlled the best lands along the rivers were those who eventually became the entrenched elite-class lineages (Coe, 1968a). Indeed, this economic and social advantage shows up in modern times; recent pioneer families who control the river lands have turned out to be those who also have the capital to go into retail trade in the small river towns and thus control the local economy. Surpluses can be used for various purposes, and that which today is used for personal aggrandisement might have been used to build up political and religious allegiances in ancient times.

Bernal estimates that the 7000 square miles (18,130 square kilometers) of heartland supported an average of some 50 persons per square mile or around 350,000 at its most densely populated (1969:17). Even if one objects to such a high density and accordingly cuts the figure in half, it still means that some 15 percent of the population were able-bodied men. Therefore, some 26,250 men would have been available for communal activities in addition to food production. This is a population based solely on slash-and-burn maize farming; and, indeed, corn makes up 90 percent of the diet today in the region. However, data from the San Lorenzo ceremonial center show that the Olmecs also derived valuable protein from sources such as deer, wild pigs, and especially from fishing. Oxbow lakes and sloughs are especially favorable for seining, and robalo, tarpon, and gar were and are all favored fishes.

Given these subsistence and demographic resources, the Olmec elite developed the ceremonial centers. However, there were also certain restraints. Slash-and-burn agriculture, with its shifting fields and necessity for holding large amounts of land fallow, means that population expanded physically as it expanded in size. Community size is generally limited, although large absolute populations can be sustained: theoretically up to 150 persons per square *arable* mile (54 per square kilometer). However, this population is dispersed over the cultivable land, and hence we have the development of civic centers which were often virtually deserted during most of the year and where only a small elite class and its supporting population lived.

OLMEC CEREMONIAL CENTERS. Functionally, Bernal considers the Olmec centers to have been dispersed cities. This is also the interpretation taken within this book for the later Maya ceremonial centers. In this view, the centers operated as urban foci for complex social, political, religious, and economic behavior, but did not have the permanent large concentrations of people that we would expect in a city.

The Olmecs built mainly in earth, the principal material at hand. Clay, either in bulk or in the form of adobe bricks, was heaped up and apparently plastered with adobe. Occasionally, the facings of small structures were made of stone, but that material had to be imported to the zone with great effort and was reserved for such uses as drains and sculpture. The amount of earth moved by Olmec builders is impressive. It is generally found in the form of very high or fairly low platforms. The Stirling Group acropolis at La Venta, a large flat platform, was made of some 16.5 million cubic feet of material. Generally, these platforms are arranged in a linear fashion, about eight degrees west of true north. Mounds are also arranged in groups about courtyards. There are up to ninety-five of the larger mounds at Laguna de los Cerros occupying about 94 acres (38 hectares). Smaller platform mounds presumably supporting housing on the commoner level — thatched huts similar to those used today — are numerous. Some 200 have been found in the vicinity of the ceremonial center at San Lorenzo. All of these structures imply effort enough, but there is also the possibility that entire artificial ridges of clay were piled up by the Olmecs to serve as megaplatforms for the formal architecture. M. D. Coe suggests that the ridge at San Lorenzo, which comprises some 140 million cubic feet of material, is such an artificial feature (1968c).

There are certainly three and probably four major Olmec sites known from the heartland area: La Venta, San Lorenzo, Tres Zapotes, and the recently discovered site of Laguna de los Cerros. Only the sites of La Venta and San Lorenzo have been somewhat satisfactorily sampled, and even these would yield a great deal more to excavation. Recent aerial surveys in the Papaloapan River Basin have revealed a number of sites with plans similar to La Venta.

San Lorenzo. San Lorenzo is located on a river, the Rio Chiquito, but has a great deal more open country around it than La Venta. The main ceremonial group is on a salt dome, which was artificially modified, and consists of the linear arrangement of mounds with closed courtyards. The ridge itself, Coe thinks, represents a bird flying east. Some twenty small lagunas, apparently water storage ponds, are found on the ridge. Large basalt conduits drain the plazas and some of the ponds on the San Lorenzo ridge. The amount of stone involved in these features is enormous; some thirty tons of basalt were used in a drain just 650 feet long, and this is only one of many such features. There was much stone sculpture in the distinctive Olmec style, representing not only artistic wealth, but also a considerable effort invested in freighting the enormous tonnage of basalt. Coe estimates the population of San Lorenzo at about 1000

persons, based on the more than 200 house-mounds he found there. These people presumably were the supporting retainers of the still smaller elite population which lived at San Lorenzo.

San Lorenzo's great period is the earliest known of all of the four major sites. The end of the site's predominance — about 900 B.C. — is marked by the extraordinary destruction of both architecture and sculpture. The deliberately mutilated sculpture was buried in lines. Some of the great stone heads may have been carried off to La Venta. Since these were probably the heads of elite-class leaders, a political as well as religious turnover is indicated. While San Lorenzo lost its power and was deserted, Olmec culture continued to flourish and entered a still more spectacular phase at the large site of La Venta.

La Venta. La Venta is an island site in a swamp and on the Tonala River, and not obviously associated with any agricultural land. It was occupied from about 1300 to 600 B.C., its great period falling entirely within Olmec II times. The site is extraordinary in the symmetrical layout of one of its mound groups. This is Complex *A* and Complex *C*, which were really one functional unit. The large pyramid, C-1, may be an effigy volcano (Heizer, 1968). It is a fluted cone whose rills and ridges have been recently argued to have astronomical significance. This interpretation has been disputed by those who believe the structure to have been originally rectangular, but modified by erosion. Be that as it may, there is a striking resemblance between this gigantic pile of earth and the cinder cones in the Tuxtlas Mountains from which came the basalt used in sculpture at La Venta. Two low flanker mounds in front of the cone lead to a kind of inner courtyard. In the late phase at La Venta the courtyard had a palisade of basalt columns erected around it, possibly for privacy. The famous group of sixteen jade figurines now on display in the National Museum of Anthropology at Mexico City has a similar palisade of six jade celts and probably represents a ritual scene which originally took place within the basalt palisades in Complex A. The figurines represent a group of jostling onlookers, a file of participants, and a principal figure backed against the palisade. The whole group of figures was found associated with the Complex A mounds. Such mounds probably supported perishable buildings, and the nearby Stirling acropolis platform possibly supported sumptuous but perishable elite-class housing. The various uses of log-shaped basalt columns in both a tomb and the court-yard at La Venta suggest that the perishable structures were made of upright logs.

A great deal of monumental sculpture and many monumental offerings are present at La Venta. The whole site itself is somewhat enigmatic: it is so rich in artifacts, precious objects, and fine sculpture. La Venta's location and size mean that very few people could be accommodated at the center, even for short periods of time. However, it does have the aspect of a religious pilgrimage center. Victor Turner has noted that the major pilgrimage centers of modern Mexico are outside the major population centers. This was also true to some degree in at least late periods of pre-Hispanic Mesoamerica. The island sanctuary of Cozumel off the east coast of Yucatan drew persons from all over Mesoamerica and Central America. La Venta as a pilgrimage center thus falls within this pattern.

Tres Zapotes. The site of Tres Zapotes is located to the west of the Tuxtlas Mountains and is poorly known except for its sculpture. There is no adequate map of the site. However, the ceramics of Tres Zapotes indicate that the center certainly was contemporary with La Venta and San Lorenzo in the Olmec II period (Stirling, 1943, Drucker, 1943b). All three sites have early Ocos horizons, or Olmec I period remains. San Lorenzo is the only place where we have adequate information on what may have happened to change the Olmec from a stodgy farming community "folk" culture to the dynamic, innovative stimulus that it became after 1300 B.C. Coe suggests that Olmec culture was developed elsewhere and that it intruded to the heartland zone possibly from the Tuxtlas Mountains (1968a). If this is so, then we have still to find the earliest, developmental, and evolutionary stages of Olmec culture history. Heizer points out that this may not be easy, because if these stages are to be found in the Tuxtlas Mountains they may be hidden under deep deposits of volcanic ash from the recently active cinder cones of the vicinity. Several distinguished Mexican scholars have argued for the origin of Olmec culture in Guerrero, or the Mixteca of the highlands. Bernal on the other hand seems to feel that a local evolutionary origin in the lowlands is the best explanation. We shall return to this question.

OLMEC ART: SCULPTURE AND PAINTING. Olmec sculpture is one of the most important defining qualities of the civilization. Sculpture tends to be massive and is found in life-sized pieces as well as larger than life size. It is both full round and bas relief. The enormous human heads, of which twelve are known, are interpreted by Coe as being representations of elite-class rulers (1965b). The football helmet garb and the heavy quality of the features all fit with Coe's characterization of these leaders as "tough warrior dynasts." Some of the sculpture is patently portraiture as exemplified by the "wrestler" monument — a magnificent specimen of a man apparently flexing his muscles in a graceful exercise. Bas relief on monuments, and on cliffs outside the heartland, tends to be much more complex and obscure in meaning. Several general themes can be detected. One is the offering of a small jaguar/human, Coe's "were-jaguar," by an adult. In other scenes adults carry the were-jaguars. Coe identifies these beings as helpers of the jaguar rain deity. This principal deity is sometimes seen as a great head within whose mouth humans stand or sit. Thus the were-jaguars would stand in the same relationship to the jaguar as the tlaloques did to the great rain god, Tlaloc, in Aztec times. However, the features of the were-jaguars remain to be explained. Characteristically, their faces combine human infantile features with everted lips, jaguar fangs, and often a cleft forehead. These features are especially clear in the many small jade statuettes depicting the were-jaguars. M. D. Coe has pointed out that there are two fragmentary sculptures which explain not only these features, but also give us a "basic Olmec myth" with which to approach Olmec art and religion.

At Laguna de los Cerros and Rio Chiquito (near San Lorenzo) two badly damaged sculptures have been found which apparently show a jaguar copulating with a human female. These must have been some of the most spectacular sculptures ever done when in their original condition. At any rate, such a union would have produced the small part-jaguar assistants to the rain-god. However, this is not the whole explanation. Coe has also suggested that the cleft forehead and infantile features are explained by a genetic anomaly which is sometimes found in inbred populations: *spina bifida*. Spina bifida infants are usually stillborn and have cleft heads and characteristic snarling expressions. If this genetic anomaly did occur in Olmec populations, it might well have been interpreted by them as the result of the woman having mated with a jaguar. These intriguing explanations are not by any means proven, but they make more sense than any others yet advanced.

Another thematic group is concerned with apparent military activity. In many bas relief sculptures warriors bash other persons with clubs, or simply hold clubs in threatening attitudes. Other depictions show "knuckle dusters" which may be what the name implies. Small floating figures above represent several of the Olmec deities, including the were-jaguars. It is especially interesting that one of the most explicit scenes of violence is from the highland site of Chalcatzingo in Morelos. It suggests that the zones outside the heartland were not controlled entirely by peaceful means.

The basalt from which most of the major sculptures of the heartland sites are made was brought in from the Tuxtlas Mountains. Petrographic and mineralogical studies leave no doubt as to the origin. This importation of tons of stone is impressive, but in fact the jaguar mask ceremonial deposits at La Venta are far greater in quantity. In these deposits, roughly shaped and finished ashlars of serpentine were laid down in layers in specially prepared pits with over a thousand tons of material. On top of the La Venta A-1-C deposit was found a large mosaic mask in Olmec style with the characteristic indented head. It has been said to represent the jaguar deity of the Olmecs, but it must be something more complex because the representation seems to have four eyes. In any case, the labor and amounts of material and skill expended on these deposits bespeaks sophisticated social organization and arcane ritual. The serpentine is probably from up-river: the foothills zone. All of the material could only have arrived at La Venta by being rafted along the coastal waterway and in through the Tonala River, or down the rivers from the edges of the highlands.

Ceremonial and ritual meaning is conveyed by the remainder of the scenes with elite-class individuals apparently participating in worship or political protocol, or acting out mythical and symbolic events. These symbolic events may have been of the sort that was used as a recurrent liturgy in the ceremonial centers.

A certain number of footprints, bird heads, and the like are present on Olmec sculptures — possibly hieroglyphic writing. However, no complicated inscriptions with mathematical data and dates are found until somewhat later. We shall discuss the invention of the calendar systems and writing in Mesoamerica in the next chapter, but it is barely possible that these achievements were made during Olmec II times, at least in rudimentary form.

Some remarkable murals discovered at the caves of Oxtotitlan and Juxtlahuaca show brightly colored scenes of pomp and elite-class ceremony with a principal figure in each case seated on what appears to be a throne (Grove, 1969, 1970b). Another scene at Oxtotitlan with a dominant figure in it has definite phallic overtones. These sacred caves are not too far from Taxco in Guerrero. Another part of the Chalcatzingo cliff sculptures recently found shows a person on a throne within the mouth of a jaguar which perhaps represents a cave, and from which cloud symbols emerge. Small clouds hang above the cave with rain falling from them. It all recalls the later Aztec belief that the Tlalocs lived in caves and that caves generated clouds and rain.

Olmec sculpture outside the heartland tends to be of a narrative style depicting both the military and ritual protocol themes. Chalcatzingo has already been mentioned. Massive boulders and outcrops sculptured in place have been found by Navarrete at Pijijiapan which is located at the entrance to the Guatemalan coastal plain. A rather imposing set of individuals, both conferring and aggressively advancing, are shown, along with depictions of one of the Olmec deities, with a sprouting maize plant in his headdress. Further south on the coastal plain, at Monte Alto, some extraordinary round heads similar to the twelve great stone heads of the heartland have been found. These Guatemalan heads lack the characteristic "football helmet," however, as well as other metropolitan Olmec stylistic elements. Recent work at Monte Alto seems to show that the site is contemporary with part of Olmec II, and therefore these heads were probably carved under stimulus of Olmec artistic canons. The farthest south that Olmec sculpture has been found is in the highlands of El Salvador at Las Victorias. Again we have a boulder carving which depicts Olmec personages in a dynamic scene in which persons of elite rank are walking about with what appears to be either clubs or plant symbols in their arms. Other Olmec sculpture has been found in this zone, as well as in the highland zones of Guerrero and Morelos, but enough has been said to make the point that there is a general distribution in two very specific zones of Mesoamerica. The artifact distribution is somewhat wider, but includes the zones where sculpture occurs.

Small Works of Art and Other Artifacts. These portable expressions of Olmec style were made of exotic materials, jade being especially favored. Jade was probably obtainable from the Balsas Valley in Guerrero (near the sacred caves of Oxtotitlan and Juxtlahuaca), from the Motagua River Valley in Guatemala (Monte Alto and Las Victorias are on the way to this place), and from other as yet unknown sources. American jade is variable with the most highly prized being apple-green in color. White streaks occasionally are found in pieces of it, and the color may run to a dark, turquoise-like blue. The small figurines of the were-jaguar were a favorite motif. Highly polished axcelts with incised designs, including what appear to be rudimentary hieroglyphs akin to certain designs found on sculpture, are also fairly common. Other, rarer forms include canoe-like pieces, were-jaguars with wings, and "letter-openers" probably used for blood-letting in religious ritual. Celts were especially favored in the heartland and in addition to the famous cache of figurines already mentioned, cruciform deposits of celts were found at La Venta. Most of the above mentioned forms are also found in basalt, serpentine, and other stone.

Masks are especially well done. One in a private collection in Guatemala City is an extraordinary, life-sized piece of jade carved into a were-jaguar mask and is said to come from La Venta. Another mask is of wood, preserved by some miracle, and depicts a human face and is encrusted with jade. Another mask is a powerful expression of the jaguar's face and is of marble.

All of these items — celts, masks, figurines — are especially prized by modern collectors and were similarly regarded in ancient times. Apparently, many of the small portable items were held as heirloom pieces, and one even has wound up in the Vatican's collections, covered with elaborate Italian gold work! It was probably sent back by a sixteenth-century Spaniard and might have come from an Aztec source, which would mean that it had been passed down through various hands for about 2800 years. Their religious symbolism made jades even more valuable to their ancient owners, although aesthetic acquisition seems to be nearly a religion in the twentieth century.

Large hollow dolls of clay, made with baby-face features, appear consistently in graves in areas outside the Olmec heartland, and as trash and discard within the San Lorenzo site. These dolls must have been exported to the Basin of Mexico and the Morelos burial site of Las Bocas, where they occur.

Iron ore mirrors, ground into concave reflecting surfaces, occur in the heartland sites, especially at La Venta and San Lorenzo. The source area for one variety of iron ore, magnetite, has been found in the Central Valley of Oaxaca, where Flannery and his associates have also located the villages and the houses of

these specialists who made the mirrors. Within one of the houses of these highland craftsmen were found the characteristic hollow doll figurines. These finds add the Valley of Oaxaca as an important zone in some way connected with the Olmec.

Obsidian from about seven sources has been detected at San Lorenzo. Mineralogical analysis shows that obsidian came from near present day Pachuca, north of Mexico City, Orizaba volcano near Puebla, and from as far south as El Chayal, near Guatemala City. Obsidian was important as the primary cutting material in ancient times.

In addition to the above items, mica, schist, flint, and bitumen were all imported into the Olmec heartland zone. Judging by the items found at the Olmec sites of La Venta and San Lorenzo, the Olmec should have suffered from a balance of payments problem since they seem to have exported only the finished products. However, we must consider the nature of the Olmec-influenced sites outside the heartland before we settle on an explanation for the matters outlined above.

OLMEC CONTEMPORARIES: COLONIES, COLLABORATORS, OR COMPETITORS?

Four major zones have been indicated as influenced or connected in some manner with Olmec culture. From north to south, these are the Basin of Mexico, the Morelos Valley-Balsas drainage, the Central Valley of Oaxaca and the Pacific coastal plain of Guatemala. A look at the individual communities of these areas will give us some information on the nature of Olmec contact.

Tlapacoya is located in the southeastern corner of the Basin of Mexico and was at least a large village in Olmec II period. Its location is at the entrance to the basin that one might use if he were approaching it from the Olmec heartland. Recent excavations by Tolstoy and Paradis indicate that Tlapacoya possesses the debris to be expected of an intensively occupied village, along with certain characteristic Olmec pottery forms, including the hollow dolls (1970). This period is dated at about 1200 B.C. Across the basin and the lake, there was a contemporary village now known as Tlatilco. It is just northwest of Mexico City. This site is famous for its spectacular burials of which some 500 or more have been excavated. Tolstoy and Paradis' research indicates that Tlatilco has about four periods represented in its burials, the earliest of which precedes the Tlapacoya material, dating about 1500 B.C. Tlatilco seems to have been a large community with perishable housing, but also possessing low, one- or two-step clay platforms which may have been specialized temple platforms. At any rate, there is a definite Olmec presence at Tlatilco from the beginning, with the characteristic hollow dolls showing up in the burials, as well as other exotic forms of Olmec pottery. Bowls in which excised jaguar paw designs are emphasized by red paint rubbed into them and a black slip surrounding, virtually replicate vessels from La Venta and San Lorenzo. Clusters of figurines with the burials show many life scenes: acrobats, diviners, and women carrying babies, for example. On the other hand much of the exotic material at Tlatilco seems to be of a native ceramic tradition. The famous "life-death" bowl, which shows a live face on one half with a skull on the other side is such a piece. It is significant that there is no earlier Preclassic culture known for the basin than this Olmec-connected period, with the possible exception of the Tlalpan phase dated at about 1600 B.C. or earlier. The location of Tlatilco is again important, representing as it does the exit point on the western side of the valley should one be traveling across it to the Toluca Valley beyond. Coe thinks that the two sites together represent the route of ac-

cess to Toluca for the possible purpose of obtaining jade from that western valley.

HIGHLAND CENTERS. The geographical placement of the two principal Olmec-connected sites in the Morelos Valley is similar to that of Tlapacoya and Tlatilco. Las Bocas lies at the eastern entrance to the Morelos plain that one should cross if he wants to go to the Balsas drainage, and Chalcatzingo is at the western exit from the plain into that drainage. Las Bocas has unfortunately been looted for its burials by antiquity hunters serving the rapacious collectors and dealers of Latin America, the United States, and Europe. However, enough is known to state that the burials are similar to those at Tlatilco in its earliest period. That is, the Las Bocas burials contain Olmec items, including the hollow dolls and jaguar-paw–decorated vessels, as well as ceramics of more local tradition. Las Bocas is probably a village site and is backed against a cliff, a circumstance that suggests to Coe that defense was a factor (1965c).

Some of the most crucial evidence bearing on the nature of these highland, Olmec-connected communities has been developed by David Grove's recent work (1974c). The site of San Pablo Pantheon on the Cuautla River in Morelos has yielded over 200 burials. The ancient graves are in a burial mound appropriately located next to the modern cemetery. Across the river is another zone with distinctive burials, locally called La Juana. Based on stratigraphic and comparative material, Grove says that La Juana is the older phase. Hollow ceramic "babies," spouted trays, roller stamps, black ware, and other San Lorenzo horizon items in these burials indicate that he is right. On the other hand, the San Pablo Pantheon mound produced pottery which is characteristically in a variety of bottle forms: stirrup-spouted bottles, composite bottles, belted bottles, tubular-necked bottles, etc. Yet, less than one percent of the other Pantheon pottery had highland Olmec affinities. Hollow D and K figures of the Valley of Mexico typology occur. The picture is generally of a regionalized Preclassic culture. Curiously there is no evidence of La Venta horizon material.

Based on this evidence and the fact that there is internal evidence at Tlatilco for multiple phases, Grove concludes that the La Juana material dates around 1100 to 900 B.C., and the Pantheon pottery, 900 to 500 B.C. However, it seems to me a possibility that the Pantheon material is earlier still. This is based on the fact that the Tlatilco graves are not properly sorted out yet and bottles occur in what may yet turn out to be the earliest of them.

Chalcatzingo is a large community, possibly even a town, principally known for its cliff sculpture, which has already been discussed to some degree. Again, the location against the cliff walls suggests that defensibility was desired. Grove's recent work at this site indicates that it was particularly active during the La Venta horizon, although it was a provincial Preclassic village earlier (Grove, 1968, 1974b). A serpentine figure of La Venta workmanship has been found, as well as a masonry altar reminiscent of the La Venta table-altars, and an intaglio sculpted stela of La Venta style. Grove has also reported a platform mound 70 meters (231 feet) long.

The Valley of Oaxaca has become better known in its earliest phases through the research of Flannery and his associates (Flannery, 1968). In a phase contemporary with Olmec II phases of the heartland, San Jose, he has found the characteristic hollow dolls. Again, as already discussed in part, we have an indication of local ceramic tradition and perhaps social stratification in these highland communities. Clay and stone platforms for more sumptuous housing for more important people of the communities suggest that formalized leadership was already in existence. Distribution patterns of iron ores used to manufacture the mirrors exported to the heartland suggest definite wealth differences among the communities and among people within the communities of Oaxaca.

The Monte Alto site on the Pacific plain of Guatemala has so far only produced information which implies that the place is a small-scale and not too impressive attempt to replicate the Olmec ceremonial centers of the heartland. A fairly intensive occupation is indicated by the heavy deposits of ceramics and other debris in association with the large sculpture. No large platform building is known.

THE SOUTHEASTERN LOWLANDS. The pleasant and fertile valley of Chalchuapa is open to the Pacific coastal plain through the Ahuachapan Pass. A long and important sequence of cultural development has been defined by R. J. Sharer (1974). Only the Preclassic phases concern us at this point.

An early Preclassic, Cuadros horizon ceramic complex, *Tok,* dates from about 1200 to 900 B.C. It has close affinities with other Cuadros-affiliated complexes, but no specific Olmec ties. In other words, it is not linked to the San Lorenzo horizon of Olmec expansion. Sharer comments that Tok is a part of Lowe's expanding, lowland, maize-cultivating tradition. These earliest populations apparently are colonists from the coastal plain.

Colos ceramic complex (900–500 B.C.) is tied into the La Venta horizon. The ceramic inventory clearly indicates this, and includes white-rimmed black ware, polished black pottery, streaky grey, and white to buff pottery, as well as specific Olmec motifs, including the double-line break. A large pyramidal structure at Trapiche is built to the imposing height of at least 20 meters (about 65 feet). Cacao, hematite, and Ixtepeque obsidian would be desirables attracting the Olmec. Twenty-five kilometers (15 miles) away at Ahuachapan, finds have been made of serpentine and jade Olmec figurines which indicate that there is probably a major Olmec trading center of the Chalcatzingo–Las Bocas variety there. Although the Olmec presence is impressive, and Sharer thinks that it stimulated cultural evolution, it is not massive. Grove's trading station model seems to fit the Salvadorean situation well.

SOCIAL AND POLITICAL IMPLICATIONS

It is at this point that some of the most controversial problems of the Olmec arise. Economic and ritual motivations for the establishment of ties with all four areas noted above can be suggested. Obsidian and jade came from the zones around the Basin of Mexico and the Morelos Valley. Iron ores for the mirrors came from the Valley of Oaxaca. The Guatemalan Pacific plain produced the best and largest quantities of cacao of all of Mesoamerica. This was the area known as Soconusco in Aztec times and was conquered by those people to control that very valuable commodity. In addition, the Pacific plain gave access to obsidian resources in the Guatemalan highlands.

In order to make some coherent sense out of this material it is necessary to deal with reconstruction of the social fabric of the Olmec heartland itself. It seems clear that Olmec society was stratified, with an elite or upper class which is depicted on the sculptured monuments. This elite engaged in religious ritual, warfare, and economic activities, judging by the depictions of them in action. They commanded sufficient labor to accomplish the building of such large monuments as the C-1 effigy volcano at La Venta. They also commanded the economically and ritually valuable commodities such as jade, magnetite, obsidian, probably cacao, and other perishable items. Socially significant,

they commanded also the services of craftsmen so skilled that they must have been full-time specialists at least by La Venta times. We therefore get a picture of Olmec society in the heartland as possessing an upper class, a group of artisan-craftsmen, and a mass of population of lower status. If this reconstruction is correct, then the Olmec set a general pattern of social organization which reappears among the Classic Maya, and thus it may have survived until A.D. 900.

Olmec centers in the heartland probably acted as religious pilgrimage centers, political capitals, and nodes of economic exchange. This seems particularly true in the case of the largest centers. There is some internal evidence, previously discussed, that the site of San Lorenzo achieved dominance first and then was succeeded by La Venta. Coe thinks the implications of these data are that the religious and political capitals were moved (1970). The positions of Tres Zapotes and Laguna de los Cerros in this political history are not clear as yet, due to lack of excavation at those sites.

The relationships of the Olmec to the outside cultures of highland Mexico are more in dispute. Covarrubias saw the situation essentially as one in which the Olmec were derived from Guerrero, colonized the heartland zone, and then developed their pattern of civilization which was adopted and adapted by all succeeding cultures in Middle America (1946, 1957). This is almost certainly too simplistic a view, since Covarrubias did not have the advantage of the new information from the lowlands when he wrote. Guerrero does not seem to be a nuclear zone of culture development in spite of early Olmec materials found there.

Bernal classifies Tlatilco and Tlapacoya in the Basin of Mexico and Chalcatzingo and Las Bocas in the Valley of Morelos as being actual colonies of Olmecs contemporary with the non-Olmec peoples living at small villages such as El Arbolillo in the basin (1971). He sees these Olmec colonies as being in the minority and exercising influence, but not necessarily complete control, of their regions. Both Caso and Bernal point out that the later empires of Mesoamerica were not physically continuous. The Aztecs, for example, were content to control the most economically valuable regions, by garrisoning strategic points and by controlling the routes of access. As will be seen, this seems a replication of the physical and social organization of the Toltec and Teotihuacan empires. As a long-standing pattern, it fits well as a template onto the physical and social arrangements of the Olmec and Olmec-influenced sites and regions. However, the lack of dense populations of the sizes later achieved probably indicates that trade and ritual relationships were more important than political and military control.

At this point we should mention M. D. Coe's provocative suggestion that the Olmec were ethnically and linguistically Maya (1968a). This is based principally on the fact that the Maya language family is spread continuously around the Gulf of Mexico from the Soto la Marina River in Tamaulipas to the Ulua River in Honduras except for a wedge of Nahuatl and Totonac speakers in southern Veracruz and Tabasco. This wedge occupies an area which includes the Olmec heartland zone. Further, Nahuatl languages have the center of distribution in the highlands. This and other data indicate that the Nahuatl speakers are not very ancient occupants of this part of the coast and that the Olmec heartland during its florescent period was probably Maya-speaking. We shall deal with certain implications of this in the next chapter.

THE OLMEC AND THEIR ROLE IN EARLY CULTURAL EVOLUTION

Olmec culture was precocious and advanced and undoubtedly influenced many later cultural developments. However, one must not make the mistake of regarding the contemporaries of the Olmec as being absolute barbarians. Flannery, in a closely reasoned argument, has pointed out that there is every evidence for relatively socially advanced communities in Oaxaca, the Basin of Mexico and the Valley of Morelos (1968). He further notes that history and anthropology most often provide evidence of acceptance of advanced cultural traits only when the donating and accepting cultures are already nearly on a par. In other words, the Preclassic societies which most successfully accepted and assimilated Olmec ideas did so precisely because they were advanced enough to appreciate them. Flannery would not regard Tlatilco and Tlapacoya nor the San Jose Mogote site in Oaxaca as Olmec colonies, but rather as advanced highland communities which accepted certain Olmec ideas and gave them their own twist and added much of their own cultural equipment.

Still another viewpoint has been put forth by Sanders and Price who are disturbed by what seems to be the appearance of the earliest civilization in the lowlands. The tropical forest areas in their scheme of things are ecologically inferior to the highland zones as a setting for civilization, if civilization means urbanism. Reserving these theoretical matters until a later chapter, we must still note that Sanders and Price regard the Tlapacoya/Tlatilco/Chalcatzingo/Las Bocas complexes as a separate cultural manifestation from that in the Olmec heartland and propose to call it Amacusac (1968). Such a culture would have near parity in sophistication with the Olmec if one accepts this argument. However, the evidence for a lowland Olmec presence in the highlands is too strong for us to accept this viewpoint. Conversely, there is little doubt as to the highland affiliations of sites such as La Venta and San Lorenzo, judging by the amounts of highland items found at those places. Flannery's suggestion looks better at this point in the game, and the model of trade-ritual network seems to fit too well with the present evidence to ignore.

It remains to discuss the crucial matter of the importance, however much that may have been, of the Olmec phenomenon in the development of civilizations in Mesoamerica. At this point we shall consider some alternative explanations and attempt to put together a reasonable synthesis of our own. Caso, Covarrubias, and M. D. Coe have all argued at one time or another for the essential uniqueness and cultural autonomy of the Olmecs. This is to say that in the Olmec II period there was no other culture or cultural area in Mesoamerica which had developed sufficiently to be considered even on a near-parity with the Olmecs of the heartland area. Although Coe and others want to derive the heartland culture from some nearby zone, they would regard that intrusive culture simply as a part of the main Olmec tradition. Thus the Olmec heartland tradition of period II would represent a kind of mother-culture that donated its ideas and stimulated developments among their less sophisticated contemporaries. The Olmec indeed did exercise influence on later Mesoamerican groups as will be seen in the next chapter. There is a continuity of sculptural style between the Olmec II material, the Izapa style, and early Maya sculptural tradition that is impressive.

Sanders and Price approach the problem of the Olmecs from more of a social structural point of view (1968). They classify as civilizations those Mesoamerican cultures which had state-level organizations and high-density urbanism. The Olmec culture, they say, seems more like a chiefdom, and there is obviously a lack of true cities or towns in the Olmec heartland. Thus, the Olmecs were just below the threshold of civilization. At this point, Sanders and Price then offer the Amacusac grouping of highland cultures as examples of contemporary highland chiefdoms and of approximately equal cultural attainments. From this point of view, the Olmec lose their unique status as the earliest civilization of the area and become more a precocious member of an interacting group of Preclassic cultures. The highland members of this group build up to state levels of political organization around 200 B.C. with towns and cities. Sanders and Price further argue that this development was only possible on the basis of irrigation farming. Therefore, Teotihuacan would become the first true (urban) civilization of Mesoamerica. Importantly, also, this would mean that the highlands are ultimately the seat of the most important cultural developments.

Tolstoy (1969) has trenchantly criticized Sanders' and Price's construction. He points out that the Amacusac sites are much more closely tied to the lowland Olmec expression than once seemed likely. He further notes that Sanders and Price relegate the Olmec to the status of a chiefdom not only because of the lack of true cities, but because of the assumed lack of such features as social classes, markets, and bureaucratic organization. However, as seen above, it is now clear that the Olmec may have possessed all of these features. Even if they did not, however, the distinction between highly developed chiefdoms and civilization is a comparison of apples and pears. Based on intellectual achievements, religious conceptions, monumental constructions, the implications of labor organization, and the trade-tribute system implied by artifacts and raw materials, the Olmecs qualify for civilized status, whatever their style of social arrangements. Tolstoy says that Sanders and Price explain the origins of urbanism within their irrigation-demographic arguments, but not the origins of civilization.

The preferred view of the Olmec taken here then, is that the Olmecs indeed did have cultural priority in Mesoamerica as a whole. They probably did invent and diffuse much of the cultural equipment utilized and reformulated in later cultures. On the other hand, they undoubtedly did interact with certain highland Preclassic cultures of near-parity in development. Therefore interaction among the regional cultures of Mesoamerica on economic and cultural levels was probably as important as it was in later times. The symbiotic relationships and interstimulation among these cultures were probably the most important factors in keeping up the evolutionary momentum of civilization in Mesoamerica.

It has already been seen that this interaction pattern was in existence in the preceding periods of incipient cultivation, and was crucial in the development of agriculture. Willey has suggested that the Olmec's crucial role was in providing a vehicle for intensifying and accelerating that interaction and thus bringing many more areas of Mesoamerica into the process of evolution of civilization (1962). He suggests that the Olmec religion was a major motivation for this step-up in interaction patterns. This might be called the "Canterbury Tales" theory. Olmec religion seems to have been a powerful ideological force and one which inspired a missionary fervor among its adherents. This proselytizing aspect included a kind of church militant which used force for conversions and to attain the resources necessary to maintain the main centers of Olmec religion. The pattern of pilgrimages by culturally and ethnically diverse peoples to the lowland centers can be inferred

from the archaeological record. All of the above fits a pattern that is somewhat like the historically recorded spread of Islam both as a religion and a cultural and political movement. Persons traveling to religious centers exchange ideas, goods, and even genes. This spiritual motivation to cultural evolution in Mesoamerica is particularly appealing, because it was important in later times and because it has become apparent that cultural ecology does not give a full explanation. Irrigation farming leading to urbanism and thus to civilization seems too mechanistic a scheme to explain all of the data, even as incomplete as it is now.

The Olmecs thus set the style for much of later Mesoamerican civilization, and their inheritance was absorbed thoroughly and carried on in a more or less direct tradition by the lowland Maya. In the highlands, there seem to have been still further qualitative developments in social organization. These were based on the greater numbers of people which irrigation farming made possible. However, this further development seems clearly stimulated in its earliest stages by Olmec's pristine state, which ultimately lay back of nearly all of the later regional civilizations. From this point of view, Olmec culture did not die out, but simply was absorbed and passed on in more or less transformed variations. It is to the evidence of the bridging cultures between the Olmec and their inheritors that we now must turn.

1 △

The Olmec and Epi-Olmec. *No one knows what the Olmec called themselves. Jimenez-Moreno has suggested "tenocelome" or "people of the jaguar." About 1200 B.C. several impressive civic-religious centers developed in southern Veracruz and Tabasco, the Olmec heartland (1). The area is one of high rainfall, many rivers, steamy climate and dense rain forest. One of the centers, La Venta (3), is located on a small island in a swamp. Supporting population had to live away from the island, in the surrounding countryside. Presumably they were drawn in to build such monuments as the large pyramid (2), and to participate in rituals in the temple precincts of complex A (3).*

2 △

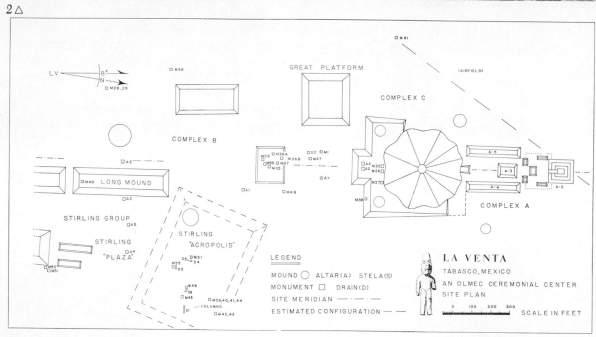

LV

8°
N

□ M56

□ M29,29

GREAT PLATFORM

(AIRFIELD)

□ M61

COMPLEX C

COMPLEX B

□ A2

□ M49   LONG MOUND

□ A3

STIRLING GROUP

□ A5

STIRLING
"PLAZA"

□ A4

STIRLING
"ACROPOLIS"

□ M50

□ M51

□ M59 □ M36A
□ M58 □ M36B
□ M35

□ S2 □ MI
□ M47

□ M57
□ 4
□ D3
□ 2
□ D5
M55

□ M46
□ D5
□ M43

□ D1   COLUMNS

□ M39,40,41,44

□ M42,43

□ A1

□ M48

□ A7

A-5

A-3

A-4

□ A3
□ M25
□ A2 □ M26

M27

M38

COMPLEX A

□ M23

A-2

LEGEND

MOUND ◯ ALTAR(A) STELA(S)

MONUMENT □ DRAIN(D)

SITE MERIDIAN — · — · —

ESTIMATED CONFIGURATION — — —

LA VENTA

TABASCO, MEXICO

AN OLMEC CEREMONIAL CENTER
SITE PLAN

0   100   200   300

SCALE IN FEET

3 △

5△

△4

△6

Radiocarbon dates indicate that La Venta reached its peak about 800–400 B.C. It was supported by a population of perhaps 18,000. At the end of this period the site was abandoned and its monuments deliberately mutilated.

Perhaps the most interesting Olmec find ever made is the group of sixteen jade, granite, and serpentine figurines and six jade celts (4). Buried two feet deep, these male figurines (6½ to 7⅓ inches) are engaged in a ritual in which some are observers and others are active.

Other La Venta finds included a pit twenty-four feet deep and fifty by sixty-one feet in size, which was lined with a thousand tons of serpentine slabs. Near the top, a mosaic pavement was built in the form of an abstract mask which has a typical Olmec cleft head (5). The large quantities of stone all had to be imported from a considerable distance, probably by water.

La Venta Altar 4 (6) shows a ruler sitting in a niche formed by a jaguar's mouth, grasping umbilical cords that tie him to his ancestors. This altar throne is made from basalt quarried one hundred miles away.

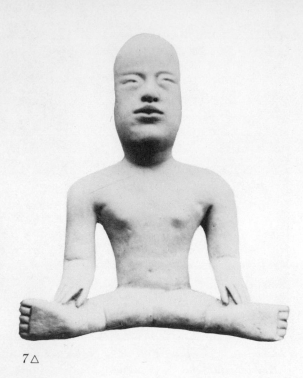

7 △

8 △

Dozens of fragments of hollow figurines, like this one from La Venta (7), have been found at San Lorenzo. The indication is that they were made in Veracruz. They were traded widely.

Sculptures of rulers glorify them as in La Venta Stela 2, which shows the central figure surrounded by supernatural helpers (8). La Venta Monument 19 (9) shows a person of status resting in the crook of an impressively large serpent, perhaps a rattlesnake.

9 △

The famous giant stone heads were very likely portraits of rulers, according to M.D. Coe. The largest found to date is the San Lorenzo Monument 1, 9 feet 4 inches high by 6 feet 6 inches wide (10). This huge piece of basalt was quarried and transported 50 miles. Another unique piece of sculpture is a figure of a kneeling man with ratchet-disc shoulder sockets (11). The arms are lost. At all large Olmec sites, the rain god or were-jaguar, such as appears on the San Lorenzo Monument 52 (12), is a common motif. The cleft-headed, feline-faced personage may have been believed to be the offspring of a mating between a jaguar father and a human mother, which seems to be depicted in a couple of mutilated sculptures.

Distribution of Olmec art is wide and ranges from West Mexico to Los Naranjos, Honduras, 600 miles distant. The defining features of Olmec art persist in pieces found both in the heartland and at great distances.

10 △

11 △

12 △

13 △

14 △

15 △

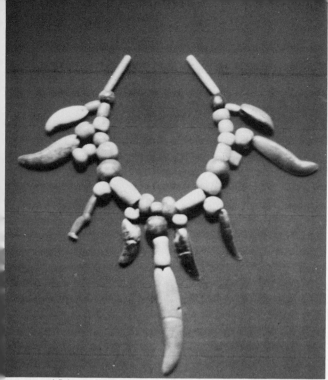

16△

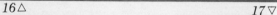

17▽

The trade of the hollow "baby" figurines to highland centers like Las Bocas (14) indicates that centers outside the heartland had accepted the Olmec complex of religious iconography. The Las Limas (13) statue shows a human holding a were-jaguar baby; it was found by country people in Veracruz who thought it was a statue of the Virgin.

The Wrestler figure (15) is a magnificent and naturalistic example of heartland style sculpture.

The "Kunz Axe" (17) is a jade celt of unknown provenience, but carries the unmistakable Olmec imprint of the were-jaguar with feline and infantile features combined. The axe is one of the largest pieces of Olmec jade ever found, weighing 15½ pounds. Like all Olmec pieces, it was apparently manufactured by patient use of reeds, cords, and wet sand. The jade necklace (16) includes replicas of jaguar claws. The obsession of the Olmec with jade was apparently because of the symbolic linkage between the green gemstone and water. Much of the trade and contact in Olmec times was sparked by the heartland center's quest for jade and other minerals filled with supernatural power.

18 ▷

The Oaxacan greenstone figure (18) is clearly Olmec in style and carries incised figures of warriors on its back and front.

An example of Olmec contact with other areas is the nearly unique wooden mask (19) inlaid with jade. This small item, 6¾ inches, was found south of Taxco in a cave of the Canyon de la Mano. It may have been meant to be worn as a pendant.

The Oxtotitlan mural, of which the central figure is shown here (20), is from a cave in Guerrero. This extraordinary painting shows a principal figure who wears a bird mask and who is seated on a throne very similar to Altar 4 at La Venta.

The Olmec style was transformed after 400 B.C. and persisted in what have been called the epi-Olmec styles. The site of Izapa, on the Pacific coast of Chiapas, has produced great amounts of sculpture from this period (21). At the site of Chiapa de Corzo a palace of the period (22) was found that had been deliberately destroyed at the end of the Horcones phase, together with a vast hoard of pottery (23). Clearly, the contemporaries of the Olmec and their descendants had developed a series of vigorous regional cultures.

19 ▽

20 ◁

21 ▽

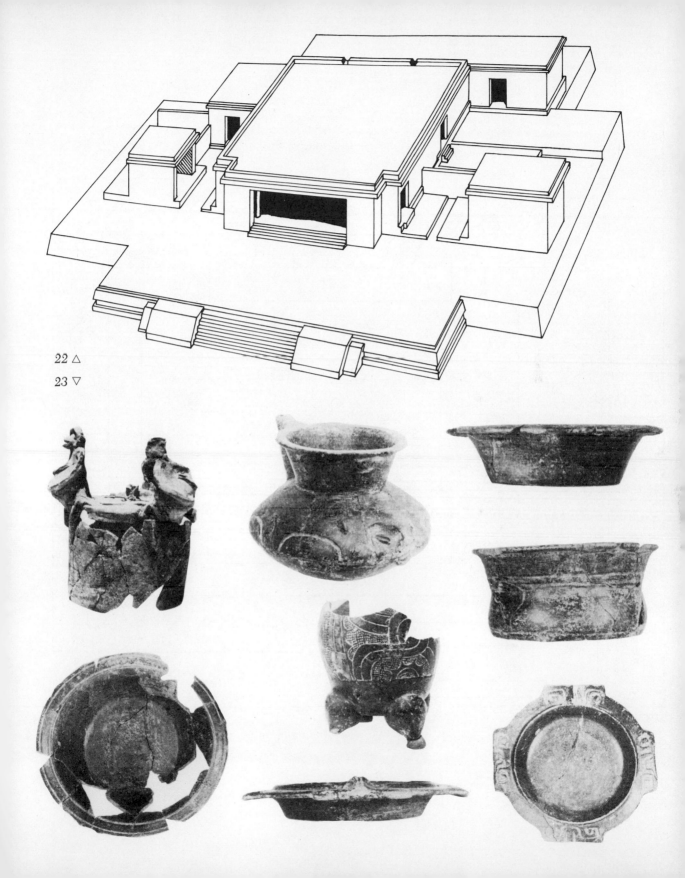

22 △

23 ▽

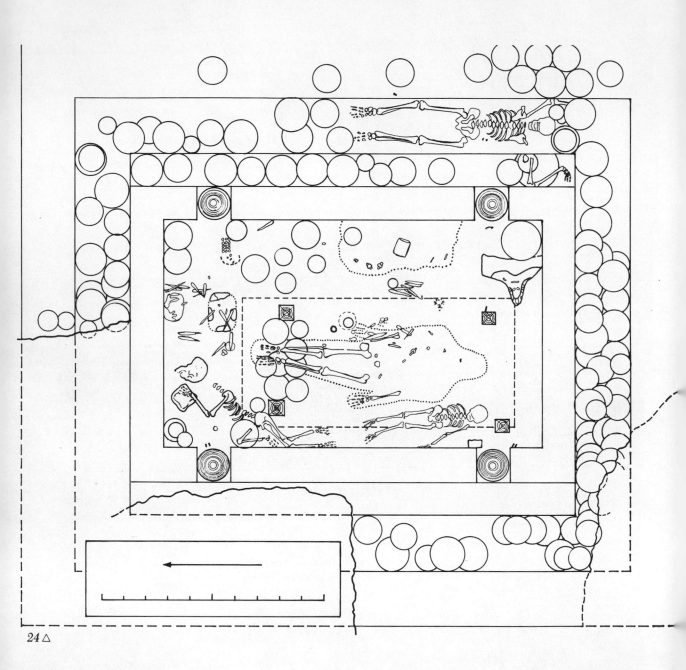

At Kaminaljuyu, one of the most powerful epi-Olmec centers evolved. The site is now destroyed by Guatemala City's growth, but huge burial temples formerly contained the tombs of rulers (24). These chiefs, buried with hundreds of pottery vessels and with sacrificed retainers and servants, had once called on the services of thousands of people. Their lives and activities were memorialized in stone monuments such as Kaminaljuyu Stela 10 (25), a tradition carried to great lengths by the lowland Maya. Stela 10 shows strong links to the other epi-Olmec cultures.

△ 25

△ 26

Kaminaljuyu Stela 11 (26), a florid sculpture that includes glyphic writing, also shows strong links to the other epi-Olmec cultures. Silhouette sculpture (27) is unique to the Guatemalan highlands during the Proto-Classic epi-Olmec period. This example shows the long-nosed god common to all the Maya cultures that may be a religious legacy of the Olmec.

In the Olmec heartland itself new centers took the places of the abandoned sites of La Venta and its contemporaries. These later cultural centers became one more regional variant on the general Mesoamerican theme that the Olmec had such a unique role in establishing. Cerro de las Mesas, Veracruz, has many stelae honoring its rulers. Stela 5 (28) shows such a dignitary and carries a Maya style date of 9.1.12.14.10 (468 A.D.).

CHAPTER 5

THE EPI-OLMEC,
THEIR CONTEMPORARIES,
AND MAYA BEGINNINGS

In the year and in the day
of obscurity and utter darkness,
before there were days and years,
the world being in deep obscurity,
when all was chaos and confusion,
the earth was covered with water,
there was only mud and slime
on the surface of the earth.
At that time . . .
there became visible
a god who had the name 1-Deer
and the surname Snake of the Lion
and a goddess, very genteel and beautiful,
whose name was also 1-Deer
and whose surname was Snake of the Tiger.
These gods are said to have been the beginning
of all the other gods.
—Mixtec origin myth in Leon-Portilla, 1969: 55.

Those who carried with them the black and red
ink, the manuscripts and painted book, the

wisdom. They brought everything with them, the
annals, the books of song and their flutes.
—Sahagun, in Leon-Portilla, 1969: 10.

Their dwelling place was as follows: . . . in the
middle of the town were their temples with
beautiful plazas, and all around the temples stood
the houses of the lords and the priests, and then
[those of] the most important people. Thus came
the houses of the richest and of those who were
held in the highest estimation nearest to these,
and at the outskirts of the town were the houses
of the lower class. And the wells, if there were
but few of them, were near the houses of the
lords; and they had their improved lands planted
with wine trees and they sowed cotton, pepper
and maize, and they lived thus close together for
fear of their enemies.
—Landa, 1941: 62.

IZAPA, Guatemala. Sculpture at this site in the coastal plain of Guatemala demonstrates the transition between Olmec and the Classic Maya traditions. Somehow Izapa, with its domination of the cacao rich zone aound it, transmitted this Preclassic heritage to Maya centers in the lowlands of the Peten as well as to nearer places such as Kaminaljuyu. Izapa is a typical Mesoamerican center with over 80 platforms arranged about plazas which contain over 200 stone stelae and altars. It is only one of many vigorous centers that enveloped the basic patterns of Mesoamerican culture and passed them on to the Classic civilizations.

THE RICHNESS OF VARIATION AMONG MESO-american high cultures has its roots in the Preclassic period. This variety of cultural texture and pattern reaches back to the early Preclassic stage, but becomes more pronounced as one moves forward through time to the cultures that succeeded the Olmec and their contemporaries. At this point in our archaeological rediscovery of these ancient predecessors of the Maya and Aztec, it is clear that there are several clusters of Preclassic cultures. In their areal distribution, these clusters are nearly templates for the major Classic civilizations. At least five of these clusters can be defined at present: the trans-isthmian block, the Maya lowland area, the Oaxacan, the central Mexican, and the west Mexican. The trans-isthmian cultures are clearly related to the Olmec patterns and have been sometimes called the epi-Olmecs, largely because they all share an art style that is derived from the Olmec — the *Izapan*. The early lowland Maya have been also sometimes called epi-Olmec on the basis of a limited amount of information, but this inclusion is debatable. The Maya, like the central Mexican and west Mexican cultures, seem largely to have gone their own cultural ways without strong direct heritage from the Olmec period. Before examining the individual clusters of cultures, we should observe that not all of them achieved civilizational status during the Classic period. We have the interesting phenomenon of a retrogression in parts of the isthmian block; and the west Mexican cultures waited for a further circumstance before they could evolve more complex forms.

THE TRANS-ISTHMIAN CULTURE BLOCK

As during the great days of Olmec dominance, the Isthmus of Tehuantepec later formed an avenue of communication between the Gulf Coast plain and the Pacific slope of Guatemala. The late Preclassic cultures in this zone are tied together by an art style which is mainly expressed in sculpture and which has been called the Izapan from the site of Izapa where great numbers of monuments occur. The name does not mean, however, that the style necessarily began there or that the site was the most important of the group. On the contrary, during the late Preclassic period (300 B.C. to A.D. 100) there seems to be a situation much more characteristic of the rest of Mesoamerican prehistory. Instead of the dominance of one locality or area, we have a series of local cultural traditions which interact, play on one another, and have certain commonalities, yet which maintain their own distinctiveness.

CERRO DE LAS MESAS. Cerro de las Mesas is located on the northern edge of the Tuxtlas Mountains, in the former Olmec heartland. Tres Zapotes is not far away. It is at both of these sites that we have the most direct continuation of the Olmec artistic tradition. Earthen mounds were built around plazas, stone monuments were erected, and about the final century B.C., a system of dating was invented.

Cerro de las Mesas may be one of the earliest Izapan-affiliated sites, beginning as early as 600 B.C. or before. Unfortunately, the site was excavated with less than rigorous methods, and there is confusion about the sequence of pottery, burials, and other minutiae that archaeologists use to sort matters out. There may well be an overlap with Bernal's Olmec II period (1200–400 B.C.), but clearly the Cerro de las Mesas site represents a culture related to the Olmec — one which survived the closing of the older ceremonial centers, and one which bridges the evolutionary gap between Olmec and the Classic civilizations. At the moment, however, the evidence is fragmentary, elusive, and tentative.

A ceremonial deposit (cache) of 782 jade and stone pieces was found, of which Bernal considers only four to be Olmec in style. They may well be heirloom items buried a long time after their manufacture. Most of the items are earspools, beads, and other personal jewelry. A burial in a small mound produced a magnificently carved turtle shell which has as its principal motif the "long-lipped god." This same deity is found on the Izapan-related sculptures. Some of the sculptures at the site also reflect the later style of transformed Olmec heritage, with seated and standing figures of rulers associated with religiously powerful symbols which no doubt lent greater authority to those rulers.

At nearby Tres Zapotes there is evidence of early writing, with Stela C probably representing the earliest found example of bar and dot numerals. Until recently, the date (31 B.C.) was somewhat in doubt, because the top of the notation was missing. The missing part has been found and fully justifies the reading that Stirling, the discoverer, made some 30 years ago (1943). Taken together with the date of 98 B.C. on a small jade carving, the Tuxtla Statuette, it is certain that a complex calendar and notation system was in use in the former Olmec zone by 100 B.C. The fact that the notation and the calendrical reading of these inscriptions are in the Maya system recalls M. D. Coe's suggestion of the Olmecs as Maya speakers (1968a). The oldest known date in the Maya lowlands is A.D. 292 on Stela 29 at the site of Tikal.

IZAPA. Across the Isthmus and down the Pacific coast from Tres Zapotes and Cerro de las Mesas is the large center of Izapa where there are more examples of the Olmec to Classic transition in sculpture than anywhere else in Mesoamerica. Izapa has its beginnings in the early Preclassic periods, and there are extensive mounds and plaza groups built even during its beginnings around 1500 B.C. Izapa was greatly enlarged and became an important political and religious center during the late Preclassic and Protoclassic periods. The location of Izapa in the cacao-rich Pacific plain was undoubtedly one of the sources of its importance. This economically important crop was a motivation for some Aztec conquests as already noted. Cacao is depicted in Izapa sculpture. The center is large and impressive, with earthen mounds and stone monuments arranged about large plazas which are formed by terraces. Some 244 stone monuments are known and are located in front of various mounds. Like later Maya sculpture, many of the monuments are upright stone shafts with round altars often placed in front of them. Over fifty of the monuments are carved.

Many of the elements from the Olmec period carry over into Izapan art, including the use of the St. Andrews cross and U-shaped elements representing the jaguar, scenes contained within jaguar mouths, and scrollwork skies or clouds. M. D. Coe says that "the hallmarks of this style are the baroque, cluttered scenes depicted and the presence of a long-lipped god derived from the Olmec were-jaguar (1965: 696)."

The pictorial aspect of Izapa "narrative style" art appeals more readily to those unfamiliar with the iconography of more arcane Mesoamerican styles. Animals, gods, and humans are combined in scenes of action. Storm gods gather water and release it; jaguars are captive participants in human rituals; bird gods fly through the sky; gods in canoes ride over waves beneath which swim realistically depicted fishes; other gods descend headfirst from heaven; seated humans tend incense burners; a warrior decapitates an enemy. Susan Miles thought that this latter represented a conquest by Izapa (1965). These apparently straightforward depictions, however, had their deeper symbolism. Stela 5 depicts a ceremony engaging several persons and dominated by a huge tree. The tree has been named "the tree of life" and possibly represents the great ceiba tree, which in later Maya mythology was thought to hold up the heavens. Whether or not this is correct, there is no doubt that the message intended is more than just the stylistic medium.

Jacinto Quirarte (1973) has pointed out that among other elements that later show up in Classic Maya art, is the double-headed monster figure (stelae 5, 7, and 12). As will be seen, many Izapan traits are to be found in early Maya art.

Moving on to the south, the plain narrows and the volcanic mountains of Guatemala are visible from the coast. There are other sites such as El Baul which also demonstrate by the presence of Izapa-style sculpture their participation in the Olmec heritage. These centers also served as a transmission route for the passage of Olmec-derived ideas into the highland areas.

KAMINALJUYU. Kaminaljuyu is an enormous site and rapidly disappearing under the edges of modern Guatemala City. Fortunately, the Carnegie Institution of Washington during the 1930s and 1940s and the Penn State project of the 1960s have preserved a rich haul of data which would otherwise have been lost forever. Among the most crucial of the information gained from the Kaminaljuyu sequence is the long sequence of apparently local sculptural expression. At this site it appears first in variable boulder pieces. These sculptures depict fat men and are perhaps as early as the Olmec, dating from the end of Olmec II. Carved and uncarved angular pieces of basalt are from the period immediately following that of great Olmec art. Finally, apparently under stimulus of and through interaction with Izapan centers, the Kaminaljuyu tradition floresces into an exuberant and unique expression which includes depictions of "squashed" frogs (*ranas aplastadas*), silhouette sculptures of extraordinary complexity, and formal erect shafts which are clearly stelae, although most of them do not carry hieroglyphic texts. The extraordinary sculpture known as Kaminaljuyu Stela 1 shows a barefoot individual otherwise richly attired standing between two blazing incense burners. An equally interesting sculpture was found in the same excavation as Stela 1 and is made of dense, black basalt. In spite of the difficult stone, skill of execution is high and the three human figures depicted in relief are among the best in Mesoamerican art. Great virtuosity is evidenced by the treatment of the feathers flowing from a backframe on the lefthand figure. Stela 10 also has a rather long hieroglyphic text which is incised to the side of a large relief-carved glyph. Unfortunately, the stela was deliberately smashed in ancient times, and in any case, the glyphs are indecipherable at present. Judging from the similar features of later Classic Maya lowland stelae, we believe that these monuments memorialize temporal rulers, and the inscriptions may give some historical data about them. In later times, succeeding rulers often smashed the monuments of their predecessors.

The Izapan sculpture at Kaminaljuyu belongs to the *Miraflores period* (100 B.C. to A.D. 200). As indicated above, Kaminal's beginnings are earlier, perhaps as far back as 800 B.C., judging by some pottery. Presumably, a regional ceremonial center was slowly developing in the rich Valley of Guatemala and then reached a first climax at the end of the Preclassic period. Thanks to recent work by William Sanders and his associates, we now see that the settlement patterns and ceremonial center arrangement seem to reflect a widely dispersed series of temple and burial mounds around which were gathered small clusters of population (Sanders and

Michaels, 1969). There are at least a dozen of these small civic centers together with a number of hamlets. The implication is that these population clusters were kin groupings with their ceremonial life focused on funerary and religious monuments. There is also an implication of a rather loose political organization perhaps analogous to that found in the Maya lowlands to the north, one based on kinship and marriage ties among the local important families. Population is estimated at 3000 to 6000 persons. There is a fascinating parallel between this local situation and the late Classic Maya lowland world, with its somewhat loose social organization; militaristic groups intruded into both situations. Although the intrusions and transformations occurred at different times and in different places, they may have undergone similar development. We shall return to this matter in considering the problems of cultural collapse and transformation at the end of the Classic period.

CHALCHUAPA. The southeastern lowlands in the Chalchuapa area retained their cultural precocity, and the later Preclassic remains are represented by three ceramic complexes. *Kal, Chul,* and *Caynac* date from 400 B.C. to A.D. 200. During this period, the Trapiche pyramid was rebuilt and extensive new construction around Chalchuapa covered about half a square kilometer (one-fifth of a square mile). Numerous individual mound groups similar to those of contemporary Miraflores phase Kaminaljuyu were the rule. Monumental stone sculpture also appeared at the end of the phase. Monument 1 at Trapiche is especially important for its long and complex hieroglyphic text which shows very advanced features of the later Maya system.

Large quantities of ceramics and debris indicate a growth in population in the late Preclassic period. Usulutan ware becomes intensively developed, and Chalchuapa may have been a manufacturing center for this important trade ware. Tons of Usulutan are found around the valley. The eruption of Ilopango Volcano apparently cut short the cultural development, and refugee populations from the southeastern lowlands possibly found their way into the Maya lowlands as well as into the adjacent highlands. The Usulutan multiple-wavy-lined decorative techniques show up at this time in the lowlands in Protoclassic and late Preclassic (*Chicanel*) complexes.

CHIAPA DE CORZO. Chiapa de Corzo is one of the most important sites in Mesoamerica because of its nearly continuous sequence which runs from 1400 B.C. to the present, some 3300 years. Pottery waterbottles, jugs, and storage jars are the main evidence for earliest human occupation of this part of Chiapas. The site is in the lowland trench of the Grijalva River. This finger of tropical lowland environment is the only part of the zone to produce early remains. The nearby highlands lack nearly all kinds of early settlements, but small villages apparently lined the Grijalva River bottom lands, taking advantage of the same features that made the area around San Lorenzo so attractive to the Olmec peoples.

Continuity of culture and population is reflected in the sequence, with a slow series of changes producing the first pyramids and other civic buildings around 550 B.C. — about the same time they first show up in the Maya lowlands. This monumental architecture becomes complex over time, and by 150 B.C. palaces of cut stone, plastered with heavy coats of polished stucco and roofed by beams and mortar, have appeared. These buildings are clearly suited for residence and are more elaborate than the thatched-roof, mud-walled houses that sheltered most of the population. Apparently, some persons were important enough to rate superior housing built at community cost.

Social stratification is also reflected in the burials of the period, with Tomb 1 obviously representing a person of extraordinary importance. Tomb 1 is a formally built chamber of unfired brick. A long lance with an obsidian blade was in the grave along with several unusual pottery vessels and jade jewelry — the latter always a symbol of high status. Also found were three elaborately carved human femurs which had been worked while the bones were fresh. Apparently the bones were originally set with feathers and used as aspergillums. Mythological subjects, such as a crocodile swimming through water, are portrayed on the bones in a style definitely related to Izapan sculpture. Another bone shows a jaguar-masked person who is very similar to Kaminaljuyu sculptured depictions of humans on Stela 11. To make the case tighter, fragments of Izapa-style sculpture have turned up at Chiapa de Corzo. Indeed, Chiapa Stela 2 may be the most ancient dated monument known, with a reading of 36 B.C., according to M. D. Coe.

One of the most extraordinary finds in Mesoamerican archaeology was that of the palace structure now called Mound 5. When archaeologists dug through the debris of the fallen roof, they found hundreds of smashed and burnt pottery vessels of outrageous variety in shape and decoration. Many of these exhibited the hallmarks of the late Preclassic period in eastern Mesoamerica: mammiform feet; multiple, wavy-lined decoration; and bridged spouts. These characteristics indicate contacts with the zones of Kaminaljuyu and the great site of Monte Alban. Some pottery from the latter site was actually traded into Chiapa de Corzo. Again there is a strong implication that political and economic ties linked these centers and provided stimulation one to another in various cultural fields. The palace and the pottery at Mound 5 were deliberately destroyed and the site of Chiapa de Corzo abandoned by its former rulers. It

was reoccupied shortly after, but the styles of pottery indicate new peoples.

About this time, the group of people known as the Zoque pushed into the Grijalva depression, according to linguistic evidence. This leaves us with the question of who built Chiapa de Corzo in its late Preclassic (*Horcones*) phase and probably earlier phases. The answer to this is still speculative, but it seems possible that we have here another case of Maya speakers being shoved out of their original positions and displaced into their historical locations. The Zoque are non-Maya. On the other hand it will be recalled that the highlands adjacent to the Grijalva were apparently vacant during most of the Preclassic. They are also the historical highland Maya groups' home. The intrusion of the Zoque or their ancestors, and the movement of the Maya into the highlands would account for the sudden appearance of early Classic period remains in that region. The deliberate destruction of the Mound 5 palace at Chiapa de Corzo, in this scheme, would have been the last act of ritual abandonment by the Maya as they left the center for a new homeland. The Zoque in turn seem to have been displaced into remoter zones of the central depression of Chiapas starting about A.D. 500. The Chiapanec were the group occupying the zone of Chiapa de Corzo in the sixteenth century.

The appearance of Izapan-style sculpture at the highland sites of Tonina and Chinkultic may indicate the areas in which the Chiapa de Corzo elite took refuge (Norman, 1973). On the other hand, these sites may merely represent contemporary centers. In any case, it is important that we now have Maya highland sites with Izapan-style sculpture which are geographically intermediate between the main Izapan area and the Maya lowlands. Robert Sharer and David Sedat have found sculpture at El Porton in the Salama Valley similar to that found at Kaminaljuyu, again a geographically intermediate position. Clearly Izapan cultures were located in positions that enabled them to contribute to Maya lowland civilization (Sharer, 1974).

THE MAYA LOWLANDS
AND MAYA BEGINNINGS

Like all of the major areas of Mesoamerica, the Maya lowlands are ecologically diverse within themselves (Sanders, 1973). Annual rainfall varies from a semiarid 20 inches on Yucatan's north coast, to an overwhelming 250 inches in a small zone of the southwestern lowlands on the Chiapas escarpment. Vegetation varies accordingly, with lower scrub thorn jungle in the north giving way about the present Guatemalan border to higher tropical forest and, finally, along the Pasion and Usumacinta rivers to three- and five-canopy rain forest. Technically, the jungle is monsoon forest, adjusted to an annual cycle of distinct dry and rainy seasons. These seasons fall into Mesoamerica-wide periods of January to May for the dry months and June to December for the rainy months. Water is carried off by the great rivers of the southern lowlands, and replenishes the lakes of the central Peten. The coastal zone of the Gulf and Caribbean consists of flood plains of substantial rivers such as the Belize up to a line running across the peninsula from Champoton to Chetumal. North of a series of fault lines which run east-west through the central Peten, there is very little ground water either inland or on the coasts. Instead, the rain drains down through the massive unbedded limestone to a water table that is far out of reach of wells. Small water catchments (*aguadas*) supply a certain amount of water during the dry season, but many dry up as May approaches. In the far northern lowlands, the water table is only twenty feet or less below the surface, and in many cases the subsurface streams have worn away the bedrock which has dropped through to form large natural wells locally called *cenotes*. Population tended to develop around these sources, and the later Maya developed reservoir techniques to stretch dry season water supplies.

Communication from one part of the lowlands to another is usually not difficult, only tedious. In the south, the main rivers give access to the interior from the Gulf and the Caribbean coasts. North of the central Peten lakes, however, it is generally a matter of walking to get through the vast spaces of central Yucatan. In fact, due to difficulties of portages and rapids, the river passages in the south were only usable to the limits of the coastal plain under ordinary conditions. Crossing the peninsula was such an arduous task in the sixteenth century for the tough long-distance merchants of Mesoamerica, that they preferred to go around Yucatan by sea. Most of the coasts are accessible by canoe, but even this means had its limits. For example, north of Campeche City there is a twelve-kilometer-wide band of mangrove swamp which is very difficult to penetrate. In ancient and colonial times, canals, which can still be seen today on aerial photos, were cut through the swamps. In earliest times these improvements were not yet made.

Mineral resources on the peninsula are scarce, but everything necessary to sustain human life is and was present. Salt was collected on the northwestern corner of the peninsula, the second largest salt-producing area in modern Mexico. Basalt and the harder varieties of limestone were available in various parts for use as food grinders. The forests, animals, birds, and sea life all provided rich resources on which early farmers with primitive techniques could draw. Only one near necessity was lacking — obsidian, the material from which the machine tool of Mesoamerica, the flake-blade, was made. However, deposits of obsidian in the highlands of Guatemala were accessible to lowland peoples through a trade network. It is well that obsidian lasts a long time and that relatively little was needed. Even from the Coban zone of the northern Guatemalan highlands, it is calculated that under good conditions it would take about two weeks to transport goods to Tikal, in the central Peten.

EARLIEST KNOWN PIONEERS. The earliest remains known from the Maya lowlands are from the Pasion River, deep in the interior, and date about 1000 B.C. Two sites, Altar de Sacrificios and Seibal, have produced pottery and other evidence to indicate that here are some of the first agricultural colonists. It is almost certain that there are earlier remains along the coasts of the peninsula which would be in MacNeish's earliest sedentary community category. Jack Eaton's surveys turned up an amazing number of shell mounds, most of which are Preclassic in date. However, none are as early as the Xe (pronounced "Shay") farming villages on the Pasion.

The Xe frontiersmen built small villages of perishable houses placed directly on the jungle floor, in contrast to the later Maya, who built their houses on platforms for drainage. This may indicate that these settlers came either from hill country where there was no need for platforms, or from an area of less rainfall. The first settled village life was undoubtedly based on agriculture, although there is no direct evidence for it. By this time, a full complement of domesticated plants was available. It is interesting that the first Maya (if they were such) chose the same ecological situation as had the Olmec — a river area.

Xe pottery is well developed, although it makes use of the tecomate and flat pan forms characteristic of most middle Preclassic Mesoamerican cultures. The major functions of pottery are as cooking pots, storage vessels for liquids, serving dishes, and transportation vessels. Water jars are invariably slippery and in a pottery-using community last about a year. Part of the solution to the slipperiness problem was the use of handles. Another was roughening the surface of the jar to make it easier to grip. Handles were used on Xe pottery but the later Maya changed to the roughening solution.

Not much pottery that can be called ceremonial was found in the Xe remains, certainly none that indicates ritual and religious life as do the later informative Maya polychromes. Small, hand-modeled, solid pottery figurines are thought to be curing and fertility ceremony items. Presumably, spiritual life was on the level of curing, shamanism, and divination, and was animistic with little community leadership. Judging by similar non-western, traditional communities, every household was probably responsible for its own spiritual well-being. No ceremonial structures have been found.

Communities were small and isolated. The two Xe communities now known probably numbered less than a hundred people each. Survival in a world of virtually untouched forest and rivers meant meeting tough daily challenges. At that time, the Pasion was full of tasty fish and turtles, but was also full of alligators. The woods contained deer, wild pigs, rodents, and other food animals, but also the formidable jaguar and an awesome tribe of snakes.

We have only hints as to the origins of these dauntless groups. A cruciform deposit of jade axes at Seibal is very similar to Olmec deposits. A characteristic Olmec artifact, a jade "letter opener," was found in this cache. Close similarities between Chiapa de Corzo III (*Escalera*) pottery and Xe also indicate that these pioneers may have come into the lowlands from the Gulf Coast zone. However, the ceramics are quite distinct in most respects. Likewise there is a similarity to simple pottery (Kal Complex) used in the Chalchuapa zone of El Salvador at this time, where ceremonial buildings were already being erected. Possible linkages to the Guatemalan highland site of Sakajut near Coban indicate that Xe and highland peoples may have been in contact or related. Certainly, Xe people were in contact with the highlands in some manner; they were obtaining obsidian. However, it is also possible that lowland people had colonized Sakajut, which is just on the edge of the highlands. Therefore, we are left with the probability that Xe people came from one coast or another, or from the highlands, but certainly not as part of a directed colonizing movement. They had no close links with the great events of the early Preclassic period such as the Olmec religious movement. The Maya lowlands was a vast untamed wilderness which absorbed a great many people and their efforts before their culture began to evolve from a backwater status.

Slow evolution. Slow, uneven population growth occurred from 1000 to 550 B.C., resulting in the proliferation of small farming communities all over the peninsula. There are indications that this erratic population growth became an explosion after 550 B.C. Very similar red, black, and cream potteries were made and used all over the Maya lowlands during the Mamom period (550–300 B.C.). At Dzibilchaltun in the north there is the beginning of a long occupation. What had been thought to be earlier pottery in Yucatan, found at the Mani Cenote, has turned out to be Mamom in date. In the central zone, around Becan, Mamom remains are the earliest. Villages are especially numerous in the southern lowlands, occurring around Tikal, on the Pasion River and in the lower Usumacinta area.

A noteworthy feature of many of these sites is the beginning of formal architecture and special buildings dedicated to ritual. The architecture is simple and variable. At Dzi-

bilchaltun, packed earthen walls with stucco floors were tried, whereas at Altar de Sacrificios, packed lime and ash floors supported the same simple thatch and pole buildings lived in by the preceding Xe farmers. At Altar, three of the buildings raised on platforms are grouped around a plaza in what is clearly a ceremonial precinct. The plaza remained a temple zone throughout the remaining 1400 years of the site's occupation. At a small site in British Honduras, greater sophistication in building techniques appears on the Mamom level. A low, two-stage platform is made of cut stone covered with plaster. Since this is the basic building technique later elaborated in the Classic civilization, it is clear that experimentation with the idea started far back in the Preclassic stage.

Small, hand-modeled figurines, most representing human females, indicate the continuation of the "fertility" and curing ideas. The appearance of mushroom-shaped pots may indicate something more. Hallucinogenic mushrooms occur in this zone of Mesoamerica and are still used as aids to communication with the supernatural in divination, curing, and other ceremonies. Stephen Borhegyi suggests that these mushroom pots reflect the religious use of hallucinogens in this period.

The population explosion, the appearance of ceremonial buildings, however simple, and the uniformity of far-flung Mamom culture at this time all demand an explanation beyond a simple statement of their existence. They reflect a lifeway centered on small villages of pole and thatch houses scattered thickly throughout the forested lowlands. An occasional village had one or more structures elevated with a few more sophisticated features. These were apparently centers of worship. The uniformity of pottery and other material culture during this period probably reflects a process of settlement extension based on slash-and-burn agriculture. The later regionalisms of Maya culture grew up partly in response to geographic isolation. We believe that Mamom, because of its peninsula-wide uniformity, represents a fairly rapid expansion through space of a population which had once been in close contact and which subsequently had not had time enough to develop regional distinctions. The use of slash-and-burn agriculture in a situation of unlimited land would produce this effect. Since relatively great amounts of land were required for relatively small numbers of people, the population would have to spread out into previously uninhabited zones as it grew.

A similar process took place in the great primeval forests of Europe about 5000 B.C. when the earliest Danubian farmers began to spread into western Europe (Piggott, 1965). Villages were established at a great rate, abandoned, and reoccupied. Slash-and-burn agriculture was used by these early Danubians, and this extensive form of cultivation led to expansion through space. Transient and shifting communities were characteristic of both the early Maya and early Europeans, but no connection is implied. We only wish to show that both were subject to similar ecological conditions (primeval forests) and used the same solution to their agricultural problems.

Again, there is no strong reflection of the startling events taking place among the Olmecs, except for one discovery recently made by J. A. Sabloff and William Rathje on Cozumel Island off the northeast coast of the peninsula. Rathje found an heirloom Olmec jade in a classic period tomb. Whether this finding indicates Olmec trade connections with Cozumel or simply was a piece traded to the Maya much later is unknown.

THE TRANSFORMATION OF MAYA CULTURE. A two-act sequence of events transformed Maya culture from a village-centered, more or less egalitarian society, to one oriented around formal ceremonial centers containing elite residents. These two acts are in the guise of two archaeological phases. The earliest (late Preclassic) is the period lasting from 300 B.C. to A.D. 150. A clear continuity between Mamom and this later Chicanel pottery is present in the waxy red, black, and cream monochromes. Again, the context is that of village life in the earliest part of the phase, and astounding uniformity in ceramics over the entire 97,000 square miles (251,230 square kilometers) of the Maya lowlands. Around the time of Christ some clearly different matters have transpired. Many centers are erecting much more elaborate architecture. Yaxuna in far northern Yucatan has a pyramid dating from this phase which is over 60 feet (18 meters) high and which measures about 200 by 420 feet (61 by 128 meters) at the base. Cut stone masonry was used to build this platform, which undoubtedly supported a temple as did the identical later pyramids. To the west of Yaxuna, at Dzibilchaltun, the use of cut stone masonry is well established, although the buildings are much smaller. At Becan in the central zone, a large platform 45 feet (14 meters) high was built, and smaller buildings with masonry and stucco platforms and walls topped with thatched roofs were being erected. Further south is one of the most elaborate of these structures and one which reflects the Izapan style in its stucco heads of serpents and jaguars. This is the famous E-VII-sub structure at Uaxactun. Twelve miles to the south, Tikal was burying its important dead in formal masonry chambers within platforms. In one of these burials the dead dignitary was furnished with a jade mask with inlaid shell teeth. Red and black monochrome pottery in the burial is distinctive only in form from the general run of Chicanel ceramics. An early temple in the Tikal north acropolis area is painted with a procession of human figures dressed in feathers and costumes. The figures are bent around the outside corners of the structure, apparently to give them more dimension. The style of these figures is clearly related to Izapan art. Fragments of carved stone indicate that the Tikalistas were experimenting with sculpture. Ninety miles to the south, on the Pasion River, the Altar de Sacrificios center possesses three temples and a possible residential structure grouped around a plaza. Also at this center is an attempt at erecting a tomb for a distinguished person who had died. As in the Tikal tomb, the tomb pottery is only distinguished from the other red, black, and cream pottery by being excellent examples in finish and form. Small incense burners and the continued use of mushroom pots give us some indication of ritual. However, for most of this period we still have pitifully little evidence and must extrapolate back from the Classic period which follows.

Direct evidence of more elaborate buildings and some ritual paraphernalia indicates a more formalized religion. However, these materials were only the stage on which the actual liturgies took place, and we have little evidence of the latter. We have even fewer ideas as to the philosophical concepts that underlie religious practices, although we can draw analogies. Presumably life crises, political and community matters, nervous farmers, and a desire to foresee the future determined many of the functions of early Maya religion. These functions are near-universals in human religions. Curing ceremonies and life crisis rites are especially emphasized in village-oriented societies. The more highly organized the society, the more functions are taken on by religion and the more need there is for specialists. Possibly the dignitaries buried in the early tombs gave not only community direction but also religious leadership. Certainly the early tombs reflect increasingly stratified society, and, at least at Tikal, the concentration of some wealth in the hands of a small part of society.

During this same period, Maya writing and the mathematical system were developed and applied to problems of time and astronomy to produce a formal set of calendars. The writing system is closely related to formal art, and there is a good deal of interchange in symbolism between the expressions of intellect and aesthetics. However, there are few early examples of hieroglyphs, numbers, and temporal periods left to us.

The epi-Olmec–related styles found at Tikal and Uaxactun in the southern lowlands indicate some contact with outside zones. However, as nearly as we can tell, the late Preclassic Maya world was still largely isolated — penetrated only occasionally by ideas diffused from elsewhere. The rest of their cultural apparatus was evidently developed on their own.

Population growth apparently reaches a plateau at the end of the late Preclassic period in most Maya centers. Whereas Mamom (middle Preclassic) had been the period of colonization of many of the vacant interior regions of Yucatan, Chicanel represents the filling in of the rest of the available space. Until about A.D. 650, in the middle of the Classic period, population grew at a moderate rate or was stable. Many more villages and centers were probably established during Chicanel times than at any other period of Maya prehistory.

At this point in their evolution (at the time of Christ), the Maya had reached more or less the point that the Olmecs had achieved at 1300 B.C. Many of the Preclassic cultures of Mesoamerica never progressed any further than this level of well-developed chiefdoms and remained at this plateau until the arrival of the Spaniards. We are beginning to see only murky outlines of the transforming events of the Maya late Preclassic stage, but one of the clearly crucial factors was the intrusion of more sophisticated Central American and Maya highland cultures and peoples into the Maya lowlands. This is called the Protoclassic period (A.D. 150–450). It is a difficult period to deal with because of fragmentary evidence. There is also the complication that only part of the Maya lowlands was directly affected by the cultural and population intrusions. However, after the appearance of this set of ideas and peoples, Maya culture is never the same.

An arc of Protoclassic cultures stretches from the Belize Valley, and swings south through the eastern Peten to the Pasion site of Altar de Sacrificios. In these zones, about A.D. 150, there is a sudden appearance of several features of later Maya civilization: polychrome pottery for ritual and elite-class use, a system of hieroglyphic writing used to transcribe elite-class doings, much more formal and larger architecture, a fully developed art style expressed in fresco paintings, and sculpture, and by inference, a rigidly stratified society.

Along the Pasion River, these developments are preceded by the appearance of Central American pottery and ideas derived from that tradition. For example, Usulutan (multiple-lined) decoration and exotic forms are grafted onto the local red, black, and cream monochromes. When the polychrome pots, hieroglyphic monuments, and the rest of elite culture appears, common domestic wares do not change, however. The fact that the domestic wares of Central America were quite distinct from those of the lowlands probably indicates an intrusion by an elite class, which took control of resident populations from a less sophisticated native leadership.

About this time the Central American highlands were shaken by volcanic eruptions. Payson Sheets has suggested that the dense blankets of ash laid down about 100 B.C. drove out the farming populations from around the powerful center at Chalchuapa (1971). He further suggests that these peoples were the ones who sought new lands and brought Protoclassic traits to the edges of the Maya lowlands.

On the other hand, a Preclassic pottery tradition continues undisturbed at Tikal with the development of greater and greater sophistication in architecture, crafts, and society. No disturbance of native tradition can be seen.

Further to the north, slate wares and architectural styles peculiar to the northern peninsula were developed. At Dzibilchaltun, we seem to have roughly parallel developments in the full emergence of ceremonial centers and directing elites.

By the beginning of the Classic period (from A.D. 200–450) we can define at least three regionalized variants of Maya culture. The northern and central Yucatecan are the most indigenous and least affected by outside influence except perhaps by example. The central Peten zone is clearly derived from the late Preclassic, but is distinct in pottery, architecture, and social organization. In addition it is affected by interaction with Protoclassic and epi-Olmec cultures. Finally, the centers on the arc from the Belize to the Pasion Rivers form a variant clearly transformed by Central American, and Highland Maya cultures, and perhaps even taken over at the top level by outsiders.

EXPLANATIONS OF THE RISE OF MAYA CIVILIZATION

It is easier for us to understand the ultimate collapse of Maya civilization than its rise. We have seen and have had recorded for us, the catastrophes and disasters that can overtake human communities, but no records or eyewitness accounts are available to us on the circumstances leading to the rise of any of the world's great preindustrial civilizations. There are good reasons for this situation. Writing, as a necessity and as cultural elaboration, is itself a feature of civilized life. History is a still later feature. Even in its earliest forms, writing did not record historical fact as we know it. Linear B of Bronze Age Greece and Crete was used for the accounts of royal households. The earliest Chinese writing records the results of arcane divination important to the elite at the court city of Anyang. In any case, it is unlikely that persons participating in these pristine civilizations understood the evolution and quantum jumps leading to new orders of society and culture. This is not to say that they did not explain matters; but their later explanations were more in the nature of myth, cosmology, and legend, and there is no reason to believe that earlier explanations were more empirical. No doubt the members of early civilizations had the same confidence in the explanatory power of their theories as we have in our theories. However, we do follow the cult of the scientific method which gives us confidence (perhaps unwarranted) that we are approximating the truth. Be that as it may, the following account combines the best understandings that we have at present of the surge of Maya culture from a village-centered, rural society to the splendor of an exotic tropical civilization.

No single event or theory accounts for the transformation. Faulty as it may be, the evidence indicates that no simple-minded theory of derivation from another culture is the answer. It is equally simple-minded and inadequate to think in terms of a strictly in-place evolution, a kind of bootstrap operation on a giant scale.

The Olmec-Izapa-Maya evolutionary chain is clearly involved but is not the only factor, as can be seen from the central Peten material, and even more from the northern Yucatan sequence. It has been suggested by Rathje that the need for obsidian and basalt and other materials not found in the lowlands led the Maya to organize themselves highly to assure themselves of these materials through trade (1971). This seems unlikely. Small amounts of obsidian are needed for everyday life and this can be obtained through casual trade on an occasional basis. Basalt is even less necessary, and sandstone and dolomitic limestone are available as an alternative for corn grinders. Trade is probably a factor, but at a later stage of development and for more exotic materials. The trade model does explain a lot of contacts developed after the Maya elite were in existence and had developed tastes for goods and manufactures not available in the lowlands.

To date, the most appealing explanation combines the important factors mentioned above and one crucial matter not discussed. Robert Carneiro has developed a theory of the origin of the state that revolves around the growth of population and the intense use of scarce resources (1970). He argues that as population grows, certain resources such as prime farm land and water assume an overwhelming importance and must be managed and enlarged. In addition, he argues that instead of seeking new lands or resources outside the ecological niche already developed, people tend to intensify their use of the resources within their original ecological zone. For the Maya, this "resource circumscription" centered around water. Water is an obvious necessity and, even in the soggy lowlands, becomes scarce during the dry season. The peculiar nature of the Maya area means that as population grew, water sources had to be managed and improved. We know of large reservoirs built during the Classic period. It seems likely that these date even further back to a period when population outgrew the natural water sources. In the south, this is not a problem since the people there had the advantage of rivers. Central and northern Yucatan, however, were hard pressed to provide water based on natural sources for much more than a thin population. Therefore, the people of those regions would modify and build waterholes which would become the focuses for the local populations. This situation, in turn, would lead to the concentration of power in the hands of those leaders who could command the manpower to construct and maintain the reservoirs. Immense political power and social control would fall to those able to control the water supplies. It is noteworthy that the major political and religious centers of later times are located near reliable natural or artificially created water supplies.

The above sequence of events is still unconfirmed, but the pressure of the late Preclassic population on water sources, the development of native religious leadership, and the necessity of organizing for improvement of resources would create a situation in which the Olmec model of society with directing elites might be attractive. The interaction of the Maya lowlands with the rest of Mesoamerica evidently provided lowland cultures with variants of the Olmec model. However, this is still not a sufficient explanation.

Competition among the Maya communities themselves for scarce resources also seemingly led to more highly organized societies. Knowledge of human nature makes it difficult to rule out the possibility of violence in these circumstances. The development of militarism on a low level might well occur. It is now known that the Becan fortress — a wide moat about 1.2 miles or 1.8 kilometers long, surrounding a number of buildings — is late Preclassic in date.

Thus we may see the rise of Maya civilization as due to population growth, and as leading to increased need for water supplies at a critical point of the year, and further, to competition among Maya communities over water and land. Ideas from other parts of Mesoamerica, and especially from the epi-Olmec cultures were absorbed and transformed. Once developed, the social, military, and agricultural systems had imperatives and consequences of their own. One such imperative would be exotic wealth to symbolically bolster the status of the leadership class. Religion would also bolster its social status, and the more complex the liturgy and philosophical underpinnings, the more the need for specialists.

In other words, the transition from village culture to civilization is not just a step, but a quantum jump. This in itself would explain the relatively sudden nature of the transformation. Once the process had begun, it moved quickly and was irreversible.

THE OAXACAN PRECLASSIC

The central Valley of Oaxaca is a highland area of mountainous beauty. It covers some 3375 square kilometers (1303 square miles) and lies at about 1550 meters above sea level. Seven hundred square kilometers (270 square miles) are located in the most desirable valley bottom.

An extraordinary amount of recent work in the central valley has produced a long sequence which begins at least by 5500 B.C. and runs up to about 3000 B.C. This beginning is in the period of incipient cultivation so well defined by the Tehuacan Valley sequence. Indeed, it seems that the Oaxacan period is mainly a regional variation of this slow buildup toward agricultural self-sufficiency. There are similar indications of experimentation with primitive maize, and, as in the Tehuacan sequence, most of the record comes from cave sites. At about 3000 B.C. there is a break in the sequence, and when it resumes at 1300 B.C., village life is already well established. Further, there is already a difference among the communities; one is more sophisticated than the others. Tierras Largas is a small village of some six or twelve households, occupying an area of about a half a hectare (about 1.2 acres). A population of from twelve to forty-eight persons is estimated. At the same period, San Jose Mogote, not far away, was two or three times this size.

Plastered community buildings occupied the center of this larger village. Both villages grew in size, and around 900 B.C. Tierras Largas doubled while San Jose jumped to at least eight times its former size (from about 30 households to at least 240).

Men's and women's work areas within households were also found at San Jose. "Women's tools" (cooking utensils) are located in the northern halves of the houses, while "men's tools" (flint knives, awls, and chisels used in skin preparation, woodworking, etc.) are found in the southern halves. This patterning is similar to that found in traditional Indian households of nearby highland Chiapas today. In addition to sex differences, wealth differences existed among households. It has already been mentioned, in the Olmec section, that magnetite mirrors were manufactured at San Jose for export to the metropolitan Olmec centers. Only some of the Oaxacan families engaged in such a craft specialty. The same three-house grouping found around the early Oaxacan plazas is found at the Olmec center of San Lorenzo at the same time.

These earliest villages are located within the valley bottom and in a zone where water is available within 10 feet (3 meters) of the surface. This is exactly the situation chosen by present-day farmers for a type of simple irrigation called "pot irrigation." Modern Zapotec farmers of the zone lay out rectangular fields and then dig wells to the shallow water table along the field's edges. They plant their corn and other crops in hills. After lowering their pots into the wells, they water the nearest plants by pouring a potfull on each hill. They then move to the next well and water the adjacent plants. Flannery believes that the earliest villages were located where they were because they used this "pot irrigation" technique (1968). A well dating to about 600 B.C. has been found in this zone and seems to bear out Flannery's theory.

It is noteworthy that this technique does not depend on large-scale construction or on large masses of people and elaborate social organization. From about 1300 B.C. to 350 B.C. what we seem to have is a series of widely spaced independent villages with their dependent hamlets. The larger communities possessed a formal leadership and more formal civic architecture, possibly associated with marketing and religious activities. Ceramics tie these early Oaxacan communities successively to the Olmec II and Chiapa II periods.

Ignacio Bernal did an extensive survey of the valley and found that from 300 to 100 B.C. a major population expansion had taken place (1965a). Thirty-nine sites were occupied during this time, including Monte Alban which was later to become the political center for the whole valley. Many of these sites have civic architecture, and one has a residential area of 80 hectares (198 acres). Expansion into the less desirable sloping piedmont zones also shows the effect of population growth. This change in quantity was followed by one in quality. For the period between 100 B.C. and A.D. 300, only twenty-three sites are known, but these are all larger than earlier sites and have massive ceremonial and civic architecture. Seven of the twenty-three are major centers, but Monte Alban, which is one of them, is not significantly different from the other six. This indicates that the valley was probably divided up into at least seven petty states at this period. Flannery and his colleagues would see this politically fragmented but culturally convergent process as a confirmation of the Palerm-Wolf theory (Flannery et al., 1967).

Briefly, the Palerm-Wolf theory states that civilization arose in zones where primitive agricultural techniques were easiest and then spread to more difficult zones as more advanced techniques were developed to meet special cultivation needs (Palerm and Wolf, 1960). A highland variant of slash-and-burn cultivation is one of the oldest systems known. Irrigation systems with long underground channels, dams, feeder ditches, and other features came much later. Primary centers were those which were able to accumulate techniques. That is, primary areas never discarded older techniques; they kept them in the repertoire and used them to keep special zones in cultivation. Therefore, primary areas tended to be those like the Valley of Oaxaca which was ecologically diverse, and which could maintain masses of populations by continually developing new subsistence techniques and bringing into cultivation what had formerly been marginal lands. We see this process in the spread of the Preclassic communities from the valley bottom of Oaxaca into the piedmont zones, and still later, into the more arid areas. Massed population and economic power gave these areas of Mesoamerica, Oaxaca included, a decisive edge over more uniform zones like that of the Olmec. The Valley of Mexico was another such zone of massed demographic and economic power.

THE CENTRAL MEXICAN PRECLASSIC

THE BASIN OF MEXICO. Archaeological work has been carried on in the Basin of Mexico since the nineteenth century. However, most of it has concentrated on the later stages of Teotihuacan and the Aztec period, and there is a good deal of confusion and uncertainty about the Preclassic phases. Recent work has shown that the one-track evolutionary model is too simplistic to deal with the realities (Tolstoy and Paradis, 1970). Again, we face the picture of a large basin with ecological diversity and, more to the point, cultural diversity from the beginning of the known sequence. The chronology chart outlines the sequences of phases. These are largely defined on the basis of pottery, however, and we still lack much of the settlement pattern and other information needed to build up a picture of the crucial centuries before the appearance of civilization.

As noted before, the basin is most favorable for primitive agriculture in its southern sector. Frosts occur less frequently, and rainfall is greater. The first agriculturally-based communities in the valley occur in this zone. There was a gradation of population density and social evolution from south to north through the Preclassic period. Cuicuilco is near the present University City, and was located on the lake shore. It is possible that the Tlalpan phase at this site dates to around 1600 B.C., and that it represents a simple farming hamlet whose inhabitants did hunting and fishing on the side. Pottery made by these people closely resembles that of the early Barra phase in the isthmus. There is no hint of ceremonial architecture.

As noted in the chapter on the Olmec, the first securely dated material from permanent settlements is from about 1300 B.C., is Olmec-related, and is found at Tlatilco in the middle valley and at Tlapacoya in the southern part. Garbage remains at Tlapacoya dating from around 1100 B.C. include tiny maize cobs. Bones of deer, rabbits, gophers, domestic dogs, and people were all found in contexts that suggest that all were used for food. Mud turtles and water birds were eaten, although fish are mysteriously absent from the earliest phases. *Ayutla* and *Justo* subphases have both these traits and Olmec features. The latter include white-rimmed black ware, large hollow doll figurines (C-9), and the use of Olmec motifs on pottery. The northern basin reflects these Olmec influences in a very pale way with Olmec-style pottery showing up only occasionally in the earliest communities.

The sophisticated traits of Olmec-related culture drop out about 950 B.C., and the villages of the southern valley seem to suffer a cultural simplification. Even if this is really the case, there is still no pause in population growth. Villages multiplied, and there are indications that by about 600 B.C. the southern lake was solidly edged with communities. Native ceramic traditions slowly evolved after the Olmec episode, and attractive monochrome brick reds, charcoal blacks, and chocolate browns were made and traded around the zone. Red and white, and red and yellow decorations relieved the single color themes, as did experimentation with form. Low bowls and large water jars are the most common forms, but long-footed plates begin to appear toward the end of the Preclassic period. Modeling in pottery continues. Jade was used in ear ornaments and other personal jewelry, although this was uncommon. Quite probably, the stone already had assumed its mystical and high status properties and was restricted to persons of high social rank.

From the earliest period of the Preclassic sequence, on into the Aztec and early colonial periods, we have an uninterrupted series of figurine styles. Made by hundreds of people, in dozens of communities, over at least 3000 years, thousands of these small relics have been collected and sold to generations of tourists and are still to be found. Many Preclassic types have female characteristics and are thought to have been associated with the idea of fertility. Human fertility and that of the earth were apparently intertwined; we know that the Aztecs hung strings of these little figures over their fields. Another likely function was their use in curing ceremonies; the figurine represented the person and his or her particular ailment. In most contemporary ethnographic societies, such figures are discarded or become children's playthings after their primary function has been completed. An extraordinary number of these figurine styles blend into and succeed one another in the Basin of Mexico. They reflect not only an artistic and aesthetic continuity but also a philosophical-religious continuum.

Clay platforms and more formal architecture appear certainly at Tlatilco by 1300 B.C. At Cuicuilco, the first round platforms made out of adobe appear about 400 B.C., soon to be replaced by a larger model made of stone. These are constructed in a large town by people using ditch irrigation for subsistence. Cuicuilco is large—at least 20 hectares (50 acres) in extent. Tlapacoya built a sophisticated stone platform for ritual purposes at about the same time. Obviously, these communities were not the only important ones in the valley. There is a good deal of difference between these small towns, with their politico-religious precincts, and the rural hamlets which continued the lifeway of the remote past. Most of the sophisticated communities were clustered in the southern valley, presumably because of its more favorable environment. In the northern reaches of the basin, population was always thinner through the Preclassic period. The Teotihuacan Valley has a few scattered villages which are contemporary with Zacatenco in the south at about 1300 B.C., and these are located on the valley floor near the springs and river.

At Cuanalan houses of this period have been found in apparent clusters inside walls. Such household compounds are reported for Aztec times and are still in use within the Teotihuacan Valley to this day. These compounds are composed of the houses of a man and his wife and their married children, together with a few shacks for cooking. The compound consists of a dusty, beaten earth floor, and most of the families' daily work is done under the shade of the trees within its wall. Preclassic hamlets in the northern valley consisted of groups of these family compounds. This extraordinary continuity of lifeway for some 3500 years demonstrates, at the least, why archaeologists are interested in traditional communities in the areas in which they work.

While Cuicuilco is building pyramids

(400 B.C.), the Teotihuacan Valley finally gets started with civic architecture. This change is accompanied by a shift of most communities in the valley up onto the tops of small but defensible hills and out of the prime farmlands. Many small projectile points are found on these sites. Central to each community is a small pyramid, at least one of which was deliberately destroyed in ancient times. All of these features suggest to Sanders, the discoverer, that during the late Preclassic stage, the Valley of Teotihuacan was divided among several warlike communities which headed six small competing states (1965). The motivations for competition were population pressures and the consequent pressures on land. More efficient and competitive social organization may well have developed as a result of this situation of scarce resources and multiplying people.

Cuicuilco was destroyed by a volcanic eruption about 150 B.C., effectively eliminating one of the northern basin's strongest competitors. The lava flow on which the modern University City is built covers the former town. Only the round platforms remain. Unfortunately, a pioneer archaeologist used dynamite to excavate the circular stone structure, and for years it was not certain which came first, lava or pyramid.

THE VALLEY OF PUEBLA. Moyotzinco is a small village that is about the size of the early Oaxacan and Basin of Mexico sites. It dates from the same era, around 1300 B.C. The village is represented by house remains, and bottle-shaped pits which are crammed with trash. Small platforms made of adobe may represent the beginning of social stratification and religious specialization if they supported housing and temples. There is not much in print in detail about the Valley of Puebla Preclassic sequence at this time, but the German Scientific Mission has accomplished a great deal of work, which is now being analyzed (Aufdermayer, 1970, 1973). Generally, it seems that Puebla underwent the same sequence of events that we have seen in the basin and the Oaxacan Central Valley. First came the appearance of village life, around 1500–1300 B.C., and the connection of some of these with the Olmec phenomenon. A slow, steady buildup of population is indicated by the increase in the number of communities through time. Elaboration of social structure and special architecture associated with religion and stratification occurred. Finally, the appearance of small towns and cities about 150 B.C. signaled the beginning of civilized life. The great pyramid of Cholula covers a smaller pyramid which was built at about the end of the Preclassic period.

The Tehuacan Valley is a part of the greater Puebla zone, and its very detailed sequence reflects these trends. Since Tehuacan has a marginal agricultural potential, we cannot assume that the vital transition phases are present. More likely, these phases will come to light through work in the main and most desirable valley: around the later major centers of Cholula, or Tlaxcala.

WEST MEXICAN PRECLASSIC CULTURES

GEOGRAPHY AND CHRONOLOGY. Western Mexico is a convenient label for an area which was a vast reservoir of ecological, human, and cultural diversity. If any one statement characterizes the area, it is that there is no apparent unifying cultural or natural pattern to it. No area of Mesoamerica is like it; but then no area of Mesoamerica is like any other. Modern political definition of the area includes the states of Michoacan, Jalisco, Guanajuato, Colima, Nayarit, and Aguascalientes, encompassing about 209,151 square kilometers (80,792 square miles).

According to Robert West, the area's geography is created by two major and related environmental factors: volcanic activity and a peculiar hydrography (1964). Large internal drainage basins cover much of the surface between surrounding volcanic features. Large, composite volcanoes, swarms of cinder cones, and many scoria mounds dot the landscape. Some 800 cinder cones are to be found between Uruapan and Morelia. The basins are most important for human habitation. A few major rivers pierce the mountainous fence around the plateau and find their ways to the Pacific Ocean. The Balsas on the south and the Rio San Pedro on the north frame the coastal zone, with at least eight other rivers between them. Culturally, the presence of so many rivers is important; they provided easy access from the coasts to the interior plateau.

As noted, the first evidence for sedentary communities in the west is from the shell middens of Puerto Marquez, which have preceramic levels certainly earlier than 3000 B.C. This estuary, seacoast gathering way of life persisted late on the Pacific Coast as evidenced by the San Blas phase in Nayarit (around 200 B.C.). The earliest sedentary interior material is only around 1500 B.C. Clearly, in this area, which is as large as the Maya lowlands, much more work needs to be done to fill in even the most fundamental data on time-space relationships of the ancient cultures.

WESTERN VARIETIES OF THE PRECLASSIC. Most of the archaeological remains of the west Mexican Preclassic cultures so far studied are of tombs and burials. Even so, it seems that this area of Mesoamerica emphasized death and death ritual more than other Preclassic cultures. Family crypts appear about 1300 B.C. and continue until around A.D. 500. These crypts include varieties of chamber tombs. Development of an exuberant and regionally varied tradition of ceramic figures is linked to an emphasis on funeral activities. The socio-

political level seems to have been that of linked or independent villages with kinship ties as the major integrating force. It is notable that west Mexico was apparently largely isolated and relatively free of interaction with outside cultures, especially with the Olmec. This would reinforce the impression that sociopolitical organization was somewhat undeveloped in the west. Flannery's argument that the Olmec tended to deal with societies of equal sophistication might explain the lack of sustained contact (1968). Only in Michoacan and Guanajuato do traces of contact with Tlatilco show up. In any case, the west Mexican area, by 1300 B.C., establishes a distinctive cultural tradition which is only disturbed by outside events beginning about A.D. 350 when the Mesoamerican high cultures begin to penetrate the area. We are not sure whether or not there were continuities between the Preclassic tradition and the historic Tarascans who inhabited some of the same area. At the moment, it seems best to assume that such continuities were indirect at the most.

EARLIEST KNOWN CULTURAL COMPLEXES. Aside from the already discussed Puerto Marquez ceramic complex in Guerrero, there is a somewhat later preceramic phase called *Matanchen* (Meighan, 1972). This is a mollusk-gathering site in Nayarit indicated by the usual mound of shells. It should be pointed out that many people died during the Russian revolution trying to live on mollusks (M. D. Coe, personal communication). There is a dietary imbalance in such a regimen. Therefore, it is entirely likely that the Matanchen represents a periodically or seasonally occupied site at the most. A carbon 14 date of 2000 B.C. was obtained for Matanchen.

At approximately 1450 B.C., a ceramic complex known as *Capacha* appears on the Colima coast, with the pottery found mainly in simple extended burials. Stirrup jars, belted jars (*bules*), tecomates, water jars, and composite forms make up the shape inventory. Decoration is by monochrome slipping, zoned punctation, zoned incision, zoned dichrome, and red-on-cream slipping. Similar pottery has been found in Jalisco, Michoacan, and Nayarit, indicating that the western ceramic tradition had begun by this early date. Further, no close relationships are known outside of the west. On the basis of the stirrup spout form, I. Kelly, the discoverer, suggests that there must be a South American connection and origin to that form (1974). As will be seen, stirrup-spouted jars elsewhere in Mesoamerica are considerably later. In South America, one example has been found in a seacoast culture of Ecuador (*Machalilla*) which is of about the same date. However, this seems quite a weak reed to lean upon. Machalilla culture itself is probably a seacoast variant of Chorrera culture, as we can see in the evidence presented by the excavators (Meggers and Evans, 1962). Yet Machalilla is said to be earlier than Chorrera! At present no resolution to this confusion can be made. Therefore, it is dubious to defer to a South American priority when basic time-space-content matters are not yet clear for Machalilla. However this is eventually settled, Capacha is the earliest widespread ceramic complex in the west.

In archaeological terms, the El Opeño chamber burials of 1300 B.C. are only a little later in date. Work by Eduardo Noguera (1965) and Jose Arturo Oliveros (1974) has produced good data on the earliest formal tombs known from the west. Nine tombs were found to be dug into a hillside in two lines, all facing west, toward the setting sun. All the crypts are similar in construction and are of the simple chamber type, entered by a flight of stairs cut into the volcanic ash subsoil (*tepetate*). Ovoid chambers are found at the base of the stairs. The tombs contained multiple burials, as many as ten individuals in one chamber. In Tomb 3 (1970), nine skulls were found piled separately from the long bones which were sorted and stacked — an indication of disturbance and rearrangement. In several tombs there was evidence of repeated entrance and reuse, not only in the piling of bones, but also in the layering of burials one above another.

The Opeño ceramic complex is actually a funerary subcomplex, lacking the almost certainly contemporary utility types. Nonetheless, the group is quite diagnostic and is related to Capacha, as well as to some late Tlatilco pottery. Late San Pablo ceramics in Morelos are also similar. All of this boils down to a stronger indication of outside contact than that known for any other early western complex. Ceramic similarities are reinforced by similarities in obsidian point types to some found at Tlatilco. Many of the considerable number of solid figurines from El Opeño are like those from the Valley of Mexico. On the other hand, some figurines are very regionalized in style and may relate to Chupicuaro types. An Olmec-style motif, the St. Andrews cross, was incised on a greenstone pectoral, and Caribbean seashells confirm wide connections at El Opeño, around 1300 B.C. Unfortunately, we do not have a clue as to the nature of the community that used the Opeño area as a cemetery.

LATER VARIETIES OF PRECLASSIC CULTURES AND CHAMBERED TOMBS. The lower Balsas River has produced a phase which is approximately middle formative, or dating around 800 to 500 B.C. Infiernillo-phase burials were made on beaches and yielded pottery which consists mainly of globular jars decorated by zoned incision, with pendent triangles and opposed triangles as a characteristic motif. One such burial also contained shell bracelets decorated with incised parrots. Small reddish bone carvings of "ducks" were found in the same grave.

By the beginning of the late Preclassic stage

(250 B.C.) a distinctive set of burial customs was in full swing in the west. The strongest expression of this funerary philosophy is in the shaft-tomb area, which is a geographic arc running from the southern Nayarit south through Jalisco and curving west into Colima and to the Pacific coast. Chamber tombs in this arc consist of deep vertical shafts 3 to 18 meters (10 to 60 feet) deep, with ovoid tombs either directly off the shafts at various levels, or connected with the shafts by lateral tunnels. Burial offerings are distinctive and patterned. Large hollow pottery figures are common and vary.stylistically from zone to zone. Mixtures of styles are common within a single chamber. Elaborate polychrome pottery accompanied the dead, as well as slate-backed pyrite-mosaic mirrors, and conch shell trumpets. This complex of offerings is also found in zones where shaft tomb burials do not occur. For example, in the Magdalena Lake district in Jalisco, the complex occurs in mound burials, "as it also does in regular burials in the Lake Chapala Basin" (M. Bond). At Cerro Encantado to the northeast, the complex is found with both simple burials and some chamber tombs somewhat like the earlier El Opeño models. The point is that, regardless of the wildly variant styles of tomb figures, a widespread funeral ritual similarity was present in the west beginning around 500 B.C., and lasted a thousand years (A.D. 500).

Worse hit by pot hunters than most areas of Mesoamerica, the west has suffered from the fact that only at the Cerro Encantado and El Arenal sites have archaeologists found undisturbed or semidisturbed burials which show stratigraphic and other associations among the artifacts. Looting has been fantastic in its proportions. Philip Weigand (1974) estimates that the Etzatlan region alone has yielded eight to ten thousand tomb figures to the antiquity market! Even so, Peter Furst estimates that only 30 percent of the tombs have been found in one badly ravaged area.

Almost endless detailed variation in the styles of the figurines has led to a rough classification of the hollow types. *Chinesca* is a grouping of figurines with vaguely oriental features. Apparently it comes from the Nayarit zone. *Colima Redware* is from Colima. *San Sebastian Red* and *Arenal Brown* hollow figures generally come from southern Nayarit and northern Jalisco. *Ameca Gray* figures are localized in northern Jalisco. *Horned* (*Cornudo*) figures come from northeastern Jalisco and southern Zacatecas. These categories are based on stylistic similarities and undoubtedly have some basis in reality. How much so, we will be able to judge only when archaeologists find the figures in context and association.

Although less revealing than the Nayarit village scenes, the hollow figures do give a good deal of information about social life and other affairs in the ancient past. Warriors in armor, men and women in everyday dress or undress, women with babies, people sitting, and other scenes give an impression of attempts at portraiture. The famous dog figures bark, snarl, sleep, and seem faithful enough. Perhaps the figures were meant to surround the dead persons in their tombs with a semblance of the actual life with which they were surrounded before death.

Until Weigand's recent work (1974) we have had practically no information on the settlement patterns and communities that supported these rich burial manifestations. Let us now turn to that work.

Etzatlan and the El Arenal Tomb. Weigand and his colleagues have examined an area of several hundred square kilometers and classified some 348 sites. Some of these sites are only activity locations: kill spots, hunting stations, and workshops. All of the other sites are grouped into patterns of habitation mounds: semicircles or circles around a central burial mound. The simplest group is that of a single burial mound with a semicircle of house mounds around it (type 4). This is the most common type of site and was probably the sort of small hamlet in which most of the ancient populations lived. Type 4 sites are eight to fourteen times as numerous as type 2 and 3 sites. The simplest tombs are found in the hamlet sites (type 4) accompanied by one or two pottery figures.

The larger sites (types 2 and 3) have correspondingly more elaborate tombs and burial goods. The famous shaft tomb of El Arenal is in a type 2 site, and in spite of its clandestine excavation in the 1930s, Eduardo Noguera recovered a great deal of valuable information about the skeletal and pottery arrangements (1965). Another tomb was found nearby at San Sebastian, and Furst salvaged information about it (1974). Some seventeen hollow figures were in a chamber along with forty polychrome vessels which probably had held food at the time of burial. The pottery figures were of several styles and were grouped around the skeletons of a dozen individuals. Boxes with covers, shell trumpets, and obsidian mirrors were also in the burial. A carbon 14 date of A.D. 250 was obtained. The figures in the Etzatlan zone tombs and burials are most often of ball players, warriors, and pregnant women. Weigand says that many of the tombs were originally painted with murals, although these had been poorly preserved (1974).

Weigand thinks that the hierarchically-arranged communities were linked through kinship ties, specifically through ranked lineages. Each tomb figure style may symbolically represent a lineage as well as a community craft specialty.

There is only one type 1 site in the valley and that is Ahualulco, which is a combination of types 2, 3, and 4. Ahualulco's mounds and ceramics cover about half a square mile, with obsidian artifacts found over about 1.5 square miles (3.9 square kilometers).

Weigand (1974) has set up a local sequence which is as follows:

Phases	Ahualulco Chronology
Etzatlan	A.D. 1200 to 1522
Huistla	A.D. 800 to 1200
Teuchitlan (late Classic)	A.D. 350/400 to 900
Ahualulco (late Preclassic– early Classic)	A.D. 150/200 to 350/400
El Arenal	1000 B.C.(?) to A.D. 150/200

At this point we are interested only in the two earliest phases, Arenal and Ahualulco. Weigand thinks that during Arenal times, all communities in the valley were more or less on a parity. After A.D. 150 or so, Ahualulco becomes larger than any other center and politically dominates the whole valley. An early contact with Teotihuacan may have something to do with the integration of the whole valley into Ahualulco's orbit. About A.D. 350 Teotihuacan contact becomes much more direct, the great city dominates the valley, Ahualulco loses its importance, and shaft-tomb burial begins to die out. The prestige of dominant local lineages may have been destroyed by Teotihuacan and therefore the symbolic and status-reinforcing burial rituals dropped into disuse.

Cerro Encantado. Betty Bell has excavated an important site in the arid region northeast of Jalisco (1974b). As noted before, the shaft-tomb artifactual complex is found at this site, even though the tombs themselves are absent. Bell found an undisturbed burial with a pair of horned (Cornudo) figures in it. Actually, these figures are typically male-female pairs, with only the males having the mushroom-shaped horns on their heads. An associated carbon 14 date indicates A.D. 100–250 for this style. Pottery at Cerro Encantado shows relationships to the Chupicuaro culture group to the east, and to the Canutillo and Alta Vista phases (A.D. 200 to 500) of Chalchihuites culture to the north.

Nayarit Villagers. The southern highlands of Nayarit was the homeland of an extraordinarily lively set of ceramic models which reflect everyday life in an amusing and detailed manner. No southern Nayarit figurine or model has ever been found by an archaeologist in an undisturbed context. Gifford thought that these belonged to a period dating from about A.D. 0 to 500 (early *Ixtlan*). This remarkable anecdotal sculpture has been categorized and analyzed by Hasso von Winning (von Winning, 1974; von Winning and Hammer, 1972). Most of the scenes fall into the following types: house models showing domestic life; ball games played in courts; and village scenes of infinite variety. War, tragedy, gaiety, life crises, and mundane, quiet domesticity are all shown. The village models show funeral processions in which catafalques are carried on pallbearers' shoulders through crowds of people. Adults mourn dead children; a small figure lies on the ground within a circle of seated persons who gaze at the child. Volador ceremonies take place on poles erected in the center of a group of houses; a man balances on his stomach on the top of a pole. Dignitaries are carried in elaborate litters by groups of men. Villagers dance and drink in riotous festivals. Family groups engage in quiet conversation outside their houses. Women prepare meals for their families. Women in childbirth are assisted by midwives. Groups of warriors on hills defend their villages against other groups. Figures strapped on beds are suggested by von Winning to be bodies ready for interment. Bloodletting ceremonies involving piercing the cheeks with rods are frequent. Sometimes the rod runs through several persons' cheeks as they stand in a line. In short, we are provided with a rare look at daily life which is as close as the archaeologist gets to doing ethnography.

The pottery models from Nayarit undoubtedly have some regional distinctiveness, but they may generally reflect the quality of life and its major features throughout these late Preclassic times.

Judging from the figures and the village scenes, there was social stratification and specialized leadership, but it stopped short of urban complexities. Villages show elaborately decorated and complex houses, but these are no more so than those of ethnographically known Chiapas villages and ceremonial centers. On the other hand, there is little depictively shown of civic architecture. Small round platforms in the centers of villages, some ball courts probably with clay walls, and rather low platform foundations for houses are the extent of formal architecture. These features do not reflect access to manpower above the village level. Nor does housing show significant differences above the ranked levels found in most village societies. The warfare pattern indicates that most men engaged in it, but that there is no sure evidence of specialist warriors. Funerary activities were extremely important, and kinship ties undoubtedly the main social organizational principle. The great men of the western villages probably were such partly because of their superior lineages. The inferences which can be drawn from these Nayarit scenes are remarkably congruent with the Etzatlan settlement pattern data.

The Chupicuaro Culture Group. The Chupicuaro site is gone forever under a lake created by a modern dam. During the archaeological salvage project in the 1940s, however, some 390 burials were dug out, many richly furnished with brilliant pottery. Some forty-six dog burials accompanied human graves. Muriel Weaver, who made the most extensive report on the site, defined two periods, early and late (1953), but Bennyhoff and McBride have suggested (to date without contradiction) that the periods as defined are reversed; i.e., that early is really late and late is really early (Chadwick, 1971). We may accept Bennyhoff's and McBride's revisionist arguments, which are based on the Valley of Mexico figurine sequence. Such figurines are found in the Chupicuaro burials, and thus they can be ordered by a knowledge of the sequence of appearance of figurine types in the valley from whence they originated. The argument is over the correct seriation of figurines. However, rather than confuse things even more and to avoid absolute bedlam should McBride prove to be mistaken, we will call early Chupicuaro, *Chupicuaro Black Ware* phase; and late Chupicuaro, *Chupicuaro Brown Ware* phase.

Chupicuaro Brown Ware phase is now probably earliest and dates from about 200 B.C. to A.D. 0 according to McBride. Common to both phases are red, red on buff, painted pattern, and black polychromes. Brown Ware phase is characterized by a heavy reliance on (what else?) brown wares, including brown polychrome, as well as by specific Protoclassic forms in all types. Tetrapod bowls with swollen feet are especially diagnostic. Shoe-shaped pots are a favorite form, as are fruit stands, boxes, and linked cylinders. Many textile-like designs are found on the black polychromes. Again, as at so many sites, we have a cemetery without information about the supporting communities. There is no doubt that Chupicuaro represents an exuberant ceramic tradition in full flower. Chupicuaro-like ceramics are distributed widely over Guanajuato state and into Tula area (Tepeji del Rio) and Teotihuacan Valley (at Cuanalan).

Chupicuaro Black Ware phase emphasizes black-slipped pottery and is apparently later. Pottery has been simplified, and red-rimmed, red ware, red on buff, and black polychromes are characteristic. In both periods, large hollow figures painted black and red on cream and figures-strapped-to-a-bed are found. The intimate connection of the hollow figure and the bed figurine traditions with the chamber tombs of the farther west perhaps indicates a commonality of burial ritual and belief.

In both periods, graves were furnished with a wealth of domestic tools and ornaments. Many items of bone possibly useful in textile manufacture were found, as well as a number of musical instruments. The latter consisted of the usual complement of Mesoamerican ocarinas, rattles, rasps, and turtle-shell drums. Clearly, Chupicuaro was an affluent variant of late Preclassic Mesoamerica.

Ortices complex in Colima is mainly known from the extraordinarily fine red-ware hollow figures of great variety. Animal, vegetable, and human effigies are cleverly and deftly done. These figures apparently come from the shaft-tombs in the southern end of their distribution arc. The Chanchopa tomb is one example, which also yielded a thin orange pot from Teotihuacan II (Miccaotli) and had a carbon 14 date of A.D. 10.

Deposition of the Morett midden site on the Colima coast probably is begun in the late Preclassic period. Certain incised types of pottery at Morett resemble Tuxcacuesco ceramics. Tuxcacuesco pottery in Jalisco is dominated by red wares. Solid figurines which are included in the complex have similarities to Ortices figurines.

A number of other regional complexes dot the west during this period, but are less well defined, and, in any case, pottery is not people. We can only say that the west seems to have been thoroughly settled by peoples with a fairly unified set of beliefs expressed in a variety of funeral customs. Ceramic linkages among the various regions indicate widespread trade and contact, but not on any basis more sophisticated than the village market level.

SUMMARY

The present heavy research into the Mesoamerican Preclassic stage is beginning to form certain patterns. These, in turn, allow certain inferences and general statements about what factors led to cultural elaboration. These features allow us to look at less advanced cultures of Mesoamerica and advance some guesses as to why they did not achieve cultural parity with the nuclear zones.

Clearly, the momentum built up by the Olmec episode carried forward into the Izapan and related cultures with considerable strength. These diverged through time and space and by the time of Christ are certainly distinctive, even though the arcane sculptured styles may share an iconographic similarity. However, even these similar elite elements exist within very different regional contexts. Much of the baggage of Olmec-derived hierarchical culture is carried in carts made of local materials. Thus, when we examine Izapan sculpture and compare it to that of Kaminaljuyu there are strikingly different sets of subject matter in the two bodies of work. Further, ceramics and other materials traditional to the regions are distinctive. This situation can probably be explained by a general model of Mesoamerican elites who were in long-distance and knowledgeable contact with one another while they ruled over native populations of regionally distinct cultures. It reminds one of the resident hacienda or coffee finca elites of the nineteenth and twentieth centuries in Mexico and Guatemala. These upper classes were quite cognizant of what went on at the capital and in other states and also of matters in the outside world. The company labor working on the estates lived in compartmentalized worlds, however. A similar compartmentalization of elite and folk culture took place during the Preclassic period and is reflected by the growing distinctions and diversity to be found within any single region.

The influence of population growth is obviously enormous during the formative periods of Mesoamerican civilization. It alone can account for many of the transformations in the quality of cultures. It makes a great deal of difference as to whether one lives in a rural hamlet of 50 people where everyone is related or in a town of 1500 where everyone does not know everyone else. The quality of differences among the communities is important. Apparently, there was never an equality or parity of communities; several were always larger or richer, or had other advantages. Sanders and Price elaborate these arguments in much more detail and with a great deal more sophistication. They also point out that sociopolitical organization is almost perforce tied to population levels. That is, what has been good enough for grandfather when he lived in a small community is not good enough for grandson who may live in a town. Efficiency of interaction, distribution, and conflict resolution demand a new social apparatus. The new way elaborates on the old structure, but, nonetheless, quantitative changes do bring about irreversible qualitative changes. Eventually, adaptation to new conditions passes a threshold, and nothing is the same again. Certainly one of those thresholds was reached with the initial formation of the petty states seen in the Maya lowlands, the Valley of Oaxaca, and the Basin of Mexico. As will be seen, a quantum jump was made in the two highland basins when they were each consolidated under a single system of sociopolitical control. Only then did maximum cultural elaboration take place. The lowland Maya are interesting in that they seem to have retained the petty state apparatus for a longer time and yet achieved considerable cultural success within that framework.

The west Mexican Preclassic seems to have stabilized at a developed village level of social organization, albeit with some very complex features, especially those aspects of culture dealing with death. The understanding of these stabilized cultures is crucial in dealing with differences in rates of cultural evolution in Mesoamerica. It is only under influence from the Valley of Mexico that part of the west eventually becomes transformed. It is also much later, in Toltec times, that all of it finally takes the step forward to civilizational status.

More of these matters will be discussed in the final chapter.

ADDENDUM

A rather extraordinary series of new carbon-14 dates have just been published by Norman Hammond and his associates (1976). These come from a deeply stratified site (Cuello) located in northern Belize near the Caribbean coast. At this small center, excavation revealed 4.7 meters (ca. 15 feet) of layered fill from which seven dates were obtained, ranging backward in time in relation to the depth of the stratum. The topmost date, 175 B.C., was from a Late Preclassic Chicanel layer. Deeper down, material associated with Mamom (Middle Preclassic) ceramics are dated at about 910 B.C., earlier than most dates previously obtained on this ubiquitous pottery. The most important and most spectacular is the date near the bottom of the pit 2000 B.C., corrected back to 2600 B.C. This is associated with a full complement of ceramics, some of which are slipped, and the forms of which are sophisticated and interesting. Therefore, the Maya area has now produced pottery nearly as early as any in Mesoamerica, and more sophisticated for its age than any yet found. Further, Hammond's discoveries have added a thousand years to the previously known Preclassic occupation of the Maya lowlands. Undoubtedly, new information will be forthcoming on this most exciting discovery.

CHAPTER 6

CLASSIC MAYA LOWLAND CIVILIZATION

Then they adhered to the [dictates of] their reason. There was no sin; in the holy faith their lives [were passed]. There was then no sickness; they had then no aching bones; they had then no high fever . . . At that time the course of humanity was orderly.
—Chilam Balam of Chumayel, 1967: 83.

[Herewith] the history which I have written of how the mounds came to be constructed by the heathen. During three score and fifteen katuns (1500 years) they were constructed. The great

. . . men made them . . . the great mounds came to be built by the lineages.
—Chilam Balam of Chumayel, 1967: 79.

Among these high hills which we passed there are a variety of ancient buildings among which I recognized habitations inside, and although they were very high and my strength very little, I climbed them, although with difficulty. These were in the form of a convent with small cloisters, and many living rooms all roofed, with terraces [outside] and whitened with lime inside.
—Father Avendaño, in Morley, 1938: 55.

PALENQUE, The Palace Group, as seen from the entranceway of the Temple of Inscriptions. Perhaps no other classic Maya building complex, with possible exception of the Central Plaza zone of Tikal, better exemplifies the highest achievement of architectural complexity and harmony of design. The Palace Group is noted for its broad stairways, unique four-storied observatory tower, low, rectilinear buildings with mansard roofs, and three sequestered inner courts. Unlike many classic Maya sites, the Palenque architects built upon the natural elevations of the site and displayed a preference for graceful integration of the architecture with the natural setting, rather than for monumental size.

MAYA CLASSIC CIVILIZATION WAS NOT created full-blown in a green flash of Olmec lightning. As seen in the previous chapter, it is regarded as the result of a number of factors which interacted, a less spectacular but more interesting process. Resource concentration, as suggested by Carneiro, the demonstrated fact of cultural variability among the farming villages, the donation of new ideas and techniques from outside the Maya area, and the food resources available to the Maya, all affected the forms of Maya high culture from about A.D. 200 to 850. Like most of the cultural superstructure in Mesoamerica, Maya classic civilization was an elite-class phenomenon. Within its broad patterns, there were plenty of variations. This diversity also operated through time, and, as will be seen, Maya culture underwent serious and drastic changes as a result of several crises in its history. In the background of all of this historical action, however, are commonalities and continuities which are connected with the everyday matters of getting enough to eat and drink and of providing shelter. Therefore, the farming and food-gathering patterns of the Maya claim our attention first.

AGRICULTURAL PATTERNS

It has been generally assumed that the prehistoric Maya practiced agriculture in much the same ways used by his descendants in the sixteenth century and even today. To assume this means that for the ancient farmer, swidden agriculture or shifting cultivation was extremely important and, indeed, the major occupation of the commoner. It also means that the principal crop, maize, or Indian corn, was the dominant crop as it is today. Recently developed data lead us to question the assumption. There is no doubt but that maize was important, but in ancient times it probably shared the subsistence scene with other crops.

Many studies have been done of the Maya system of shifting cultivation, and although there are variations from zone to zone, a general pattern prevails for the whole area. Maize cultivation was a variant of slash-and-burn or swidden. This is an extensive form of agriculture most used where the circumstances do not permit intensive techniques such as the chinampas of the highlands of Mexico, and in areas where land is plentiful. It is also much more common in the tropical lowlands than in the highlands. Typically, a patch of jungle is cleared off and burned and the crop planted in the ashes at the beginning of the rainy season. A family of five needs about 3000 pounds of maize per year given the present-day diet and food habits of the Maya. There is reason to believe that these food habits were the same at the time of the Spanish conquest and have changed little in the traditional villages since then.

However, there would seem to have been a radical shift in food emphases sometime after the catastrophic collapse of Classic civilization about A.D. 900. In any case, swidden agriculture imposed its own limitations on Maya life if it followed the present-day pattern. For one thing, the field must be fallowed after about three years of cultivation, and a four- to eight-year rest period allowed. Thus, from four to eight times the amount of land in actual maize cultivation is locked up in fallow ground. Any shortening of the rest period would not allow the land to sufficiently recover its nutrients and would ultimately lead to catastrophic crop declines. The large amount of land necessary for a single family thus imposes one other limitation—the number of people that can live together in one place. If most people wish to live within even a half-day's walk of their fields, then the number of people living together in a permanent farming village is finite. Thus, as population expands absolutely in numbers, it also tends to expand through space, eventually filling up all available land and becoming fairly evenly distributed over the cultivable parts. Even so, agronomy studies by Ursula Cowgill, admittedly controversial, indicate that just using the shifting cultivation system with its dependence on corn as a main crop, the carrying capacity of the land would be about 150 to 200 people per square mile (or 76 per square kilometer), supporting a much larger urban population than did the Maya rural sector (1961, 1962). This is a considerable density (rural population in France averages 85 per square mile).

It is possible that the Maya lowlands had an even greater carrying capacity through the utilization of arboriculture. Theoretically, the use of the ramon nut resources would allow two or three times the number of people supportable only by maize as the main crop. In other words, the staggering figure of up to 450 people per square arable mile was possible. It should be pointed out here, however, that the use of this food would not have significantly changed the settlement pattern inasmuch as the population, although higher, would still tend to be distributed fairly evenly through space. This sort of situation seems to be reflected fairly well in the distribution of house mounds, or small platforms which supported the perishable houses of the commoners. The survey by Bullard, confirmed by others, has shown that practically anywhere there is arable land, there are certain to be house mounds (1960). The density of these structures rises as one approaches a ceremonial center, but seems never to approach the high nucleation of population found in the cities of the high plateau of central Mexico.

At this point, let us review the yearly activities of the Maya farmer, both ancient and modern, who depended wholly on the shifting cultivation system and on maize as the main crop.

MAYA YEARLY CYCLE. Selection of the piece of land takes place sometime during the previous year. Choice is based on the soil — clayey soils are avoided — and drainage. Crops must be drained or they will rot either at the seed stage or later. So the farmer looks for sloping land with enough top soil on it to guarantee sufficient nutrients for his plants. By planting on the slopes, the farmer also avoids some of the danger of frosts which occur in the lowest ground. A piece of land is then cleared during the dry season — from January to April for most of the area. This means arduous and difficult work chopping out trees and bushes, and dealing with snakes, thorny bamboo, poisonous trees, and other hazards. A man's friends and family may help him, but much of the time he does it alone.

When a sufficient amount of land is cleared, then the cut-down vegetation must dry. On a suitable day, the vegetation is burned. This is a spectacular and dangerous business, and the criteria for a suitable day vary through the lowlands. In the northern lowlands farmers prefer a windy day which will drive the fire through the field. In the Peten, they wait for a windless day to avoid setting forest fires in the higher jungle of those parts. In any case, the burning requires cooperation among neighbors, since the fires are set in many places simultaneously to get a "good burn." The field may burn and smoulder for several days, although most of the fire has done its work in a few hours. Another important decision then follows — when to plant. If one plants too soon before the rains, then the birds may get the seed corn. If one waits too long, then he may not be able to get into the field, the seed corn may rot before it germinates, or it may be washed out of the ground.

Planting is done by making a hole in the

ash of the burned field with a sharpened stick. A kernel is dropped in, and with a swipe of the foot the farmer covers it up. Once the crop germinates, he need only occasionally weed it, but although he has a temporary respite from his labors, his anxieties continue. Hail lurks in the dark, rainy season clouds; high winds may also destroy or decimate the young corn plants. Later, insects, birds, and wild animals are an ever-present menace. Where corn fields have been cleared from the jungle, the small Yucatec deer multiplies in response, being very fond of corn and very quick to take advantage of the tasty meals at hand. Of course, the farmer is not entirely the loser; he may hunt the predatory and well-fed deer, thereby balancing his diet with animal protein. Deer may also have been at least partially domesticated as indicated in Spanish accounts of tame deer found in sixteenth-century Maya villages.

Several other crops are planted in corn fields among the plants. Most common are varieties of beans, squashes, and pumpkins. Kitchen gardens also provide nutritional balance to the Maya diet, adding chile peppers, tomatoes, and other vegetables such as *huisquil*, with which North Americans are not familiar. Papayas and other beneficial fruits are available. Avocados are cultivated, as are the chocolate bean and vanilla.

All of this information on Maya diet and farming practices comes from ethnographic and early chronicle sources and fits the present-day Indian as well as the prehistoric situation (Cook, 1921; Reina, 1967; Sanders, 1973). Although some of the most recent and revolutionary findings on Maya diet demonstrate that Classic farmers probably used quite different combinations of foods, the great emphasis on corn or maize is the same today as in the sixteenth century. Many writers have emphasized the religious aura which surrounds the sacred crop in the mind of the

traditional Maya and ritual which accompanied the varying parts of the agricultural cycle in historic times. The same mystical attachment to the planting and raising of corn still obtains today. There is also the "machismo" factor, which means that a man is not demonstrably "male" unless he wrests a living from nature. This prestige element probably operated in ancient times also, as we shall see, but for different reasons.

Recent work by D. Puleston of the Tikal Project, has produced a revolutionary new perspective on the possibilities of subsistence in Classic times (1968, 1971). Puleston's surveys of the residential zones around Tikal, extending out as far as twenty kilometers, have indicated a strong correlation between the distribution of house mounds, chultuns, and the ramon tree (*Brosimum alicastrum*). The ramon is an exceedingly useful tree, as it produces a highly nutritious nut that is equal, and in some ways superior, to maize. Indeed, when the maize crop fails today, the Maya depend on the ramon tree as a substitute source of vegetable protein. By ingenious experiments, Puleston has found that one type of underground chamber (*chultun*) is suitable for the storage of ramon nuts, but unsuitable for practically anything else. Ramon nuts will survive up to eighteen months in good condition in the multiple-chambered chultuns; maize, for example, deteriorates within two weeks and becomes inedible. The association of the ramon tree groves with the residential mounds of the ancient Maya seems too close to be fortuitous; there is a positive correlation of about .85. By careful recording, Puleston has found that the wild trees will produce up to 1000 pounds of nuts per acre, and further, that they always produce nuts, even during the years when the rain fails, although the crop may be smaller. Corn has the disadvantage of having to reproduce the entire plant each year, and only then is the food-giving ear brought forth. Ramon trees last nearly one hundred years, and a grove, once started, requires no care. The nut can be eaten in tortilla form and, in addition to its nutritional value, is tasty, having a bran-like flavor.

Puleston argues from this and other data that the ancient Maya depended on the ramon during the high population periods of the Classic stage and that maize was a high-prestige crop which may have been limited in regular consumption to the upper classes. If this argument is correct, the implications are enormous. It means that the population density could have been raised up to 450 persons per square arable mile, as noted above. Moreover, since women and children can harvest the ramon crop by simply picking up the nuts, the amount of manpower available for work under the direction of the elite classes was significantly increased. Energy expended in the shifting cultivation cycle was significantly decreased.

The *milpa* or maize agricultural cycle absorbs up to six months of labor a year. If a man is not wholly dependent on maize, he can devote much more time to other things. Thus, the presence of the ramon tree may explain how so much labor could have been expended on the monumental works of Classic Maya civilization. Many more people may have been present than we have previously believed, and much more of their time may have been available for "civilized" activities.

Marine resources were also quite important in the diet of those people living near the coast (Ball and Eaton, 1972; Lange, 1971). This is evidenced by large amounts of shell and fish bones in middens near the shores and on the beaches of the peninsula. As a colleague has observed, the peninsula is surrounded by one vast soup, teeming with food resources. Finally, we do not doubt that many root foods were used including, probably, yucca. However, camotes, and many other roots are also available for the digging. Again

the investment in labor and resources is minimal and the return is great (Bronson, 1966; Cowgill, 1971; Sanders, 1973).

POPULATION SIZES

As has been seen for the Preclassic period, most of the population lived in thatched-roofed huts, clustered in small kinship units or, at the most, in small villages. The picture changes during the Classic period with its great ceremonial centers only to the extent that some nucleation takes place around the centers and that nonfarmers reside in the centers. Even if we grant the dispersion of supporting populations, we will have difficulty in associating the housemounds and the ancient population they represent with the ceremonial centers. Only by accurate estimation of the sustaining populations can we develop any certain idea as to the nature of Maya society. Recent work by G. R. Willey and his associates in the Belize River Valley gives us the chance to accomplish this goal (Willey et al., 1965).

The Belize River situation is unusual in the Maya lowlands in that the house mounds and ceremonial centers are strung out linearly along the river. Most of the house mounds are next to the river, probably to allow access to the water, more convenient travel, and the cultivation of highly prized cacao crops in the alluvial soils near the river. Present-day maize farming is limited to the slopes on both sides of the river, but no ancient house structures are found there. Here then is a way around the difficulty of drawing boundaries around the zones of sustaining populations associated with the various ceremonial centers. Careful estimates of the populations would indicate that perhaps as many as 24,000 people were living on about 600 square kilometers (about 232 square miles). It is estimated that about 6000 persons were associated with each of the major ceremonial centers of the Belize Valley. However, this figure is conditioned by the limitations of maize agriculture. If one accepts the additional use of ramon nuts, then the population associated with a center might be from 6000 to 18,000. Coming at the problem from another direction, Bullard estimated from his survey of the northeastern Peten, that districts of roughly forty square miles were associated with major centers (1960). Taking the middle-sized center of Uaxactun, which has been excavated, as a test case, and calculating with the figures of maximum population density allowable, less the land not suitable for cultivation, we reach a population of about 15,000.

S. G. Morley (1946) estimated very much lower population densities for the northern lowlands in Yucatan, 44.6 persons per arable square mile, but this was before the ramon studies and also did not include the agronomy studies of U. Cowgill. However, there seems little doubt that there was something of a population gradient from south to north, with the higher density to the south and lower to the north. This difference was due to the increasingly stringent limitations on agricultural activities as one goes north. E. W. Andrews, however, has estimated a population of 250,000 in the extreme north around Dzibilchaltun (1967). However, in the absence of any detailed documentation for this figure and the many indications to the contrary, we must disregard this extreme possibility for the present.

One can play at length with these and other figures, and it may be that the reader has given up in disgust at the imprecision of the exercise. However, it seems clear that new techniques and more information will soon allow us to formulate more accurate estimates. In the meantime, we have reached at least a measure of the order of magnitude of populations involved. In other words, we can say with some confidence that, at the height of the Classic period, Maya ceremonial centers involved the interaction of probably thousands of people — surely not many tens of thousands, but surely more than just hundreds. This is a distinct improvement on matters as they existed only a few years ago.

We shall have to return to the matter of the size of the elite classes and their retainers after considering the functions of their ceremonial centers.

CEREMONIAL CENTERS AND THEIR FUNCTIONS

A good deal of scholarly blood has been spilled over the issue of whether or not what J. Eric Thompson has called ceremonial centers were cities. This matter of urbanism can block further understanding of more important matters such as what kind of society operated from these collections of monumental architecture. We shall approach the matter from a functional viewpoint, examining the major classes of buildings within the Maya Classic centers, assigning them functions from evidence available, and then showing how centers varied in their combinations of the major elements. Maya centers seem to have been functional urban centers (Steward, 1961), performing urban functions for dispersed populations, lacking only the criterion of high-density permanent population to take their place with the other forms of cities known. The interesting point is not so much that the Maya cities were formally unlike other cities, but that they functioned as cities for that society in the special circumstances of dispersed population.

There are several major formal classes of monumental architecture in Maya ceremonial centers: temples, palaces, ball courts, *sacbes*, and reservoirs. At some sites fortifications must be added, but these are not invariable components as the other elements seem to be.

Buildings were made of cut limestone masonry covered with a strong stucco plaster to protect the building from the rains. With the lines and angles thus softened and smoothed off, buildings were thus flowing and more curvilinear than we see them today. Rubble cores of rough stone, sometimes mortar, earth, and even wood, made up the mass of the structures. The limestone walls often, especially later in the Classic period, formed a sort of veneer over the rough hearting. Generally good quality mortar was used to cement the stones in place. As pointed out by Laurence Roys (1934), the ultimate structural strength of Maya buildings is really that of a concrete structure tied together by the mortar and rubble mass with not much integrity given by the masonry skin. Roofs were built using the corbeled system, which involved edging the stones on opposing walls toward one another, course by course, until the space was small enough to be bridged by a capstone. This form of vault allowed rooms up to fifteen feet in width, but the usual size was smaller, and Maya rooms tend to be long and narrow and high.

TEMPLES. Maya temples are generally elevated on terraced substructures. The substructures vary in height and width but are generally solid and without chambers except for tombs and associated passages. The temple structure itself is usually small compared to the mass of the substructure and has relatively little space inside, and even that may be occupied by benches and altars. Very few people could be accommodated within such a structure. The rooms were high and narrow due to the use of the corbeled vault, but they were deliberately made so. The roof of the temple often carried an ornamented wall, called a *roofcomb,* decorated with modeled stucco. Most temples show remnants of such stucco decoration and red paint, often on much of the building other than the roof-comb. Burn marks on the floors, masonry altars, and walls indicate the repetitive use of *copal* (pine resin) incense. The fragrant smoke of copal permeates the atmosphere today in Maya communities when religious affairs are being conducted. Other evidence indicates the use of these buildings as foci for ritual activities. Elaborate caches of exotic materials, precious to the ancients, are found beneath the floors and in masonry altars. These offerings include items of jade, stingray spines, imported sea shells, and other symbolic items. At Tikal such caches are so consistently patterned that archaeologists can predict the nature of the caches and their locations. The traditional interpretation of temples has been that they were centers for the worship of the impersonal deities represented in Maya art. This is probably true, but, with new evidence, it seems we can go further.

Carved wooden beams occasionally span the doorways in the most important temples. These are resplendent with the florid and symbolic depictions of gorgeously attired persons, surrounded with scrollwork, serpents, jaguars, etc. — the panoply of power and authority. Complex texts of hieroglyphs accompany the depictions. As will be seen in the discussion of stelae, these texts usually include some historical information.

In the modeled stucco decoration similar subject material is found on a giant scale. Super-sized human figures seated on elaborate benches and surrounded with the symbolism of divinely attributed authority, can still be made out on some of the badly battered roofcombs. Hieroglyphic texts accompany the depictions in at least some cases, perhaps in all. The major key to the interpretation of the function of the temple type of building lies to some degree in the sumptuous tombs often found in them, and in the nature of the carved stone monuments called stelae.

In 1956 Michael Coe suggested that one of the functions of the Maya temple was as a resting place for distinguished members of society. Indeed, it seems that if one searches long enough through the often immense mass of rubble of temple substructures, an elaborate burial will often be found. The famous tomb found by Alberto Ruz in the Palenque Temples of the Inscriptions is one of the most elaborate examples of this sort of mortuary structure. In both this tomb and in others at Palenque, there is a feature called a *psycho-duct*, which is a small tube leading from the tomb up through the masonry to within a few inches of the floor of the temple building. Several other tombs at Palenque have the same feature. It seems clear that here we have an attempt at maintaining communication with the person placed in the tomb below. This would be something like the *sipapu* in southwestern kivas, which allows communication with the spirits underground. Thus both the occurrence of elaborate tombs and the psycho-ducts seem to confirm Coe's idea (1956). However, there is more to be said, and we must now consider the nature of the stelae, and the content of their texts.

STELAE. Stelae are carved stone shafts erected most often in association with temple buildings. T. Proskouriakoff's revolutionary studies indicate clearly that stelae are not simply impersonal monuments to the operations of celestial mechanics, and the figures not simply priests or god-impersonators associated with a calendrical cult (Proskouriakoff, 1960, 1961, 1963, 1964). There seems no question now that these are historical monuments, erected to record the exploits of a ruler, his genealogy, and circumstances of his birth, probably in justification of his political power. Groups of these monuments were associated with single temples at Piedras Negras, each stelae group dealing with a single individual's lifetime. The historical texts include information on birthdays, dates of accession to power, conquests, personal names, and

probably names of ceremonial centers. The frequent physical association of Maya stelae with temples suggests a ritual and functional association. Indeed, at least one temple on which the stucco decoration was fortuitously preserved (at Rio Azul) seems to duplicate, in arrangement of texts and depictions, the arrangement of the same material on stelae (Adams and Gatling, 1964). Specifically, the human figures are on the broad surfaces of the roofcomb and building, and the hieroglyphic texts on the narrow sides of the structure. This physical analogy suggests a functional analogy, and that temples in some way were historical, commemorative monuments.

Pulling it all together, temples would seem quite often, perhaps always, to be memorials to the distinguished dead, as well as places for the worship of the more impersonal supernatural. The implications of this will be further discussed when we consider the nature of Classic Maya society.

PALACES. "Palace" is a catch-all term to designate what are usually multiple-room, occasionally multiple-story buildings with a nearly endless variety of ground plans. As will be seen, some were truly luxurious residences. Others are more suited for administrative functions. Still others include dim and dark rooms which seem only usable as storage facilities. Finally, there is little doubt that many palace rooms have features which fit them for ritual and ceremonial practices.

Many scholars have objected to classification of palaces as elite-class residences. Objections have been made on the grounds that the buildings are dim, dark, slimy, damp, cramped, and unfitted for comfort. This seems an excessively ethnocentric and unimaginative approach. At the present, palaces indeed deserve all of those opprobrious adjectives, but this is after 1100 years or more of abandonment and neglect. Moreover, judging from their own depictive sources, the Classic Maya elite class had their own ideas of what constituted comfort.

In many ways the elite life-style seems to have been something like that of traditional Japanese culture. The commonest sitting position is cross-legged. The Maya seem to have used relatively little furniture of any size. Most is in the form of low tables, boxes, and other portable items. Most domestic life seems to have been carried on either on elevated benches built into the palace rooms, or on benches elevated on feet. The rooms with benches are commonly the widest to be found in palace structures, and the benches occupy up to 95 percent of the floor space. With mats, cushions, and a minimum of portable furniture, rooms could be changed in function as need arose. Indeed, the floor plans of what seem to be "apartments" in the A-V palace at Uaxactun provide some evidence that there was relatively little interior space for any single occupying individual or family. Cupboards built into the walls presumably stored items needed only at night, such as light blankets. Thus, the multiple uses made of rooms, the cross-legged sitting position, the use of portable furniture, and the ready availability of outdoor space all would make the larger rooms with benches quite suitable for living areas. Paved courts and terraces are often found in front of such rooms; with the use of canopies, or temporary awnings, some of which are shown in Maya murals and evidenced by post holes in the courtyards, these pavements would be supplementary living areas.

Simple maintenance would take care of a great many of the other objections to the use of Maya palaces as residences. Cutting down the present vegetation, restoring paved courts around the buildings, cleaning walls, keeping up water-tight roofs, all would contribute to creature comforts. Under such circumstances, with the major buildings surrounded by acres of heat-reflecting pavements, the dimness and coolness of the interior rooms would have been absolute assets.

Certain palaces have been found with built-in conveniences. It seems clear that Becan Structure IV palace has an interior drainage system which could be used with a shower or bath (Potter, 1973). The floor slopes to the drain in this case. In the same building, a built-in fireplace has been found. These features are unusual, however, and it seems that domestic necessities such as kitchens and latrines were located in supplementary and even perishable minor buildings. At Edzna and Becan, steambaths were available for the use of the inhabitants of the palaces on the other side of adjacent courts. A kitchen in what was probably a thatched hut was found at Tikal conveniently located to the palaces of the central acropolis. Unfortunately we don't know much about sanitation facilities, but perhaps some of the more humble types of Maya pottery functioned as "thundermugs." There is evidence that the courts, buildings, and rooms were kept swept and clean, and that debris was carried to selected dumps.

The question of the size of populations resident in the parts of the palaces given over to living quarters is one to which an answer can only be approximated at the moment. However, by considering the probable functions of the rooms with benches, and making a couple of other assumptions, we can arrive at ceilings on the numbers of people that could have been accommodated. One way to get at this figure is through consideration of sleeping space. Sleeping quarters are the minimum requirement for residences. Assuming that we are correct on the functions of the benches as primary living spaces, and assuming that these functions included sleeping, then the benches were also beds. There is equivocal evidence for the use of hammocks in pre-Hispanic times, and this device, so popular now among the lowland Maya, seems to have been introduced from the West Indies about the time of the Spanish conquest. In any case, there is no evidence that the hammock was very popular even if present. Protected sleeping space for the inhabitants of the palaces is limited to the benches, and these can be measured for maximum capacity. Assuming also that the proportional mix of ages and sex in such a palace population was something like that of the ethnographic Maya, one can make certain estimates. For all the palaces at Uaxactun, this would mean a maximum population of about 185 persons, which would break down into the following categories: 125 adults, and 60 children. At Uaxactun, these persons would be perhaps controlling and directing a supporting population of about 9000. Considering that adult males are most often mentioned in the hieroglyphic texts, and therefore probably were politically most important, it may be that about 20 adult males managed affairs at places such as Uaxactun (Adams, 1974a).

The activities of the elite class embraced politics, religion, and economics. Administration was assisted by a kind of civil service, made up perhaps by the elite, but more likely by a lower ranked group of specialists. In order for the ritual and ceremonial context that seems to have surrounded Maya nobility to operate, properly arranged quarters were necessary. There are many palaces which have parts fitted out for religious affairs, and perhaps for court protocol. Long narrow rooms, largely open on one side, with a central throne or altar, probably served these functions (Smith, 1950). Administration could have been carried out in subsidiary rooms which are suitable for living but near the deadend space most suitable for storage. The Group III quadrangle at Holmul might have been such an administrative and storage headquarters. In the center of the quadrangle there is a building with the large rooms and benches characteristic of the living zones. Perhaps a

chief bureaucrat lived here. The rooms surrounding the quadrangle are mostly without benches and narrow, and many are interior without ventilation or light. Presumably here were kept the food surpluses that supported the elite, the servants that cared for them, the bureaucrats that administered for them, and the craft specialists that they supported (Adams, 1970). Here too would be kept the elaborate costumes, the valuables which gave prestige, and arms (Merwin and Vaillant, 1932).

MARKETPLACES. Institutionalized trade is a long-standing trait of Mesoamerican civilization, but the Maya seem to have been peculiar in their trade patterns. For most people, trade during the Classic period took place in an interior and closed system. It seems clear from the distribution of artifacts and from technological studies that certain communities, hamlets, and villages, specialized in Classic times in the manufacture of certain items. This would fit with the present-day pattern of conservative Indian culture in such areas as the highlands of Chiapas where certain towns specialize in such crafts as pottery-making. These specialty manufactures are now distributed through a regional market system. Textiles, pottery, flint and obsidian tools, feathers, food, drink, salt, raw goods, artifacts of wood, and much else must have circulated through a regional economy in Classic times by means of a system based on the local ceremonial center. Combined with the model of an aristocratically led social structure, the evidence for internal circulation through a region implies more of a redistributive arrangement. This is an economic setup which is more characteristic of chiefdoms than state-level societies. Personal and kin relationships form the basis for reciprocal economic relationships. Certain goods and services are given the heads of kin groups, who in turn redistribute these items in return for still other goods and services. This model would better explain the apparent lack of formal markets in Maya ceremonial centers (Webb, 1973; Rathje, 1972). Aztec regulatory agencies required large buildings to carry out their work, but no such buildings are apparent in the ceremonial centers. We would expect these to be associated with the broad paved open spaces of the plazas, but such does not seem to be the case. This is still an arguable point.

Open plazas functioned for public ceremonies of importance to society as a whole. Such events are depicted in Maya art and include the judgment of captives after conquest, as well as religious rituals.

Finally, open spaces also functioned often as simply additional living space for the inhabitants of the palaces, their retainers, and perhaps even for people temporarily come to town.

SACBES. Elevated roads or causeways, *sacbes*, often connect important building groups within the ceremonial centers. Especially in northern Yucatan, these roads also sometimes connect separate ceremonial centers. These roads are elevated up to fifteen feet above the terrain and are up to sixty feet wide. They are made in the usual Maya manner, with a rubble core and cut stone judiciously used to give them a finished appearance. Finally, they were paved with a hard plaster. The traditional suggestion has been that the intercenter causeways were used for commerce. General ritual use for the interior sacbes at ceremonial centers has been argued. J. W. Ball recently has brilliantly argued and demonstrated that probably all these roads were ritual in purpose. In regard to intercenter roads, he points out that it is much preferable today to travel over any distance in the Maya lowlands in the shade of the jungle and on the springy surface of the ground, rather than on the modern paved highways. Further, the con-

nection of sacbes with temple groupings is very common. A much more reasonable explanation of such roads in ancient times, Ball suggests, is the projection back in time of a religious custom which still exists in the Maya area. This custom is the regular visiting of one saint — really his statue carried by the congregation — to another and the return of such visits. These visits are made between town quarters, and in some cases, between towns. The visits imply the respect of one saint for another, but also of social units whose religious patrons are the saints involved. Thus social solidarity is maintained, ties are strengthened for various purposes, and in the case of dispersed populations, allegiances reinforced. This custom of visiting may have been practiced in the case of the ancient deities. As will be seen further on, there is an indication that, in ancient times, the political and religious power was expected to shift from group to group along with the calendrically regulated shift of deities from shrine to shrine. These shifts may have been formally made over the sacred roads.

FORTIFICATIONS: MOATS AND HIGH BUILDINGS. In most Mesoamerican centers, the ultimate refuge in war was the chief temple of the town. The weapon systems of the time (bows, arrows, spears, rocks, slings, etc.), made the height and steepness of such buildings a formidable advantage. In addition, the interlocking nature of the buildings would allow mutual support by the groups fighting from them. The Maya were probably no exception to this. Of course, the scenes of warfare depict mainly what seem to be raids, and conflict is a knightly activity. However, recent research has indicated that there are more formal fortifications in the Classic period. Thus far, these consist wholly of moats, their palisades, and associated features. The largest known moat was found by Puleston to cover the northern approaches to Tikal and runs for nine and a half kilometers from swamp to swamp. Narrow causeways cross the great ditch. There seems to be a southern fortification also, of similar nature, but this has only recently been discovered.

The best known moat at present is at Becan in Campeche, where the ditch is about one mile in circumference, and was found by Webster to have originally been about forty feet deep and some sixty feet across (Webster, 1974). Formidable parapets increase the height of the interior lip of the ditch, and these may have been strengthened by the addition of log palisades. Seven narrow causeways cross the Becan moat; they show signs of having been cut in the ancient past, evidence that the fortification was probably used in earnest. One causeway had been cut and left open in late Classic times. In the combination of its isolation in the midst of surrounding swamps, in its carefully guarded access to water, and in its enclosing ring of fortification, Becan is unique in the Maya lowlands, a true fortress.

Many other Maya sites, however, are potentially defensible in their locations on ridges and next to formidable ravines. Seibal is an example. We have no idea at the moment, moreover, how many sites may have been defended by perishable military works which are detectable only with careful excavation. Deliberately fostered tangles of thorny second growth jungle in belts around the classic sites could have acted as deterrents to attack. Bolstered by palisades, fields of sharpened stakes, deadfalls, and the occasional features of formal construction, Maya centers would not be the defenseless, open communities that they seem at first sight. The dates of the Becan and Tikal moats are at the beginning of the early Classic (about A.D. 350) and the Becan ditch may be late Preclassic. As will be seen, these features may not be wholly

unique; they may reflect cultural-evolutionary processes.

BALL COURTS.   Another major functional class of formal architecture found in Maya sites is the ball court. This is a manifestation of the Mesoamerican ball game played with a solid rubber ball. The game varied in style and rules from place to place and through time, as reflected in the bewildering variety of courts from all over Mexico and Guatemala. However, certain common features probably tie these games together. It seems that either individual players or teams could play, judging by accounts of the conquerors and native sources. Sometimes the idea was to score points on the other side, and, within an alloted period of play, the highest score won. A variant seems to have been that a single score won the game. This happened when the goal was so difficult to make that only one score could reasonably be expected.

In conquest-period Mexico, the game had both recreational and divinatory functions. There is no knowing, at this point, how much of this sixteenth-century data we can extrapolate back in time. The Maya Classic ball courts are so distinct in form and style from later courts that the game may have differed radically. The safest thing we can say is that the game was played in some form, that it was popular, and that it was associated with elite-class life. The courts occur only in the ceremonial centers. This does not mean, however, that play may not have taken place on informal courts away from the centers. Indeed, the game is still played to this day in an impoverished form by peasants on the west coast of Mexico, and the court is marked only by a few stones at the corners, and by lines drawn in the dirt.

RESERVOIRS AND OTHER WATER STORAGE DEVICES. Water may not seem to be a concern for a people living in a tropical forest. However, because of the peculiar nature of the drainage of much of the Maya lowlands, water impoundment becomes a necessity. Most of the peninsula of Yucatan is massive, porous, unbedded limestone with little topsoil. These conditions become exaggerated as one goes from south to north. North of Lake Peten Itza in Guatemala, there is little permanent ground water in the form of lakes, ponds, or streams. Most of the heavy rainfall goes right through the soil and into the bedrock and down to the water table. At Tikal this is at least 550 feet below ground level. In the northern part of the peninsula the water table is about 70 feet down. During the dry season of three to four months, the small rain catchments often dry up. Modern settlements, even small ones, suffer greatly because of this circumstance, and water often has to be brought from up to twenty miles away from the settlement. In the north, sinkholes, locally known as cenotes give access to water all year round. Caves with permanent springs were used from earliest times and remains of thousands of special jars have been found in them, broken while carrying water up to the surface.

Artificial means supplemented the sources in the north and south. In the north, special types of chultuns, or underground storage chambers, bell-shaped and plastered, were dug. Some are in use to this day. The one at Kabah has been refurbished and serves the local community. In the south, with less access to the ground water table, large reservoirs were favored. At Tikal it is estimated that the maximum capacity of all the reservoirs amounts to about 40 million gallons. The permanent population of Tikal is estimated at about 50,000 people. This would mean that over a long dry period, 120 days, there might be 800 gallons per person, if all impoundment zones were full. These reservoirs took advantage of the great areas of pavement, which were slanted to drain into them. The

runoff must have been extraordinary, judging by the rate at which the somewhat reexcavated reservoir around the Tikal archaeological camp filled. It was nearly filled to its present capacity of 3 million gallons within 70 days after the rains began in 1958.

The matter of water becomes crucial in a high density and absolutely high level of population. Impoundment of water means resource concentration in Carneiro's terms and as has been noted, may be one of the stimuli to high culture involved in the Maya tropical forest zone. Assuming the eventual maximum expansion of human population on the basis of optimum conditions, and the consequent expansion beyond the support capacities of most natural means of water impoundment, then artificial means would have been an absolute necessity at some time early in the Maya settlement of the lowlands. Later, as an elite class developed, the reservoirs and other water storage devices may have become a means of social control.

South of Lake Peten and in certain other regions, far fewer problems are involved in providing a dry season water supply. Permanent lakes, large streams, and rivers are all dependable. Curiously, not many of the largest sites are located around these favorable sites. Perhaps (and this is only a guess) the people with independent means of water and food supply were less amenable to submitting to social control if they didn't have to. This would fit with, although not confirm, the idea of water as the resource which was concentrated.

REGIONAL AND CEREMONIAL CENTER VARIATION. Stylistic variation is plentiful among the regions of the Maya lowlands and among the centers themselves. These variations undoubtedly reflect in some manner the variations among local social systems and the relative importance of the individual sites. To take the technical styles first, there are at least five major architectural regions of the Classic period. These are indicated on the accompanying map with archetypal examples included. It will be noted that the *Greater Peten* style is the most widespread. This style is characterized by extensive use of polychrome painted, modeled stucco in decoration and an essential conservatism of conception in room dimensions. The elaboration of relatively few themes and the recombination of these architectural elements in a multitude of ways is characteristic of most Peten-style sites including the outlying site of Coba in the north. Tikal, with its complexities of palace groups and jumble of temples in groups typified this style.

Florid architectural decoration in the form of mosaic facades of carved stone is typical of the two north central styles, the *Puuc* and the *Rio Bec–Chenes*. This ornamentation takes the place of and carried the iconographic messages of the modeled stucco in the Greater Peten group. The differentiation between Rio Bec and Chenes styles has been demonstrated on the basis of recent field work to be invalid. Chenes facades are typically low, one story high, but with the motif of the earth monster as the primary one, with the central doorway ornamented as the mouth of the monster. Rio Bec buildings are typically ornamented with large towers which are nonfunctional temples. That is, the staircases are too steep for use and the dummy temples at the top are solid masonry. However, there are suitable tomb chambers in the mass of the substructures, although no undisturbed grave has ever been found. These towered structures are contemporary with the Chenes style and, indeed, in such sites as Becan and Chicanna, face Chenes structures across a plaza, forming what undoubtedly was a functional unit. Therefore we shall combine these previously separated styles into one unit.

Puuc structures are floridly decorated with rain god masks and earth monster facades. They are also characterized by alternation of the carved mosaic zones with severe or undecorated zones. Columns seem to set Puuc apart as well. Both the Rio Bec–Chenes and the Puuc styles are notable for their daring in architectural conception compared to the Greater Peten style. Rooms tend to be larger and higher, and the massiveness of the structures in general is notable. In other words, the monumentality typical of Maya ceremonial centers is emphasized in these regional styles, making them probably the most impressive of Maya buildings. The sites of Uxmal, Kabah, and Labna are exemplary of this impressiveness. Care in conception and execution of construction and carving is also typical of these northern styles. Greater Peten architecture often conceals construction faults under the heavy coatings of stucco and plaster.

The two other major style zones, are the frontier zones of Maya Classic culture, the *Southwestern* and the *Southeastern*. The former is epitomized at the site of Palenque. The use of physical isolation as a means of emphasizing a building, and the delicacy of stucco ornamentation set this site and associated centers apart from the rest of the Maya area. Certain features, such as mansard-style roofs and inner shrines also distinguish Palenque architecture. Copan is the prototypical site for the Southeastern style unit, and in its emphasis on the temple form and architectural sculpture nearly in the round is quite distinctive. The general emphasis on three-dimensional forms in Copan sculpture is notable, even in the stelae.

Although it has been argued otherwise, it seems quite clear on the basis of recent work and the accumulation of data from previous research that all of these regional styles are essentially contemporary at least in the late Classic period, and especially about the eighth century A.D. We are not so certain about the early Classic other than the Greater Peten style group, since not as much work has been done to reveal the early prototypes of the fully developed styles in the northern and frontier zones. Indeed, there are indications that the Southeastern and Southwestern groups are results of relatively late elite-class expansion into these zones in the late Classic period. We shall consider this point more below. The Rio Bec–Chenes and Puuc styles seem to go far back in time in the north.

Different combinations of the functional elements discussed above are remarkable. For example, at Uaxactun in the A-V palace, we seem to have temples and palaces in nearly all their functional permutations represented in one complex. This combination would seem to be analogous to the Mycenean "great houses" of the early Bronze Age in Europe, in that it served for political, economic, ceremonial and elite residence purposes. As noted above, almost nothing can be designated as elite-class residences at Copan. Perhaps here as at Altar de Sacrificios the upper classes lived in sumptuous residences built of perishable materials. On the other hand, moving north into the Rio Bec–Chenes zone, we find towered palaces apparently isolated from the ceremonial centers. These buildings in their isolation seem akin to the manors of the Middle Ages in Europe. The Puuc sites again give the impression of grandiosity implementing the designs of an elite who were housed better there than elsewhere.

Special function sites existed, the best understood of which are the burial islands on the Gulf Coast of Campeche, Isla Jaina, and Isla Piedras. Here, especially in the late Classic period, the distinguished and perhaps even the less socially prominent were buried with special ritual and special mortuary figurines. These figurines may represent scenes from the lives of the persons buried with them. They have been highly prized by the rapacious collectors of pre-Columbian art in recent years, because they are much more naturalistic than most Maya art.

DEPICTIVE MEDIA AND COMMUNICATION SYSTEMS

Technical qualities of writing and art are discussed in a separate section. The plethora of styles and media, and the richness of symbolism and iconography are distinctions of Maya art viewed either in a Mesoamerican or more broadly comparative context. Intimately connected with the art, and indeed, in one sense, part of it, were the hieroglyphic writing and calendrical systems. Both the depictions and the more abstract symbolic messages are inextricably connected with the cosmology and religious concepts of the Maya. Much of the function of these communications media was to attempt an understanding of the universe, to divine the possibilities for man both as an individual and as a social group, and to record his historical experience.

History was regarded by most Mesoamericans as cyclical. They believed that history literally repeated itself. Disasters would come at regular intervals as well as more favorable events, and these could in some way be anticipated or perhaps even forestalled by intimate knowledge of the regularities of the stars and other phenomena regarded as supernaturally controlled. The Maya of the sixteenth century believed in these cycles, and used art, calendrics, and writing to explain the forces behind the cycles. Although there may be something of a disjunction between Classic culture and Postclassic cultures of the Maya lowlands, a good argument can be made for projecting these basic concepts back into time. The beliefs implicit in the conceptions of segments of time as deities themselves and of specific metaphorical allusions such as the passage of time as being carried by the deities as burdens, all indicate a basic continuity of belief. However, added to these and other long-lasting traditions, there was probably a greater emphasis on ancestor worship among the elite class and possibly among broader segments of the populations. There is no doubt but that the concerns reflected in high art styles are essentially those of a small and elect class. We can see this in the fact that the historical and genealogical information deals exclusively, as nearly as we can tell, with the upper-class rulers.

Proskouriakoff's epochal discoveries have also established the stelae as elite-class monuments. Thanks to her work we can now confidently regard them as historical records of temporal rulers who had divine or semidivine attributes (Ruppert, Thompson, and Proskouriakoff, 1955). The sumptuously dressed individuals are not, as once thought, priest-impersonators of gods, or the gods themselves, or mythical beings engaged in mythically significant events. Groups of monuments are usually associated with the funerary, memorial temples, forming both a ritual and historically significant complex. The writing on the monuments and in the temples carries a load of historical data as well as the more esoteric astronomical and mathematical information. The calendrical system with all of its arcane permutations is at least in part historical in function, recording dates of rulers' births, accessions to power, conquests, and so forth. Genealogical information is also recorded, and often other ceremonial centers and their elite class are mentioned in the texts. Other depictive art, principally murals, can be interpreted in the same way and again the messages primarily concern upper-class matters. The famous Bonampak murals are undoubtedly historical in nature; the complex ceremonies, the raiding scene, and the more domestic scenes are all profoundly connected to circumstantial events and quite distinctive individuals. The newly found murals of Mul-Chic near Uxmal in Yucatan depict rather appallingly violent scenes of warfare. Bodies are strewn on the ground; one hangs from a tree; people bash one another with stones; and three grisly Maya warriors, decorated with

necklaces of skulls of what were probably previous victims, stalk through the scene taking trophy heads. A reconstruction of Maya warfare can be made from such depictions, which indicate something about war itself and also about the nature of society that was associated with such a style of warfare (Piña Chan, 1962a, 1962b).

From the sculpture, we can say with some confidence that trophy heads were common; in other words, the Maya were headhunters. We can also say, judging by the dress of individuals most often depicted with the trophies and in battle, that war was principally an elite-class activity. Prestige was connected with these activities. Certain rulers are quite prominently referred to as "conqueror of so-and-so"; for example the ruler "Bird-Jaguar" of Yaxchilan is known as "Conqueror of Jeweled-Skull," Jeweled-Skull being the name or title of another ruler. Given the weapon systems of the times, this kind of aristocratic warfare makes considerable sense. Depictive sources seem to show that Maya Classic warriors limited themselves to spears, rocks, and knives, and combat seems most often to have been hand-to-hand. There is no indication of highly organized, state-level warfare with standing armies, sophisticated tactics, and anything approaching large-scale casualties or genocide. Hand-to-hand combat generally does not produce a high casualty list. Likewise then, there is little indication that warfare was a socially disruptive activity. Probably the subsistence farmers were left alone much as the peasants in England's Wars of the Roses. After all, such people and their subsistence production would be the spoils of warfare.

Classic warfare, according to our model, allows for violence, but in such a form that it did not seriously disturb social stability. However, it is a warfare pattern that may have made Maya society vulnerable to a more formal and sophisticated pattern like that of the

Toltecs who later invaded Northern Yucatan. On the other hand, this model does leave us with some problems of explanation of the formal fortifications at Tikal and at Becan. The Tikal ditches are especially difficult to explain in the face of the unsophisticated formalized violence. We shall turn to historical material to explain these features later. Here we will be satisfied with one final observation about Mesoamerican warfare in general: even among the highlanders where war was apparently more endemic ,and societies more militaristic, there is a notable lack of elaborate formal fortifications. Thus, as noted before, Maya buildings, arranged around closed courts, would be naturally defensible.

LUXURY GOODS AND THEIR IMPLICATIONS

Polychrome pottery is especially a hallmark of the Maya lowland Classic cultures. Exuberant development of design, color combinations, and vessel forms all indicate a great deal of creative effort, as do the sheer amounts and distribution of polychromes. About 5 to 7 percent of the total pottery production was devoted to polychrome pottery during the late Classic period, and polychromes are found during this period even in the humblest housemounds. Naturally, the quality and complexity varies greatly, and there is a gradient in quality from the mundane examples of isolated residences, up to the often exquisite types found in elite-class tombs. It seems likely that polychrome pottery among the Classic Maya filled the function of "best china" among ourselves. It was like the "Blue Willow" China of our grandmother's day. Everyone had some, but some people had better pieces than others.

Other luxury items are severely restricted to tombs and other contexts of the upper class, indicating that only the elite had access to these craft products. Fabergé-quality human figures were produced for certain ritual occasions at Tikal. These are of excellent workmanship and are composed of several kinds of materials, but they were ruthlessly smashed during some ritual. Superb flint blades and eccentric flints are found in association with stelae and altars, especially at Altar de Sacrificios. At Tikal again, some carved bones with exceedingly fine-lined depictions of water scenes, people and animals in canoes, fishing, and so on, probably produced on the Usumacinta, have been found in a tomb. Great art-quality pottery has been commonly found in many elite tombs throughout the Maya area. The limited distribution of all of these things and many others indicates limited access to the resources and the craftsmen capable of manufacturing the items. Doubtless there were equally magnificent perishable items which have not come down to us except as they are depicted in Maya art.

Especially noteworthy for their complexity are the costumes of the Maya elite, each of whom seems to have dressed in a unique manner. Common elements in Maya hieratic dress include the following: headdresses of carved wooden elements with attached plumage and, occasionally, encrustations of other materials; fine quality cloth of various kinds ranging from fine open weave to what may have been patterned and tailored items, such as the trousers depicted on the "Altar Vase"; kilts and long robes of cloth or animal skin are often depicted; elaborate sandals, presumably of leather or cloth; and jewelry of a bewildering variety. The favored substance for jewelry seems to have been jade, and both men and women of the upper classes wear beaded necklaces and bracelets. Trophy heads, or alternatively, depictions of trophy heads, often set off a warrior's costume. The head may have been made of jade at times. There was simply not enough jade to go around, at least at certain sites. At Altar de Sacrificios a middle-aged woman of high social status was buried with various sumptuous items that included jewelry both of real jade and "fake jade." The latter items were necklace beads of stucco covered with green paint and presumably represented the lady's "costume" jewelry. Or, perhaps, she passed on the real items to her survivors and was buried with the imitations.

The amounts and variations of the above items alone are impressive, and the list could be nearly indefinitely expanded. However, enough has been said to make the following points: Maya society was affluent enough to afford to support craftsmen of impressive skill. For the most part these craftsmen seem to have produced many items only for a small group in Maya society and certainly nearly all of the best and unique items were for their use. The one exception to this seems to be in the production of polychrome pottery which, at least as regards run-of-the-mill quality, was apparently available to everyone. The means of distribution, however, as discussed earlier, may not have been through a formal market system, but through a more redistributive system based on ties between social classes, with goods controlled by the upper classes exchanged for services by lower classes. At this point we have laid the basis for an examination of the nature of Classic Maya society.

RECONSTRUCTIONS OF SOCIAL STRUCTURE AND SOCIAL CHANGE

Several alternatives are open to us in reconstructing the social fabric of Maya society during the Classic period. A structure from ethnographic sources is suggested by Vogt (1971). Briefly, this structure centers on a system of rotating religious and civil offices of increasing importance; the fulfillment of the less important qualified a man for the more important. Theoretically, every man in Maya society had a chance at the most important offices and the attached political and religious power. Vogt has suggested that this may fit the Classic Maya case and solved for them problems of social integration of a dispersed population. As we have seen, this model might well fit the late Preclassic societal picture with the evidence of ranked social positions rather than class distinctions. However, the archaeological data strongly contradict the egalitarian, rotation-of-power model as the prime organizing principle of Classic society. Genealogical data in the hieroglyphic texts used as the justification for assumption of power, argues that ascriptive principles were at work in social organization. Indeed, into what social ranking one was born seems to have had a great deal to do with the degree of access to all kinds of things, from the sumptuous items and housing to nonmaterial affairs such as political and religious power. An increasingly aristocratic principle seems to have been characteristic of Maya society as time goes on. We will discuss this in an historical perspective below, but suffice it to say that an elite class at the top of a pyramidally organized social structure better fits the empirically derived evidence. However, a rotational kind of cargo system could have been combined with aristocratic organizational principles to modify them. This, as we have seen in our study of the Aztecs, was indeed the kind of society that existed in several parts of Mesoamerica at the time of European contact. Other scholars have discerned possibilities of relatively low levels of chiefdoms for the Classic period, arguing that such societies were perfectly able to create the monumental architecture without having the political and social organization of a complex order. Although this may be so, and it will be seen that we can indeed pick out chiefdom characteristics in the Maya Classic, it seems best to start with the archaeological data and attempt to derive from it some sort of social model which we may then compare with the ethnographically or ethnohistorically derived structures.

One may approach the problem from the point of view of occupational specialization. Quantities and the quality of certain productions of Maya society indicate that certain people spent all of their time in manufacturing or construction activities. Taking the late Classic as our time period, since it is best known, we can use the evidence for an elite class as our anchor and then arrange occupational specializations in order of lessening complexity away from the upper class. That is, the more complicated the skills and the more the knowledge required in order to perform the skill, then the closer that practitioner is set to the native elite. This assumes that we can first make a strong case for the existence of an aristocracy based on birth, or ascriptive principles.

William Holland argues that ancestor worship was a strong feature during the Classic period and that the pyramid-temples with their elaborate tombs indeed represent the resting place of the ancestors (Holland, 1964). We have seen that Maya temples are indeed mortuary and memorial structures and that they can be interpreted as places of ancestor worship. The genealogical emphasis in the later texts also would fit with this. Not confirmatory, but suggestive, is the increasingly exclusive appearance of sumptuous housing during the late Classic period, with residence limited to relatively few people, and those persons being physically isolated from the mass of society.

Depictive sources — murals, sculpture, and figurines — suggest that this elite class engaged in several occupations. Architectural planning certainly took up a good deal of time, inasmuch as most Maya monumental architecture has been seen to be for the use of the small, exclusive upper class. The constant construction, demolition, and refurbishment of residences, funerary monuments, sacbes,

and other features must have taken a great deal of time and energy even if the upper classes did not engage directly in the execution of plans. Warfare was another interest of the nobility, one which lent prestige, and one which absorbed more and more interest and energy as time went on. A model of Classic warfare as raids in which only the small upper class took part has been established above. Political administration would have been the other main concern of the upper class. Their very existence depended on political and kinship arrangements, and there is little difficulty in attributing this function to them. However, they must have had assistants in dealing with the tedious and time-consuming tasks of administration, and this leads us to a discussion of possible non-elite-class occupations.

Some modeled stucco reliefs at Palenque in the tower of the palace seem to show scribes. Moreover, these persons are kneeling and in such an attitude as to indicate perhaps a subordinate position in society. Certainly, judging by the plethora of writing in the form of sculpture and on murals which have survived, perishable documents must have been present in great quantity. Such documents do not survive in the rainforest, however, and all we have are pictures of people using such documents and the surviving books in use at the time of conquest, in addition to a few piles of painted stucco in tombs, which presumably represent the remains of books or painted screenfolds. Both quantity and complexity of the art of writing among the Maya argues for full-time practitioners — scribes — then, and this occupation must have been fairly restricted to small groups of craftsmen and the elite. The lack of writing among the few survivors of the collapse of Maya culture suggests this. Glyphs are drawn on the walls of buildings after the severe diminution of populations, but it is of rudimentary and unskillful aspect and seems to be the product of persons attempting to imitate a complexity for which they are not trained. Another argument for the existence of something of a scribal class is that one cannot imagine the most exalted members of the elite class, as depicted on their stelae, worrying over the exact amounts of black beans, maize, squash, chiles, and other mundane items provided periodically by 20, 50, or 100 small villages for the support of the ceremonial center. Either lesser nobility took care of this, or a scribal class managed such affairs. Perhaps these groups were the same.

Sculpture and fine pottery are obvious craft specialties, considering the large quantities of both produced in the Classic. A high degree of knowledge of the canons of art and hieroglyphic writing, as well as of specific skills all argue this. Manufacturers of elite-class costumes undoubtedly occupied a special place. A wide range of exotic materials and manufactured items were involved as well as problems of tailoring and fitting. It seems likely that there were specialists something like western culture's couturiers. Musicians and other entertainers are depicted in the art, especially in the Bonampak murals where a full-fledged orchestra tunes up for a ceremony.

Servants are also depicted in the art, although these are personal servants. Again in the Bonampak murals, servants are shown dressing certain august persons in elaborate costume, adjusting jewelry, and carrying headdresses. Servants are also depicted as taking care of children, and they must have performed many other domestic chores. Maya palace buildings are often quite high and difficult of access, and persons must have been available to carry the necessary water and food to upper apartments. Large numbers of people, especially sweepers, would have been necessary to keep the ceremonial centers clean. Perhaps this duty was performed on a rotational basis, with the duty going to younger and less important members of society, somewhat in the manner in which the streets and the town headquarters are cleaned in present-day Guatemalan Indian towns.

Construction specialists are only present by inference, but again the mass of building and complexity of skills involved demand the presence of at least cadres of specialists in such things as stucco modeling and stone cutting. Much of the work involved with Maya monumental architecture, however, could have been done by part-time specialists. Every Maya man today learns how to build a house without a nail, and such skills can easily be applied to building scaffolding for large-scale building. The Maya masons reconstructing the Temple of the Dwarf at Uxmal covered that immense structure with scaffolding made of poles, planks, and rope in 1968. The directing and supervisory skills may have remained in the upper class or there may have been foremen and master masons who ran things.

Judging by R. L. Rands' recent work in the Palenque region (Rands, 1973), there seem to have been various specialist communities, and thus there may have been concentrations of such specialists as suggested above in satellite communities around the ceremonial centers. Rands' data also suggest that the local craft products seldom went beyond the bounds of the individual ceremonial center's domain, in Palenque's case, an area of about 125 square kilometers or about 85 square miles. Other information also suggests that trade of manufactured items between regions was relatively sparse. Closed economic systems would seem to be the best models.

One can rank Maya society according to the complexity of skills involved in the occupational specializations and wind up with something of a possible social organization. However, there were matters of kinship involved as we have seen, which modified society and made it a class society as opposed to a ranked society. William Haviland's evidence from Tikal seems to indicate the presence of ranked lineages which lived together as residential groups (1968). Certainly there is evidence among the ethnographic Maya for patrilineages and these are a long tradition in Maya kinship. Finally, circumstantial factors must have also been involved in Maya society. Personal servants may, as in so many other societies, have had a necessarily closer relationship to the elite than their status warranted.

Social mobility to a certain degree may have been involved through the rise of a skilled and talented person to a prestigious position. However, judging from the genealogical data on the stelae, the elite may have been a rather closed class, almost caste-like in its features. In the lower realms of society, social mobility may also have been possible if the cargo system of rotational religious offices was in operation. This system cannot reasonably be reconciled with the picture of Maya society as reconstructed above except in terms of restriction to certain classes below the elite.

POLITICAL ORGANIZATION

Again the best data are from late Classic times and indicate that Maya polities were, at the most, groups of associated ceremonial centers, and, at the minimum, major centers with associated minor centers and rural population. Certainly, different orders of magnitude of political organization are reflected in the differences of internal organization of the ceremonial centers. Tikal, with its massed palaces and temples and immense size, is clearly distinct from Uaxactun with its "great house" pattern. Uaxactun, in turn, seems to contrast with the kind of "manor house" pattern in the Rio Bec area.

Other direct evidence is available on the nature of Maya political organization from the written texts. In the Usumacinta centers,

it seems that accession to power was based on exalted genealogical credentials. However, this might be modified by a usurper as seems to have been the case at Piedras Negras in the late eighth century. It may be that the ruler of Yaxchilan took advantage of the legitimate heir's youth to place his own candidate on the throne of this important neighboring city. Even this usurper, however, then justified his position by reference to certain prestigious kinship ties. At this point Yaxchilan and Piedras Negras seemed to be tied together in a larger-than-city-state unit by this kinship tie.

Two burials at Altar de Sacrificios lend weight to this picture of elite kinship and marriage ties as the basis for political alliance. Three groups of pottery manufactured at places other than Altar de Sacrificios match the home areas of three individuals depicted as at a funeral ceremony which took place at Altar. One of these persons is the ruler of Yaxchilan, Bird-Jaguar (so nicknamed after the elements that make up his name glyph). Another person is from Tikal, and still a third seems to be from the Alta Verapaz region of the north Guatemalan Highlands. All of these persons seem to have been drawn to the Altar funeral by kinship and marriage ties to the middle-aged woman being buried. The funeral took place in A.D. 754 according to the date on the Altar Vase which depicts the event. Bird-Jaguar, incidentally, came to power in A.D. 752. These persons brought the pottery placed in the tomb, among other things, and presumably perishable things, too. This suggests a pattern of funerary visitation among the Maya elite which corresponds to the gathering of European nobility on similar occasions. Examining the inventories of other elite-class burials throughout the Maya lowlands, we see that few have pottery foreign to the zone in which they are found. This suggests that perhaps Maya city-states made only occasional alliances on the basis of kinship and marriage and that only the most important of the elite were involved. If this were so, then such alliances, as we know historically from other instances of similar arrangements, were fragile, transitory, and shifting. It also means that, at least as reflected by the grave inventories of most Classic period Maya, their kinship ties were severely localized, even on the elite level, and that their worlds revolved around the local ceremonial center.

The distribution of emblem glyphs may eventually give us some indication of inter-center alliances and their shifts. Tikal emblem glyphs, for example, are common at the large site of Naranjo to the east, and even more common than at Tikal in the inscriptions of Dos Pilas to the south. These glyphs may not actually indicate geographical locations, but kinship; they may be the devices of ruling lineages. Without more information, we are somewhat at a loss presently to resolve some of the alternatives of interpretation. However, these glyphs do not conflict with the model of essentially autonomous city-state polities, ruled by local elites who are tied more or less loosely to neighboring elites by blood and marriage.

The distribution of ceramic goods in the Palenque region suggests the same sort of situation on an economic plane. The sort of trade and distribution of goods that took place within a Maya ceremonial center's orbit would seem to fit well with the redistributive system of reciprocal obligations rather than with the more formalized market systems that we have seen in operation in Aztec society. If we accept this argument, Maya society was indeed in this feature a kind of high chiefdom. However, as we shall see in the historical review, there is strong evidence of a trend toward more state-like characteristics in other fields.

Thus we see Maya elite civilization with its proud and exalted leaders. Everywhere they gazed within their ceremonial centers they saw symbols of their power, authority, and prestige. The polychromed and red temples dedicated to their ancestors rose above the plains of white plastered courts, and a well-ordered society kept them in comfortable ease in the sumptuous palace buildings. Servants waited on their needs, and an administrative apparatus of which they were part took care of administrative matters. The gods were well attended, and indeed, their most exalted servants in this world could probably look forward to becoming part of the supernatural world after their deaths. In the meantime, the balance of the universe was taken care of by continual and careful intercession with the ancestors who had gone before and who could be contacted by their surviving relatives. War was a matter of high social concern but more for prestige than much else, although economic gains may have entered in from time to time.

Agriculture and the forces of nature were matters of high religious moment, for the upper class as well as for the farmers. At this point the class structure probably came together in a kind of psychological overlapping which lent strength to a society in which much of the population was physically dispersed. Religious ceremonies in the centers would assuage anxieties over the problems of rain, crops, and threats of agricultural failure. Indeed, the justification for the exalted social position of the elite was just this, that they acted as intercessors for mankind in a capricious universe filled with protean and unpredictable deities. If we accept this synchronic interpretative and elite-class point of view, it must seem to have been a well-integrated and successful system which would go on indefinitely with only minor adjustments. However, we will see that the Classic period was one of repeated crisis and possibly even collapse at one point, leading to the even greater catastrophe which brought eventual cultural and biological destruction to the Maya.

HISTORICAL RECONSTRUCTION OF THE CLASSIC PERIOD

The Classic period can be viewed as a series of crises. This may be too apocalyptic a stance to take in consideration of what essentially was about 900 years of dazzling cultural success. It may also be a point of view too much conditioned by our foreknowledge of the ultimate failure of Maya civilization. However, the crises are more detectable in the archaeological record than the more mundane events at this time, and they form a convenient framework within which to work.

The Classic period begins variably through the lowlands and might be regarded as starting as early as 100 B.C. at some sites and as late as A.D. 300 in other regions. The end of the period comes variably also, depending on the site, starting around A.D. 800 and ending about A.D. 900.

It has been remarked that the Preclassic Maya villages were communities in which an anthropologist, somewhat inured to sociocultural exotica, would probably feel comfortable. Early Classic civilization, however, is a different world from that of which we have direct knowledge. The sculptural record possibly influences our view too much, but certain aspects indicate that elements of the fantastic, both in behavior and world view, were commonplace in this period. A very distinguished archaeologist once said it more simply; he said that he had often thought that the Maya of that period were all "nuts." That was a facetious comment, of course, but shows the distance between that culture and our own. This is an ethnocentric difficulty, however, and we must attempt to overcome the screen that time and our own culture place between us and these ancient people if we are to begin to understand the inner workings of their society. We can better understand the external pressures on them because we may have, in some cases, a better view of these matters than did the people who were themselves involved.

Sculpture from the early Classic period is the most difficult to deal with historically. The earliest known Maya stela is presently Stela 29 at Tikal (A.D. 292), but certainly there must have been earlier monuments than this. For one thing, there is evidence of a custom of constant demolition of monuments at Tikal after certain determined periods of time. Thus the earliest structures and sculpture are likely to be destroyed or buried under later monuments, and difficult to find. Then too, the earliest known monuments carry a relatively sophisticated version of the hieroglyphic system, which would indicate that some considerable time of experimentation preceded the now known earliest stelae. Fragments of stone sculpture are found in the Preclassic levels at Tikal, as well as fragments of impressively complex murals painted on the exteriors of temple buildings. As time goes on in the Classic, moving toward A.D. 350, an increasing sophistication of sculpture, writing, architecture, and polychrome pottery is evident. Altogether this indicates the beginning of the functional relationships outlined above — between monumental architecture, craft specialties such as sculpture, and the needs and demands of an emergent elite class.

Symbolism in the sculpture and ceramic motifs is extraordinarily psychedelic for this period, with small animals intertwined about poles, and vegetation transformed, mutatis mutandis, into animals — but animals which often have no parallel in the reality of nature. Grotesquerie and, in some cases macabreness seem to be ends in themselves. Central figures gloatingly lift up human heads, and wear others on their belts. One wonders if the hallucinogenic mushroom cult entirely died out, or if it had simply been integrated into a new religious form with depictive symbolism sparked by the resultant fantastic visions. Mesoamerican cultures did not distinguish between supernatural and natural; one was a reformulation of the other, and the gods operated in this world as well as men who were the objects of their capricious conduct. This kind of world view seems to lie behind the early Maya sculpture. A rather animistic approach to the world also is present, in that natural objects of all kinds seem to have had supernatural power. Incense burners of the same periods reflect much more abstract symbolism and more complex references to religious concepts than later. What may be a reference to a creation myth is a favorite theme.

Maya society might not look so strange to us if we used the west African chiefdoms and kingdoms of historic periods as models. The styles are distinct and the cultures differ in detail, but the divinely ascribed or justified leadership is present in both cases. Sumptuary activities center on such leadership, and the leadership has religious as well as economic and political responsibilities. A court ritual, or at least some sort of protocol, is associated with such chiefdoms. Yet there are some relatively personalistic and unbureaucratic features about societies on this level. One such feature is in the realm of economics and is the lack of formalized market systems. Circulation of goods within the chiefdom-level societies tends to be in terms of reciprocal arrangements based on kinship ties. Thus a man is tied in a loose fashion by fictitious or actual kinship links to a chief who demands certain labor and other services from that man. On the other hand the man can also expect reciprocal favors in the form of food or manufactured items or other forms of wealth distributed by the chief. This is a redistributive type of system and it works well enough in relatively small social groups. It is the model of economic behavior which seems best to fit the archaeological distribution of goods.

Monumental architecture can be manufactured by relatively small numbers of people as has been shown by C. J. Erasmus' experiments (1965), but the capital investment in the knowledge of how to plan and build a large structure implies a specialist class whose skills can be directed by the elite. Thus early Classic society is elaborated beyond the form of most anthropologically known chiefdoms and might better be called "high chiefdoms." Certainly this kind of petty city-state chiefdom society is extant by the end of the early Classic, and probably by the beginning at precocious places like Tikal. There is conflict among the elites of these centers as indicated by the trophy head depictions, and other scenes of martial prowess. The intensity of interest in these affairs and their inextricable connection with the elite class imply a crisis of the leadership class when we reach the enigmatic break in sculptured texts which occurs at 9.15 in the Maya calendar (A.D. 434) and lasts about sixty years. This also seems to be a period of strong influence of the great urban center of Teotihuacan on the Maya. An understanding of this event is crucial for understanding of the way in which Maya society attempted to shift gears from an essentially chiefdom-level society to more of a state-level organization.

The evidence of Teotihuacan intrusion into the Maya lowlands is sporadic, varied, and in some ways vague. All of it seems to be associated with upper-class activities, however. Teotihuacan tomb pottery shows up in Maya elite-class burials at Uaxactun and Tikal. It is absent at many other centers, especially those on the Pasion and Usumacinta Rivers. Sculptured representations of Tlaloc, the patron rain deity of Teotihuacan, is on stelae found at Tikal. Further, the magnificent Tikal Stela 31 shows a Maya priest-ruler on the front of the monument, but on the sides are two Teotihuacan warriors, outfitted with spears, spear-throwers, and shields. Again, Tlaloc imagery decorates the shields of these men, as well as their headdresses. They support rather than intimidate the central Maya figure. Finally, the find of a magnificent cache figure of Teotihuacan style at the fortress site of Becan is suggestive. A ritual deposit of a slab-footed tripod vessel was made in the back room of a building with Teotihuacan architectural features just before the structure was interred under an outer structure. The pot itself is of Teotihuacan form, but the motif is strictly Maya, suggesting to J. W. Ball, the ceramic analyst, that the pot was exported as a blank to be finished by native craftsmen of the recipient region of Mesoamerica (Ball, 1974a). Seated in the vessel was a large hollow figure of undoubted Teotihuacan origin. Inside the hollow figure were eleven solid figures, also of Teotihuacan style. Other caches of identical makeup have been found at Teotihuacan. The importance of this cache is that it seems to date from the period of the construction of formal defenses at Becan and that, in combination with the other information, it tells us something about the nature of the Teotihuacan intrusion.

Formal fortifications of the kind found at Becan and Tikal do not fit with the model previously given for Maya Classic period warfare. The Becan moat is about a mile in circumference and, based on excavation, was originally about forty feet deep and sixty-five feet across. At a time which may be the same as that of the hiatus in stela texts, the causeways leading into Becan were all cut, sealing off access to the ceremonial center within. The Tikal fortifications are even more formidable. Both sets of defenses have one problem; they need sophisticated military organization to take advantage of them. This means state-level organization with cadres of professional soldiery and appropriate tactics. The only good candidate for this sort of military apparatus in Mesoamerica at this time is Teotihuacan. Therefore it seems possible that these defenses were built by or directed to be built by Teotihuacan people. The following is a plausible reconstruction of the possible role of Teotihuacan in the Maya lowlands.

Chiefdom-level organization would be vulnerable to state-level societies in several ways, but especially if a violent confrontation came about. The competition among the Maya elite may have led one or more of the city-states to ask for outside help from these highland Mexicans. Alternatively, the Mexicans may have seen an opportunity to intervene to their own advantage and taken it. This was a period of imperial expansion of Teotihuacan. At any rate, Tikal, Uaxactun, and Becan probably were centers that accepted, either voluntarily or forcibly, such aid. Teotihuacan elite themselves either took over or backed certain native elite factions in the Maya lowlands. The kind of fortress represented by Becan is the sort of security maybe felt necessary by a minority ruling class which is in a sea of, at best passive, and at worst, hostile, population. This disruption would explain several things. It would explain the hiatus in native elite records and would also explain why, afterwards, places like Tikal may have become bigger than others. They had absorbed some of the state craft of the urbanized and nucleated Mexican highland state. The crisis would be one of the elite civilization, and in a sense, a collapse from which there was a recovery. Finally, it would explain why Maya society in the late Classic period, after the Teotihuacan episode, made an attempt to shift more to a state-level organization.

The episode was relatively short; Teotihuacan influence is gone sixty years after it appears. We apparently have an absorption of foreigners in the same manner that China has absorbed so many conquering outside groups. Part of the explanation of the disappearance of Teotihuacan influence is to be found in the fact that the great city itself is in trouble about this time and withdrawing to itself from outer areas of Mesoamerica. However, Maya Classic culture is not the same afterward.

Late Classic Maya culture displays aspects of elite-class megalomania. Gigantic funerary monuments and memorial temples are built at the cost of the labor of casts of thousands; for example, the five great memorial temples at Tikal and the immense structures of Mirador, and the Temple of the Magician at Uxmal. Large palace areas indicate an expansion in numbers of the people who lived and worked there — the elite, and their immediate retainers. A physical expansion of the total population size of the Maya is also quite clear. These and other features made Classic society vulnerable to many internal and external stresses, leading to increased military competition among the Maya and ultimately to the final catastrophe of the ninth century. Before we consider this event and its implications, however, we should examine the other polarity of Mesoamerican civilization for this period, the great and splendiferous center of Teotihuacan.

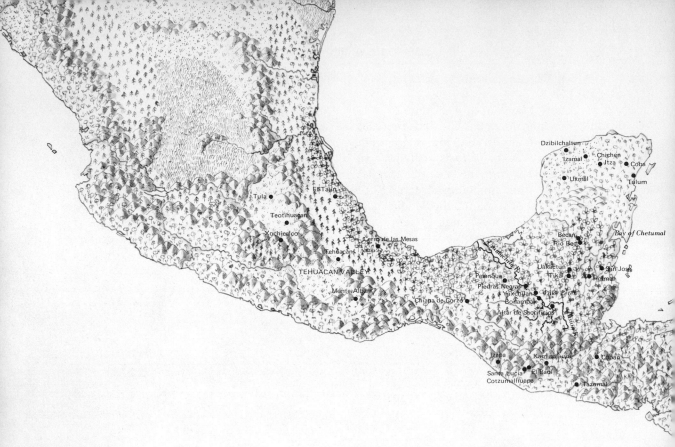

Dzibilchaltun
Izamal
Chichen Itza
Coba
Uxmal
Tulum
Tula
El Tajin
Becan
Rio Bec
Bay of Chetumal
Teotihuacan
Xochicalco
Cerro de las Mesas
Uaxactun
Tikal
San Jose
Tehuacan
Palenque
Holmul
TEHUACAN VALLEY
Piedras Negras
Lake Peten
Monte Alban
Yaxchilan
Bonampak
Chiapa de Corzo
Altar de Sacrificios
Izapa
Kaminaljuyu
Copan
Santa Lucia
Cotzumalhuapa
El Baol
Tazumal

1 △
2 ▽

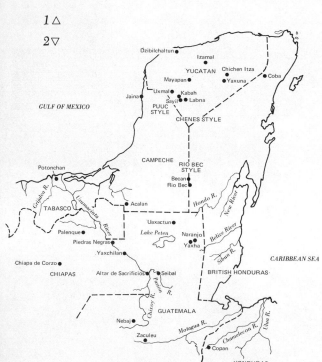

Dzibilchaltun
Izamal
YUCATAN
Chichen Itza
Mayapan
Yaxuna
Coba
GULF OF MEXICO
Jaina
Uxmal
Kabah
Sayil
Labna
PUUC STYLE
CHENES STYLE
Potonchan
Grijalva R.
TABASCO
Usumacinta River
CAMPECHE
RIO BEC STYLE
Becan
Rio Bec
Acalan
Hondo R.
New River
Palenque
Uaxactun
Lake Peten
Naranjo
Yaxha
Belize River
Piedras Negras
Yaxchilan
Sibun R.
CARIBBEAN SEA
Chiapa de Corzo
CHIAPAS
Altar de Sacrificios
Seibal
BRITISH HONDURAS
Pasion R.
Chixoy R.
GUATEMALA
Nebaj
Motagua R.
Zaculeu
Chamelecon R.
Ulua R.
Copan
HONDURAS

Classic Mesoamerica. *The long evolution of the Preclassic resulted in several cultural climaxes between the first and ninth centuries* A.D. *Rapid growth in population, creative arts, trade, empirical knowledge, and the rise of true cities took place (1). The extreme contrasts of these developments were centered in the Valley of Mexico and the Maya lowlands (2).*

Teotihuacan (3, 4) was the greatest and most highly structured prehispanic urban center. Two gigantic temple-platforms, the Pyramids of the Moon (3) and of the Sun, were built during the first two centuries A.D. *The massive volumes of these and other contemporary structures imply vast numbers of people and a sophisticated social organization. The Street of the Dead, the main north-south axis (15), runs from the Moon pyramid to the Citadel (4) and on past for another kilometer. The principal temple of the city, the largest palace, and fifteen other temples are contained in this fortified administrative complex.*

3 △

▽ 4

5△

6△

7△

8▷

The ideological strength of Teotihuacan was manifested in its many gods and in the power of expression in varied art forms as, for example, the embellishment of the large temple within the Citadel with the sculpted images of Tlaloc and Quetzalcoatl (6).

The gods and some of the art forms appeared at far-flung places in Mesoamerica. For example, the hollow figurine containing smaller figurines (7) is nearly duplicated by one found at Becan in the Maya lowlands. Some gods came from the ancient past as in the case of the "Old, Old One," the Fire God (5). Quetzalcoatl and Tlaloc (6), the main gods of Teotihuacan, were exported along with Teotihuacan political and economic control. Other deities were more local manifestations, such as the rain goddess (8), who may be a deity ancestral to the Aztec Chalchiuhtlicue.

166

9 △

10 △

11 △

12 △

△ 13

◁ 14

The thousands of high quality items found at
Teotihuacan indicate that the city contained
many skilled artisans. Such productions as this
mosaic-decorated mask (12), fine ceramics (9),
and excellently carved ball game marker (13) are
examples. This fragment of mural (10) represents
the irrigated fields, perhaps chinampas, that
supported Teotihuacan's diverse population. The
millions of pieces of common pottery used for
domestic purposes (11, 14) were mass produced
by other specialists.

△15

Ultimately, the true nature of the city of Teotihuacan is best seen in a map (15).

The great center of Monte Alban represents the climax of a public building tradition which began about 1300 B.C. From the commanding position on its ridge above the central valley of Oaxaca, Monte Alban (16) dominated its fellow city-states. The major temples (16, 17) at the center of the complex were built in a highly distinctive regional style.

16▽

17▽

18▽

19▽

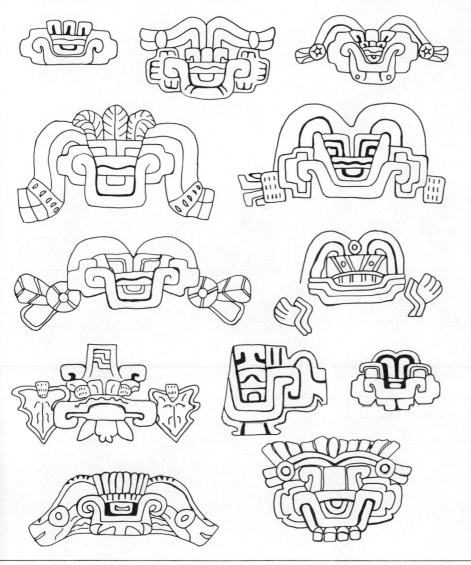

△ 20

21 ▽

22 ▽

Palace and residential buildings were built around open patios (18), but were smaller and less complex than those at Teotihuacan. The ball court at Monte Alban (19) was fitted into a small space and was distinctive in features. Monte Alban's rulers were memorialized on stelae (21) and in a formal writing and numerical system (20, 22).

△ 27   28 ▽

Oaxacan family tombs held the remains of the ancestors, and distinguished people were buried with great ceremony. A distinctively Oaxacan trait was the elaborate development of incense burners for funerals. These often depicted gods (23, 25) or, sometimes, the deceased (24).

Some of the earliest of the stelae were decorated with the *danzante* sculptures (26), which depicted mutilated captives.

One of the most extraordinary expressions of classic civilization arose in northern Veracruz at El Tajin. In architecture (27) and sculpture (28), as well as in its emphasis on the ball game, Tajin was distinctive.

171

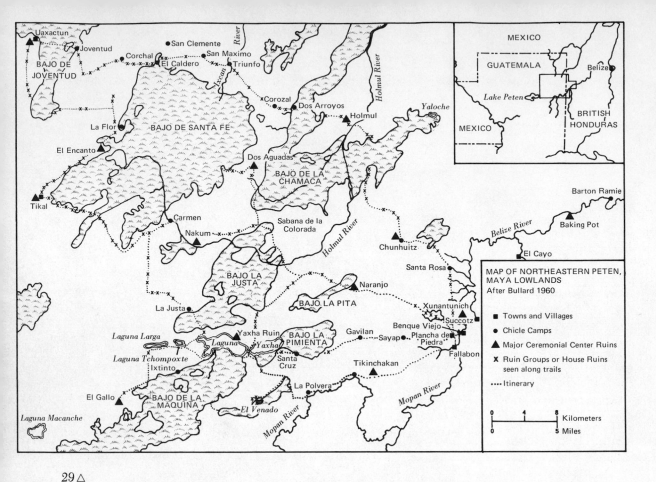

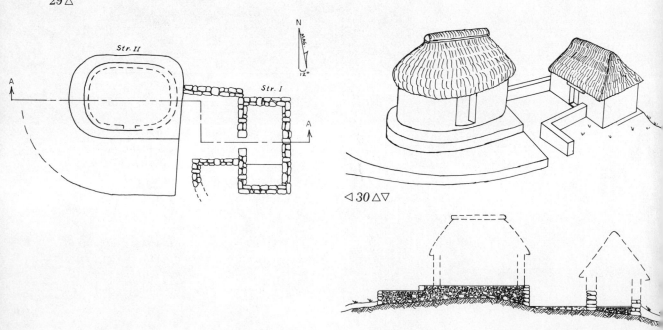

MAP OF NORTHEASTERN PETEN, MAYA LOWLANDS
After Bullard 1960

■ Towns and Villages
● Chicle Camps
▲ Major Ceremonial Center Ruins
✕ Ruin Groups or House Ruins seen along trails
···· Itinerary

29 △

Str. II

Str. I

A

N
12°

◁ 30 △▽

172

31 ▽   32 ▷

33 ▽

The Classic Maya have often been characterized as a civilization without cities. This mistaken idea was based on the assumption that
slash-and-burn agriculture (32, 33) was the only
system in use in ancient times. Slash-and-burn
cultivation demands a dispersed population because of continually shifting fields. However, it is
now known that many Maya areas shifted to
intensive agriculture by 600 A.D. Drainage of vast
areas of swamps (29), terracing of hillsides, and
the rise of thousands of farmsteads (30) signal the
presence of high density populations. It now
seems that the late classic Maya elite in their civic
centers ruled over multitudes as large as those of
most highland city-states.

Maya relationships with other Mesoamerican
cultures are indicated by imported trade goods,
in this case a pot (31) probably exported from
Teotihuacan as a blank and carved by a Maya
artist.

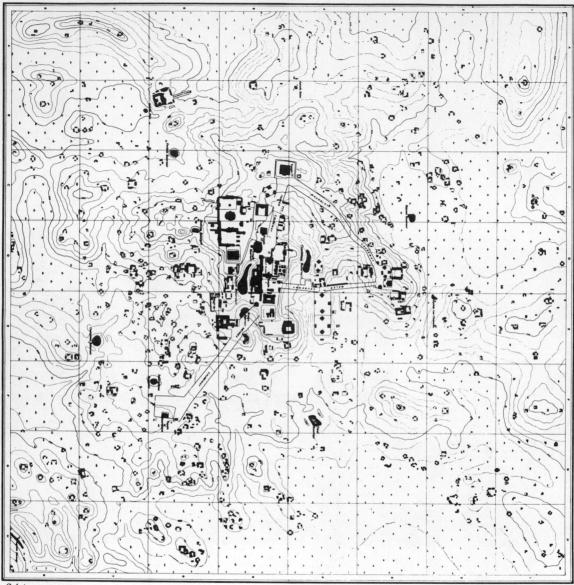

34 △

Tikal was one of the largest Maya centers, its central zone covering an area of 16 square kilometers (34). The loose arrangement of buildings contrasts dramatically with the tight urban planning of Teotihuacan. Maya centers were primarily intended for the use of the elite class, as shown by the functions of the main types of buildings. However, Tikal at its height may have contained as many as 49,000 people.

36 ▷

37 ▽

35 △

Temples were monuments to the distinguished dead, as in the case of Tikal Temple I (35), which contained a sumptuous tomb. Such tombs also contained fine ceramics (36, 40) and other possessions of the dead. Associated with the temples, carved stone monuments (stelae) gave life histories of rulers and dynasties. Tikal Stela 4 (37) may show a Mexican ruler of the late fourth century, according to Clemency Coggins.

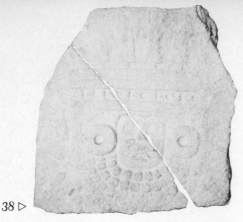

38 ▷

Tikal Stela 32 (38) shows the same Mexican ruler as does Stela 4, but with the Tlaloc headdress typical of Teotihuacan. Such patterns of memorialization were established long before, in the Preclassic. Beneath the Early Classic North Acropolis at Tikal (42), crowded with its memorial temples, lie the remains of similar Preclassic temples and tombs decorated with stucco masks (43). Tikal Stela 2 (39) is one of the earliest Maya monuments. The presence of skilled artisans is evidenced not only by the mass of complex architecture and sculpture, but also by smaller, delicate objects such as chert and flint chipped into eccentric shapes (41). Ball courts, such as the court at Tikal (44), served the demand for the popular ball game.

Palaces served as elite residences, administrative headquarters, and storehouses, and for state functions. This example from Uaxactun (45) closely resembles in function the Mycenaean "Great Houses" of Greece and Crete.

39 △

41 ▽

40 ▷

42▷

43▷

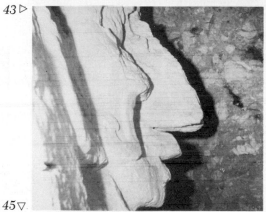

45▽

◁44

46 △

47 ▽

Maya centers varied greatly in style and setting. Copan in the southeast lowlands (46) had
the advantage of ready access to both highland
and lowland areas. Its architecture is ornamented with florid stone sculpture (49) also
manifested in its stelae (48, 50). Copan's ball
court (47) is one of the best examples extant.

During the period, many smaller centers arose
which produced art of surprisingly high quality.
This rubbing is of several glyph blocks from the
small site of Machaquila (51). These blocks were
originally in a frieze around the top of a palace
and their proper order has been lost. However,
the text seems to refer to a married couple and
several noble women, with local names and titles.

48 △

49 △

50 ▷

◁ 51

52 △   53 ▽   ▽54

The marvelous site of Palenque lies on the edge of the foothills overlooking the coastal plain of Tabasco. It is like most classic centers in its informality of planning. The Temple of the Inscriptions (52) is the location of one of the most famous tombs to be discovered, that of the eighth century ruler of Palenque, Pacal. This same ruler's palace (55) is largely intact, having been somewhat restored. Palenque's buildings were originally decorated with vast amounts of modeled stucco, of which these portrait heads are examples (53, 54). Baroquely complex incense burners (58) have been found near the site.

The great center of Yaxchilan is famous for its sculpture and the hieroglyphic texts that celebrate its rulers. Bird-Jaguar II is shown in two of Yaxchilan's stelae. Stela 11 (57) shows the ruler's accession to power. Bird-Jaguar stands before three captives and wears a sun-god mask. Lintel 26 (56) shows Bird-Jaguar and his consort, with the latter holding his jaguar mask.

55△

56△

57▷

◁58

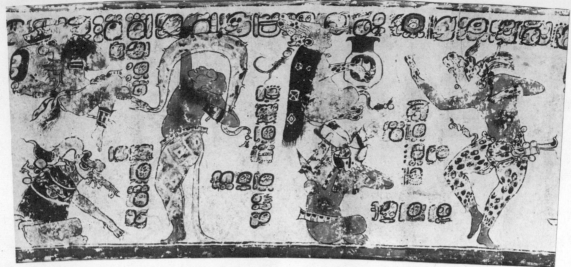

59 △

60 ▽

61 ▷

Bird-Jaguar dances at a funeral for a relative in 754 A.D. as shown on this polychrome vase (59, 60). Another relative, from Tikal, offers a sacrifice and is identified by a hieroglyphic caption (61). The small nearby center of Bonampak has murals showing contemporary nobles dressing for a ceremony (62), while lesser personages gossip.

In the southern center of Seibal the late rulers of Seibal are memorialized by monuments (64, 65) around and near a temple (63). These rulers, however, came not from the southern lowlands but from a northern center that usurped power in the ninth century A.D.

62 ▽

63△   64▽   65▽

66 ▷

67 ▷

△68

◁69

Smaller classic centers, such as Altun Ha (66), have yielded great amounts of valuable information on ancient trade routes and commercial networks. All of these centers were in contact, often competing, sometimes cooperating, as in this meeting of dignitaries (67) preserved for us on Altar Q at Copan.

To the north of the Peten are the great sites of the Chenes and Puuc zones. Uxmal is the largest and possibly the most important. The usurpers at Seibal probably came from the Chenes or Puuc. A temple structure with several phases, the Adivino (68) is associated with a massive palace quadrangle, the so-called nunnery. On the stone mosaic facades are intricate designs, such as thatched huts (69).

185

70 △   71 ▽

Raingod masks (71), form part of the nunnery facade (70).

Maya centers such as Labna with its famous arch (72) are too often nowadays the targets of vandals and looters. The latter feed the international art markets with pieces such as this facade from Calakmul (73). This large item was recovered but, more often, stolen objects are not. Even restored palaces such as at Chicanna (74) are in constant jeopardy from people who care more for money and the possession of things than for understanding the cultural heritage that such monuments and artifacts represent.

72 △

73 △

74 ▽

CHAPTER 7

TEOTIHUACAN, MONTE ALBAN, AND OTHER EARLY CIVILIZATIONS

. . . there at Teotihuacan, as they say, in times past, when yet there was darkness, there all the gods gathered themselves together, and they debated who would bear the burden, who . . . would become the sun.
—Sahagun, Book 3, 1963: 1.

And there [Teotihuacan] all the people raised pyramids for the sun and for the moon; then made many small pyramids where offerings were made. . . . And when the rulers died, they buried them there. Then they built a pyramid over them. . . . For so it was said: "When we die, it is not true that we die; for still we live; we are resurrected. We still live; we awaken."
—Sahagun, Book 10, 1961: 191.

LAMBITYECO, Dynastic Tomb, Valley of Oaxaca. When Monte Alban was abandoned at the end of Period IIIB, the Zapotec tradition, as Monte Alban IV, was carried on in the valley at sites such as Lambityeco. Characteristic of this period were plaster tomb friezes realistically depicting people. Radiocarbon dates from Mound 195 indicate a Period IV date of 690 A.D. ± 105 years. Lambityeco may have continued into the fifteenth century, with a blending of Zapotec and Mixtec traditions.

MOTECZOMA II, WORRIED BY EVENTS OF ill omen, is said to have made a pilgrimage to the dead city of Teotihuacan a few years before the arrival of the Spaniards (Vaillant, 1941: 65). There he made sacrifices and communed with the gods. As it turned out, his prayers were futile, but his worries were justified. Moteczoma was following a long tradition of pilgrimage established in a past so distant to the Aztecs that they had lost the history explaining the enormous fossil metropolis. Even in ruins, Teotihuacan was so impressive that the sixteenth-century people of the Basin of Mexico thought that the city had been built by the direction of the gods. The myth of the successive suns has the gods assembling at Teotihuacan in the primordial darkness to bring light to the cosmos. Two of the gods were believed to have sacrificed themselves in a fire and thus became the sun and the moon. After that, humanity gathered at the place and built the great city (Leon-Portilla, 1961: 23–27).

A major and sustained effort at understanding Teotihuacan began with Manuel Gamio's 1917 project and continues today with a fourth generation of scholars. Fortunately, the work of excavation and study has focused on the entire Valley of Teotihuacan and not just on the civic center.

CHRONOLOGY. A series of phases with the usual difficult names divides the cultural history of the city into several periods lasting from about 200 B.C. to about A.D. 650. The terminal date is still in dispute, and it may be that the city lasted until about A.D. 750. The important point is that, even if this is so, Teotihuacan had apparently lost its imperial and dominant status by 650, surviving as a large, regional city-state, delaying only its physical destruction until A.D. 750. On the other hand, there is no dispute over the major features of Teotihuacan's rise and cultural apogee.

It seems quite probable that the giant Pyramid of the Sun was built about A.D. 100. Just before this, the population of the urban area rose sharply, from about 2000 at 200 B.C. to about 60,000 at A.D. 100 and, finally, to about 150,000 at A.D. 600. There is strong evidence that this resulted from the concentration at Teotihuacan of most of the population of the Basin of Mexico, and not from a population explosion. It is clear that Teotihuacan must have had political and social control of the basin to be able to accomplish this aggregation. To understand this overwhelming dominance, not only of the basin, but of great areas of Mesoamerica, it is easiest to begin with an examination of the city at its height. This will indicate the functional relationships of the parts of the city, and show some of the imperatives that drove Teotihuacan to its position of preeminence.

THE URBAN CAPITAL: A SURVEY. According to the recently completed mapping project directed by Rene Millon (1970), Teotihuacan at about A.D. 600 sprawled over a huge irregular area of about twenty square kilometers (about eight square miles). The space was occupied by avenues, markets, plazas, temples, palaces, apartment compounds, a grid system of streets, slums, waterways, reservoirs, and drainage systems. The city was laid out on a north-south axis of about 15¼ degrees east of north. This orientation was also typical of other contemporary centers on the central plateau under the domination of Teotihuacan. The major north-south avenue is now known as the Street of the Dead. This is a name, like all others at Teotihuacan, applied by the Aztecs and archaeologists at best or by tourist guides at worst. Another major avenue is on an east-west axis, and the two axes intersect at the location of the administrative, religious, and market center of the city, the "Citadel" zone. Along the north-south main street are clustered sumptuous and lavish elite residences jostling with large and small temple platforms. The street is also the location of the two gigantic pyramids of the sun and moon, as well as of the Citadel and the Great Compound. Away from the north-south street and arranged on a grid system of smaller streets are one-story apartment houses. Most of the population of the city lived in these formal structures. On the edges of the city, less formally planned clusters of rooms built of poorer materials are found. These were probably Teotihuacan's slums. Springs arise from the ground in the southwest section of the city and were led away to fields and chinampas. Some still-extant canals are oriented to the Teotihuacan grid. The location of the ancient city was determined by these springs. The sources of the San Juan River are separate and derive from runoff and tributary streams some distance up the valley. In ancient times this river was channeled and fed through the city, winding down its eastern edge and then turning west and running around the Citadel and Great Compound zone. Ultimately the river gave access to the great sheet of lake water that lay to the southwest of the city. Reservoirs were built and side channels dug which gave more of the city's inhabitants access to the river and spring water. Wells have been found within the city, sealed under later floors (Cowgill, personal communication).

One of the many significant findings of the Teotihuacan mapping project was the discovery of walls which are at least partitions and may also be defensive. Such walls set off large parts of the city from one another and define their boundaries. Examples are the east-west walls located just north of the moon pyramid. These walls tie in with another which runs north-south, protecting or delimiting the western city limit until this

function is taken over by the Barranca de Malinalco. Millon notes that the chinampa district in the southwest would also slow any attacker and on the east the San Juan River would serve the same purpose. Millon makes a convincing case that Teotihuacan may have been a clumsy giant but was certainly not a defenseless city (1973). If belts of cactus were added to the other features, defenses would have been strengthened.

The oldest part of the city is in the northwestern quarter, where architecture dating to Tzacualli times (about A.D. 100) has been found. This section also became the most densely populated of the city. Everything noted above except for the slums points to urban planning and controlled growth from at least Tlamimilolpa times (A.D. 200). Whether the entire city followed a master plan or simply grew by accretion within the quadrants formed by the avenue is unknown, but is also somewhat irrelevant. From the point of view of urban definition, Teotihuacan shows every evidence of having been a sophisticated and gigantic center.

Construction Techniques, Materials, and Style. The favorite building technique at Teotihuacan was to use a kind of pudding made of chunks of porous volcanic stone (*tezontle*) set in a matrix of clay, gravel, and mortar. Walls, ceilings, and floors were covered with a heavy coat of plaster, finished by polishing, which made it both attractively glossy and impermeable. Large amounts of wood were used to construct roof beams, vertical supports within the walls, centers for masonry pillars, and door lintels. Huge tree trunks were incorporated into platforms to transmit weight to the ground. It has been suggested that deforestation probably resulted and led to erosion of agricultural lands (Millon, 1967). At first sight then, Teotihuacan architecture might seem concrete enough to satisfy the most demanding fire marshall, but it concealed within the plaster and mortar highly flammable materials. Add to these the equally flammable textiles, wood, feathers, and mats in the buildings, and the fire rating would probably have been very high (Margain, 1971; Marquina, 1964). The fire hazards were similar to those at Casas Grandes, where a fierce conflagration also destroyed the town (DiPeso, personal communication). When Teotihuacan was finally destroyed, it was an enormous fire that did the work of destruction, leaving a blanket of ash and debris that is found nearly anywhere one excavates.

Teotihuacan had a characteristic architectural style which archaeologists depend on in detecting Teotihuacan influence on other cities of the time. Buildings were single-story and flat-roofed, whether they were placed directly on the ground, on low platforms, or elevated. The edges of the roofs were decorated by large ceramic elements. Spouts from the roofs and underground drains from the patios carried off rain water and sewage. Large and small interior courtyards allowed fresh air and sunshine to penetrate the windowless structures. Porches, arcades, and wide doorways relieved the otherwise faceless exteriors. As in later Tenochtitlan and much traditional Mexican architecture, the most attractive features of the buildings are concealed within.

Pyramidal platforms supported both temples and some elite dwellings. These platforms are distinctively styled into a set of terraces using what has been named the *talud-tablero* (terrace–wall panel) form. The concept is best grasped visually; it consists of a slanting terrace wall topped by a vertical framed panel. The terrace top recedes to the base of the next terrace wall, and so the talud-tableros continue to the top of a platform. Decorative and symbolic painting is often found in the panels.

Civic and Religious Structures. The largest buildings at Teotihuacan are the Pyramids of the Sun and Moon. Both platforms undoubtedly supported temples. A recent discovery of an ancient tunnel leading to a natural cavern under the sun structure suggests one of the functions of these huge piles. The now dry cavern once seeped water. Therefore, it may have been conceived of as the house of Tlaloc, the principal deity of the city. Tombs of distinguished persons may also be located within the mass of the two large structures. The two pyramids both have frontal platforms similar to those used as locations for burials at the Teotihuacan-influenced city of Kaminaljuyu.

To the south of the Sun Pyramid (Tlaloc's home?) and across the artificially channeled river is the famous and fortunately named Citadel (*Ciudadela*) complex. The major part of this complex consists of a huge platform surrounding a great square. The platform supports smaller platforms which in turn once supported temples facing inward to the open square. The base platform once also supported an encircling wall which would have been defensible. On the eastern side of the square is located what must have been one of the major temples of Teotihuacan, perhaps dedicated to the rain god, Tlaloc, or to the feathered serpent, Quetzalcoatl. Two building phases are now visible. The outer structure is plain and relatively unadorned, consisting of severe talud-tablero terraces. In ancient times it probably was brightly decorated with painted stucco. The inner and earlier temple is a spectacular example of Teotihuacan architectonic sculpture. Great feathered serpent bodies writhe across the tablero panels, punctuated regularly by projecting heads of serpents and what is perhaps goggle-eyed Tlaloc. A grand staircase with balustrades decorated by toothy serpent heads leads to the top of the pyramid. The sculpture is highlighted by painting in greens, reds, and white. Seashells and other water symbols strongly suggest that one is in the presence of Tlaloc. The temple atop this glorious structure is long since gone, no doubt destroyed in ancient times during the refurbishment of the square or in the ultimate catastrophe that overtook the city. Enough of its floor remained to show that it had the two-room arrangement typical of most Mesoamerican temples.

Clusters of rooms like those found in the apartment compounds and palaces were found on the terrace abutting both sides of the main Citadel temple. Temple attendants may have used these rooms as Aztec priests used similar apartments which also were adjacent to their temples. However, in this case, the rooms seem too extensive for priestly quarters alone. Rene Millon suggests that more likely this was the principal palace of Teotihuacan (1967: 43). If there was an emperor in Teotihuacan or even a city-state ruler, then probably this was where he lived and administered.

The Great Compound, across the road from the Citadel, is thought by Millon to have been the central market of the city. Today it is covered by a modern parking lot, tourist shops, museum, and restaurant. Thus this complex continues to function somewhat along its ancient lines. The building complex is the largest in the city, reflecting its importance.

Referring to a map of Teotihuacan, one sees clutches of "lesser" temples oriented around small courtyards in groups of three. These "lesser" temples are bigger than most Maya temples. Such courtyard groups are found in all parts of the city, but cluster especially along the north-south street. There are often low platforms in the courtyards which served as places for public ritual and dances. These dances were not simple entertainment. A mural from Atetelco apartment compound shows gaily clad but armed warriors whose dance steps are diagrammed by

footprints on the platform floor in true Fred Astaire style. More soberingly, these warriors carry elaborate curved knives on the ends of which are stuck bleeding human hearts.

Murals and models found at Teotihuacan depict temples as single-story and highly decorated with feathers, paintings, and cloth on the walls and roofs. A mural fragment depicts such a small temple sitting by a road on a single-terrace, talud-tablero platform. All such depictions of temples show what is apparently a wooden armature on the roof supporting the feathers and other decoration. (See Sejourne's reconstruction of Zacuala, 1966: fig. 28.) The green feathers waving and swaying in the breezes on the temple tops perhaps symbolized the bright green corn plant leaves stirred by the wind in the vast fields around the city.

If they followed what seems to be a common Mesoamerican pattern of the time, these temple groups were dedicated to gods associated with specific kinship groups. Excavations in such buildings should produce the remains of tombs with ancestral burials in them if this is the case. However, it also seems certain that the greatest of these temples attracted worshipers from outside the city. The remains of offerings from other parts of Mesoamerica have been found at Teotihuacan. Pilgrimages from these far-flung places, as well as those from the basin and nearby places, no doubt provided people with some of the needed means of ideological identification with the city.

Palaces. The famous Quetzalpapalotl Palace (quetzal bird/butterfly) is incompletely excavated, but shows the magnificence in which the elite lived. A set of deep porches leads to a central courtyard which is surrounded by an arcade and three large rooms. This part is altogether unsuitable for habitation and seems to have been an administrative and audience area. The rear of the audience area gives into several room clusters which are for living purposes. These room clusters are similar to those found in the apartment structures. The Quetzalpapalotl Palace is located on the edge of the courtyard in front of the Pyramid of the Moon and therefore is probably one of the most important and elaborate of such structures. If this palace is more or less typical, however, the pattern of deep porches giving access to an audience area with adjacent and secluded living quarters may be repeated elsewhere in the city. Certainly these palace buildings are distinguished from the apartment structures by larger size, complexity, and special features which are not found in other structures (Acosta, 1964a).

Apartment Compounds. Of the 2600 buildings in Teotihuacan, over 2000 of them are apartment compounds. As of 1974, only twenty-five or thirty of these had been even partially excavated. These buildings are highly consistent in general pattern. Clusters of rooms are arranged around several patios, and a common outer wall surrounds the whole maze. The structures are arranged on a grid system of streets which averages about 60 meters (197 feet) on a side. However, both the grid and sizes of the houses are variable. The latter vary from 625 to 6000+ square meters (6750 to 64,800 square feet) in extent. There are probably a few larger and smaller examples. Millon estimates that about 100 persons lived in the largest compounds and about 20 in the smallest. From these figures he estimates the total population at about A.D. 600 as at least 75,000 and perhaps more than 200,000 with a mean figure of 125,000 (Millon, 1970: 1080).

There is no doubt that these buildings were residential. Each apartment apparently had its own kitchen, within which have been found cooking places and large amounts of cooking, serving, and storage pottery. Sufficiently careful excavations to detect such evidence have been made in only a few cases. The apartment compound named Tetitla perhaps had a cistern for rainwater storage which was fed by roof drains, according to Laurette Sejourne (1966). However, the evidence is puzzling and not at all certain. There are also sanitary facilities taking the forms of patios or blind alleys where the results were available to turkey buzzards. Fortunately, the high altitude and strong sunlight helped promote rapid sterilization of effluents. Below-floor drains carried the rains away from the patios and into the streets.

Each apartment compound varies in number of rooms and patios, but most have at least 50 and Tetitla has over 100. All apartment houses thus far excavated have their own temple or shrines. In many ways the apartment houses were self-contained units. Even burials, presumably of former occupants, were made inside the structures.

Millon writes of these buildings: "The residential areas of Teotihuacan must have presented a somewhat forbidding aspect from the outside; high windowless walls facing on narrow streets. Within the buildings, however, the occupants were assured of privacy. Each patio had its own drainage system; each admitted light and air to the surrounding apartments; each made it possible for the inhabitants to be out of doors yet alone" (1967: 43). Millon has also commented on the defensive nature of these structures. It is worth noting that these structures provided a far higher quality housing for most of the city's populace than that available in the valley since the Spanish conquest (Sanders, 1965).

Slums. Tlamimilolpa is apparently an apartment structure but more extensive than most. Its rooms are smaller and its plan is much more complex and maze-like. Further, it is built of inferior materials, principally of adobe. Its location is on the eastern edge of the city and away from the most important structures, suggesting that its inhabitants were of relatively low social status. Certainly, Tlamimilolpa does not live up to the standards of construction and the amenities of a house like Tetitla. In modern Mexican terms, the contrast is between the modern government apartment buildings (*multi-familiares*) and the adobe tenements (*vecindades*) described in *Children of Sanchez.*

Summary. Obviously, our classifications of palaces, apartment houses, and so forth are artificial separations. The city was an organic growth. The functions of these buildings overlapped and melded into one another. There is the great palace wrapped around the temple in the Citadel; apartment houses have their own temples; palaces combine many functions, even as sumptuous burial places; some apartment houses are nearly palaces in elegance and appointments. The Great Market was probably involved with religious activities. The Tlamimilolpa slum in its earlier phase seems to have been more affluent. Certainly, at least one person who died during those early days was given an elaborate funeral and was accompanied by a large quantity of excellent pottery. Perhaps the fortunes of the kinship unit occupying Tlamimilolpa later shifted for the worse. Barrio divisions seem to be clear, with the most emphatic example being that of the Oaxacan Barrio. Each of these neighborhoods has its own temple.

ART AND RELIGION. No one source gives us as much information about the Teotihuacanos and their lives as the brilliant murals to be found on the interior walls in practically every building of the city. As sculpture and modeling were the artistic media favored by the

Maya for architectural decoration, so was mural painting preferred at Teotihuacan. Nicholson notes that Teotihuacan sculpture is cubistic, massive, and stylized (1971b). It is typified by the giant and blocky sculpture of Tlaloc in the National Museum. However, for what their stone sculpture lacked in vitality, the Teotihuacanos made up in their mural art. Over 350 examples of painting are known from only 13 locations. Since there are over 2600 buildings in Teotihuacan and most are unexcavated, there must have been a very rich mural art form in the city.

Clara Millon (1972, 1973), Esther Pasztory (1974), George Kubler (1967), and Kubler's student, Arthur Miller (1973), have made the principal studies of mural art. According to Kubler, there are at least forty-five images of life forms in the paintings, and these are far surpassed by the number of geometric and stylized motifs. There are also about fifty elements which are probably glyphs. Kubler characterizes Teotihuacan murals as being strongly liturgical, especially in the early phases. That is, there are repetitions of religious symbols and graphic obeisances arranged in a kind of polychrome litany.

The liturgical murals fall into five thematic clusters which probably correspond to specific religious cults. The Raingod Cluster is the most common. An example of this is the speech scroll of the singing priest of the Maguey Mural. In the scroll are richly various signs for water, and the scrolls' edges are trimmed with a Tlaloc headdress, a serpent's eye, and a possible lightning symbol. Avatars and variable manifestations of the rain god occur in the forms of feathered serpents (recall the Citadel temple), starfish, jaguars, flowers, and warriors. In an extraordinary tour de force, the porticos of the three temples in the Atetelco apartment house are covered from floor to ceiling with the life-giving figures of the rain god. The human face in the Tlaloc costume is replaced by coyote and eagle heads in some murals, while water-drooling jaguars prowl at the bases of the walls. Tlaloc in a full front view is shown, at Tetitla with water flowing from his hands (Lothrop, 1964). Symbolically, within the water streams are pieces of jade, human heads, animal heads, and perhaps grains of corn.

In the fascinating "paradise" mural from Tepantitla, Tlaloc, grasping Tlaloc dolls, presides over a scene which Caso has interpreted as a depiction of Tlalocan, the afterworld of the rain god (1942). A great waterspout gushes upward in the center of the mural, spewing people into paradise. The spout seems to result from two rivers flowing from springs guarded by jaguars in the corners of the mural. Interestingly, the rivers are bordered by neatly divided and irrigated fields. Paradise is indeed a happy place, and speech and song scrolls issue from the many who have arrived. One man is so happy to be there that he weeps and makes a magnificent utterance, judging by the ornate speech scroll issuing from his mouth. Tlaloc's goggle-eyed butterflies flit through the scene which shows humans engaged in games and other pleasant pursuits. This promised afterlife no doubt gave the Teotihuacan priesthood a powerful moral and psychological lever to use for social control. This unitary view of the "Tlaloc" figures has been challenged recently by Pasztory, who thinks that several gods are represented by these figures (1974).

The Butterfly Cluster of themes is often found on incense burners used in funeral rites, suggesting that the butterfly may be a symbol for the soul. Owls, arrows, and shields are members of a third complex and are probably the symbols of war. Kubler suggests that the combination of owl and quetzal birds in the Quetzalpapalotl Palace designate a specific dynasty and its association with war.

A fourth complex of themes centers around the depiction of a cult object and its worshipers. In a mural discovered in 1889 in the Temple of Agriculture, and since destroyed, chanting worshipers look at two smoking altars while they offer pottery, a dove, food, and bundles of what may be incense. Cremation was one way of disposal of the dead at Teotihuacan, and this scene may show just that sort of funeral together with the symbols of the presiding city.

The fifth cluster of themes is grouped around rain, ground water, lightning, and fire. In many scenes, jaguars, symbols of the underworld, prowl below blowing shell trumpets, which drip water and which produce thunderous sounds as indicated by noise scrolls.

Changes through time in mural subject matter and style indicate both changes in basic cultural values and the more subtle aesthetic trends. Clara Millon's important work has been oriented toward these diachronic matters, as contrasted to Kubler's essentially synchronic approach. Millon has sorted the trends in painting into six major periods (1972). Specific qualities which persist through all periods include the following:

1. A use of flat colors
2. A general absence of spatial depth
3. A prohibition against portrayal of human sexual characteristics

Period 1 painting seems to have been largely supplementary to sculpture. Sculpture was more important than painting early in the city's history. A few ancillary depictions on the Quetzalcoatl pyramid typify this art.

Period 2 murals include the "Mythological Animals" painting and those from the Superposed Structures building. The general characteristics are small bodies combined with large heads, increased polychromy, and complexity of composition.

In Period 3 a more monumental style was developed. The giant jaguars painted on exterior walls of the Street of the Dead are good examples. Much experimentation in style is in evidence, indicating that many painters were at work in a period of canonical flux. Clara Millon comments that, "Among the paintings we find artistic disasters and magnificent successes" (1972: 9).

Period 4 is one of a fully developed art style with a realized potential. The famous Tepantitla "Tlalocan" mural is from this period as is the sequence of "kneeling jaguars" at the Tetitla apartment compound. Clara Millon sees Maya and Zapotec influences in some of the Tetitla paintings. Again the style is rich and varied, but is tied together in its concern with the transcendental. Brilliant polychromy is characteristic.

Period 5 painting is distinguished by the trend toward painting almost entirely in tones of red. The netted design in the Atetelco white courtyard (*Patio Blanco*) is an example of one thematic development. Clara Millon has recently interpreted a motif from this mural and others as representing temporal and sacred power combined. This grapheme is a tassel attached to a tablero (Millon, 1973).

Period 6 is the final period and seems to feature a narrower color range than preceding periods. The upper paintings of the Quetzalpapalotl Palace exemplify this period. Ornateness and simplicity exist side by side, continuing the divergent traditions established long in the past.

In my opinion there may be a distinct shift in cultural values through time reflected in thematic changes. From an emphasis on the exaltation of nature, the Teotihuacanos, late in their history, shifted to glorification of warriors and rulers. As noted above, Teotihuacan religion seems to have been strongly animistic in its earliest phases and then to have moved to a focus on humanized deities and even deified humans. The Mural of the Mythological Animals is thought by Millon to represent the myth of cyclical creation and destruction and is early in date (C. Millon, 1967: 48). Another example of this earliest cosmology is on a decorated pot found at Las Colinas, Tlaxcala, but probably made in Teotihuacan. In a fascinating analysis, Hasso von Winning demonstrates that the figures on the pot represent Tlaloc in four aspects: serpent, coyote, quetzal bird, and water. The four may symbolize the four kinds of rain associated with the four world directions (von Winning, 1961). Later murals show armed figures with spear throwers, darts, and shields, and even depict symbols of human sacrifice.

TEOTIHUACAN SOCIETY.   From settlement pattern data which show differences in housing, we can recover something of the structure of Teotihuacan society. Evidence for occupational specialization indicates considerably more than just a two-part stratification — rulers and ruled. At present, we can only see the outlines of the fully developed and sophisticated system extant in the latest period; the earlier periods are even hazier. The correctness of the following survey of social classes depends on the correctness of the functional interpretations that we have made of the various city structures, murals, artifacts, and other information.

Farmers.   The support of the more than 125,000 persons living in Teotihuacan was based on farmers who lived both in the city and in nearby communities. It also depended on tribute from satellite cities and on the control of large zones of the central plateau. The huge market in Teotihuacan was the redistribution mechanism for the urban center. Farmers living in the apartment houses and slums managed the surrounding, irrigated farmlands shown in the murals. Rural towns such as Maquixco provided specialized agricultural products. Satellite cities such as Tula and Xochicalco must also have contributed foodstuffs.

Maquixco (technically known as site TC-8) is located on the northern slopes of the Teotihuacan Valley, a few kilometers west of the city. It is in the piedmont zone and therefore in an area of poorer soil and less water than the valley bottom settlements. This rural community consists of about fifteen houses similar to the Yayahuala apartment complex in the city. The apartments of Maquixco are quite different in detail from those in the city, however. The building materials are inferior, being mainly of adobe as contrasted to the concrete of the urban dwellings. Apartments are smaller, and there are fewer rooms within each building: 12 to 15 versus the 50 to over 100 rooms in most of the urban houses. At Maquixco, because there is a much greater expanse of vacant terrain, a grid plan is lacking and, instead, the apartment houses are grouped around plazas. Murals at Maquixco depict only relatively dull geometrics, and lack the lively, variable forms of the city art. Five hundred to six hundred people lived at Maquixco at its height.

Today the area is exploited for the production of maguey which provides fiber and pulque to the region. Beans are another important crop. Maquixco performed the same functions from about A.D. 400 to 600. Special obsidian blades used for processing maguey are found in large numbers over the site. The Fat God, the god of pulque, is the most common type of figurine in the village. Maquixco produced very little else for itself, however. Pottery and obsidian and other stone tools are identical to those found in the city and were undoubtedly made there. In other words, the town was firmly tied into a trade network and probably marketed its products in the central market of the city, exchanging them for obsidian, fine ceramics, stone corn grinders, and other necessaries. Undoubtedly, Maquixco also depended on the city for religious reassurance in its agricultural activities (Sanders, 1965). A mural, now unfortunately in the Cleveland Museum, shows a singing priest striding over a nicely cultivated field into which are stuck unmistakable maguey leaves. A spiny crocodile-serpent, symbol of the earth, frames the scene.

Maquixco may be typical of the towns of the hinterland which were tied into the subsistence base of the city. There were relatively few of these communities during the great period of Teotihuacan. Jeffrey Parsons' surveys of the eastern and southern basin have shown that most of it was thinly populated during this time. The implication is that most of the people were congregated in the city (Parsons, 1968, 1974).

It has been suggested that chinampa agriculture was developed at this early date and helped to support the city. Armillas' recent work has shown that the great period of chinampa farming came when water in the lakes fell to relatively shallow levels in the Postclassic period (1971). However, the chinampa technique may well have been instituted during this period. Certainly, the area just outside the southwest part of the city seems to have been so exploited, not to speak of any lake activity farther south.

Craft Specialists. Although most of the farmers lived either in the city or in small farming villages like Maquixco, perhaps 25 percent of the city's population were craft specialists. This means tens of thousands of people. Rene Millon and his colleagues found a tendency for people living in the same compound to engage in the same occupation. They also found over 500 workshops, the vast majority of which were obsidian workshops. More specialized craftsmen made other stone items such as the famous stone masks, while still others manufactured elaborate and exquisite pottery. Stuccoed, slab-footed tripod vessels were a Teotihuacan specialty, as distinctive as Wedgwood pottery. Much utility pottery was also made. The murals indicate that there were also couturiers, who fabricated the elaborately feathered and bedizened elite costumes. Leather sandals for the elite and probably a woven type of grass sandal for commoners were made. The huge amount of formal architecture and some specialized tools indicate that there were full-time masons, plasterers, carpenters, quarrymen, and other construction trades workers. Painters of murals were certainly a specialist class. As with the lowland Maya, painters had to command not only technical aspects of fresco painting, but also the sophisticated iconography which gave meaning to their efforts. As has been done for the Classic Maya, one could construct a complicated and stratified model of these specialties. The most prestigious presumably would be those involving arcane knowledge largely shared with and derived from the elite classes. If this were the case, then the construction trades and common implement crafts were probably the least prestigious. Producers of luxury and sumptuary items with ritual significance such as the stucco-coated tripod ceramic bowls and the sophisticated murals would have been highest on the craftsman social scale.

Presumably there were also merchant-craftsmen who dealt with the transactions of the city's marketplace. There were also long-distance merchants who handled the transport and exchange of goods to far-off areas. These antecedents of the Aztec pochteca class were probably of higher status than the resident craftsmen merchants.

If we make analogies to the earliest cities of Mesopotamia and the protohistoric cities of Mesoamerica, we find that there was probably a group of specialties that were the province of a bureaucracy. These civil servants may have also been the elite, but more likely were ranked according to their responsibilities. Teotihuacan had a more complex arrangement and was larger than the later Aztec capital, although Tenochtitlan may have had more people. It is therefore unlikely that Teotihuacan was any less complex in social organization. Sanders has suggested that kinship units consisting of groups of related families or lineages lived in the apartment houses (1965). This arrangement is analogous to that of the "small ward" (*barrio pequeño*) of the Aztecs which was probably the residential area of a lineage. Therefore, calpullis or similar units larger than the lineage may have existed and performed the calpulli functions. Social organization and kinship structure is probably the most conservative part of human culture. Assuming that the Aztec period peoples inherited much of their cultural apparatus from Teotihuacan, it may be that the social forms also came from this period.

Foreigners in the City. One of the most interesting findings from the work of Rene Millon and his colleagues was that of the presence of at least one barrio set aside for foreigners. This zone was apparently occupied by people from Oaxaca. Excavations in this ward on the western edge of the city produced one genuine Oaxacan-style tomb which had been looted. However, the ancient tomb-robbers had left in place a stone stela carved with an Oaxacan glyph. Bones of several individuals suggest that the tomb may have been a crypt reopened from time to time for burial of a newly deceased person. In addition, two Monte Alban-style funerary urns were found in other nearby excavations. Several sites near the eastern edge of the city have produced unusual concentrations of fine pottery from the Gulf Coast area. This is the region that Millon has at times called the "Merchants Barrio." Excavation in at least one case indicated an adobe structure of much lower quality than the usual apartment compounds. Millon has conjectured that this may have been a merchants' storehouse or warehouse. Maya lowland wares, such as the fine, glossy polychromes, are much rarer and are scattered throughout the city, as if these were occasional exotic pieces in the homes of the wealthier Teotihuacanos (Millon, 1973: 40). One implication of this evidence is that Teotihuacan supplemented the income from its tributary areas with long-distance trade connections to Oaxaca, the Veracruz lowlands, and the Maya lowlands. The nearer Huastec area may have been represented by a resident group of people in the city, as evidenced by a round temple in the northwest section of the city. The Quetzalcoatl-Ehecatl wind god cult and its round temples were particularly strong in the Huastec area.

Teotihuacan Elite. Elite-class specialties included religion, politics, and warfare. As indicated above, long-distance trade may also have been an elite activity.

Although, as noted before, formal religion had changed in response to other cultural evolution, it began as animistic and ended with great similarities to that of Aztec times. That is, the latest manifestations of Teotihuacan cosmologies and ritual practices seem to glorify humans who were historical personalities and who were eventually identified with the supernatural. Among the thousands of figurines produced through the several hundred years of the city's life are depictions of gods or godlike humans known from later times. The flayed god (Xipe), the rain god (Tlaloc), the feathered serpent (Quetzalcoatl), and the fire god (Xiuhtecuhtli) were all present. Sanders argues that the same association of religion with warfare and ritual cannibalism was present in the final stages of Teotihuacan as in Aztec times. Maquixco, for example, produced large quantities of split and splintered human bone fragments in general garbage and trash heaps, indicating that humans were being used for food during the A.D. 400–600 period. The murals showing human hearts on the ends of knives brandished by Teotihuacan warriors suggest the same. Jaguar and eagle deities shown in late Teotihuacan murals were later Toltec and Aztec warrior society patrons. Large numbers of projectile points are found in late Teotihuacan debris at Maquixco. All of this may add up to a picture of an aggressive Teotihuacan, able to move against its neighbors with military force partially rationalized by religious ideology sanctioning human sacrifice.

Among other motivations for aggressive warfare was the one familiar in our own day, that of the demands of a large and growing population. Conquered areas could be made to yield valuable tribute of food. The role of the warrior became more and more important to Teotihuacan, setting a pattern carried on up to the Spanish conquest. Teotihuacan had the organizational jump on most Mesoamerican cultures during its first centuries, but as time went on the gap narrowed, and the city finally came into peril.

TEOTIHUACAN AND THE REST OF MESOAMERICA: EMPIRE OR ALLIANCES? Bernal (1966) suggests that Teotihuacan was an empire along lines initially invented by the Olmecs. He distinguishes between the metropolitan culture of Teotihuacan and Teotihuacan influences found in regional cultures. Metropolitan culture was as has been defined above. The distribution of this culture certainly includes the valleys of Mexico and Puebla, and possibly the Valleys of Toluca and Morelos. One large city within this metropolitan zone, besides Teotihuacan, was Cholula.

Cholula, in the Valley of Puebla, is pitifully little known, considering its pre-Hispanic importance and the size of the site, and in spite of forty years of intermittent excavation. From nearly any point in the valley one can see the vast bulk of the great pyramid glowering over the small provincial town that now occupies the site. Most investigations have concentrated on the pyramid. Tunnels into the structure have revealed some earlier pyramids which date from the Teotihuacan period. These earlier platforms have the talud-tablero feature. Painted in the panels around the terraces are various polychromed motifs: black, red, and blue stripes with seashells; insects which may be the Cholulan version of the sacred butterflies of Teotihuacan; and geometrics.

The most extraordinary murals were discovered in 1965 painted on the panels of a Teotihuacan style structure adjacent to the inner pyramid. These are the so-called "Drunkard Murals" (Marquina, 1971). Groups of rather elastic formed persons vigorously enjoy themselves drinking cupsful of what is probably pulque. These people roister, gesture, pour pulque from jugs into larger jugs while dogs bark and run. All in all, the scene gives the impression of a carefree gaiety unusual in somber central Mexico. Marquina (1971) suggests that the scene is that of a harvest or planting celebration like those described by Sahagun.

Other examples of Teotihuacan-style architecture have been discovered at some distance from the main pyramid group. Clearly, during Teotihuacan times, Cholula was not the major center that it was later. The great pyramid had not yet been built. The area of its location was occupied by a group of Teotihuacan-style buildings. What sort of a settlement surrounded those buildings is yet unknown, in spite of the thorough work of the German Puebla Scientific Mission. Teotihuacan pottery is quite regular and probably locally made.

Xochicalco, near Cuernavaca, may have been another such city. Sanders has noted cell-like residential structures at Xochicalco similar to those found at Teotihuacan. However, these are not necessarily grouped into apartment compounds. Beyond the central plateau area the evidence is of strong regional cultures which were more or less influenced by Teotihuacan. Using the model of the protohistoric empires, we find it likely that any empire built by Teotihuacan had large geographic holes in it. That is, there were undoubtedly zones in Mesoamerica only controlled by alliance, intimidation, or isolation, with only the most crucial zones and routes physically occupied and controlled by Teotihuacan. This fits the classic model of empire in many world zones and, more to the point, fits the Aztec case. Patterns of Teotihuacan's influence and control indicate that it too fits this model. An examination of the most important cases in point will demonstrate this analogy.

Maya Highlands: Kaminaljuyu. Sanders' work at Kaminaljuyu shows a dramatic change about A.D. 300 from the scattered plaza settlement pattern we have seen in the late Preclassic period (Sanders and Michels, 1969). Teotihuacan presence is marked by a shift to a single massive acropolis in Teotihuacan style. Talud-tablero temples, oriented about closed courtyards, were built in adobe. Frontal platforms on these temples concealed and protected successive elaborate tombs. Within the tombs are masses of pottery, carved bone, and other materials, much of which is clearly within the stylistic canons used at Teotihuacan itself. Stuccoed, slab-footed tripods, with scenes featuring Tlaloc, and thin orange effigy vessels are examples of items exported to Kaminaljuyu from Teotihuacan. However, much of the painting on the stuccoed tripods is in Maya style, and recent studies by Jacinto Quirarte have shown that many of the tripods themselves were manufactured in the Maya highlands. In other words, Maya craftsmen at Kaminaljuyu made their own versions of the tripods and exported these variants back to Teotihuacan. The strength of Teotihuacan influence at Kaminaljuyu was so strong that Kidder, who dug out the famous tombs, suggested that it is an example of a military takeover by Teotihuacanos and the subsequent exploitation of a native population (Kidder, Jennings, and Shook, 1946). This idea fits the later pattern of military takeover of the Maya highlands by small Mexican groups who established ruling houses in Protohistoric times. The size of Kaminaljuyu increases at this time to about 600 acres and the population in and around the center was about 10,000 or 15,000. Rural population also increased during this period. By around A.D. 500 three subordinate towns had been established along the route between Kaminaljuyu and the south coastal plain of Guatemala, a distance of only twenty-five air miles.

Coastal Guatemala: Cotzumalhuapa and the Middle Classic. The Pacific coastal plain was at least partially controlled by the Olmec in earlier times. It was also an important zone to the Aztecs because of its cacao (chocolate) bean production. Recent bulldozing operations on the coast have destroyed dozens of mounds and produced immense quantities of Teotihuacan-influenced pottery. Most of this pottery is made of a local ware called *Tiquisate* ware, which has also been found in Teotihuacan itself. Teotihuacan-style incense burners have been found by skin divers in the lake of Amatitlan, less than ten miles from Kaminaljuyu. Sanders and Price say that the motivation for a Teotihuacan takeover of Kaminaljuyu was control of the coastal plain, and the trade route out to the Maya lowlands (1968). Kaminaljuyu evidently acted as a major outpost of Teotihuacan power and had connections with the important center of Tazumal in El Salvador as well as with Tikal and other Maya lowland centers to the north. Teotihuacan undoubtedly extracted more than just chocolate beans from the Maya area. For one thing, the Pacific coastal zone produces high quality cotton today and may have done so in the past. Manufactured goods of great variety could have been exported from the Maya area, including such high prestige items as green quetzal feathers.

The site of Bilbao on the Guatemalan coast particularly reflects an art style deeply influenced by Teotihuacan and its cultural allies. Around the present-day town of Santa Lucia Cotzumalhuapa are a number of ceremonial centers, one of which is Bilbao, and another the ancient center of El Baul. El Baul was occupied at least as early as Izapan times, and handsome examples of that epi-Olmec style of sculpture have been found there. Later sculpture at both sites shows strong influence from the Gulf of Mexico, specifically from around the Tajin zone. If Teotihuacan controlled the Cotzumalhuapan region, it was probably through a group from the Tajin zone. Tajin was either an ally or under the domination of Teotihuacan at this time. Parsons and Borhegyi worked for some time at Bilbao, and Parsons has developed the concept of the Middle Classic (L. Parsons, 1967–1969). Briefly, he thinks that the period of Teotihuacan influence over all of Mesoamerica was so pervasive that a separate time period should be set aside for it. The Middle Classic period is thus one of rapid and widespread distribution of Teotihuacan ceramic and other cultural forms. It lasted from A.D. 400 to 700 and is divided into two phases.

The earliest phase (A.D. 400–550) is that of the establishment of commercial and military colonies throughout Mesoamerica. Bilbao was one of those colonies. The last phase (A.D. 550–700) was the period during which Teotihuacan influence was assimilated into the regional art styles, producing new styles, which are syntheses. At this period, the great city's outposts were abandoning their ties with it and becoming independent.

Parsons sees the art style of the Cotzumalhuapa region as resulting from the above process. Even in terms of Mesoamerican art, the style is somewhat bizarre and unrelieved by much aesthetic merit. Subject matter falls into narrative and portrait categories. Human busts, full seated human figures, and colossal heads make up the second category. As Parsons says, the human figures have ". . . the aspect of sober puritanical New England sea captains" (1969: 143). Stiff, awkwardly portrayed people engage in the sacred ball game, human sacrifice in a multitude of forms, and various symbolic acts such as climbing ladders and offering human hearts to a diving figure which is probably the sun. A preoccupation with death is pervasive, and there are many death's heads and skeletal figures. Many of the large scenes are carved on gigantic boulders, and among the figures twine vines, on which are human heads, birds, and leaves. The art style, the ball game scenes and the ball game equipment (stone yokes, thin stone heads, and "palmas") all link the Cotzumalhuapa style to that of Tajin.

Today the zone around Cotzumalhuapa is occupied by sugar cane fields and coffee plantations. The Pacific coastal plain of Guatemala is hot and sticky, and the vegetation is a dense, intense green. One is always in sight of the huge volcanoes of the nearby highlands. At Bilbao, one plunges into the shady coffee groves and walks on soft, damp, springy earth, accompanied by the constant sound of small streams. Two Tlaloc figures carved from a boulder nestle in the mossy bank of a stream at Bilbao. The huge boulder sculptures with their grotesque figures rest on the terraced zones among the earthen mounds of the ceremonial center. Altogether, it is a fascinating, repellent, and exotic place for either Mesoamerican highlanders or modern travelers. The variant of Teotihuacan influence at Bilbao was certainly not directly imported from Teotihuacan as was that at nearby Kaminaljuyu. The hieroglyphic system used on the sculpture stones is distinct from either that of the Maya lowlands or the Mexican highlands. Cotzumalhuapan culture is an excellent example of the sort of regional cultural development which took place over and over again in Mesoamerican prehistory.

Maya Lowlands: Tikal, Uaxactun, Becan. The fact and nature of the relationships of Teotihuacan with Classic Maya sites is dealt with in detail in the chapter on the Classic Maya. To briefly recapitulate, the view taken in this book is that the early Classic Maya were on a political level which loosely might be defined as that of a "high chiefdom" or roughly equivalent to that achieved by the metropolitan Olmec. Teotihuacan influence was carried to the lowlands by combined commercial-military groups who assumed a variety of positions according to circumstance. At Tikal and Uaxactun, they may have become the ruling elite or a part of it. At the fortress of Becan they may have been responsible for the early fortifications protecting a cross-peninsula trade route leading from the Gulf of Mexico to the Caribbean. They probably exercised an influence out of proportion to their numbers — bringing ideas, statecraft, and sophistication in military and political matters which caused an initial shock to Maya society and then a transformation of it. In other words, the Teotihuacan groups and their legacies were the stimuli by which the lowland Maya changed from the "high chiefdom" level to that of the urban state. W. R. Coe sees the Tikal evidence as reflecting a later Teotihuacan period, one which may have been more tied to Gulf Coast variants of this culture than to that of the great city itself (1965b: 35–37). After the fall of Teotihuacan, there may have been a diaspora of craftsmen and other refugees some of whom landed in the Maya lowlands. This second wave of Teotihuacan influence would date about A.D. 700.

CLASSIC VERACRUZ CENTERS: CERRO DE LAS MESAS AND MATACAPAN

While Tajin in the north was still a small and undistinguished center, Cerro de las Mesas in the south became the most important place in the Veracruz plain after the epi-Olmec period. The site underwent great expansion, and some dozens of mounds were built. Although little of the site has been dug, it is clear that it was of great importance if only because of the fifteen stelae and eight other monuments found there. These early Classic sculptures echo some Izapan traits, but are largely distinctive. Stiff human figures stride or stand on the stelae in poses which are reminiscent of early Maya styles. These persons are accompanied by hieroglyphic texts, some of which include long count dates written in the Maya lowland system. There are also many unread texts which seem to deal with names, places, and conquests.

Tlamimilolpa-Xolalpan (Teotihuacan III) pottery is found at Cerro de las Mesas together with a locally developed set of gigantic clay sculptures. The latter include gods also represented in the figurines and murals at Teotihuacan, the old fire god, for example. Even so, a majority of ceramic types are strictly of local tradition. The accumulated wealth of the elite at Cerro de las Mesas is shown by the enormous cache of about 800 items which Drucker found there (1943a). The cache included such things as Olmec heirloom pieces, other jade carvings, jewelry of calcite and serpentine, and much other paraphernalia. Perhaps this represents a burial of the ritual equipment of a great person. It seems significant that when Teotihuacan influence disappears in the coastal plain, Cerro de las Mesas is abandoned. It is into this power vacuum that Tajin expands.

Matacapan is a large center consisting of some seventy mounds and located in the Tuxtlas Mountains by the sea. The one mound excavated by Valenzuela was a typical talud-tablero Teotihuacan platform. Ceramics include Teotihuacan pottery along with the locally made wares. M. D. Coe believes that Matacapan will prove to have been as intensely reflective of Teotihuacan influence as is Kaminaljuyu (1965a). Indeed, Matacapan may be the waystation established and used by Teotihuacan groups on their way to the coastal plain of Guatemala and hence to Kaminaljuyu.

LATE CLASSIC CENTERS IN THE SOUTH: NOPILOA AND EL ZAPOTAL

While Tajin dominated matters to the north, Nopiloa was apparently the prime center of the south. It is not as large or impressive as Cerro de las Mesas. Indeed, Coe thinks that the culture of the area may have stepped back to essentially a village-style, late Preclassic stage (1965a). A pancoastal art style was developed which was mainly expressed in figures and small stone sculpture. The *Yoke-palma-hacha* small sculpture complex is widespread. The "Smiling Figurine" complex develops and reaches its height. These famous figurines with their unwarrantedly broad grins, are found throughout the area.

A recent excavation at a Mixtequilla site not far from Nopiloa, El Zapotal, has produced some evidence of their function. A mound was found at El Zapotal which contained many burials in association with a remarkable shrine made of modeled clay. The shrine included a large and bony image of the death god. One nearby multiple burial was guarded by smiling figures which brandished knives in their hands, as if warding off the many hazards of the afterlife to which Mesoamerican souls were subject. An ossuary in the same mound consists of a stack of eighty skulls, about ten feet high and buried in a pit. It is difficult to know if these were burials of persons dying normal deaths, or the remains of bodies of sacrificial victims disposed of in a ritual manner. The fact that late Teotihuacan pottery was found with the burials indicates that Teotihuacan may have been a power in the plain after A.D. 500, but likely no later than A.D. 600.

EARLY CIVILIZATION IN NORTHERN VERACRUZ: TAJIN

The coastal plain of Veracruz is divided into compartments by rivers which flow from the highlands to the Gulf of Mexico. As one proceeds north from the old Olmec heartland, the climate becomes progressively drier. However, even in the northern compartment where Tajin is located, mists and rain prevail much of the year, but a longer dry season occurs than in the south. This was apparently the case in ancient times and caused problems for the inhabitants. Water is scarce during the dry season, and even the sea is thirty kilometers from Tajin.

THE PRECLASSIC BACKGROUND.   Long sequences

of ceramic complexes have been found by Ekholm and MacNeish to the north of Tajin at Tampico (Ekholm, 1944; MacNeish, 1954). These sequences begin about 1500 B.C. and continue to a period linked with the earliest Tajin occupation, about A.D. 100. Ceramics and figurines of great variety have been found all over Veracruz, one of the most famous stylistic groups being the *Remojadas* "sequence." This pottery is derived from the zone around the mouth of the Tecolutla River. Although the excavator has divided the pottery into lower (early) and upper (later) periods, it is apparent that both complexes represent enormous spans of time and varieties of materials. Lower Remojadas includes middle and late Preclassic items, and upper Remojadas is made up of early and late Classic pottery and figurines. There is practically no settlement pattern data for the central and northern Veracruz Preclassic period. An exception is some late Preclassic housemounds from Chalahuites found by Garcia Payon to be made of river cobbles (Payon, 1971). We must assume that village-level life was the rule during most of the Preclassic period, but have no idea whether or not there were Olmec-influenced towns of greater sophistication. Neither do we know the nature of the transition from village-level society to civilization. Few of the many Preclassic sites were used in the Classic period. There are no indications of an epi-Olmec period or centers of any great importance during this transition period. Presumably, there was a population growth pattern similar to that in the rest of Mesoamerica, accompanied by cultural elaboration, and then a shift from dispersed villages to more concentrated centers. At least toward the end of the Preclassic stage, the non-Olmec area of Veracruz shows distinct regionalization. Carved stone yokes, large figurines with smiling faces, and special ceramic forms such as chili grinders are all well-developed. Some scattered finds in the

Tajin zone show that that area was thinly occupied during the Preclassic period.

THE CLASSIC FLORESCENCE. Tajin itself has been excavated for over thirty years but no detailed architectural sequence has yet appeared in print. Therefore, some of the chronology which follows is an interpretation of Garcia Payon's work.

Chronology. There are two major periods in the city's history. During the first period (A.D. 100–550) Tajin is a minor center with relatively small pyramids and a few elite residences. Ceramics from this era show great Teotihuacan influence, especially in qualities which link it to the *Miccaotli* and *Tlamimlolpa-Xolalpan* (Teotihuacan II and III) phases. Trade wares from the Valley of Mexico are present as well as thin orange materials which are probably from northern Oaxaca. Teotihuacan may have established Tajin as a commercial-military colony. You may recall that a possible Classic period Veracruz quarter has been found in Teotihuacan itself.

Teotihuacan influence begins to wane about A.D. 500 and it is after this date that Tajin reaches its greatest development. This second phase (A.D. 550–1100) is one of dynamic expansion of Tajin culture through the coastal plain and even possibly as far as Cotzumalhuapa in Guatemala. The spectacular architecture and sculpture that the visitor today sees at Tajin is nearly all from this second period (Marquina, 1964).

Building and Site Function and Sculpture. Tajin is situated among dramatically abrupt hills, with much of the 5 square kilometers (1.9 square miles) of the site laid out on relatively flat ground in a valley. An adjacent hillside has been terraced and otherwise modified for an enormous mass of structures. There are more than 200 mounds (Krotser and Krotser, 1973). The basic plan is made up of a series of courtyard groups. The plan is thus more like that of Classic Maya centers than it is like that of more highly organized Teotihuacan. Buildings fall into the familiar temple, elite residence, and ball court categories. There are eleven ball courts at Tajin, reflecting the extreme ritual importance of the game in the lives of these ancient Veracruzanos. Architecture is decorated by a baroquely elaborate style in both sculpture and modeled stucco. A hallmark of the building style is the common use of a jutting cornice on terraces.

The center is dominated by a large temple-pyramid about 60 feet (18 meters) high which is fantastically decorated by 365 niches. It has been suggested that these represent the days of the tropical year and that there were originally small stucco figures in the niches. Other, smaller temples dot the site. Large, elaborate palace-residential buildings imply an enlargement of the elite class at Tajin from earlier times.

Sculptural style reaches its fullest expression in ball-court and temple slabs which show human sacrifice, warriors, and the ball game. All of these elements seem to be tied together into one ritual activity. M. E. Kampen (1972) says that the one major theme in Tajin art is human sacrifice. This situation parallels that of the Cotzumalhuapan sculpture some 900 miles away. Other subjects include the watering of maguey plants with sacrificial blood. Hieroglyphs which accompany the sculpture refer persistently to a "13 Rabbit," possibly the calendrical name of a great ruler. Particularly interesting are depictions of what appear to be Eagle Knights, a military order later widespread over Mesoamerica. Enormous amounts of small sculptured objects were produced, most of which had either a ritual or functional use in the sacred ball game. Yokes, thin stone human heads, turkeys carved into the "palma" form, and other attractive items are known. Palmas were stuck into ballplayers' belts while yokes were worn around the waist. These items were widely traded during this period and are found in highland Guatemala.

Based on the Krotsers' recent work, it seems clear that a large population was scattered about the center in house lots which contained gardens and fruit trees, like the pattern at Tikal. Using the Tikal density of 600 to 700 per square kilometer, and accepting the Krotsers' estimate of Tajin's extent as five square kilometers, an estimated population of 3000 to 3500 results. Tajin dominated much more territory, of course, and total population may have been about three times the core population, totaling about 13,000.

Given the above information, incomplete as it is, we do not find it difficult to think of Tajin as being one of the more militaristic allies or colonies of Teotihuacan, and one which went on to establish tributary colonies of its own, one of which may have been Cotzumalhuapa. It is particularly significant that Tajin expands and undergoes a florescence only when Teotihuacan influence is removed. It is also clear from pottery found at the site that the great period of Tajin corresponds with important periods at Monte Alban in Oaxaca and at Xochicalco and Cholula. The abandonment of Tajin about A.D. 1100 meant the lapse of the zone back into its late Preclassic stage, one of fragmented social and political units. Tajin had politically dominated the coastal plain, but when it declined, new centers arose along the central coast which controlled the region until the arrival of the Spaniards.

SUMMARY. Veracruz clearly had a crucial role in transmitting Teotihuacan influence throughout southern Mesoamerica during the Classic period. The sites of Cerro de las Mesas and Matacapan may have been Teotihuacan colonies or allies during the early Classic. Tajin is a small unimportant center in the north during this time. When Teotihuacan influence and power is withdrawn, the early Classic centers deflate like exhausted balloons. Tajin then begins a rapid cultural and military florescence and probably dominates the coastal plain and perhaps the transisthmian zone, including the former Teotihuacan colony in the Cotzumalhuapa district.

THE OAXACAN CLASSIC: MONTE ALBAN

CHRONOLOGY. The major periods of civilization in Oaxaca are named after phases defined by work at Monte Alban and thus are denominated Monte Alban I to V. The information has been expanded by work at other sites of the same periods; Monte Negro has provided some for period I, for example. The following chart summarizes the phasing and gives equivalent Christian dates.

The Chronology for Oaxaca

Monte Alban Period	Christian Dates
I	400–200 B.C.
II	200 B.C.–A.D. 200
III	A.D. 200–700
IV	A.D. 600–1521
V	A.D. 800–1521

TRANSITION TO CIVILIZATION AND PREEMINENCE. Flannery's work has shown that the Oaxacan Preclassic cultural development was functionally tied to population growth, elaboration of social structure, and innovations in farming technology (Flannery et al., 1967). It has been seen that large farming villages evolved, some of which were socially stratified. Evidence of superior housing for village leadership was found at San Jose Mogote in the form of a stone platform which supported a residence. By about 400 B.C. there were seven petty states in the valley. At about this time, one of these, Monte Alban, began to outstrip its competitors and eventually rose to preeminence. The reasons for this success are obscure. Developmental theories such as the Palerm-Wolf hypothesis explain the enabling circumstances. No doubt the massed demographic and economic power of the valley within which such historical events take place was important, but not the whole story. In the specific case of Monte Alban, terrain was also a factor.

Topographically and scenically, Monte Alban's ridge system dominates the central valley. The valley is divided into three arms. The Etla branch runs northwest to southeast, and then splits at the ridge. A southeastern branch runs off to Tlacolula and beyond, with the southern arm reaching down to the area of Zaachila. Any community wishing to physically, politically, and militarily control the entire valley had to control the ridge system at its crux.

Some of the most interesting work of recent years has been done by Richard Blanton who has surveyed the slopes of the ridge and located over 2000 terraces (personal communication). These terraces were used for both agricultural and housing zones. Recent excavations by Marcus Winter (1974) have shown that at least some of this terracing and housing dates back to the earliest part of Monte Alban I (period Ia). Although it is not yet certain how many persons lived on the ridge at this time, there were undoubtedly several thousand. This concentration of population must also have been a powerful factor in the rise of Monte Alban to power. By 400 B.C. then, a populous and well-organized community was in control of the dominating ground in the valley. Moreover, the community supported a leadership which resided and directed affairs from a civic center built on top of the ridge. Some hints of historical circumstances attending Monte Alban's rise

are present there (Bernal, 1965a; Paddock, 1966a, 1966b).

MONTE ALBAN I AND II (400 B.C.–A.D. 200). The entire top of the Monte Alban ridge has been artificially sculptured into a series of flattened and filled plaza areas around which is arranged the formal architecture of the center. Later massive construction has covered the earliest buildings, but there is no doubt that large-scale building was done in period I. The only major piece of architecture known from this phase is the Danzantes structure, a stone platform on the edge of the main plaza. A small inner platform some ten feet high was the first built on the spot and may have supported wood and thatched buildings. The most interesting feature of the platform is the sculpture which is set into the walls. These are the famous *danzantes* or "dancers."

Danzantes are boneless-appearing humans depicted by grooved lines incised on slabs of rock. Many appear lifeless, all are nude, and many are sexually mutilated, leading M. D. Coe to suggest that they represent dead and tortured enemies (1968a). Many of the danzantes have hieroglyph names. Caso notes that both the writing system and sculptural style bear a good deal of resemblance to those in use by epi-Olmec cultures of Veracruz, Cerro de las Mesas for example (1965).

Period I ceramics were surprisingly complex, making up for what they lacked in color by a wide variety in form. Human and animal effigies began their long-lasting popularity. Grey wares were especially typical, and a popular bottle form with attached spout was traded as far south as Chiapa de Corzo.

Hieroglyphic texts on stone include dates in the 260-day sacred almanac and the 365-day year. Other notations are probably personal and place names. Simple stone tombs ("box tombs") are found within the center. All of these features imply a fair level of sophistication among the elite class at Monte Alban.

CONTEMPORARY CENTERS: MONTE NEGRO AND DAINZU.

In the Tlacolula branch of the valley there is an enormous site called Dainzu, the main structures of which are backed against a large butte. It may be significant that this position is also militarily defensible, although not as strong as that of Monte Alban.

Ignacio Bernal has excavated at the site and found a very large stone platform which supported a masonry building. Set into the walls of the platform and its stairway are sculptures similar but not identical to the Danzantes. A great many of the Dainzu sculptures show ball players. Bernal also found a large ball court nearby which dates to the same period as the platform and much of the sculpture: Monte Alban I (1967). Similar tombs occur at both centers at this time. Dainzu was likely the capital of one of the competing petty states eventually incorporated into a larger state headed by Monte Alban.

The Monte Negro (Black Mountain) site is of especial interest. It is located north of the central valley in an area later known to be occupied by the Mixtecs. The top of a ridge was modified as at Monte Alban, and a town with thatched roofed houses erected. The ceremonial buildings were grouped around an open courtyard. One of these civic structures had the unusual feature of large columns carved from single pieces of stone. In general, Monte Negro represents a paler and less developed version of Monte Alban I culture. No writing or sculpture has been found. The pottery is poorer in variety. It possibly represents a provincial version of Monte Alban I culture, and one which is that of the ancestral Mixtecs.

Some thirty-nine Monte Alban I sites were found by Bernal in the Central Valley, but many of these finds are based solely on pottery samples. Clearly, if Monte Alban was not the dominant site at the beginning of this period, it became so by the end of it.

In period II we see an enlargement and development of complexity which signals the accession of Monte Alban to fully civilized and sophisticated status. The full-scale sculpturing of the Monte Alban ridge tops into flattened and terraced areas took place during period II. The scale of this effort indicates that Monte Alban could call on resources of manpower not available to it before. Certainly the period of political unification of the central valley was necessary in preparation for this effort. Within the great plaza at Monte Alban, the arrowhead-shaped observatory (building J) was built; apparently its peculiar plan was dictated by its function in making astronomical observations. Other platforms appear which have the characteristic Oaxacan balustrades with a decorative feature reminiscent of the talud-tablero. These platforms supported temples with two rooms and thatched roofs. Presumably the elite class which directed these construction activities lived in the center, but no palaces have been excavated from this period.

Stelae and bas reliefs with hieroglyphs were put up. Many of the bas reliefs show human heads hanging downward from glyphs which are apparently place names, and Caso suggests that these are records of conquests (1965). There are more of them than before, indicating a relatively violent era.

Tombs are more elaborate and some of them show the features which lasted until the Spanish conquest. Under the courtyards were stone burial chambers with steps leading down to antechambers. These were used for sepulchres in which only one principal person might be buried. In other tombs retainers and servants accompanied their masters into the afterlife. Some of the period II tombs are decorated with wall frescoes. Large incense burners or burial urns were placed with the dead. These urns represent various gods with one of the most popular being Cocijo, the local god of rain.

Other ceramics became more complex with delicately painted stucco applied to some vessels. As in so much of period II development, the major changes are in the elite sector of Oaxacan culture. Much of the elaborate pottery seems to be linked with ceramics of Veracruz and Chiapas. It is very difficult to detect any significant changes in the folk culture away from the centers, indicating that for most of the people, daily life went on much as before.

APOGEE: MONTE ALBAN III (A.D. 200–700). The two major cultural and linguistic groups occupying Oaxaca at the time of Spanish contact were the Mixtec and Zapotec. The culture fully developed during period III is undoubtedly Zapotec. The features of Zapotec civilization as known from the conquest period are so similar in both general features and in detail to that of period III that there is little doubt that Monte Alban periods I to IV represent Zapotec culture. Thus we probably have a Zapotec state established by A.D. 200 (period I), developing during period II, and expanding during period III.

The major historical features of period III are: (1) the establishment and expansion of a unitary Zapotec state in the Central Valley; (2) the expansion and enormous size of both civic center and population at the capital, Monte Alban; and (3) the independence of Monte Alban from Teotihuacan.

Chronology. Traditionally, the end of Monte Alban III has been set at A.D. 900, or at about the same time as the Maya collapse. However, recent carbon 14 dates and other discoveries indicate that the end of III may come about A.D. 700, more coincident with the fall of Teotihuacan. The period is divided into two phases, IIIa and IIIb. Trade, pottery, and other influences from Teotihuacan are present in IIIa, but are missing from IIIb. This is a principal distinction between the phases. The late phase seems more and more inward-looking and isolated. At the end of IIIb Monte Alban is abandoned. However, cultural and ethnic continuity beyond this event is indicated by the fact that pottery from IIIb and the following phase IV can be distinguished only by close study. The Zapotecs simply had lost their ancient capital about A.D. 700, but were as culturally distinctive as ever.

The City of Monte Alban. Bernal defines Monte Alban during period III as a true city (1965a). Formal, public architecture and surrounding terraces and housing areas covered over forty square kilometers (about fifteen square miles). Density was not nearly so high as at Teotihuacan, but Blanton's surveys have shown, as noted before, that more than 2000 terraces, all with one or more houses, occupy the slopes of the main ridge system. Many small ravines were dammed for water. The whole ridge was probably dotted with these small ponds used by the households. Population growth was spectacular during period III. Blanton's preliminary population estimates are that between thirty and fifty thousand people lived at Monte Alban during period IIIb (personal communication). Bernal's survey of the valley turned up fifty to sixty sites from IIIa and over two hundred from IIIb. Eighteen of the late sites are classified as large, with over ninety medium-sized sites known. Therefore, Monte Alban was only the most prodigious example of a generally vigorous growth in population and size.

Monte Alban had developed into a splendid center by this time, and it was during period IIIb that it assumed its most complex form. It is this architecture that the modern visitor sees when at the site. Monte Alban is arranged on a north-south axis with two enormous platforms at either end of a very large plaza. The platforms support complex arrangements of pyramid-temples, palaces, patios, and tombs. The east side of the great plaza is lined with six residential buildings and a small ball court. The middle of the plaza is occupied by three buildings jammed together into one unit. The ancient observatory structure (building J) sits detached in front of the grand staircase leading to the south platform. The west edge of the plaza is occupied by three units, two more or less symmetrical architectural complexes called "systems M and IV" which flank the ancient danzantes structure. The south platform may date entirely from period IIIa, but most of the rest of the buildings mentioned were modified or enlarged during IIIb. Ancient sculpture was retained and moved around and reused. Thus some of the danzante sculptures were shifted. New stelae and slabs commemorated new conquests and other events of dynastic importance. One stela on the south platform shows a conqueror symbolically driving his lance through the name glyph of a town. Other stelae in the same zone show bound captives standing on the name glyphs of their home towns.

The architectural style of Monte Alban was characterized by something called a *doble escapulario* or double recess. Some 90 percent of the buildings at Monte Alban have this feature, which is very regional. It is not clear whether Monte Alban architecture was painted and elaborated by modeled stucco, but certainly most of it was plastered.

One hundred and fifty-three formal tombs have been found at the site. Most of these date from period III and have a characteristic form. They are built of masonry slabs and are placed below the courtyard floors. Some have been found in the great plaza and many more under the patio floors of the apartment houses

on the upper slopes of the ridge. Most period III tombs are entered by a flight of steps leading down below ground level to an antechamber. The facades of the tombs are nearly identical to the facades of temples once extant at Monte Alban. Above the doorways there is often a niche within which rests an elaborate incense burner (funerary urn). Carved and plain slabs close the tombs off from the antechambers. The interiors of the tombs are mainly rectangular with deep wall niches within which rest pottery and other offerings to the dead. Most often the tomb was occupied by a single person surrounded by ceramics and other items which presumably belonged to him during his lifetime. Again, the remarkable incense burners are highly characteristic of these offering groups. Occasionally, murals decorate the tomb walls. Some of the most interesting of these paintings were found in tombs 104 and 105. In each case, there are certain similarities to the mural art of Teotihuacan in the lines of gaily costumed figures with speech scrolls who parade around the walls. However, there are also some vague Maya characteristics in the glyph-like forms. Taken as a body, the mural art seems to show a nonderivative regional Mesoamerican style. It is securely Oaxacan in origin, although it may share certain common ideas and conventions with other Mesoamerican cultures.

A hint of the elaborate ritual which surrounded the lives and deaths of the elite at Monte Alban is given by a remarkable group of figurines which were found above Tomb 103 (see Paddock 1966b; fig. 151). A dead man is represented by a mask set on a miniature pyramid. An orchestra and five priests surround the mask while another person impersonates the old fire god. This figure group is probably a record of a memorial ceremony for someone of great importance already buried, perhaps for the person buried in Tomb 103 below. As in the case of the group of Olmec figurines from La Venta, it is as close as we will ever get to a "snapshot" of the culture in action.

Crafts and Specialists. The amounts of ceramics found around Monte Alban are enormous even by Mesoamerican standards. Much of the material was made for household use, but a great deal of specialty pottery was also produced. A polished gray ware is the most characteristic of Monte Alban III. Teotihuacan flower vases (*floreros*) and other forms show up in IIIa along with significant and persistent amounts of a trade ware called *thin orange*. Recent studies have shown that thin orange pottery was probably made in an area which lies between Puebla and Oaxaca. Other Teotihuacan forms were also made from local clays. The baroquely elaborate incense burners were almost certainly made by craft specialists. Aside from these urns, IIIb represents a simplification of IIIa ceramics. During the late phase, Teotihuacan influence disappears entirely from the ceramic complex.

Other crafts are not particularly well developed, especially when measured against the exquisite productions of the later Mixtecs. Some carved jades come from tombs but are relatively simple in technique and motif. The best were imports from the Maya highlands.

Social Structure and Religion. The sumptuous palaces and what are apparently dynastic records at Monte Alban imply a hereditary elite. Ancestor worship is indicated by the funeral complex and the nature of the tombs. The reinforcement of social status by religious sanction seems to have been in operation among the Zapotec as it was among the Classic Maya. Zapotec rulers are clearly shown as receiving divine aid in their activities, and their burial places under and near temples indicate that when they died they assumed their places in the supernatural order.

Very specific ideas as to the nature of Monte Alban III religion can be gained from a study of the incense burners and murals. This has been masterfully done by Caso and Bernal (1952). Some thirty-nine gods have been identified, most with calendar names derived from the sacred almanac. Eleven of these gods were female. Nearly all of them are grouped around several major themes which are strikingly similar to those defined for Teotihuacan. One theme is that of the rain god–lightning complex. The jaguar is associated with this group and is at least partly symbolic of Cocijo, the rain god. Another cluster of deities is organized around the maize plant. The maize god himself, Pitao Cozabi, took the form of a bat. A number of serpent gods include Quetzalcoatl in his guise as the wind god. Bird-masked gods, goddesses, the "flayed god" Xipe Totec, and an opossum deity make up the rest of the period III Zapotec pantheon. Nearly all of these deities were still worshipped at the time of Spanish contact, and therefore there is a certain amount of information that comes down to us from the early Christian missionaries. It is again clear that there is an extraordinarily strong continuity between the culture of Monte Alban III and that of the contact period Zapotecs. On the other hand, there are also enough distinctions to also make clear that period III culture may have been somewhat more elaborate than that of 1521.

Relations with Teotihuacan or the Ñuiñe? The fact that we have two powerful and culturally vigorous states coexisting in Mesoamerica is of interest. Even more interesting is the question of their relationships.

It used to be thought that the influences in ceramics of Monte Alban II and IIIa indicated a very powerful general influence on Monte Alban from Teotihuacan. There is still a body of opinion that feels this way. In reviewing the nature of the contacts, however, it is remarkable to us how few and ephemeral they are. Principally, outside influence assumes the aspects of Teotihuacan ceramic forms made from local wares, the import of thin orange pottery, and reminiscent stylistic links in architecture and mural art. These links and influences are quantitatively small. Furthermore, John Paddock has noted that the thin orange trade ware came from a zone intermediate to Teotihuacan and Monte Alban, a zone called the Ñuiñe, or "hot land" (1966b). Thin orange was exported from about A.D. 200 to 500. Paddock has defined a style named after the origin area, the Ñuiñe. It is intermediate in style of sculpture and in its glyph system to both Teotihuacan and Monte Alban. Paddock argues convincingly that the traits noted above were most likely not transmitted directly from Teotihuacan but through the intermediary culture of the Ñuiñe area. This zone was apparently a buffer area under the control of Cholula. However, this still leaves us with the problem of the "Oaxacan Barrio" at Teotihuacan. Apparently the Oaxacan group was of relatively high status, and they represented an essentially autonomous political and cultural zone. Cowgill comments that although Monte Alban may have been independent of Teotihuacan, the two states were certainly not on a par. Teotihuacan, on the other hand, certainly prevented Monte Alban from extending its area of influence much beyond the valley of Oaxaca (Cowgill, personal communication). Paddock's evidence and interpretation makes a strong case for the relationships between the two great centers being on a basis of uneasy alliance or detente rather than strictly dominance and subordination.

Period III is the apogee of Monte Alban and also of Zapotec culture. The great city existed and grew in the midst of ever-extending populations and subordinate centers. The nature of the probable relationships between the rulers and the mass of the population has been very well described by Paddock:

> Monte Alban was a place electric with the presence of the gods. . . . Every temple stood over half a dozen temples of centuries before. Buried in the great temples were ancient high priests of legendary powers, now semi-deified; centuries of accumulated mana in ceremonies, centuries of power and success lay deep inside that masonry. But with their own humble hands, or those of their remembered ancestors, the common people had made the buildings. No whip-cracking slave driver was needed. The satisfaction of helping to create something simultaneously imposing, reassuring, and beautiful is enough to mobilize endless amounts of human effort (Paddock 1966b: 153).

And yet at the end of period IIIb, about A.D. 700, Monte Alban was abandoned by rulers and ruled.

SUMMARY

Teotihuacan, Cholula, and Monte Alban were the urban centers of early highland civilizations. Later cities such as Xochicalco and Tula in the highlands and Tajin in the lowlands were small and provincial places at the time of Teotihuacan's greatness. Teotihuacan, in this view of things, was probably not the overwhelmingly dominant city it has sometimes been portrayed as. It exerted enormous influence, but there were strong regional cultures outside its homeland which resisted or assimilated its influence. Cholula was most susceptible to this influence, being physically close. Monte Alban was apparently safe behind its mountain walls from domination. The relationship between the Oaxacan city and Teotihuacan must have been an alliance at the most. The outposts of Teotihuacan, such as Kaminaljuyu, depended largely on the goodwill of the states in the Gulf region, the Maya lowlands, and the Oaxacan highlands. Perhaps this is the explanation for the foreigners' quarters at Teotihuacan. They were in the nature of embassies and trade missions rather than being delegations from subservient states. In short, impressive as it was, Teotihuacan had rival centers which were beyond its power to dominate. The time came when Teotihuacan, weakened by whatever factors, found itself threatened by states within its homeland. This situation set the stage for the sequence of collapses and transformations that attended the ends of these first civilizations.

CHAPTER **8**

TRANSFORMATIONS
COLLAPSE OF CLASSIC CULTURES
AND THE RISE AND FALL OF THE TOLTEC

And they left behind that which today is there . . . the so-called serpent column. . . . And the Tolteca mountain is to be seen; and the Tolteca pyramids, the mounds, and the surfacing of Tolteca [temples]. And Tolteca potsherds are there to be seen. And Tolteca bowls. . . . And many times Tolteca jewels. . . .
—Sahagun.

Then there was a change of the katun, then there was a change of rulers. . . . Whereupon a numerous army was seen, and they began to be killed. Then a thing of terror was constructed, a gallows for their death. Now began the archery of Ox-halal Chan. Then the rulers of the land were called. Their blood flowed, and it was taken by the archers.
—Chilam Balam of Chumayel, 1967.

CHICHEN ITZA, The Caracol. This round structure, convoluted inside like a snail shell and rising over 70 feet above the flat Yucatan landscape, may have been used as an observatory. From inside the viewing chamber, sightings could have been made of the moon and sun at such times as solstice and equinox.

APOCALYPTIC VISIONS ARE MORE CONVINC-ing and easier to sell than they used to be. Even in the recent past, however, when archaeologists talked of the great disasters of prehistory, the spectacular catastrophic aspects tended to be emphasized, and those features which illuminated the events as transformations were given short shrift. The remarkable successes of ancient cultures tended to be overshadowed by the sense of impermanence lent by foreknowledge of their doom. It is significant that many of the disasters of the past led also to cultural reformulations and ultimately to new heights of cultural and social success. On the other hand, there is no question but that some collapses led to a kind of devolution which resulted in drastic simplifications of cultural forms. Therefore, to truly understand what happened, it is necessary to take each of the events on its own terms.

Simply stated, Mesoamerican civilizations collapsed when they had overdeveloped in imbalanced and inefficient directions. This made them fatally vulnerable to various stresses exerted by natural or cultural factors, or combinations of the two. Prehistorians have been too prone to attribute these rapid cultural transformations to single causes. As an example, it has at one time or another been fashionable to attribute the fall of Maya civilization singly to soil exhaustion, moral collapse, climatic change, grass invasion of farmlands, military invasion, disease, and earthquakes. In recent years, however, archaeologists have fortunately been exposed to the revivifying effects of systems theory, feedback models, general model building, and multiple causation. At the same time, information about cultural and social collapses has become more complex and sophisticated. It has become increasingly clear that multiple factors were involved in all of these events. Therefore, the latest explanations tend to be complex and multifactored. With these points in mind, let us approach the subject of the fall and transformations of the earliest Mesoamerican civilizations.

THE COLLAPSE OF TEOTIHUACAN

The explanation that one advances for a collapse is obviously affected by the perspective one has of the nature of that society. An older view of Teotihuacan and its sociopolitical nature is that advanced by Wigberto Jimenez-Moreno (1966a). This distinguished scholar argued that Teotihuacan was less an empire as we historically knew this form and more a religious confederation like traditional Tibet. He drew an analogy between the chief priest of Teotihuacan (an incarnation of Tlaloc?) and the Tibetan Dalai Lama who was constantly being reincarnated. The dominance of Teotihuacan in this view, then, was due to its moral force, which dissipated with the erosion of the religious enthusiasm which had originally proselytized Mesoamerica. This erosion of moral primacy led to vulnerability. Jimenez believes that Teotihuacan was ultimately overthrown in its weakened condition by a group of militaristic barbarians from the north known as the Otomi. However, Jimenez clearly admits that such an invasion would only be symptomatic and that the ultimate causes of the fall remain unidentified.

Teotihuacan, through the aid of recent research, looks more and more like a gigantic city-state bound to other city-states by tribute and alliance systems. Its heartland was the central Mexican plateau and especially the Basin of Mexico. The social and political structure at the point of supreme crisis seems to have been a somewhat secularized form of divine kingship, bolstered by considerable military power. A noble administrative class controlled highly organized kinship groups living in city wards which were the base of society. These kinship units were probably occupationally specialized, with most of them including farmers. Teotihuacan's power was largely derived from this highly organized and large mass of about 200,000 people and from the control that they exerted over various economic resources outside of the heartland. In Sanders and Price's terms (1968), the Teotihuacanos had put together the Central Mexican Symbiotic Region within the context of a single political and social system. The gradual withdrawal of Teotihuacan influence from the outlying areas, beginning about A.D. 600, would indicate that the great city had more pressing problems nearer home than the maintenance of an imperial system.

Recent work at Xochicalco, Cholula, and around Monte Alban demonstrates that Teotihuacan was not alone in its sophistication during its terminal great period of A.D. 500 to 650. Work lately done at Tula, and reviewed below, indicates that an incipient Toltec state may have existed seventy-five miles to the northwest. Jaime Litvak-King suggests that Xochicalco to the southwest was powerful and hostile enough to block Teotihuacan influence and its access to the resources of the Balsas River basin (1970). As we have seen, Monte Alban certainly seems to have been quite independent of Teotihuacan although in contact with it. If we accept these tentative interpretations as correct, then a suggestion by Sanders makes considerable sense. Sanders argues that Teotihuacan was overcome by a coalition of city-states which included Tula to the northwest, Xochicalco to the southwest, Cholula to the southeast, and possibly, Tajin on the Gulf Coast. He says that this is demonstrated by the fact that all of these states expanded following the fall of Teotihuacan (Sanders, 1965). However, it should be noted that this expansion might well have happened even if the Otomi were the villains who brought down Teotihuacan. Much more convincing is the evidence that Cholula, Xochicalco, and perhaps Tula were powerful regional states, contemporary with the end times of Teotihuacan.

According to Sanders, Teotihuacan's world may not have ended with a crack but with a squeak. The postcollapse Oxtoticpac-Xometla phase materials of Teotihuacan are found within a much shrunken and perhaps devastated city. There is some question as to when the city was physically destroyed by fire. A layer of ash and burnt debris lies over the remains of many buildings in Teotihuacan. This fire may have been the coup de grace administered to a small and remnant Xometla city or a physical destruction attached to the earlier and major political and social disaster of about A.D. 650 (late Xolalpan and Metepec phases). In any case, much of the destruction has the characteristics of an "inside" job. Caches of sacred and valuable items were dug from their hiding places and tombs systematically looted. Both of these hidden depositories yielded luxury pottery, perhaps textiles, and certainly the carved jade jewels which were the highest form of Mesoamerican wealth. More important, and more basic, was the apparent loss of prime agricultural lands. Xometla complex ceramics appear first in the lower valley and are associated with Tula-related populations. This indicates to Sanders that Tula-Toltec peoples may have moved into the area as early as A.D. 700. This preemption of arable land would have undercut Teotihuacan's economic base and made it die on the vine (R. Millon, 1973).

Ultimate explanations of Teotihuacan's downfall still elude us. It may be that the very success of Teotihuacan in developing and spreading a new urban order of society and politics led to the rise of rivals. These rivals, newer and less tradition-bound, may have had the edge on the older, more ponderous city-state. Their motivation to overthrow the mother city may have been a drought, as suggested by Armillas. In any case, it seems clear that a few hundred dusty barbarians from the north would have had a very difficult time making a serious impression on a well-organized city of 200,000. It is also clear that internal weaknesses and rival military powers of equal sophistication were necessary to bring down Teotihuacan and ultimately loot it and destroy it by fire.

The collapse of the city and its political system had several important effects. One of the most important was the release of inhibitions on regional centers which had previously been suppressed by Teotihuacan. Jeffery Parsons' surveys in the Texcoco and Chalco sides of the basin show a dramatic resurgence of population after Teotihuacan's fall (1974). Texcoco was established shortly thereafter. Reciprocally, within the valley of Teotihuacan, population fell from 200,000 at A.D. 650 to about 30,000 at A.D. 900. During this time the large center of Azcapotzalco, on the western side of the lake, showed a growth spurt. The expansions of Tajin, Xochicalco, and Cholula have already been noted.

Another effect was that of a diaspora of Teotihuacan craftsmen over Mesoamerica. It probably is no coincidence that a second, late injection of Teotihuacan influence shows up in the Maya lowlands at this time. A small temple, possibly Tlaloc, is built near an important precinct in Tikal. Along with the craft technologies that no doubt were spread in this manner by this dispersal of Teotihuacanos, political expertise may also have been carried by former civil servants and nobility of Teotihuacan. In any case, the period immediately following Teotihuacan's fall is one of reverberating clashes and military competition among the expanding and elaborating city-states. It was also a time of opportunity for groups which had heretofore been on the fringes of the major cultures and major states. Such groups as the barbarians from the north penetrated southward into the basin and be-

yond. Jimenez's Otomi would have come in at this time. Within the jumbled and locked-up valleys of northern Oaxaca, Mixtec states were being formed and reformed. Certain groups located in the Gulf Coast zone were in contact with the Classic Maya and began to press them, perhaps as early as A.D. 750. There is no doubt but that the Classic Maya lasted longer than Teotihuacan. The wonder is not that they eventually fell, but that they lasted as long as they did in the unsettled conditions after Teotihuacan's fall.

THE CLASSIC MAYA COLLAPSE

If we accept the idea of a forced dispersal of Teotihuacanos throughout Mesoamerica in the late seventh century, then the first inklings of trouble for the Maya are in the appearance of the god Tlaloc on a late Classic polychrome plate and on a stela at Copan. Pushing this line of thinking too far implies that the fall of Maya civilization was a result of external causes. However, this is probably not the case at all. A recent conference on the Maya collapse has developed an explanation which combines external and internal stresses with known historical events (Culbert, 1973).

According to what we know now, Maya civilization began reaching a series of climaxes about A.D. 650. About A.D. 830, there is evidence of disintegration of the old patterns and by A.D. 900, all of the southern lowland centers have collapsed. An understanding of the Maya collapse must be based in large part on an understanding of the nature of Maya civilization. During the terminal Classic period, A.D. 750 to 900, cultural patterns of the lowlands can be briefly characterized as follows. Demographically, a high peak had been reached at least as early as A.D. 600 and perhaps earlier. This population density and size in turn led to intensive forms of agriculture and the establishment of permanent farmsteads in the countryside between the ceremonial centers. Hills were terraced, swamps drained and modified, water impoundments were made by the hundreds, and land became so scarce that walls of rock were built both as boundaries and simply as field clearance deposits. These masses of people were also highly organized for political purposes into city-state units, which were occasionally amalgamated into larger regional states, such as one dominated by Tikal in the eighth century (Marcus, 1973). Society was organized on an increasingly aristocratic principle by A.D. 650. Dynasties and royal lineages were at the top of the various Maya states and commanded most of the resources of Maya economic life. Most of the large architecture of the centers was for their use. A small group of craft specialists and civil servants supported the elite. The mass of the population was engaged in either part-time or full-time farming. Trade was well organized among and within the states. Military competition was present but was controlled by the fact that it was mainly an elite-class and prestige activity which did not disturb the economic basis of life. Thus Maya culture at the ninth century A.D. seems well ordered, adjusted, and definitely a success. Yet a devastating catastrophe brought it down.

CHARACTERISTICS OF THE COLLAPSE. A brief characterization of the collapse includes the following features.

1. A relatively short period of occurrence: 50 to 100 years.
2. The failure of elite-class culture involving the abandonment of palaces and temples, and the cessation of manufacture of stelae and luxury goods.
3. The rapid and relatively complete depopulation of the countryside and the civic centers.
4. The geographical focus of the first collapse was in the oldest and most developed zones, the southern lowlands and the intermediate (Rio Bec–Chenes) area. The Northern Plains and Puuc areas probably survived for a while longer.

In other words, the Maya collapse was a demographic, cultural, and social catastrophe in which elite and peasant went down together. Drawing on all available information about the ancient Maya and comparable situations, the 1970 Santa Fe Conference developed a comprehensive explanation of the collapse. This explanation depends on the relatively new picture of the Maya summarized above. That is, we must discard any notion of the Maya as the "noble savage" living in complete harmony with nature. Certainly, the Maya lived more in tune with nature than do modern industrial peoples, but probably not much more so than did our nineteenth-century pioneer ancestors. As we shall see, some dissonance in the Maya nature symphony was at least partly responsible for its failure.

Stresses. Maya society had a number of built-in stresses. Many of these stresses had to do with high populations in the central zones. Turner's studies (1974) indicate that from about A.D. 600 to 900 there were around 168 persons per square kilometer in the Rio Bec zone. The intensive agricultural constructions associated with this population density are also found farther south, within 30 kilometers of Tikal. They are also found to the east in the Belize Valley (Siemens and Puleston, n.d.), and there are indications elsewhere to the south that high populations were present. According to Saul's studies of Maya bones from the period, there was a heavy load of endemic disease carried in the population (1972). yellow fever, syphilis, and Chagas' disease. The latter is a chronic infection which leads to cardiac insufficiency in young adulthood.

Chronic malnutrition is also indicated by Saul's studies. Taken altogether, these factors meant a precarious health status even for the elite. Average life span in the southern lowlands was about 39 years. Infant mortality, however, was high. Perhaps as many as 78 percent of Mayan children born never reached the age of 20. Endemic disease can go epidemic with just a rise in malnutrition. In other words, the Maya populace carried within itself a biological time bomb which needed only a triggering event such as a crop failure to go off.

With population pressing the limits of subsistence, management of land and other resources was a problem, and one which would have fallen mainly on the elite. If food were to be imported or if marginal lands were to be brought into cultivation, by extensive drainage projects for instance, then the elite had to arrange for this. There were certain disadvantages to this arrangement. Aristocratic leadership is a poor way to approach matters that need rational decisions. One need only consider the disastrous manner in which the seventeenth-century European armies were mishandled by officers whose major qualifications were their lineages. There is a kind of built-in Peter Principle in such leadership. One is born to his level of incompetence. Maya aristocracy was no better equipped to handle the increasing problems of increasing populations than European aristocrats. There were no doubt capable and brilliant aristocrats, but there was apparently no way in which talent could quickly be taken to the top of society from its lower ranks.

There are also signs in the terminal Classic period of a widening social gulf between the elite and the commoners. At the same time, problems were increasing in frequency and severity. The elite class was increasing in size and making greater demands on the rest of Maya society for its support. This would create further tensions. Intensive agriculture led to increased crop yields, but also put Maya food production more and more at hostage to the vagaries of weather, crop disease, insects, birds, and other hazards. Marginal and complex cultivation systems require large investments of time and labor, and that things go right more often than not. A run of bad weather or a long-term shift in climate might trigger a food crisis. In addition, there are periodic locust outbreaks in the Maya lowlands. Recent work on tree rings and weather history indicates that a Mesoamerican-wide drought may have begun about A.D. 850.

These stresses were pan-Maya and occurred more or less in every part of the civilization. Competition over scarce resources among the political units of the Maya probably resulted from these stress situations. The large southern center of Seibal was apparently grabbed off by a northern Maya elite group about A.D. 830. Warfare increased markedly along the Usumacinta River during the ninth century A.D., according to hieroglyphic texts and carved pictures from that area. There are hints that the nature of Maya warfare may have changed during this last period. A lintel from Piedras Negras seems to show soldiers in standard uniform kneeling before an officer. In other words, organized violence may have come to involve many more people and much more effort and therefore became much more disruptive. Certainly, competition over scarce resources would lead to an increasingly unstable situation.

The above stresses can all be considered internal, but there were certainly external pressures on the Maya. Some were intangible and were in the form of new ideas about the nature of human society and new ideologies from Mexico. The northern elite which captured Seibal seems to have absorbed a number of these new ideas. For example, they included the depiction of Mexican Gulf Coast deities on their stelae as well as some Mexican-style hieroglyphs. Altar de Sacrificios seems to have been invaded by still another foreign group about A.D. 910. There is some dispute about this group and whether it represents a truly Mexican group from the Gulf Coast or a group of Chontal Maya who were non-Classic in their culture. (See J. E. S. Thompson, 1970, and R. E. W. Adams, 1973, for both sides of this question.)

There is a progressive pattern of abandonment and disaster on the western lowlands which is suggestive. Palenque, on the southwestern edges of the lowlands, is one of the first major centers to go under. It is abandoned about A.D. 810. The major Usumacinta centers of Piedras Negras and Yaxchilan (Bird-Jaguar's city) are next to go. They put up their last monuments about A.D. 825. Finally, it is Altar de Sacrificios' turn about A.D. 910. Clearly, there is a progressive disintegration from west to east, and it seems likely that it was caused by pressures from militaristic, non-Maya groups. These groups in turn were probably being jostled in the competitive situation set up after the fall of Teotihuacan and may have been pushed ahead of such groups as the Toltecs and their allies. In any case, it seems clear that these groups were opportunists. They came into an area already disorganized and disturbed and were not the triggering mechanism for the catastrophe, but a symptom.

At any one Maya center, the "mix" of circumstances was probably unique. At Piedras Negras, there is evidence that the elite may have been violently overthrown from within. Faces of rulers on that site's stelae are smashed and there is other evidence of violence. Invasion finished off Altar de Sacrificios. At other centers, such as Tikal, the elite were apparently simply abandoned to their fate. Without the supporting populations, remnants of the Maya upper classes lingered on after the catastrophe.

In short, ecological abuse, disease, mismanagement, overpopulation, militarism, famines, epidemics, and bad weather overtook the Maya in various combinations. But several questions remain. What led to the high level of population which was the root of much of the disaster?

The Maya had had a high chiefdom political system during the early Classic period. The Teotihuacan episode may have led them to try new political arrangements more along the lines of the urban states in the Valley of Mexico. Using general historical and anthropological experience, Demitri Shimkin observes that village-level societies approach population control very differently than do state-level societies (1973). Village societies are oriented plainly and simply toward survival. There are many pre-pill, traditional ways of population control. Female infanticide is a favorite and was practiced widely even in eighteenth-century England. Use of herbal abortion, late marriage, ritual asceticism, and other means keep population within bounds for a village.

A state-level society, on the other hand, is likely to encourage population growth for the benefit of the directing elite. The more manpower to manipulate, the better. In the case of the Maya, we have noted a certain megalomania in their huge, late Classic buildings. An unfinished Brobdingnagian temple at Tikal under construction at the collapse was larger than any previous Maya structure. Such efforts required immense manpower reserves and a simultaneous disregard for their welfare. The Maya may have tried to shift political gears into a more sophisticated and maladaptive state organization.

Another question to be considered is, Why didn't the Maya adjust to cope with the crises? The answer may be in the nature of religiously sanctioned aristocracies. Given a crop failure, a Maya leadership group might have attempted to propitiate the gods with more ritual and more monuments. This response would exacerbate the crisis by taking manpower out of food production. Inappropriate responses of this sort could easily have been made, given the ideology and world-view that the Maya seem to have held.

The rapid biological destruction of the Maya is an important aspect of the collapse. From a guessed-at high of 3 million, the population was reduced within 75 years to an estimated remnant of about 450,000. The disease load and the stress of malnutritional factors indicate that a steady diminishment of Maya population probably started about A.D. 830 and rapidly reached a point of no recovery. An average increase of 10 to 15 percent in the annual mortality rate will statistically reduce 3 million to 450,000 within 75 years. Obviously there was not anything like a steady decline, but the smoothed-out average over the period had to have been something of that order of decline. The disruptive nature of population declines can be easily understood if one considers the usual effects of epidemics. In such a catastrophic outbreak of disease, those first and most fatally affected are the young and the old. Even if the main working population survives relatively untouched, the social loss is only postponed. The old take with them much of the accumulated experience and knowledge needed to meet future crises. The young will not be there to mature and replace the adult working population, and a severe manpower shortage will result within fifteen to twenty years. Needless to say, much more work on population estimates and studies of the bones and the general health environment of the ancient Maya need to be done to produce a really convincing statement on this aspect of the collapse.

A last, although not by any means final, question is about the failure of recovery. This feature may involve climatic factors. If shifts of rainfall belts were responsible for triggering the collapse, then the persistence of the drought conditions until there were too few people left might be an answer. More likely,

the Maya were confronted with the situation of having overcultivated their soil. Temporary abandonment of fields would lead to their being rapidly overrun with thick, thorny second-growth jungle which is harder to clear than primary forest. Thus a diminished population may have been confronted with the problem of clearing heavily overgrown worn-out soil of which vast amounts were needed to sustain even small populations. Second-growth forest springs up overnight and is even today a major problem in maintaining archaeological sites for tourists. Another possible answer to the problem of no recovery is that the Maya may have been loathe to again attempt the sort of brilliant effort which had ultimately broken them. Just as they preferred to revert to swidden agriculture rather than maintain intensive techniques, they probably found it a relief to live on a village level instead of in their former splendid but stressful state of existence.

The above is the integrated model of the Maya collapse. It explains all of the features of the collapse and all of the data that we now have in hand, but it is not proven by any means and in some respects is more of a guide to future research than a firm explanation. If the model is more or less correct, however, it should be largely confirmed within the next ten years of research. Indeed, this seems to have already begun. The 1970 conference, which developed the model, could explain certain features of the archaeological record only by assuming much higher levels of ancient population than were otherwise plausible at the time. The 1973 Rio Bec work of Turner (1974) and Eaton (1976) turned up a vast amount of data which indicated that these higher levels of ancient population indeed had been present. This lends further credibility to the model.

DELAYED COLLAPSE IN THE NORTH. The vast and very densely distributed centers of the

Puuc area survived for a time. It may be that these Puuc cities turned into predators, exploiting their less fortunate southern neighbors. Even so, it seems that such large centers as Uxmal, Kabah, Sayil, and Labna lasted only a hundred years longer. The northern chronology is much more disputed than the southern, but it seems likely now that the Toltecs penetrated Yucatan by A.D. 1000 and perhaps as early as A.D. 950. There are clear indications that Uxmal was in contact with Mexican ideas much earlier. Certain motifs, such as eagles, show up on Puuc building facades late in the Classic period. We are now faced with at least three possible explanations of the Puuc collapse: they may have succumbed to the same combination of factors that brought down the other Maya centers; the Toltecs may have been responsible for their decline; or a combination of these factors may have been at work (Pollock, 1965; Potter, 1973).

Chichen Itza, in the north, is a center which was clearly culturally allied with the Puuc cities in architecture and perhaps politically. Puuc centers have been found in the far northeast of the peninsula. At Chichen, Puuc architecture is overlaid and succeeded by Toltec architecture. The data available now make it likely that the Toltecs and their allies penetrated Yucatan about A.D. 950 and established themselves at the former Maya center of Chichen Itza. Toltec raids and battles, combined with the internal weaknesses of Classic Maya culture and perhaps with changing environmental factors, brought about a swift collapse in the Puuc.

The aftermath of the collapse was devastating. Most of the Maya lowlands have not been repopulated until the last fifty years. Eleven hundred years of abandonment have rejuvenated the soils, the forests, and their resources. Modern man is now making inroads on these forests. Kekchi Maya Indians have been migrating into the lowlands from the Guatemalan highlands as pioneer farmers in recent years. The Mexican government has colonized the Yucatan and Campeche areas with dissatisfied agriculturists from overpopulated highland areas. The forests are being logged and cut down. Vast areas have been reduced to low scrub jungle, and large amounts of land are now being converted to intensive agriculture. One looks at the modern scene and wonders.

MONTE ALBAN AND ITS COLLAPSE

If we know relatively little about the Teotihuacan collapse and a lot about the Maya disaster, almost nothing is known about the demise of Monte Alban. It began to lose importance about the same time as Teotihuacan and was reduced to only a sacred cemetery by A.D. 700. We can only suggest a few factors that may have been involved.

Monte Alban seems to have been fully urban, but without the topographic and water advantages of Teotihuacan. Therefore, one handicap was its location, as defensible as it was. Certainly, the 30,000 or more persons living in and around Monte Alban presented problems of support. There were many other centers with dense populations in all parts of the central valley of Oaxaca. Although Monte Alban was the head of a unified Zapotec state and could call on a multitude of resources, it certainly was an inefficient user of those resources because of its location. About this same time, A.D. 700 to 900, the Mixtec states located to the north and northwest began making raids and encroachments and generally exerted pressures on the Zapotecs. The nearest that we can come to an explanation of the abandonment of Monte Alban at present is that it simply became too large a burden to support the spectacularly placed ceremonial center.

Unlike the other catastrophes at Teotihuacan and in the Maya area, the fall of Monte Alban allowed the Zapotec leadership to survive. This undoubtedly was because the leaders adjusted to new conditions. At the time of the Spanish conquest they had split their capital into two distinct functional centers. One, Mitla, was located in the Tlacolula branch of the valley, and was primarily a religious center. Zaachila, in the branch of the valley of the same name, was the political capital. We shall return to the Mixtecs and Zapotecs in Chapter 9, but at this point suffice it to say that they seem to have weathered the crises of Classic civilization much better than did the Teotihuacanos and the lowland Maya.

THE LEGENDARY
AND HISTORICAL TOLTEC

THE CHRONICLE OUTLINE. Itzcoatl, the fourth Aztec emperor (1427–1440), did no one any favors, least of all when he ordered a purge of the state archives and the burning of all of the most ancient history books. In that particular act of anti-intellectualism perished the documents which could have unscrambled the history of the Toltecs. As it is, Toltec traditions and history are a mass of contradictions, conflicting dates and king lists, overlapping and telescoped events, and plain fraudulent rewriting on the part of the Aztecs to support their claim that they were descended from the Toltecs. Fortunately, Wigberto Jimenez-Moreno and other distinguished scholars have been able to make sense out of the major features of Toltec history and to inject a good deal of convincing documentary detail into the archaeological record.

There are two major lists of Toltec rulers. One is derived from Ixtlilxochitl's *Historia Tolteca-Chichimeca,* which is an account of the origins and history of Texcoco written by an educated Texcocan after the Spanish conquest. The other source is the *Anales de Cuauhtitlan,* a generalized history of a Valley of Mexico city-state whose inhabitants claimed that their ancestors had come from Tula. The author is unknown. The two lists are different, but overlap. G. C. Vaillant and others (Sanders, 1965:182) believe that the two lists are of different dynasties, but that they overlap with Topiltzin-Quetzalcoatl who is named in both. The table following is the summary of the lists and correlation as presented in Sanders (1965: 182). Numbers in parentheses are the lengths of reign.

Of the nine dated reigns from the Ixtlilxochitl list, six are of fifty-two years each. This corresponds to a complete cycle of the sacred almanac and inspires less than complete confidence in the accuracy or even the truth of this list. The very irregularity of the reigns and their lesser lengths in the *Anales de Cuauhtitlan* list lend somewhat more credibility to it. Huemac, an extraordinarily important figure as the last Toltec ruler, had a reign of seventy-five years, somewhat suspect by its length. Notice also the conflict in the length of reign assigned to Topiltzin in each list: fifty years' difference.

By checking one document against another and the historical information against the archaeological material, Jimenez-Moreno has developed a framework for Toltec history and prehistory (1941, 1966b). What follows is largely his synthesis. There are other reconstructions, notably that of Paul Kirchhoff (1961).

During the period of Teotihuacan dominance, peoples of Mesoamerican culture from in or around the Valley of Mexico colonized to the north, penetrating even into Durango and Zacatecas. Jimenez-Moreno suggests that the great fortress of La Quemada may be the Tuitan of the chronicles. This expansion took place during the period of A.D. 100 to 300, and colonial centers thus established lasted until around A.D. 600, when many of them were abandoned. The expansion was in many

Correlation of Toltec Rulers

Ixtlilxochitl List		Anales de Cuauhtitlan		
Huemac—				
Migrant priest leader				
Chalchiuhtlanetzin	A.D. 510–562 (52)			
Ixtlilcuechahauac	562–614 (52)			
Huetzin	614–666 (52)			
Totepeuh	666–718 (52)			
Nacoxoc	718–770 (52)			
Mitl Tlacomihua	770–829 (59)	Mixcoamazatzin—		
Xihuiquenitzin (Queen)	829–833 (4)	Migrant military leader	(?– ?)	
		Huetzin	869– ?	(?)
		Totepeuh	? –887	(?)
Iztaccaltzin	833–885 (52)	Ihuitimal	887–923	(36)
		Topiltzin (Quetzalcoatl)	923–947	(24)
Topiltzin (Quetzalcoatl)	885–959 (74)	Matlacxochitl	947–983	(36)
		Nauhyotzin I	983–997	(14)
		Matlaccoatzin	997–1025	(28)
		Tlilcoatzin	1025–1046	(21)
		Huemac	1047–1122	(75)

Sanders, 1965. Adapted from G. C. Vaillant, *The Aztecs of Mexico*, rev. by S. B. Vaillant. Copyright © 1941, 1962, by Doubleday & Company, Inc. Reprinted by permission of Doubleday & Company, Inc.

cases connected with extensive mining activities.

The first major period of Toltec history began when, after the fall of Teotihuacan, people from the northern colonies flowed back south into the central mesa zone. Barbarian groups from the northern deserts also moved south. Jimenez-Moreno would see the Toltecs as a Mesoamerican group led to the Valley of Mexico by their legendary leader, Mixcoatl (Cloud Snake), who established their capital at Ixtapalapa.

The second and greatest period began when, pressured by the historic Olmecs who controlled Cholula, the Toltecs moved to Tula and placed their capital there. Tula was already a town, and had been established in the period of Teotihuacan dominance, possibly as a colony of the main city. Tula is the most frequently mentioned Tollan of the chronicles, although there are other places which were also called Tollan. The Toltec move was made under the leadership of Topiltzin, also known as Quetzalcoatl. He was also called Ce Acatl, or "1 Reed" after his birthday. This move was probably made about A.D. 960, according to the chronicles (Carrasco, 1971).

During this period, Topiltzin, the high priest of the Quetzalcoatl cult, became involved in a power struggle with another religious and political faction. In the chronicles, there is mentioned a series of events in which Quetzalcoatl and Tezcatlipoca are pitted against another. Quetzalcoatl is defeated by trickery and is exiled. Jimenez-Moreno argues persuasively that this is historical truth, and that Quetzalcoatl was actually the high priest of a religious cult and that his faction was defeated and sent into exile. According to the legends, Quetzalcoatl abhorred human and blood sacrifices and urged that flowers, fruits, and some animals be offered to the god he represented. The Toltec-Chichimec followers of Tezcatlipoca, the lord of darkness, wished to promote human sacrifice and all of the bloody terror that went with it. Sanders suggests that the faction of Tezcatlipoca represents newcomers from the barbarian north (1965). Walter Krickeberg has compared Topiltzin-Quetzalcoatl with the Egyptian heretic king, Aknahton (1956: 209). Like Aknahton, who also sought to reform a dominant state religion, Quetzalcoatl seems to have had a relatively ephemeral effect. In any case, Topiltzin-Quetzalcoatl, with his followers, the Nonoalco, moves off the Toltec stage at about A.D. 987 and reportedly goes to Cholula and then to Yucatan. The great period of Tula continues, and Aztec chronicles speak with unvarnished admiration of these Toltecs.

Sahagun's informants said that "The Toltecs were wise. Their works were all good, all perfect, all wonderful, all marvelous; their houses, tiled in mosaics, smoothed, very marvelous" (1961: Book 10, 165–166). The Toltecs were righteous, not deceivers. Food, especially maize, was produced in abundance. "They were tall; they were larger [than the people today]. Because they were tall, they ran much and so were named [the tireless runners]" (1961: Book 10, 169). They are also claimed to have spoken Nahuatl. Paul Kirchhoff (1961) has attempted to define the extent of the Toltec empire using chronicle material. It is clear that the main focus of the empire was north and west of the Valley of Mexico, with main centers at Tula, Tollanzinco, and Tenanco, with parts of the Bajio of Jalisco included. Thus most of the Valley of Mexico and all of the Valley of Puebla were excluded. The two central valleys were controlled by the historic Olmec Uixtotin who apparently ruled with an iron hand from Cholula. The chronicles speak of an "Olmec tyranny."

Tula dominated this large political unit and lasted until about 1156, when it was overthrown. The third and last period of Toltec history began when Huemac, the last Toltec king, transferred the capital south to Chapultepec, where he died in about 1162. This is the end of an independent Toltec dynasty, and by this time new waves of barbarians were again breaking through the northern frontiers and penetrating even into the Valley of Mexico. The breakup of the Toltec empire meant that again Mesoamerican refugee groups and newer, rawer barbarians began a series of intrusions against the cities of the central zone.

THE ARCHAEOLOGICAL RECORD AT TULA. *Environment, Chronology, and Physical Layout.* Very little direct information about the Toltecs pertains to the first period of their history. The second period is reasonably well documented by Acosta's work at the main acropolis of the civic center (1956, 1964, 1974). Thirteen seasons' work in the civic architecture has given us a basic sequence upon which to build (Acosta, 1940 et passim). This is presently being supplemented by Matos' excavations and area surveys (1974) and by Diehl's excavations in residential structures (1974).

Tula is located about sixty-five kilometers (forty miles) northwest of Teotihuacan and is laid out along one major ridge with groups on adjacent spurs. The Tula River, which is a tributary of the Rio Panuco, flows north past the ridge, giving easy access to water. It also forms a route of communication to the Veracruz coast. Generally rolling countryside broken by sharp ridges characterizes the zone inhabited by the Toltecs. To the east lies the ancient Teotlalpan or "Land of the Gods" and still further to the east and north was

Huastec country. The Teotlalpan contains the important Pachuca obsidian mines and was also an extremely important agricultural zone at one time. Both the Teotlalpan and the immediate Tula area were ravaged during the colonial period by the destructive effects of overgrazing by sheep, goats, and cattle, continuing a drastic decline in fertility begun in the fourteenth century through erosion and overcropping. What are now exhausted, eroded, deforested lands were fertile, well-watered, and extensive croplands and forests at the time of Toltec domination (S. F. Cook, 1949).

Recent work by Robert Cobean (1974) indicates that at least six ceramic phases are present. However, these fall into three major time periods. Two early ceramic groups correspond to a period of contemporaneity with Teotihuacan. Settlement for this period indicates no large communities. Communities consist of small Tlamimilolpa, Xolalpan, and Metepec phase housemound groups scattered over the countryside between Tepeji del Rio to the south and the present Endo Dam on the Tula River to the north. No significant architectural remains from this period have been found at Tula itself, although it is possible that Tula Chico dates to this period. Pottery shows certain Teotihuacan affinities, and a good deal of it belongs to a ceramic group called *Coyotlatelco*. A large, unexcavated ceremonial precinct at the center of the ridge (Tula Chico) may date to this period, but this is uncertain.

The second ceramic period correlates with the major architectural period of Tula and is characterized by orange-colored pottery decorated with multiple wavy red lines, the *Mazapan* style. Various monochromes and dichromes make up most of the complex, with the major forms comprising chili bowls, water jars, and simple bowls with nubbin legs. A few sherds of late Classic Maya polychrome have been found. By far the most important imported pottery, however, is *Plumbate*, from the Pacific Coast of Guatemala. Plumbate, a lead-colored and glazed pottery widely traded about A.D. 1000, is found in great quantity and variety. Nicoya Polychrome from Costa Rica and Fine Orange from the Maya Gulf Coast were also imported (Diehl, Lomas, and Wynn, 1974).

The third ceramic period dates from after the fall of Tula from its status as a great power center. Black-on-orange potteries similar or identical to those from the Basin of Mexico are found over the site. Aztec 2 material is clearly from a widespread occupation whereas Aztec 3 ceramics are limited and sporadic in distribution, indicating more of a squatter occupation. It may have been during the Aztec 3 period that the main occupation center shifted from the ridge to the modern location of Tula. The modern town probably rests on the site of the sixteenth-century community, which was sizeable. Chalco-Cholula polychromes show up in this later complex, as do quantities of black-on-white pottery from the Huastec area (Huastec 6 period).

At about the time that Tula became the capital of the Toltecs, the archaeological record shows a great expansion of the center. The second ceramic phase, the Mazapan, is associated with this expansion. Mazapan pottery shows some stylistic affinities to later "Aztec" black and orange wares. The city grew to cover about 11 square kilometers (about 4.2 square miles) by A.D. 1000. Some 1000 mounds are scattered over the zone. However, there must be at least as many more undetected low structures, many residential.

R. A. Diehl and his colleagues have excavated a group of thirteen houses located northeast of the Tula Chico zone in the center of the ridge. The houses are grouped into what Dan Healy argues are corporate residential groups built for extended families (1974). The houses are rectangular and arranged around central courtyards in each group with restricted access. The architecture is of small stones set in mud in the lower parts of the walls and adobe block above. Beam-and-mortar roofs finished off the rooms. Food processing areas have been located in many of the houses, and there are areas used for textile manufacture and maguey fiber processing. A kiln was found which seems to have been used for production of the subfloor drain tubes so common throughout Tula. Healy suggests that the houses are big enough and arranged in such a way as to imply that the groups accommodated about 4.5 persons per house. A temple-type structure has been found in one group. An altar was found within a courtyard with a burial inside it. The skull was missing, and whether this implies human sacrifice or ancestor worship is impossible to say at the moment. What is certain is that the housing groups at Tula are quite different from the great apartment compounds at Teotihuacan. The terrain at Tula would have made a gridded arrangement difficult, but more important is the fact that, as Rene Millon points out, there was apparently no social necessity either at Tula or later for the apartment compound developed at Teotihuacan (1973). A spectacular cache of Plumbate and Nicoya Polychrome vessels was found in one house.

Near these residential structures is a civic center group, Tula Chico or El Corral. Acosta's excavations revealed a two-stage temple structure, part of which was round. This suggests that the temple may have been dedicated to Quetzalcoatl in his guise as Ehecatl the wind god. An attached altar carried a frieze that shows skulls, crossed bones, and Toltec warriors. Associated with the temple was a platform which contained the only Tula artifact that lives up to the reputation of the Toltecs for fine craftsmanship. The piece is a Plumbate jar covered with mother-of-pearl carved to represent feathers. The motif is that of a coyote with the mouth open

to reveal a man. Apparently it represents a Toltec warrior with an animal headdress. Acosta argues that this is an actual representation of Quetzalcoatl. The coyote is known to have been Quetzalcoatl's nahual or animal soul and therefore the symbolism would be appropriate.

The main group of late civic architecture is elevated, acropolis-like, on the southern end of the ridge with artificially terraced slopes. It contains about 35 percent of the 1000 mounds at Tula. Diehl reports terrace walls 15 to 18 meters (50 to 60 feet) high on the north and west sides. Other, smaller civic plazas, such as Tula Chico, are known within the city, but the main temples, those of the sun (or White Tezcatlipoca of the East) and Quetzalcoatl, are in the acropolis group. The group is oriented 15½ degrees east of north, like Teotihuacan.

The focus of the southern, late, and most important civic group is structure B, or the Temple of Quetzalcoatl in his form as the morning star (Tlahuizcalpantecuhtli). Structure B faces south onto the square and is a squat mass of masonry built with talud-tablero features. It had been enlarged and renovated at least six times. In its latest phase, the whole platform was encased in sculptured panels depicting prowling, slavering jaguars and pumas, heart-devouring eagles and buzzards, and Quetzalcoatl himself. Toltec warriors and more abstract designs are also shown. The motifs of these panels were emphasized with bright greens, reds, blues, and white. Most of the paneling has been destroyed or removed since the city fell, and only a few zones remain intact.

The superstructure was entirely missing when excavated, but judging by Toltec architecture in Yucatan (Chichen Itza), there was probably a large, two-roomed temple on top of the platform. The temple was approached by a broad staircase, at the top of which were banners held by human and jaguar figures of stone. A stone *Chacmul,* or reclining human figure, sat in front of the doorway. The main door was framed by the columns formed from stiffened serpent bodies, the heads of which rested on the floor. Inside, gigantic human figures in the form of caryatid columns held up the flat roof in the front room, while square, carved columns supported it in the rear chamber. There was probably a large flat stone table altar supported by small columns carved in the shape of men who raise their hands to carry the table. These are the famous Atlantean figures named from their posture of burden-bearing. Alternating wooden columns and adobe brick sections made up the walls if the temple followed the general pattern of construction at Tula. Elsewhere in Tula walls were plastered and painted with bright murals, and it is likely that the major temple was decorated similarly. Perhaps structure B shows us in somewhat diminished form what the greater temples at Teotihuacan looked like.

Altogether, the effect of the theoretical reconstruction of the Temple of Quetzalcoatl is bizarre, magnificent, and powerful to our minds. It must have been at least as impressive to the Toltecs and their contemporaries, who also vested the building with the supernatural power of an important god.

The major temple on the square, structure C, faces west and is possibly a temple to the Sun or the White Tezcatlipoca of the East. In later times, the White Tezcatlipoca was sometimes a manifestation of Quetzalcoatl. So much of structure C was destroyed at the time of the city's downfall that nothing is left but the immense platform, which was apparently undecorated. A feature reminiscent of Teotihuacan is the large subsidiary platform attached to the center line front of the main platform. Atlantean figures were found in the debris of this building.

An elaborate wall called the *Coatepantli* (serpent wall) is curiously located to the rear (north) of the Temple of Quetzalcoatl. A row of lively serpents is shown apparently devouring skeletal figures and is set into a panel between frames of frets. The frets are the same as those that appear as part of the name glyph for Tula in the Mixtec codices (*Codex Bodley* 9–11, Caso 1960: 38). The wall is capped with the capital G's or shell cross-sections which are also found on the edges of the palace roofs at Tula. The serpent wall closed off the northern zone from access to the sacred precinct. A similar wall performed the same function in Aztec Tenochtitlan.

Jammed among and against the temples were colonnades and palaces. The large main square was marked off on two sides by such colonnades. Structure 3 is west of temple B and is largely formed by a row of three patios within which are altars, daises, and benches all placed under arcades. Built-in plastered firepits and huge pottery incense burners were found in the palace. Enormous masses of burned debris were found on the patio floors giving structure 3 the name of the Burnt Palace. However, it is noteworthy that, other than deliberate burials, no skeletal remains were found within the structure. Everyone evidently escaped when the palace burned down, or had abandoned it long since.

The interior of patio 1 was sumptuously decorated around the edge of the courtyard's roof with a carved stone frieze made up of slabs similar to those found on nearby structure B. Reclining human figures, sacred green stone symbols (*Chalchihuites*), capital G forms, and a depiction of a blood and heart receptacle make up the major motifs. Within an altar in patio 1 was a closed stone box which contained, among other things, a carved jade plaque, one of the few precious items recovered from the site.

Scratched into the plaster of the floor of patio 3 of the Burnt Palace are what were probably boards for the playing of the popular Mesoamerican game, *patolli*. The boards vary somewhat among themselves, but generally look like a "Monopoly" board with a cross of squares in the center. The game was played by advancing counters around the board using bone dice. One can imagine that the end patio may have been the zone where the palace guard or other permanent functionaries were stationed and that the patolli games were a means of whiling away the endless hours. The later Aztecs gambled on the outcome.

An altar or dance platform was placed in the middle of the main plaza. A cache found in its masonry consisted of thirty-three ceramic vessels, many of which were precisely like early (Aztec 2) black-on-orange pottery from Culhuacan in the Valley of Mexico. It is interesting to note that when Tula was abandoned, part of its population settled in Culhuacan. Three hollow female figurines were also found in the platform cache, and these also are greatly similar to contemporary figurines from the Valley of Mexico.

A very large ball court is located on the west side of the main square and is similar in its closed plan to one at Xochicalco. It is about 110 meters (361 feet) in overall length. Another ball court lies north of the Coatepantli. At least three more are known from elsewhere in the site, making a total of five at Tula.

Acosta comments that the site of Tula and its principal building show meticulous and excellent planning, but that execution of those plans was careless and characterized by poor workmanship. Many or most of the features of the civic architecture and the building groups were present at Teotihuacan, but the Toltecs added their own contribution in their use and conceptualization of those elements. One innovation which took hold and lasted until the Conquest was the use of masses of columns around open courtyards. These columns, usually carved, supported roofs and sheltered stone benches. A comparison of the great market of Aztec Tenochtitlan with the central square of Tula shows great similarities in this regard. The emphasis on the ball game and the ball court as a formal structure begins in this period, and the lavish use of architectonic sculpture in place of or supplementing mural art was another change in emphasis from Teotihuacan times.

Sculpture and Other Art. Most of Tula Toltec art survives in the form of sculpture. Apparently, however, all of the sculpture was colored, and unsculpted surfaces were painted. Most of the fragments of painted walls are geometric in motif. Bands of red, blue, yellow, and black decorated the walls of a passage between temple B and the Burnt Palace. The only life scene recovered from Tula so far is that of a sketchily drawn deer hunt, but this is from a much earlier structure which may date back to Teotihuacan times.

A hallmark of the Toltec horizon in much of Mesoamerica is the *Chac mul* sculpture. These stiff and ungainly reclining human figures were probably always placed in front of temple doorways to receive preliminary offerings. Free-standing sculpture includes four stelae, long since removed from the site. These may have depicted rulers of Tula. Certainly to be included in the inventory is a petroglyph on a rock of a nearby mountain which shows Quetzalcoatl and which includes his calendrical name, Ce Acatl. Production of a great mass of small sculpture which supplemented the architectonic sculpture is highly characteristic of the Tula Toltec and later Basin of Mexico cultures.

However, most of the sculpture was architectonic and consists of stone slabs designed to be fitted into continuous bands or friezes. Columnar sculptures make up the other major groups. Many of the motifs have already been noted, but an important feature not yet mentioned is that of hieroglyphic writing. Several panels include bar and dot and day sign notations, "2 serpent eye," for example. The distinctive features of Tula writing seem to be closely related to the system found at Xochicalco, according to Acosta (1964b). The glyph for *cipactli* (alligator) is often found at the top of columns.

One of the most interesting sculptural scenes at Tula is that found on a dais in the antechamber of a palace between temples B and C. Quetzalcoatl himself is depicted against the background of a feathered serpent. He faces a file of Toltec warriors, and a line of feathered serpents undulates above the whole scene. This scene and sculpture and dais are practically duplicated at Toltec Chichen (Temple of the Warriors) in Yucatan.

TRADE, METALLURGY, AND NORTHERN EXPANSION. Tula was said by Sahagun's informants to have been a place where a number of different peoples lived who spoke different languages. Certainly it was large enough to have been an ethnically diverse city. Comparing its size with those of better known Mesoamerican cities, we find that it should have contained 40,000 to 50,000 people at its height. As in Teotihuacan, there were craft specialists, many of them obsidian workers. Also as in Teotihuacan, there were ties with the rest of Mesoamerica through long-distance trade. Diehl's recent work detected a cache of ceramic vessels located in an apartment compound. The pottery was Plumbate and Nicoya Polychrome, both made outside Tula. Several vessels are Plumbate. Plumbate was made in the Izapa and Tajumulco areas of southern Guatemala, which also produced cacao. The rest of the pottery is Nicoya Polychrome from the Pacific coast of Nicaragua and Costa Rica.

These long-distance trade connections are of more than ordinary interest because they may indicate the means by which metallurgy was introduced into Mesoamerica. Metalworking in western Mexico appears at about A.D. 800 at the earliest, but is much older in South

America and dates back to at least 800 B.C. in the Andean area. It has long been thought that metallurgy was introduced to Mesoamerica from South America. There was also a long-standing tradition of metalworking in the intermediate zones of Central America, Colombia, and Ecuador. Although it is not by any means clear at this time, it may be that fairly sophisticated metallurgical techniques were learned from Central Americans and transmitted by Mesoamerican traders. It may also be that long-distance voyages from South America introduced the craft through West Mexico.

The Toltec era was one in which metallurgy spread over Mesoamerica. Yet it is also frustratingly true that not a single shred of metal has been reported from Tula. Superior examples of Toltec-style metalworking are known from Yucatan, but these probably were produced by Maya craftsmen. However, these Maya had to have learned the technique from the Mexicans inasmuch as metalworking is not present in Classic Maya culture. Thus, we can only make the most circumstantial surmises at the present. These are that metallurgy was probably introduced into Mesoamerica via the Pacific Coast, and ultimately from South America through Central America. The Tula Toltecs probably had a great deal to do with the development and spread of the craft throughout Mesoamerica, via their long-distance trading activities.

A line of outpost settlements of Mesoamericans was established through expansion into the frontier areas of Durango and Zacatecas during Teotihuacan times (J. C. Kelley, 1971: 768). These peripheral and frontier Mesoamerican cultures are grouped together generally as the *Chalchihuites* culture. The earliest penetrations were made about A.D. 100. This was during a period of greater rainfall, which was encouraging to agriculturalist expansion. There is evidence of conflict between these cultivators and the more nomadic groups of the zone, and many of the Mesoamerican sites are fortifications protecting agricultural communities or mining areas. Hematite, weathered chert, flint, and possibly jadeite and turquoise were the principal objects of mining operations. Vast areas of churned-up gravels as well as the ancient mines themselves indicate that it was an expansive and considerable operation (Weigand, 1968). Withdrawal of Mesoamericans began about A.D. 600, and by A.D. 850 the Suchil and Colorado drainage areas of the Chalchihuites area had reverted to their original inhabitants, who had absorbed much Mesoamerican culture themselves.

The Toltecs expanded into the northern frontier zone or Gran Chichimeca about A.D. 900, this time to both the coastal and eastern sides of the western Sierra Madre, apparently making contact with the southwestern cultures of what is now the United States and transmitting metal objects, but not the craft (Meighan, 1974). Charles DiPeso thinks that about A.D. 1050 Casas Grandes was converted from a small village in Chihuahua to a major Mesoamerican trading center (DiPeso, 1968, 1974: Vol. 2, 290–309). From this and other centers such as Zape, pochteca made trips into the Hohokam and Anasazi areas of Arizona and New Mexico trading copper bells and other items for turquoise, slaves, peyote, salt, and other commodities that the southwesterners provided. Cultural influences followed commerce, and it is believed that many traits in ethnographic southwestern religions derive from Mesoamerican influence. Murals from Awatowi in the Hopi area seem to show southwestern versions of Tlaloc. Quetzalcoatl shows up in several areas. Chaco Canyon in far-off northwest New Mexico shows impressive architectural parallels with Toltec building.

A more detailed examination of the debated and complex cultural history of western and northern Mexico and their role in Mesoameri-can relationships with the United States southwest is outside the scope of this book. Suffice it to say that several northern Mexican trading centers were built after A.D. 1050. "Each appears to have [had] its own internal history and each collapsed due to a combination of local factors and pressures, triggered in part by unrest within the Mesoamerican governments, their main consumers" (DiPeso, 1968: 54). These centers, as will be seen, outlasted the Toltecs, and in some cases, the Mexican trading connections on which their existence largely depended.

TOLTEC INTRUSION TO YUCATAN: THE BACKGROUND. Within this segment of Maya prehistory, we again enter an era on which ethnohistory and archaeology bear and within which they sometimes conflict. Fortunately, several excellent minds have considered the problems and produced syntheses that are more or less convincing in their major features (Ball, 1974; R. Roys, 1965a, 1972; J. E. S. Thompson, 1966; Tozzer, 1957). The scheme followed below owes much to all, but especially to J. W. Ball's most recent attempt to reconcile all pertinent data (1974).

With the simultaneous collapse of Maya civilization in the intermediate and central lowlands, there were intrusions of northern Maya elite to such places as Seibal on the Pasion River. These northerners already had absorbed significant influence from Mexican highland cultures. As early as the eighth and ninth centuries, new motifs in sculptures at centers like Kabah show the influence of Mexican religious concepts. At Dzibilchaltun a stone platform for use as a skull rack for sacrificial victims (*tzompantli*) dates to this period. Giant, and not so large, phallic stones appear at Uxmal. Censers with Tlaloc faces applied to them show up in a raingod shrine deep within a cave near Chichen Itza (Balankanche) dated by C-14 as having been placed there about A.D. 860 (Andrews, 1970).

One major question has always been whether or not the northern Maya centers went under with those of the Peten or survived for a longer time. E. W. Andrews has argued forcefully that the Rio Bec, Chenes, and Puuc areas all survived the southern centers for a number of centuries (1965). He seems to have been partially right. Based on recent work, the Rio Bec sites, including the Becan fortress, seem to have weakened as major military-political centers by around A.D. 750. As was the case farther south, diminishing populations held on in the hinterlands and even in the centers for as much as another century, but the intricate social and political arrangements deteriorated and finally disappeared. The Chenes area also seems to have suffered the same collapse. The Puuc area, however, is the exception to Andrews' argument.

At the archetypal Puuc center of Uxmal, there is a Chenes-style building which was later buried under the gigantic platform of the Governor's Palace. The latter is pure Puuc in style. This and similar physical evidence at Uxmal indicate that Puuc outlasted Chenes and Rio Bec architectural styles and therefore also survived the general disaster to the south. It also seems likely that Puuc was a style which spread over the entire Northern Plains area and was not just confined to the hill zone from which it takes its name. Indeed, the center of Chichen Itza has a Puuc phase of building. Yaxuna, to the east of Chichen, also is known to have Puuc building, and recently discovered sites in that same area also have Puuc features.

J. W. Ball ties these events of the late eighth and early ninth centuries to the first coming of the Itza, a ruling group of Mexican derivation which settled at Chichen Itza. Various chronicles give dates around A.D. 800 for this event. It is probably through these ruling families that Mexican ideas were introduced to Yucatan, and the subsequent predatory raids and intrusions to the south (Seibal) took place. Yucatan is an unprepossessing place for exploitation, being mainly barren rock, and we are puzzled at first as to what would motivate such a political and military intrusion to the area. Ceramic linkages and hints from the chronicles seems to show that the Itza and their colleagues were probably Chontal from the lowland Tabasco area at the bottom of the Gulf Coast. In such a location, they traditionally were probably middlemen in trade relationships between the Maya area and Mexico and would be familiar with the resources of the Peninsula. The largest salt fields in Mesoamerica are and were located at the northwestern corner of Yucatan and as such were a prize worth risks. Another principal resource of Yucatan for an exploitative group might have been its dense population. Even Yucatan can be a very comfortable place with enough people to act as servants. Ball suggests that the "abandonment" of Chichen mentioned in the chronicles is really the departure of *some* of the Itza for Seibal, where they established themselves about A.D. 830. Ball identifies the archaeological Seibal with one of the historical Chakanputuns mentioned in the Maya chronicles.

It will be recalled that about A.D. 910, there is an invasion of Altar de Sacrificios downriver from Seibal. This invasion is probably by another group of Chontal from the Tabasco region. Seibal and Altar are both subsequently abandoned by A.D. 950. These events would correlate with the attack of one Itza group on another mentioned by the chronicles. If one accepts Ball's identification of Chakanputun as the archaeological Seibal, then its abandonment is mentioned in the chronicles.

All of the above goes over events already discussed, but with the addition that historical detail is added to the historical process outlined before. It is important because it leads to an explanation of one of the most interesting episodes in Mesoamerican prehistory, the establishment of a Toltec center in northern Yucatan.

Relationships between the native Maya and the early intrusive Chontal-Itza seem to have been relatively harmonious. Ball notes that an early Mexican-influenced building at Chichen has a wall relief showing what is apparently a peaceable meeting between Maya and probably Chontal leaders (Tozzer, 1957: 33). These amicable relationships did not last.

TOLTEC INTRUSION TO YUCATAN: THE EVENT. According to the above reconstruction then, the superb Puuc variant of Maya Classic culture was still thriving in the Northern Plains at about A.D. 987 when the chronicles mention the second coming of the Itza and the arrival of Kukulkan, the Maya name for Quetzalcoatl. It was as a result of this intrusion and take-over that the great and magnificent Toltec center at Chichen Itza was established. A great deal of excavation of the Toltec period ruins at Chichen has been done, and it is to that archaeological evidence that we now turn.

Chronology and Trends. As usual in the Maya area the chronology is in part based on a ceramic sequence and on Maya dates, thirty-four of them at Chichen. No reliable carbon 14 dates are available, although the above-mentioned Tlaloc censers were found in a nearby cave at Balankanche and contained twigs which have been processed. All evidence gives Chichen's sequence three major periods.

Period A lasts from about A.D. 692 to 968 with nearly all of the Maya dates falling into the short span from A.D. 869 to 889. This is the already-discussed period of Puuc-related late Classic culture. Toward its end the period brought an infiltration of influence from Mexican sources. Chichen at this time con-sisted of widely scattered groups of civic architecture which included the "Old Chichen" zone with the famous round Observatory and the Monjas palace structure with its annexes. These groups are connected by sacbes of which nine are known. Other groups include the Temple of the Phalli, and a number of other small but elegant Puuc-style residential structures. According to Roys, Chichen's name at this time may have been Uucil Abnal (Seven Bushy Places).

Period B is a transitional Maya-Toltec style represented by the inner Temple of Kukulkan and the Temple of the Chac-mul under the Warriors' Pyramid. It would overlap in time between periods A and C and possibly represents 100 years.

Period C is about 200 years long and lasts from about A.D. 987 to 1187. It is the period of the Toltec-Maya and the phase of construction of the most magnificent of Chichen's buildings. Tohil Plumbate and Silho Fine Orange potteries are introduced at this time through trade.

Location. A functional description of the Toltec center must take account of the natural water sources which attracted settlement in the first place. There are many cenote-wells in the Chichen vicinity, most of which are now choked with naturally fallen debris. In ancient times, however, many of these may have been open and furnished water. If so, then Chichen was indeed a favored spot with much more of a secure water supply than most of the Northern Plains, and might be looked on as specially favored by the rain god. Two large cenotes are the foci for the major architecture. One cenote (the *xtoloc* or iguana) was the main water source. The other, larger, and almost sheer-sided sinkhole was apparently used exclusively as the focus of a rain-god cult. According to Bishop Landa, the first Spanish Bishop of Yucatan, "Into this well they have had, and then had, the custom of throwing men alive as a sacrifice to the gods, in times of drought, and they believed that they did not die though they never saw them again. They also threw into it a great many other things, like precious stones and things which they prized" (1941: 179–181). Indeed, dredging the well has produced an immense amount of valuable material as well as human bones. Legend has embroidered fact by stating that the sacrificial victims were beautiful young virgins. A. E. Hooton, who analyzed the bones, cogently observed that it was difficult to tell from them if their owner had been either beautiful or virgin. What he did find, however, was that most of the victims were children (21) or adolescents, with a sprinkling of adults (maybe 15) (Hooton, 1940).

Much of the valuable material, especially dozens of extraordinary pieces of carved jade, found in the well is late Classic in date (Proskouriakoff, 1974). A considerable amount had been imported from other parts of the Maya area or from outside of it, including Cocle goldwork from Panama (Lothrop, 1952). It therefore seems likely that the Toltec simply took over an established center of a religious pilgrimage which drew people from much of eastern Mesoamerica. This would partially explain the location chosen by the Toltecs for their colonial capital. Finally, Chichen is geographically located in the center of the northern plains and is well situated for military and political control of that area.

Architecture.   The major Maya-Toltec buildings are built on a vast platform in the middle of which sits the most important temple, that of Kukulkan-Quetzalcoatl. This structure is more or less in line with a sacbe leading out of the civic precinct and north some 300 meters (984 feet) to the sacred well. Another sacbe leads south to another large plaza with a large temple in its center, the so-called High Priest's Grave. "Dance platforms" and

a tzompantli are scattered around the Kukulkan plaza. The northwest corner of the precinct is occupied by a monumental ball court, the largest in Mesoamerica. It measures about 150 meters (492 feet) long and is magnificently adorned by small temples and ornamented by sculpture. The eastern side of the Kukulkan plaza is occupied by a row of three temples, one of which, the Temple of the Warriors, is much larger than the others. A very large colonnade closes off the rest of the eastern plaza. Behind this colonnade is the Group of the Thousand Columns, a subsidiary plaza surrounded by large structures built nearly at ground level somewhat like the palaces at Tula. Another large ball court lies to the east of this group with a jumble of structures around it which includes a sweatbath.

If Tula suffered from shoddy workmanship, such is not the case at Chichen. This colonial capital of the Toltecs is magnificent in both conception and realization. No doubt the availability of Maya masons who were used to producing the superbly cut and fitted stone of Puuc structures made a difference. Stonework is excellent. Toltec Chichen is clearly central Mexican in plan and many features. However, Maya building practices of long standing are also apparent. In short, the architecture is a blend of two strong and distinctive cultural traditions.

The introduction and use of multiple columns for roof support allowed vastly greater spaces to be enclosed within buildings. The Maya arch was combined with the use of columns. Although the Temple of Kukulkan (the Castillo) is somewhat Maya in plan, with an inner sanctuary, most other buildings consist either of one large room or of two rooms, one behind the other. As at Tula, long and spacious roofed colonnades furnished with benches afforded vast cool areas for large numbers of people. The great numbers of columns were decorated with stiff Toltec warriors and priests on all four sides, invariably framed between the sun god above and Quetzalcoatl below. Also as at Tula, one major temple, the Temple of the Warriors, was decorated with bas reliefs set in panels around the terraces of its platform. These panels depict the heart-devouring eagles and jaguars also to be found on the "dance platforms." Stiffened, feathered serpents frame the temple doorways, and Chac-mul figures rest outside the doors, waiting for offerings. Banner holders carved in human form have been found. Atlantean figures hold up large table altars in several temples. By analogy with later and similar central Mexican buildings, there are buildings in the eastern group suitable for use as palaces, barracks, and a marketplace.

The so-called High Priest's Grave is a somewhat smaller version of the Temple of Kukulkan. Feathered-serpent doorway columns and all of the other Maya-Toltec features are to be found on it. E. H. Thompson lifted the stone floor and found a stone shaft penetrating the platform. Several burials were on several levels within the shaft. Ultimately Thompson found that he was on bedrock. A stone cover concealed the entrance to a natural cavern which had been used for the burial of an important person. Years later, J. E. S. Thompson analyzed the burial furnishings and concluded that the person buried there was probably a member of the ruling class at the time of Toltec or Itza domination (E. H. Thompson, 1938). Functionally, then, at least one of the major temples at Chichen was a funerary temple.

Architectonic sculpture is a strong feature. Bas relief covers large areas in several monumental structures. In the great ball court, scenes of sacrifice accompany the ball game scenes, indicating that it did not pay to have a losing team. Bas relief human skulls decorate the platform which supported a wooden framework with real skulls. Scenes of conquest decorate the walls of some buildings, the Temple of the Tigers, for example. The Toltecs memorialized their conquests in some superb mural art found in the Temple of the Warriors and other places. An infinity of detail makes it clear that Tula and central Mexico are the sources of derivation of the new ideas. Roof frets occur in the form of the Toltec glyph for war, for example. On the other hand, the Maya rain god, Chac, decorates panels and corners of the Temple of the Warriors. Toltec Chichen was truly the seat of a hybrid culture.

Art. Sculpture, murals, and small portable objects make up most of known Toltec-Maya art. As seen above, the style is definitely a synthesis of two distinctive traditions. The subject matter is also definitely weighted toward the martial and toward ritual violence. The hundreds of columns in the buildings and colonnades are carved with hundreds of warriors and priests, each distinctive and unique. Could these be portraits of the individual invaders? There are over 900 known human figures carved on the walls and columns. Gods depicted or impersonated emphasize Quetzalcoatl-Kukulkan, with his old antagonist, Tezcatlipoca, and Tlachitonatiuh, the sun god. Scenes of battle are found in murals, in sculpture, and on the repousée decorated gold disks from the well of sacrifice. Toltec and Maya warriors are quite distinctive with the Maya usually wearing individualized feathered headdresses and carrying flexible shields and feathered back frames. The basic Toltec hat is a cylinder set with feathers and sometimes with ear flaps. Round shields, loincloths, and sandals rounded out the basic Toltec uniform. Battle scenes show raids on seacoast villages, combat within villages, and fighting on lakes and along the shoreline. The gold disks are the most explicit in showing the Toltecs as conquerors throwing spears at fleeing Maya, interrogating prisoners, sacrificing a human, pursuing in canoes Maya who are escaping on rafts, and other thematic variants. Sky deities, including the feathered serpent, attend the battle scenes. Disks L and M from the Cenote of Sacrifice show Tula-Toltec eagles attacking Mayas. A carved and painted dais shows lines of warriors who face each other in the center. It is noteworthy that each of these figures is backed with a feathered serpent. At Tula the strikingly similar dais has only one person with a feathered serpent behind him, leading to his identification as Quetzalcoatl. At Chichen, all are protected by the feathered serpent.

Much of the mural art is lively, informative, and interesting. Fragments from the excavation of the Temple of the Warriors show us a jaguar crouched on a masonry pyramid, cactus and other plants in bloom, gorgeously clad elite-class people, tantalizing scenes of combat, a humble man offering burning incense in a bowl at the foot of a pyramid, birds and bees, and much else. A magnificent scene reconstructed by Ann Morris shows a peaceful seacoast village with people at their daily tasks. Porters carry burdens, a woman attends a boiling pot, three canoes loaded with warriors cruise just offshore through waters filled with fish, stingrays, snails, and other shellfish. The local elite discuss matters in a building over which the feathered serpent writhes (A. A. Morris, 1931). Grimmer subjects are depicted in the north temple of the great ball court. In scenes fraught with symbolism, prisoners are interrogated, houses and a temple burn, a sleeping person's throat is cut, and two Toltecs perform an act of phallic worship. Some small-scale Faberge-quality turquoise mosaics tend to confirm the Toltecs' legendary reputation as craftsmen. These mosaics depict the feathered serpent and were used as dedication offerings in temples.

Social and Political Implications. The chronicles say that the Itza and their Toltec colleagues ruled at Chichen for about 200 years. Ralph Roys believes that they dominated nearly all of the peninsula. At some point during this period, probably fairly early, the last variant of Classic Maya culture, the Puuc, is extinguished. Very little is known of this delayed part of the Maya collapse, but it may have been that the new order at Chichen with its superior military organization was too much competition. It is a fact that no Plumbate or Silho Fine Orange potteries, hallmarks of the Toltec period, have been found at Puuc sites, and therefore, they must have been off the trade routes and then soon extinguished. At present, we know practically nothing else about the Puuc collapse, although it would not be surprising if its general nature were the same interrelated downward spiral of decreasing populations, disrupted agricultural systems, health problems, social disorder, and military activity.

The later Maya had scant respect for the intruding Itza, magnificent as the Chichen capital may have been. The Itza were considered to have been those who introduced lewdness (phallic worship?), promiscuity, incest, and other perversions to Yucatan. They were also said to have spoken Maya brokenly, which would fit the Chontal, who spoke a distinct dialect of Maya.

The chronicles give us a puzzling account of the end of Chichen Itza. Apparently, the ruler of Chichen stole the bride of the ruler of Izamal. Hunac Ceel, head of Mayapan, who was an ally of Izamal, avenged the abduction and led the sack of Chichen Itza. The Itza abandoned their capital and journeyed south to Lake Peten, their historical location. Apparently, this all occurred about A.D. 1187. It is probably not coincidental that Tula had fallen shortly before this date. The Chichen center had been set adrift without the Mexican support it had once enjoyed. Hunac Ceel then turned on Izamal, defeated it, then at Mayapan rapidly put together the short-lived urban center and small conquest-state which lasted until 1446 (R. Roys, 1966).

In terms of broad historical perspective, it is certain that any ruling class remaining 200 years in the midst of an alien people must have become highly acculturated. The Chontal were Maya speakers to begin with and by the end of Chichen's domination must have handled Yucatec well. Altogether, Chichen's fall is more to be explained by external competitive politics and the internal stresses of a weakening dynasty than by any grand cultural-historical theory. As will be seen, Mayapan represents a renaissance of the native Maya tradition, although in a transmuted form.

THE COLLAPSE AT TULA. Huemac's departure with his followers for Chapultepec about 1156 signals the end of Tula as a capital. Actually, the center had probably been hard pressed for some time. There is evidence from the United States southwest that a series of droughts affecting the whole Gran Chichimeca began about the middle of the twelfth century. The northern frontier areas of Mesoamerica were so marginal in rainfall that minor precipitation shifts would have major effects. It seems likely that colonial and frontier Mesoamerican settlements were abandoned and that the populations began flowing back to the south, creating pressures on the cities there. As will be seen, the invading groups were all called Chichimecs, but there were varieties of them. Some were the frontier Mesoamericans and others were acculturated peoples from the northern deserts and mountains. Still others drifted south who were genuine unacculturated barbarians from the Gran Chichimeca. The Toltec chronicles mention dissensions and conflict among factions within Tula as well as external wars. In any event Tula was abandoned. The city was also savagely destroyed. As in the case of Teotihuacan, the destruction has the marks of be-

ing an inside job. Huge trenches were put through the major temples, perhaps in search of tombs and their valuables, but also clearly for the purpose of extirpating Toltec symbols. The giant caryatid columns of Quetzalcoatl's temple were thrown down and battered. The sun god's temple (building C) was so thoroughly trenched that it was exceedingly difficult to make much architectural sense out of it later. Adjacent palaces were burned; hence the name for structure 3, the Burnt Palace. No extensive excavations have been done in other parts of Tula, and so it is unknown whether or not they were burnt out along with the civic buildings.

After the destruction of Tula, various Tula-Toltec groups joined the general drift south into the Basin of Mexico, where they settled in several communities.

A kind of golden haze fell over the Toltecs in after years and great prestige accrued to those who could claim descent from them. A diaspora of people from the broken Toltec state throughout Mesoamerica seems to have taken place. The noble houses of several regions, including the Valley of Mexico and the highlands of Guatemala, traced their ancestry back to the illustrious Tollan.

More than social prestige was involved, however. For the Aztecs, the age of Tollan represented something of a lost golden time which filled them with nostalgia, in somewhat the same way that the era before World War I is regarded in our own day:

And they were also very rich — of no value were food and all sustenance. . . . And these Toltecs enjoyed great wealth. They were rich; never were they poor. Nothing did they lack in their homes. Never was there want. And the small ears of maize were of no use to them. They only [burned them to] heat the sweatbaths (Sahagun, *Florentine Codex:* Book 3, 14).

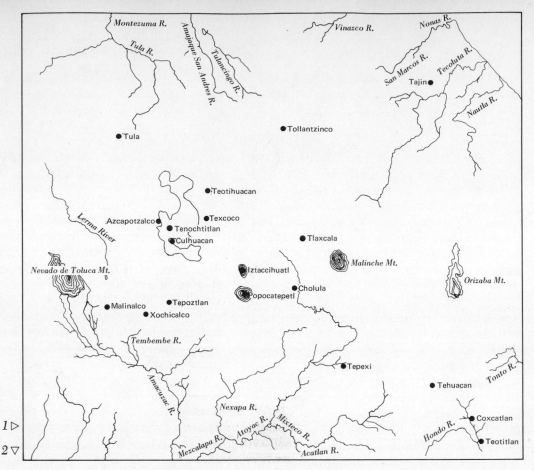

Montezuma R.
Tula R.
Amajaque San Andres R.
Tulancingo R.
Vinazco R.
Nonas R.
San Marcos R.
Tecoluta R.
● Tajin
Nautla R.

● Tula
● Tollantzinco

● Teotihuacan
Lerma River
Azcapotzalco ●
● Texcoco
● Tenochtitlan
● Culhuacan
● Tlaxcala
Nevado de Toluca Mt.
Iztaccihuatl
Malinche Mt.
Orizaba Mt.
Popocatepetl
● Cholula
● Malinalco
● Tepoztlan
● Xochicalco
Tembembe R.
● Tepexi
Amacuzac R.
● Tehuacan
Tonto R.
Nexapa R.
Atoyac R.
Mixteco R.
● Coxcatlan
Hondo R.
Mezcalapa R.
Acatlan R.
● Teotitlan

1 ▷
2 ▽

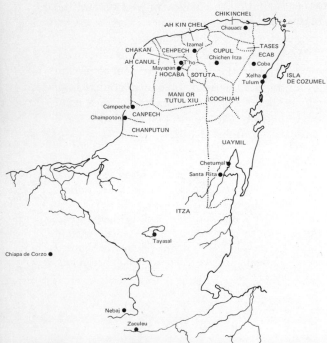

CHIKINCHEL
AH KIN CHEL
● Chauaca
CHAKAN
CEHPECH
● Izamal
TASES
CUPUL
ECAB
AH CANUL
● Tho
Chichen Itza
● Coba
Mayapan ●
● Isla
HOCABA
SOTUTA
Xelha
DE COZUMEL
Tulum
MANI OR
COCHUAH
TUTUL XIU
Campeche ●
CANPECH
Champoton ●
CHANPUTUN
UAYMIL
● Chetumal
Santa Rita ●
ITZA
Chiapa de Corzo ●
● Tayasal
Nebaj ●
Zaculeu ●

The Tula Toltec and the Rise of the Protohistoric States. *The last 800 years before the Spanish conquest was a period of rise and fall of kingdoms and empires. The central plateau (1) was the focus of the greatest of these empires, beginning with the Toltecs at their capital of Tula, whose domain included Yucatan (2).*

Architecture in the administrative center at Tula (Tollan) was heavily decorated with military themes suggesting the Postclassic period conflicts. Structure B (4) was once decorated with eagle and jaguar symbols of warrior societies. Six stone atlantean columns fifteen feet high (5) supported the temple roof. A typical Chacmul sculpture (6) was found in a nearby palace. Stelae of Tula show soldier rulers in dress uniform (7).

In contrast to this splendor, commoners lived in a surrounding city of low one-story houses (3) reminiscent of today's dwellings or those of later Tenochtitlan.

3 ▷

4 ▽

△ 6

◁ 7

5 ▽

243

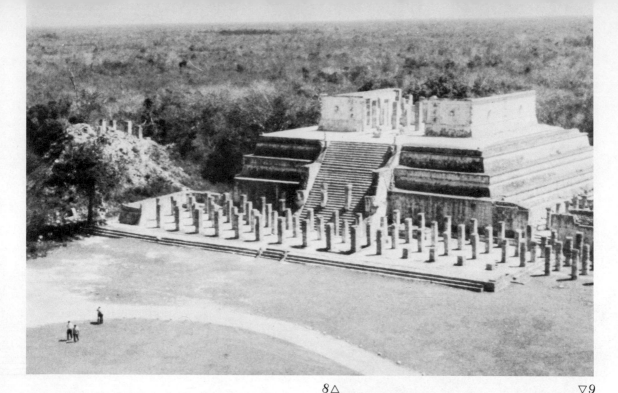

8△   ▽9

Toltec hegemony over the Yucatec Maya lasted for two centuries (987-1250 A.D.), and was exercised from their colonial capital at Chichen Itza. Magnificent architecture outshone that at Tula, and the Temple of the Warriors at Chichen (8) is an excellent example of the fused Maya-Toltec style. This style is shown by the Temple's inclusion of Maya Chac raingod masks at the corners (9), Toltec-inspired feathered serpent columns at the doorway (10), and Toltec sculptures in wall inserts (11 left) and in the form of atlantean altar supports (11 right).

Toltec domination of Yucatan was possibly sparked by a desire to control the salt fields in the Northwest. Many battle scenes showing conflict between Maya and Toltec have been found, including land and sea battles portrayed on Gold Disc G (13) from the sacred cenote.

The gold disc also evidences the introduction of metal into the Maya lowlands. Obsidian continued to be used extensively and trade was built upon it as in Olmec times. These prepared blade cores from Michoacan (12) show one processed form in which obsidian was shipped all over Mesoamerica.

244

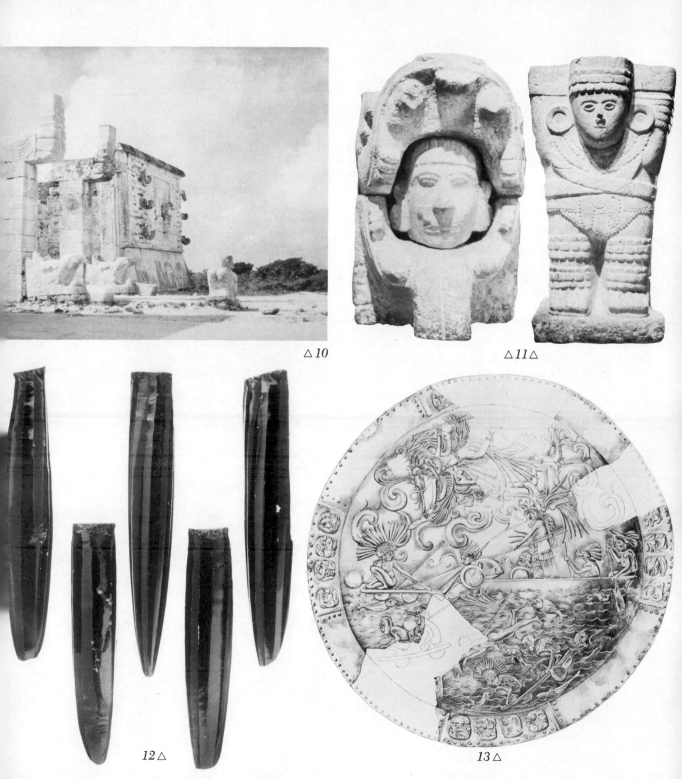

△10

△11△

12△

13△

14△   ▽15   ▽16

▽17

Toltec chronicles say that Quetzalcoatl himself led them to Yucatan. Indeed, the largest temple at Toltec Chichen (15) is dedicated to Kukulkan, the Maya name for the feathered serpent. At Chichen, with Maya master builders doing the work, the Toltecs built the largest ball court in Mesoamerica (16), over 300 feet long, with vertical walls and small stone rings through which the solid rubber ball had to pass. Quantities of Toltec sculpture covers the ball court, showing scenes of sacrifice and war (14, 17). Both scenes had symbolic connections with the ball game.

246

18△

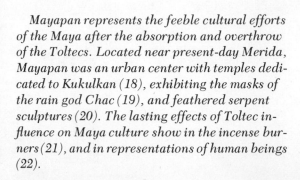

Mayapan represents the feeble cultural efforts of the Maya after the absorption and overthrow of the Toltecs. Located near present-day Merida, Mayapan was an urban center with temples dedicated to Kukulkan (18), exhibiting the masks of the rain god Chac (19), and feathered serpent sculptures (20). The lasting effects of Toltec influence on Maya culture show in the incense burners (21), and in representations of human beings (22).

▽19

◁21

▽22

△20

247

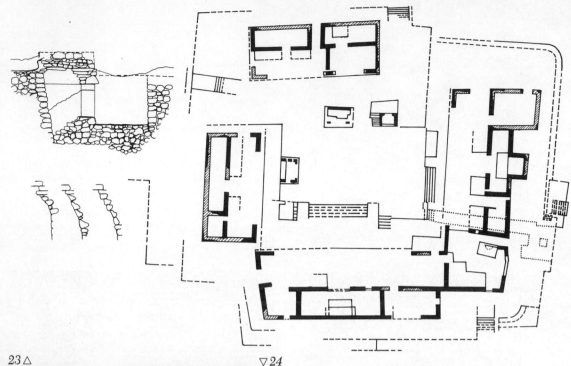

23 △   ▽ 24

Mayapan was the shabbily built administrative capital of a confederation held together by force. The city was fortified with a wall and nobles from subject cities were forced to reside within as hostages, although in palace residences (23). Family tombs are found in the palaces. Mayapan was destroyed by a revolt in 1446 A.D., and thereafter the Maya independent city-states existed in continual conflict up until the Spanish conquest.

One Protohistoric center is Tulum (24) on the east coast of Yucatan. Small, walled, poorly built, and dominated by a single, large temple residence (25) which backs up to the sea (26), Tulum is typical of centers of the period. Murals decorate the interiors of the buildings. This restored painting (27) shows a noble performing a sacrifice before an altar, perhaps at a roadside shrine. "Diving Gods" (28), which are in reality patron deities of bees and beekeepers, plunge toward the ground from niches over building doorways.

▽ 25

▽ 26

▽ 27

▽ 28

29 △
30 ▷

Maya influence in Postclassic highland Mexico
is perhaps signaled by a mural (29) recently
found at Cacaxtla, Tlaxcala. A battle scene from
this mural includes other Maya figures, suggesting that among the militant groups moving
around Mesoamerica in those days were bands
from the Maya lowlands.

New religious emphasis in the Postclassic
period are indicated by the rise of such cults as
the Xipe Totec (30) fertility rites.

Far to the south of Yucatan, in the Guatemalan
highlands, other Maya groups built fortified
cities such as Iximche (31), capital of the Cakchiquel, and Chutixtiox (32), a Quiche strong-
hold. Late highland Maya cultures showed Mexican cultural influences similar to those in Yucatan, in architecture, murals, and social structure.
The noble rulers of the Quiche, for example,
claimed descent from the Tula Toltecs. They
engaged in continual armed struggle for
domination.

33△   34△

35△   36▽

In Huehuetenango, Guatemala, the Mam Maya built the protohistoric center of Zaculeu. Structure 4 (34) is a combined temple-residence complex, perhaps dedicated to the wind god. The main temple has been restored, even to its white stucco finish (35). Zaculeu was tied to the Post-classic trade networks, as seen by fine pottery: Plumbate from nearby, fine orange from Tabasco, and incense burners in the Mixtec style of Oaxaca (33).

The once-thriving city of Cempoala in Veracruz (36, 37) was the first large Mesoamerican center encountered by Cortez in 1519. Teayo, not far away, yielded this pulque deity (39). A long regional tradition of brilliant polychrome pottery is exemplified by this early Postclassic piece from Misantla (40). All of these centers were gradually or abruptly destroyed during the Spanish conquest and early colonial period. The native aristocracy became, at best, the administrators of Spanish exploitation but were no longer memorialized as in this sculpture from the Mixtec city of Tilantongo (38).

37 △

◁ 38

39 ▽   40 ▷

41 △   ▽ 42

A page from the Nuttall Codex (41), a Mixtec document, shows an attack on a town in a lake by warriors in canoes. Note the similarity of the hieroglyphs to those found on the Aztec stone of Tizoc (42). The highland writing systems were less flexible than the Maya system and depended heavily on oral explanations learned by heart in special schools. Hundreds of these documents were burned during and after the Spanish conquest, forever destroying invaluable information on native history and customs.

The Protohistoric cult temple of Malinalco (43) was Aztec sponsored, although located in Tlahuica country to the west of the Basin of Mexico. It is carved from the rock of a cliff. Near Toluca, the center of Calixtlahuaca rests abandoned in fields of maguey cactus with its wind god temple platform (44).

 43

43
44

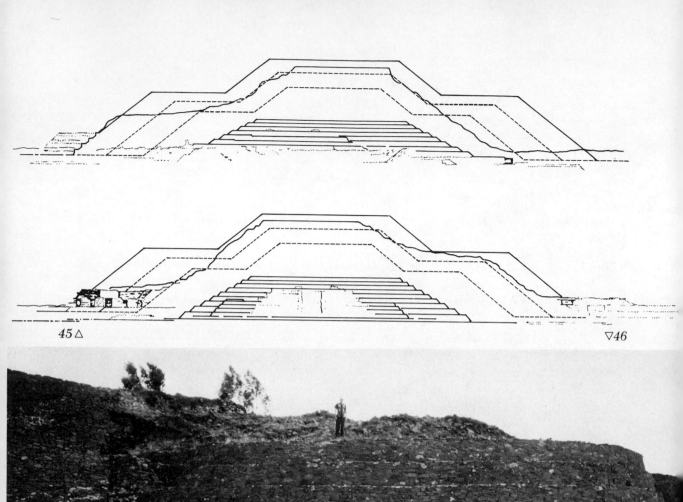

45 △   ▽46

47 △

48 △

With the disruption of Mesoamerican cultures
by the Spanish, the centuries of building great
pyramids came to an end. Cholula's Great
Pyramid (45) displays five major building phases
beginning in the Preclassic period and ending late
in the Protohistoric. The once large capital of the
Tarascans, Tzintzuntzan, possesses the remains
of Yacatas (46), temple-burial places of the
Tarascan kings. Frontier fortresses, such as La
Quemada (47, 48) dating from Classic times, now
lie fallen and silent.

257

CHAPTER 9

PROTOHISTORIC MESOAMERICA
MIXTEC, TOTONAC, AND OTHERS

Before the Spaniards had conquered that country [Yucatan], the natives lived together in towns in a very civilized fashion. They kept the land well cleared and free from weeds, and planted very good trees.
—Landa, 1941.

Now in those days when Mayapan was captured in battle, they confronted the katun of affliction. . . . Although after the days of shooting down the multitudes we pleaded for mercy, they then kindled fires over the whole province. The heavens were sealed against us. When they had succeeded in reducing the population, the compassion of heaven set a price upon our lives.

Should we not lament in our suffering, grieving for the loss of our maize and the destruction of our teachings concerning the universe of the earth and the universe of the heavens.
—Chilam Balam of Tizimin.

The first [ruin] that attracted my attention was a massy pile of building apparently designed for the defense of some interior structure. . . . It stands on the projecting angle of rock surrounded by vast precipices, [and protected by] innumerable serpents, fostered by a climate so intensely hot as that of the lower Misteca.
—G. Dupaix, in Gorenstein, vol. 63, 1973.

MAYAPAN, YUCATAN, Temple of Sacrifices. The walls of the Mayapan temple were crude by comparison with the fine veneer walls of Uxmal and Chichen Itza. Rough blocks, mortared with mud or plaster, were covered over with an adobe stucco and have not survived the passage of time well. Abandoned about 1441 A.D., it represented one of the last of the Maya Postclassic centers of occupation.

B Y THE THIRTEENTH CENTURY, CIVILIZATION within Mesoamerica had a history of some 2600 years. It had assumed certain patterns of ebb and flow, rise and fall, and reformulation. In some ways, the situation resembled the ancient Middle East in pre-Islamic times. A. L. Kroeber has pointed out the cyclical nature of patterns and cultural reformulations which occurred in the late prehistoric period of fully developed Middle Eastern civilization (1963: 761–825). That this was the case in Mesoamerica, and that it was somewhat recognized by the Mesoamericans, is hinted by the myths of cyclical creations, the endless cycles of time, and the belief among some of them that history literally repeated itself in accordance with the calendrical rounds. This was the "insider" view of what was happening. On the short run, the cyclical manner of viewing things does explain some events. Our "outsider" view, however, shows us a different reality, at least over the longer perspectives of time given us by archaeology. We will now resume the various stories of various parts of Mesoamerica bringing them — Mixtecs, Mexica, Huastecs, Maya, and others — down to the terrible event of the Spanish conquest which truncated all of their culture histories, cycles or not.

This chapter covers the final three to four hundred years before European contact. In some areas, such as western Mexico, we will cover more time, but topically the focus is the same: the development of the formal and dynamic qualities of the civilizations encountered by the Spaniards. The Aztecs are excepted from this consideration. The period is sometimes referred to as Protohistoric or late Postclassic. We will use the former term.

THE MAYA LOWLANDS

At some point about A.D. 1200, the Toltec episode came to an end in a manner not at all well understood. It seems likely that intermarriage and long residence over several generations had assimilated the Toltec rulers into the Maya mainstream. It also may be that the lapse of contact with the Toltec centers in central Mexico made the colonial capital at Chichen vulnerable in the always fierce competition among Maya political units. In any case, Chichen and its Mexicanized elite, the Itza, lost their primacy.

E. W. Andrews has suggested that the east coast of Yucatan, with its isolated location, preserved the more strictly Maya traditions and that after the Toltec colony's fall, these influences flowed back into the northern plains area (Andrews, 1965). The reestablishment of this more native tradition took most vigorous form at Mayapan. As noted before, Hunac Ceel, having overthrown Chichen and Izamal, made the small center of Mayapan the capital for a unified Maya state.

THE MAYAPAN PERIOD. *Ethnohistory.* "In that guardiania [Mani], near a mission-town called Telchac, a very populous city once existed called Mayapan in which (as if it were a court) all the caciques and lords of the province of Maya resided and there they came with their tribute" (Landa, in R. Roys, 1962).

A substantial body of historical information survives about Mayapan which has been sifted and organized by Ralph Roys (1962). Prophecies for the twenty-year *katun* periods contain historical material in accordance with the Maya penchant for mixing prophecy with reality. The *Relaciones de Yucatan* was written in the sixteenth century and is replete with data. The Hunac Ceel episode is related in these sources as an explanation of the intrigue by which that ruler as the head of the Cocom family gained ascendancy over the rest of the Maya ruling lineages. A unified government was established, with the local rulers required to reside at Mayapan in order to guarantee political control.

Diego Landa in his *Relacion* (1941) says that Quetzalcoatl himself (Kukulkan) was the founder of the city and that he ordained the political arrangements. It is true that the principal temple at Mayapan is dedicated to Quetzalcoatl-Kukulkan. However, it seems likely that the god was the patron deity of the ruling family and unlikely that the actual historical personage of the Quetzalcoatl myth was involved. Myths of Quetzalcoatl's doings are too far-flung, demand too much accomplishment, and take up too much time for any single historical individual to have been referred to. According to accounts, all was well ordered and harmonious at Mayapan for a while. Lords lived in Mayapan with stewards who attended to their needs, arranging for their support by their native provinces. Mayapan, however, was rent by dissension under a later Cocom ruler who brought in Mexican mercenaries from Tabasco to tyrannize the rest of the people. A conspiracy among the other lords was set in train which finally exploded with the systematic killing of the Cocom family, the destruction of their houses, and the abandonment of the city of Mayapan. Only one son survived, whose descendants later took a terrible revenge in the sixteenth century. With this revolt, the league of Mayapan was dissolved into its component parts. According to R. Roys, there are hints that the sixteen independent states found by the Spaniards represented the various former provinces of the Mayapan league (1957). However, the correspondence is certainly not exact, because some of the former provinces had expanded at the expense of others during the 90 years or so since the fall of Mayapan.

Archaeology. Mayapan is an unimpressive bunch of stone heaps set in some of the poorest agricultural land in the northern lowlands. A number of cenotes are located in and around the site, which seem to be its only natural advantage. A low stone wall fortifies the city enclosing 4140 buildings, large and small, within an area of about 4 square kilometers (1.5 square miles). Two major periods are to be found at Mayapan, the earliest corresponding to the Toltec phase at Chichen. Mayapan was apparently a small and insignificant center at this time, seemingly established for the worship of Kukulkan and probably as a subsidiary administrative center for the Toltecs. This phase is dated about A.D. 1100 to 1250. The second period is that of the city's political importance, about A.D. 1250 to 1450.

Nearly all of the construction now visible dates from the second period. No central planning is evident from a study of the detailed map of Mayapan, except for the general features of the enclosing wall, the location of the ceremonial center roughly near the center of the city, and the location of the major houses on natural rises to catch the breezes.

The ceremonial precinct of the city constituted about 121 buildings arranged in functional assemblages, which more nearly resemble the central Mexican patterns of the Aztec period than those of their Classic Maya predecessors. A basic ceremonial group at Mayapan included a colonnaded hall, a shrine, an oratory, and associated service buildings. Temple groups included the temple, of course, along with colonnaded halls which may have been used either by pilgrims to the temple or by young men being trained for the priesthood. The colonnaded halls are reminiscent of the *calmecac* (bachelors' quarters) buildings to be found in Tenochtitlan. In many ways Mayapan is also reminiscent of Toltec Chichen with its principal temple being a smaller version of Chichen's Kukulkan temple. There are also contrasts. Mayapan lacks a ball court, skull racks (tzompantli), and sweatbaths. On the other hand, there are distinctively Maya patterns such as the survival (or revival?) of the stela cult: at least twenty-five sculptured and plain monuments. This is an astounding number considering the short period of time

Mayapan was occupied. Altogether, however, as Proskouriakoff points out, the ceremonial center of Mayapan is very reduced in proportion to the other construction at the site (1962).

Of the 4140 buildings in the city, about 2100 were used as dwellings, housing an estimated maximum population of 12,000 (30 persons per hectare or 74 per acre). These houses, as noted, were sited for cooling by the wind and therefore are scattered at random. Stone property walls surrounded each house or group of houses, resulting in a maze of alleyways instead of planned and formal, straight streets. House plans varied from the simple two-room structure, which was most common, to the more elaborate structures which seem to have been homes of the nobility. The latter are quite interesting in several ways. There is a clear emphasis on home worship with nearly every house having its own shrine. The larger houses also had what appear to be family tombs. This evidence for ancestor worship is somewhat in contrast to the more restricted "royal cult" seen in the Classic period. All houses, large and small, are furnished with built-in benches which we have earlier interpreted as sleeping, eating, and general living spaces. That interpretation seems confirmed here by the high incidence of benches in domestic housing.

In nearly every way, and by nearly any criterion, Mayapan represents a cultural decline from the Toltec or the Classic period. Masonry work is poor, with defects covered by heavy coats of plaster. Buildings are smaller and less well planned. Sculpture is crude compared to even the ordinary productions of Classic times.

Mayapan pottery is overwhelmingly utilitarian and mainly lacks the elaborately decorated wares of earlier periods. An exception to this is the incense burner group, which is very elaborate indeed. These are often massive pottery cylinders with attached molded heads, hands, arms, legs, and costumes of various deities. These deities are overwhelmingly related in form to those of central Mexico. That is, iconographic symbols and colors are quite similar to those found in central Mexican codices. However, a quite popular deity is Itzamna, the sky serpent–creator deity of the Maya. The Pinocchio-nosed Yacatecuhtli (god of merchants) is prominent and was known among the Maya as Ek Chuah.

Mayapan then, although not a large city, was a tribute-based urban administrative city in all formal senses. There are many signs of dissolution of unifying cultural features which had held the Maya distinct and together before, in contrast to central Mexico. Its culture represents not so much a resurgence of Maya tradition as an incomplete fusion of Toltec and Maya, according to Proskouriakoff. Perhaps this ideological fragmentation was one reason that Mayapan could only be held together by force. Provincial lords were virtually captive in the city, and finally, outside mercenary troops were called in to keep the lid on. The successful conspiracy of 1446 is evidenced in the archaeological record by the fact that the ceremonial center was torn apart; deliberate destruction and burning are evident in the excavations. The city was abandoned and had become a ruin at the time of the Spanish conquest, about 100 years later.

THE SIXTEENTH-CENTURY MAYA STATES. In 1517, when Cordoba first sighted Yucatan, the peninsula was divided among sixteen separate states. Most of these were dominated by a capital city or center which was the seat of a provincial ruler called the *halach uinic*, the equivalent of the *tlatoani* in central Mexico. Lineages of these rulers and nobles were important in determining succession. Each town was ruled by a *batab* who was administrator, judge, and commanding officer, according to R. Roys (1957). Records were kept in the hieroglyphic books. Chief exports from Yucatan were cotton cloth, salt, and slaves, with honey and beeswax also being shipped. Nobles, commoners, and slaves made up a three-class social structure.

An example of a Maya province is Chikinchel, or Chauaca. It was located roughly in the north central coastal zone of the peninsula, back of a long lagoon which yielded the highest production of salt in Yucatan. In 1605 the yield was stated to be 80,000 to 90,000 bushels. Copal was also exported from the province. The Spaniards report very high populations for the area, whose subsistence was based on milpa farming and on fishing. In this case, the province was one of those ruled not by a halach uïnic, but by a council of the town rulers or batabs. R. Roys quotes the Spaniards to the following effect: "The people of Chikinchel are more precise in their reasoning and more polished in their language, although the latter is the same all over Yucatan" (1957: 104).

The sixteen states occupied most of the northern plains and stretched down both coasts to Champoton in the west and to Chetumal in the east. To the interior and south of these states were the Cehache, about whom we know little more than their name. The Itza inhabited the interior around Lake Peten, but, as with the Cehache, their territory was not considered one of the sixteen provinces; that is, it was not considered as part of the northern Maya by the latter.

East Coast Yucatan: Tulum, Xelha, and Santa Rita. Although the site of Tulum was probably occupied during the Classic, its major period of construction is Protohistoric. Its sixteenth-century name was Zama, according to R. Roys, and the Spaniards reported it as early as 1518. Juan Diaz, expedition chaplain for Grijalva, wrote: "Towards sunset we saw from afar off a town or village so large that the city of Seville could not appear greater or better; and in it was seen a very great tower" (in R. Roys, 1957: 147).

Tulum is a fortified town enclosed by a wall on three sides and by the sea on the fourth. It is today a somewhat better example of Protohistoric Maya architecture than Mayapan, which was deliberately destroyed. Again, if we judge from a technical point of view, the buildings are inferior to those of the Classic centers. Sloppy construction techniques led to the slumping and leaning of walls so that certain buildings have a drunken appearance. Then, too, the architecture is not massive or tall. Defects, as at Mayapan, are covered by heavy plaster coatings. Withal, the site has a certain charm beyond that given by its exquisite natural setting on the edge of the sea. There is an architectonic unity which is readily grasped, and which the more grandiose centers such as Toltec Chichen lacked.

Mural art is one of the most interesting features of Tulum; one building, the temple of the frescoes, preserves several nearly complete scenes. Although more hieratic, and less lively, than those dealing with daily life found at Chichen, there is nonetheless a great deal of information in them. Gods are shown which are readily identifiable with those seen in one of the Maya books, the *Madrid Codex.* These deities engage in various ceremonial activities, and in one scene, according to the interpretation of J. W. Ball, visit one another using the sacred roadways or sacbes.

Modelled stucco motifs embellish the Tulum buildings at the corners and especially in niches over the doorways. So-called diving gods in these doorway niches are actually depictions of the bee gods, the Ah Muzencabob, according to R. L. Roys. Wings and antennae are clearly modeled, and the resemblance is great to depictions of honey bees in the *Madrid Codex.* Indeed, the importance of bees at Tulum and the fact that the *Madrid Codex* has an entire section devoted to a beekeeper's almanac suggest that the manuscript may have been made on the east coast, possibly at Tulum. Honey was probably an important export, as noted, and Tulum lies along the traditional trade route around the peninsula to Honduras. The pilgrimage island of Cozumel lies off the coast from Tulum, and the latter could have served as a port of embarkation from the mainland, although other places are more convenient.

Tancah is another nearby and contemporary site which is smaller, but which acted as a port, as did Xelha farther up the coast from Tulum. Arthur Miller has recently found murals at Tancah resembling those at Tulum. A series of lighthouses and watchtowers are placed at intervals along the east coast. Tulum is in sight of two of these, one to the north and one to the south, not only convenient to navigation, but also as outposts for the city. All of these centers and ports are within the old province of Ecab, but it is not understood what hierarchy of authority existed among them, if any.

To the south of Ecab was the province of Uaymil. Peter Harrison has been doing extensive archaeological reconnaissance in the zone recently and has found large numbers of crude house platforms which date to the fourteenth and fifteenth centuries, to the Protohistoric period, in other words. No masonry structures are found on these platforms, and the only ceramics are Mayapan style censers which were in use long after the fall of Mayapan. It has been suggested that in the general simplification of culture during the Protohistoric period, utilitarian ceramics were replaced by gourd vessels, *jicaras,* and indeed, fragments of Protohistoric wooden vessels have been found in caves in Belize (Harrison, 1974).

Chetumal province includes the modern town and bay of the same name and was Uaymil's southern neighbor. The famous site of Santa Rita is located near the bay and within the old provincial area. Thomas Gann found some extraordinary Protohistoric murals on a stuccoed wall, which are clearly related in stylistic detail to Mixtec art (1900). In this sense, Santa Rita shares in what Donald Robertson calls the "international style" of late prehistoric times in Mesoamerica (1970). However, as Jacinto Quirarte points out, there are distinctive Maya treatments of the subject matter (1975). Many gods or god-impersonators engage in sacred actions. A Yacatecuhtli figure (merchant god) taps a drum, while another personage faces him, with a severed human head in hand. Both stand on what may be fields planted with various crops. Chac, the rain god, and others show great resemblance to their images as depicted on the incense burners. Mayapan-style incense burners were found in association with the murals as well as small ceramic figures depicting motifs characteristic of Mayapan.

Fragmentary as the archaeological record is, there is every evidence of a well-organized, culturally and economically linked series of centers along the east coast of Yucatan reaching down to Honduras, which was the major source of cacao. Columbus, on his fourth voyage, encountered a Maya sailing canoe out of sight of land in the Bay of Honduras. The reason that one son of the Cocom family escaped from the Mayapan massacre was that he was on a trading expedition to Honduras. Sabloff and his colleagues have argued that after the Toltec fall the new Maya rulers were a merchant class, their power ultimately based on long-distance trade (Sabloff, personal communication).

On the west coast were the plains of Tabasco, the homeland of some of the greatest traders of sixteenth-century Mesoamerica, the Chontal Maya, including the Acalan. These Chontal were ultimately related to the Itza and to those groups which had broken into the Classic Maya area. In the sixteenth century they acted as middlemen between the other Maya groups and the rest of Mesoamerica. The dominant group within Acalan was the merchant class. No doubt much of the canoe traffic that went past the east coast

centers originated in Xicalango and Poton-
chan, the "free ports" near Acalan. Both were
neutral ground where normally hostile groups
could meet in peaceful trade. Cozumel island
acted in the same way, bolstered by its status
as a pilgrimage shrine. It is interesting that
Cozumel even today is a free port. Acalan is
a symbolically appropriate name, meaning
"canoe land." The area is criss-crossed with
the estuaries of a number of major rivers.
A. H. Siemens and D. E. Puleston (1972)
have recently found a series of short canals
along the Candelaria River, which J. E. S.
Thompson suggests were fish ponds (1970:
3–47; 1974). There is some ethnohistorical evidence for this. Raised-field techniques were
also used in the Candelaria bottoms. These
techniques are tied to the high populations reported for the zone by the Spaniards. It was
no accident that Cortes contacted the Acalan
people when he proposed to march across the
peninsula to Honduras. These far-ranging
traders knew the major and minor routes of
the area intimately. Enclaves of Nahuatl
speakers from the highlands occupied several
towns in Tabasco and Xicalango itself had
Nahuatl rulers. Commerce was indeed the
chief motivation for many features, events,
and characteristics of the Protohistoric.

THE ITZA REMNANT: TAYASAL, TOPOXTE, AND
MACANCHE. It is ironic that the last surviving
remnant of Maya culture was that of the Itza,
who had been expelled from Yucatan in the
thirteenth century and who were not considered Maya enough to be included in the list
of Protohistoric states. The historic center of
the Itza was a town called Tayasal located on
an island in the large lake of Peten Itza.
Cortes himself visited the Itza, and was received by them in 1526 on his epic march to
Honduras. He was in straitened circumstances and did not attempt to conquer the
Itza. We have his description of them as well

as those of several Spanish priests who visited
Tayasal during the sixteenth and seventeenth
centuries. It was not until 1697, however, that
the Spaniards made a serious effort to reach
Tayasal with military power enough to destroy the Itza state. When they did, it took
only a one-day battle to bring an end to the
last fragment of native American civilization.

Tayasal's site is today occupied by the town
of Flores, which effectively blocks much excavation. The best hope of information on the
Itza comes from historical sources and from
William Bullard's work at contemporary sites
(1970b). George Cowgill's work in the area
sets the archaeological stage for such information (1963). Using such combined data, the
sequence and nature of events from the end
of the Classic to the arrival of Martin Ursua,
the conqueror of 1697, can be traced.

Tayasal was only one of a number of Postclassic settlements around the favored ecological zone of the central Peten Lakes, including Lakes Peten, Macanche, and Yaxha.
Evidently, population concentrated around
these lakes after the disasters of the ninth and
tenth centuries. Small Tulum- and Mayapan-
style centers were established. One of the earliest of these was Macanche. Later, in the thirteenth century, Topoxte was developed as a
small, compact capital of a petty state containing about half a dozen temples and a like
number of open halls. The halls are like those
found at contemporary Mayapan. Architectural similarities to the Tulum group of sites
are so striking that they are clear indications
of contemporaneity and of the same specific
cultural tradition. Bullard thinks that Tayasal
must have had much the same appearance
as Topoxte, judging by Spanish descriptions
(1973). Topoxte evidently overlapped with
Tayasal in their occupations, although it was
abandoned by 1697, whereas Tayasal obviously was not. Bullard notes that ceramic and
architectural continuities indicate that when

the Itza moved south in the thirteenth century it was as an elite group and they took over an already developed resident population around the lakes.

The Itza were only following a pattern established long in the past and one which they apparently had practiced with success several times in their own history. During the whole of the Postclassic period, the large Classic centers of the area remained abandoned but not forgotten. Stelae were moved about, and at Tikal Protohistoric people in the thirteenth century put a grave into the inner rooms of temple I, leaving burnt copal, incense burners, and characteristic pottery. But Tikal and other Classic sites were mainly left to molder. Today, the Maya of the northern and central lowlands burn incense to the "kings" and "queens" on the stelae to propitiate their spirits. The Lacandones until recently made prayers and burned incense in special burners in the Classic temples at Yaxchilan, which still have special status and the power to awe.

THE MAYA HIGHLANDS

The chronological definition of the cultural histories of the various regions of the Maya highlands is generalized as follows:

Early Classic   A.D. 300–600
Late Classic   A.D. 600–900
Postclassic   A.D. 900–1250
Protohistoric   A.D. 1250–1540

Although useful for schematic purposes, this chronological control is highly unsatisfactory in other ways: measuring culture process, for example. For only two valleys from the Guatemalan highlands have continuous sequences been defined, those of Las Vacas (Guatemala) and the Cotzal, and both are as yet unpublished. To the west, the Chiapas highlands does have a long sequence defined mainly by ceramics, worked out by T. P. Culbert (1965), but it was a distinctly marginal region even within the Maya highlands. Eventually, chronologies will have to be worked out for each small region, a very complex job, but rewarding in the variety of cultural events that they will reflect.

In the fragmented and broken topography of the Maya highlands, small Classic states arose about which we know little. We know that they apparently consisted of a number of small ceremonial and elite residential centers surrounded by relatively dense populations. These centers consisted of the temples, palaces, and burial places of the elite, along with a number of ball courts which were very popular. These Classic sites were generally located on the floors of the valleys and were more or less open and unfortified. Nebaj is more or less typical of these open centers. After about A.D. 1000, there is a striking transformation with the dominant centers in each area being relocated to defensible ground, usually on the tops of ridges or mountain spurs. These sites were bolstered with defensive ditches, high terraced walls, and freestanding walls. The site of Rio Blanco, located on a river bottom, and Chutixtiox, located on a high ridge, exemplify the change and contrast in a single region. Both are in a zone later dominated by the Quiche, and it is possible that these centers represent the Classic and Postclassic Quiche.

In certain isolated and no doubt backward areas, such as the Cotzal Valley, life continued more or less undisturbed. No disturbance of the basic pattern laid down in the early Classic is to be seen until the Spanish conquest smashed the cultural structure. The religious focus in these areas was on ancestor worship, as reflected in family tombs which were used for several generations of dead, accompanied by several phases of pottery offerings.

Small ceremonial centers were built around the tombs of the more important lineages. In the sixteenth century these lineages were known as *tinamitl*, and Pierre Becquelin has excavated several such centers in the Acul zone (1969). In one tomb near Ilom, Postclassic and Protohistoric pottery was found along with a clay figure of a horseman from the early colonial period. Many of the old lifeways went on in the sixteenth century in isolated and marginal areas.

Certain of the larger fortified centers in the larger and most populous regions became the nuclei of the Protohistoric highland Maya states. The Cakchiquel had a capital at Iximche and the Quiche at Utatlan. Like the Itza state at Tayasal, these groups were directed by elite ruling houses which were Mexicanized in certain ways, especially ideologically. These houses claimed descent from the Tula Toltecs and documented such claims after the conquest in manuscripts such as the *Titulo C'oyoi*.

Perhaps 100 years before the Spanish conquest, the Quiche, under a ruler named Quicab, were actively engaged in a series of aggrandizing moves which had greatly enlarged their territories. Their capital at Utatlan was a somewhat larger version of the usual temple–open hall groups (Carmack, 1973). The Cakchiquels then revolted against the Quiches and established their own state. About 1524, the Cakchiquel king was in dire straits due to plagues from the newly introduced European diseases, revolts, and wars with the Quiche. He made the fatal error of sending to the Spanish for help, who came and promptly, under the cruel Alvarado, conquered Quiches, Cakchiquels, and all.

The Cakchiquel capital of Iximche has been excavated and partially stabilized by George Guillemin (1966). The site is located on a defensible and beautiful spur of land. Large temples, dance platforms, ball courts, and multiple-roomed structures, presumably palaces, make up the center. Guillemin has found some excellently preserved fragments of polychrome murals, and they show skulls, hearts, and other motifs reminiscent in subject matter and style of central Mexico.

Utatlan and Iximche were the capitals of monarchically centered states. Zacaleu in the west was the capital of the Mam, and Mixco Viejo to the east was the chief town of the Pokomam. There were others. Bolstered by their fortresses, which acted both as frontier security and regional places of refuge, these states were continually in contention with one another. In political organization, size, and warlike nature they resembled the Mixtec states.

Most of the highland Maya groups were conquered by Alvarado in 1522 and their descendants live, in many cases, near their ancestral centers. The remnant of the Pokomam inhabitants of Mixco Viejo, conquered in blood and fire, were settled in present-day Mixco, near the city of Guatemala.

The Chiapas highlands show a set of interesting trends. Like the northern highlands of Guatemala, this area was sparsely settled or vacant during the Preclassic. During the Classic a pattern of small open centers was established. Late in the early Classic a considerable growth in population is seen, followed in the late Classic by the development of large, nucleated fortified towns. R. M. Adams argues that independent communities were the dominant political form at this period (1961). During the Postclassic and Protohistoric periods, the trend is toward larger centers which forcibly organized large numbers of peoples and the most productive lands into larger political units. These never reached the sizes of those to the east or north, however, and Chiapas remained a backwater area until the Spanish conquest and, in fact, until today.

THE BASIN OF MEXICO

Within this richest of all the central plateau zones, there is a confused period (about A.D. 1175–1425) which follows the collapse of the Tula Toltecs. In a period of about 250 years several chronically documented events occurred. There is a major movement of peoples from north to south. Some were civilized remnants of the cultured groups at Tula itself. Others were regional Mesoamerican peoples from the outskirts of the Toltec empire. Still others were fierce barbarians from the northern desert steppes. All were called Chichimec with notable lack of discrimination in many of the chronicles.

Pedro Carrasco masterfully separates these various groups and traces their fortunes (1971b). The Nonoalca were a group present at Tollan-Tula and settled in the Itzocan region of the Mixteca-Puebla. Another group from Tula came to rest at Colhuacan, in the northern Valley. The Mexica were part of the least civilized groups. Xolotl was a legendary leader of some of these hunting tribes and a famous codex records the wanderings of the various sub-groups. Xolotl reputedly established the ruling dynasty of Texcoco on the eastern lake shore.

After the fall of Teotihuacan, the various city-states of the basin revived and, although evidently under the domination of Cholula and Xochicalco, maintained the traditions established by Teotihuacan. Azcapotzalco, on the western edge of Lake Texcoco, is especially noteworthy for its epigonic forms of Teotihuacan traditions in figurines, pottery, and presumably architecture. At some point fairly soon after the fall of Tula, Carrasco suggests that Colhuacan and Coatlichan may have formed an alliance with Azcapotzalco. However, Azcapotzalco came to dominate the alliance and the rest of the Valley, especially under a redoubtable leader named Tezozomoc.

The final reformulation of these shifting alliances came in 1428, when the Aztec-Mexica of Tenochtitlan formed the Triple Alliance with Texcoco and the small state of Tacuba and overthrew Azcapotzalco. After that, the Acolhua from Texcoco and the Aztecs came to dominate the alliance. After the death of the great Nezahualcoyotl, the Aztecs moved gradually into the position of major partner in which they were found when the Spaniards arrived. The chronicles of various of the city-states from the basin are replete with dynastic details and ethnic migration stories which in their Byzantine intricacy rival the tangled affairs of the European principalities. In many cases, however, not a great deal of cultural-historical significance is to be found in the tales of intermarriages and lineage rivalries. The Aztecs, being brash and barbarous outsiders, however, depended for their very existence on the alliances that they could make with more powerful neighbors. In these arrangements, until 1428 they were very like many other petty Mesoamerican states. Their quantum jump in social organization apparently led them irreversibly into a new order of things, especially under Tlacaelel and during the spread of the empire beyond the basin.

WEST MEXICO: CLASSIC TO PROTOHISTORIC

CHRONOLOGY AND TRENDS. Present evidence based on carbon 14 dates (and largely ignoring the obsidian hydration material) indicates that west Mexico can largely be correlated with the rest of Mesoamerica using the early Classic, late Classic, and early and late Postclassic rubrics. However, these are strictly chronological in utility and do not by any means explain the cultural rhythms of the west, which were quite distinct from those of central Mexico. The distinctions between western Preclassic cultures and those of the early Classic period are minimal in many regions, although Teotihuacan items do show up on horizons in the period of A.D. 350 to 600. The late Classic period is again a matter of fine chronological and technical distinctions in the main, except at a few centers. Amapa in Nayarit is one of those centers which shows a quantum jump in the late Classic stage or just at the end of it. Early Postclassic dates are from about A.D. 900 to 1200; this is a time of more general disturbance and development than seen before. Most of the metal from Amapa dates from the early Postclassic period, which may indicate Central American and even South American contacts. Tula-related items show up in many western sites in the Postclassic period, perhaps distributed through a pochteca network. Cojumatlan in Michoacan is occupied at this time.

The date of Tarascan culture's emergence as a distinguishable entity is uncertain; Borbolla's date of A.D. 1000 as early Tarascan is strictly an estimate. It seems likely that Tarascan culture had to have been in existence at least by A.D. 1250 in order to have developed to the complex extent that it did before the Spanish conquest. Therefore, A.D. 1000 as a starting date may not be far off the mark. According to documents, A.D. 1390 represents the starting date of Tarascan expansion through the west.

Classic to Postclassic (A.D. *300–1200*). By the end of the Preclassic period, as seen in a previous chapter, west Mexico had generally achieved the level of village-centered, regional cultures. Special burial modes, particularly the shaft-tomb complex, seem to indicate ideologies related to the proper disposal of the dead. These religious cults, if that was what they were, began to die out during the Classic period, and by the beginning of the late Classic period, shaft-tombs were no longer

being built. The regional centers continued, but with some rearrangement of settlement. Red-on-brown became a generally distributed group of styles during the late Classic period. The site of Amapa in Nayarit provides a crucial sequence for understanding what happened (see Pendergast, 1962; Grosscup, 1961).

Amapa is located between two large rivers, only fifteen miles from the sea on the coastal plain of northern Nayarit. Easy access to the ocean was thus available. The site itself is 1.5 square kilometers (.6 square miles), and consists of some 200 mounds, large and small and of all shapes. Apparently, during the Early Period (A.D. 250–700), Amapa consisted mainly of wattle and daub houses and apparently was only a large village. After a period of abandonment, the site was reoccupied and dramatic changes took place. Most of the large construction at Amapa was built during the Late Period (A.D. 900–1200). Many small mounds supported only wattle and daub houses. However, large platforms of dirt and river stones supported temples of perishable materials. An I-shaped ball court was built.

Perhaps the most interesting thing to happen at Amapa occurred with the introduction of metals around A.D. 900. A cemetery which largely dates from this period provided many of the metal items found, 205 in all. These consist of needles, awls, tweezers, fishhooks, wire, pins, and many types of bells. Mazapan-style figurines like those found at Tula and throughout Mesoamerica on the Toltec horizon are associated with metallurgy at Amapa. Also found in the metal-yielding graves were finely decorated incised bowls, and many handsomely painted polychrome vessels. The chili-grinder, *molcajete,* form is characteristic of this period. Both forms and motifs show close affinities with Postclassic central Mexican cultures, and there is little doubt but that western Mexico was more fully integrated into Mesoamerica at this time than at any time before. For example, many of the animals painted on the polychromes are very similar to those found in the *Borgia Codex* group from the Mixteca-Puebla area. At least one Amapa monochrome vessel has a Plumbate form. At the same time, acting as the undoubted agency for the introduction of metallurgy to Mesoamerica placed the west in an unaccustomed and innovative role.

Together with metals, molcajetes, and Mazapan figurines, Lister has also defined the Postclassic by the appearance of *malacates,* or spindle whorls. It may be that superior strains of cotton from South America were introduced at the same time as metals, but in any case, spinning (and presumably weaving) becomes a widespread Western activity after A.D. 900.

In Michoacan, during the early Classic period, red-on-brown pottery shows up at Apatzingan in its cemetery. Molcajetes and malacates both appear at Apatzingan in the succeeding phases, and many other sites show this sequence of events, confirming the widespread nature of these horizon markers.

The general picture of Classic and Postclassic western Mexico is one of regionalized cultures, mostly village centered, but occasionally with a larger ceremonial center as a focus. Ixtepete and Ixtlan del Rio, large sites in Nayarit, are examples of the larger centers. These small regions responded differentially throughout the A.D. 300 to 1200 period to influences from central Mexico, possibly from South America, and probably from Central America. The northern part of the zone was involved in the expansion of Mesoamerican cultures northward in Teotihuacan times and later, during the Toltec period. Internal motivations to cultural complexity may have been largely based on population growth. All indications are that during the Classic to Postclassic period, population increased and that elaboration of sociopolitical arrangements was one sign of increasing complexity. At the time of the Spaniards, most of the area was either dominated by regional centers such as Cojumatlan, or incorporated into the Tarascan empire (Chadwick, 1971; Meighan, 1974).

THE TARASCANS (A.D. 1000–1521). The Tarascans are anthropologically famous for having a language that is unrelated to any other known Mesoamerican language, and for having developed a politically complex "empire," at least in legend. The historic capital of the Tarascans was the city Tzintzuntzan, located on Lake Patzcuaro. The major work of excavation has been in the five large platforms, *yacatas,* at Tzintzuntzan. These platforms are recorded from several other sites, nearby Ihuatzio, for example. A yacata is distinguished from other Mesoamerican platforms by a peculiar ground plan somewhat reminiscent of a women's liberation symbol, and by being built of masonry with mud mortar. They may have been temples to the wind god, as indicated by the round part of the platform at the rear. Yacatas seem also to have been funerary locations, and many burials have been found in and around them. These burials contain exotically shaped ceramics, including many "foreign vessel" forms, but decorated by negative painting. Also found in the burials and elsewhere are examples of virtuoso metalwork in gold, silver, and copper. Excellence in metallurgy is matched by many fine productions in obsidian, turquoise, and other stone. Palace-type structures are located near the yacatas, but little is known of their features. Stone sculpture emphasized coyotes, but seated human figures and chac-muls were also common.

The *Relacion de Michoacan* gives considerable information about the Tarascans, and the Tarascans themselves are still around to be consulted, at least on their language and other surviving matters of interest. Swadesh, with characteristic daring, has linked Tarascan to Zuni in the Gran Chichimeca, and with Quechua in South America (Chadwick, 1971).

This fits somewhat with the possibility of west Mexican contact with South America, as evidenced by the introduction of metalworking. A bit of possible additional archaeological evidence has been found near Arcelia, Guerrero, in the form of a two- or three-story adobe building which has a trapezoidal doorway, according to reports. Trapezoidal doorways and multiple-storied buildings are characteristic of the Inca area, which is also Quechua-speaking. However, Arcelia is possibly outside of Tarascan territory. This is still a question of great complexity and one on which too little evidence bears.

The *Relacion* relates that the Tarascans were ruled by a priest-king-god who governed a large political unit. In terms of area, it seems to have been the largest political unit in Mesoamerica at the time of the Spanish conquest. The Tarascans resisted the Aztecs with a chain of fortified cities and by a standing army. The empire was administered by a wide variety of officials who handled such matters as taxes and censuses. There were many craft specializations (as confirmed by the archaeological finds), and each guild had its patron deity. War was waged after the harvest was in, in good Mesoamerican manner. Spies (perhaps pochteca) were employed for intelligence purposes. The king was buried with great pomp, and several retainers went with him to the afterlife. Armillas interprets the evidence to mean that the Tarascan empire was essentially a rural one, although it had a high-density population.

Several of the most basic questions remain open regarding the Tarascans. Was Tzintzuntzan urban or a ceremonial center ministering to an essentially rural population? What are the origins of the Tarascans? Are they Mesoamericans or transplanted South Americans? What is the period at which the Tarascans can be distinguished in the archaeological record? Obviously, this is one of the most open of the frontiers in Mesoamerican research.

OAXACA

THE ZAPOTECS. *The Postclassic Period or Monte Alban IV* (A.D. *600–1250*).   Three major sites that have occupations dating from the period after the abandonment of Monte Alban have been at least cursorily examined. These Monte Alban IV sites are Lambityeco, Yagul, and Mitla, all in the Tlacolula arm of the central valley.

Lambityeco is an open site on the valley floor. It is dated within Monte Alban periods IIIb and early IV. The site was occupied by at least A.D. 600, judging by some early types of fine orange pottery found there. Over two hundred mounds constitute the site and cover an extensive area. Similarity to Monte Alban IIIb culture is to be seen in the site plan. The same style of patio arrangement of large buildings, with the same sort of subpatio tomb, are present. One large tomb at Lambityeco has the usual antechamber with a formal facade over the entrance to the burial room. The facade includes finely done stucco heads. These may be portraits of the persons buried inside. The building immediately above the tomb carries a stucco decoration, the figures, and calendrical names of persons who may have been the parents of the man buried below. Celebration of distinguished and ruling lineages continued, therefore, from Monte Alban III times and certainly into the historic period. John Paddock, the excavator, sees in Lambityeco a reflection of the decadence and decline of Zapotec culture (personal communication). It does appear possible that differences between Monte Alban and Lambityeco could simply be those between a metropolitan center and a county seat. In early Monte Alban IV, Lambityeco was one of several large centers surrounded and supported by massive populations. However, it seems to have been abandoned well before the end of period IV. Perhaps the population moved to nearby and more defensible Yagul.

Yagul is located on a flat spur running away from a large butte or mesa. It was apparently occupied as early as Monte Alban I, but so much period IV and V material lies over Yagul's earlier occupations that it is difficult to say what the site may have been like in earlier periods except that it was very small. However, excavations at the site have revealed evidence of a "building boom" at the beginning of period IV and coincident with the abandonment of Lambityeco.

Period IV sculpture and ceramics reveal the same sorts of attitudes toward the distinguished dead as in earlier periods. The burial urn tradition continued (though with a notable decline in technical and esthetic quality) throughout the valley and no less at Yagul. Effigy vessels in the form of "bat-claw" feet are particularly characteristic of the period. Carved rectangular stones are finely detailed and carry scenes of what are apparently married couples seated facing each other, although differing in technique and subject from these of earlier times.

Mitla is located about six miles farther east in the Tlacolula arm, on a small river. Traces of Guadalupe phase and Monte Alban I and II occupation have been found, but no information of substance is yet available. Two groups of major structures dominated by temple buildings and several tombs and burials represent the known IIIa and IIIb period ruins. However, the modern town of Mitla lies around these buildings, and the site may have been much more extensive than it seems. The location of these two temple groups is open and undefended. Period IV pyramids are located in a fortified zone above the river but have not been explored. The shift is impor-

tant, however, and reflects more disturbed times.

All of the above sites date from a time during which the Mixtecs were pushing into the central Valley from the north, down the Etla arm. According to Spores, the major period of successful Mixtec aggression was in the late Postclassic, but certainly, the fragmentation of early Postclassic Zapotec cultures and the breakup of the centralized state held together by Monte Alban indicate considerable pressure beforehand, that is, during Monte Alban period IV.

The Protohistoric or Late Postclassic Period (A.D. *1250–1521*). In some ways, the mysteries of quasars and "black holes" in outer space are easier to explain than Monte Alban periods IV and V and their relationships. The recent work of Donald Brockington (1973, 1974), Ronald Spores (1972), and John Paddock (1966c, 1974a, 1974b) has made the situation somewhat clearer. The difficulty lies in the history of Oaxacan archaeology. The site of Monte Alban was the first to be intensively excavated. Its periods were naturally thereafter "stretched" to apply to the whole valley. However, ethnic terms were then applied to the valley-wide periods. Monte Alban IV became, ipso facto, Zapotec and Monte Alban V became Mixtec. It is hard to distinguish the ethnicity of the ancient owner of a piece of pottery. Paddock, Brockington, and Spores have pointed out that trade of luxury (elite) goods can distribute them far beyond their origin points. There is documentation which indicates that Mixtec products were distributed through an elite trade network that stretched over central Mesoamerica. Further, it is known that Mixtec and Zapotec elite were intermarrying as early as about A.D. 1250. Brockington, in the Mixtec area of Miahuatlan, south of the main valley, found that the "Mixtec" grey common wares were distinct from those of Nochixtlan-Yanhuitlan and other still undefined parts of the Mixtec area, indicating that there was a great deal of variation within Mixtec culture itself. Finally, a conference of Oaxacan specialists in 1970 found that "Mixtec" grey ware distribution in the Valley of Oaxaca during periods IV and V was nearly identical to the distribution of the Zapotecs immediately after the Spanish conquest. Bernal, some time ago, suggested that Mixtec and Zapotec culture fused in some respects during the later periods, and offered some evidence for this having happened in period V (1965b).

Considering all of the above, we shall use the following principles to deal with late Prehistoric Oaxacan culture. Elite cultural material found in formal tombs and particularly Mixtec polychrome pottery may indicate either Mixtec or Zapotec elite culture, and the decision must be made on other grounds. Documents such as the local *Relaciones* and Burgoa's writings have proved to be quite accurate and can be used to so distinguish. Tribute networks in Protohistoric times included towns with foreign ethnic groups within them, and therefore different cultural products could show up in elite contexts. Brockington's Miahuatlan work shows that Zapotec and Mixtec cultures were widely differentiated within themselves. In other words, as we have known for many years, linguistic uniformity does not mean cultural uniformity. On the other hand, there was apparently a considerable uniformity of culture among the common folk of both linguistic groups in single geographical regions, especially during the final prehistoric period.

The main cultural-historical process of the last two periods therefore seems to be the progressive fusion of Zapotec and Mixtec cultural variants in the Valley of Oaxaca. The period of maximum differentiation between Mixtec and Zapotec cultures seems to have been IIIb.

Even in that period some "Mixtec" traits show up in the ceramics, however. Therefore, it seems reasonable here to deal with Monte Alban IV and V as they were probably originally intended to be treated, *as purely chronological blocks of time* against which we can draw the major features of prehistoric events. In these terms we may define Monte Alban IV as A.D. 900 to 1250. Monte Alban V takes over at 1250 and continues to 1521, the date of Spanish conquest.

Stratigraphic evidence from Yagul and Mitla developed by Bernal indicates that period V can be subdivided (1965b). The earliest phase is characterized at Mitla by the appearance of stone mosaic decoration and the fine grey pottery in tombs. Monte Alban's period V tombs date to this earliest phase except for tomb 7 and its great treasure. Bernal dates this phase between A.D. 1250 and 1400.

The latest phase in period V would be that represented by Mixtec polychrome pottery and the latest palaces at Mitla and Yagul distinguished by their room arrangements. Zaachila tombs 1 and 2, and Monte Alban tomb 7, date from this period. The phase started about 1400 and ended in 1521.

During Protohistoric times, Mixtec penetration of the central valley reached its maximum and then receded under a Zapotec reassertion. Apparently, the Mixtecs had practical political control of most of the communities of the valley at one point. According to Bernal's survey data, this occupation may have constituted as much as 75 percent of the 200 sites in his sample. However, by the time of the Spanish conquest in November 1521, the Tlacolula and Zaachila arms of the valley were under partial Zapotec control, and Bernal's conclusions may be biased by factors discussed at the beginning of this section. This comeback was consolidated and expanded by the Zapotecs in the early colonial period. Cuilapan in the western valley represented the major Mixtec outpost in 1521, perhaps having as many as 70,000 inhabitants. In 1519, the total valley population was approximately .5 million, or much less than that of the Basin of Mexico. As in the basin, Zapotec and Mixtec communities were organized into tributary networks typical of the Protohistoric city-states. For example, Macuilxochitl was tributary to Zaachila. Thereby, a loose political control was exercised by Zaachila (originally named Teozapotlan) over the other continually bickering communities. Valley towns were often multi-ethnic, having barrios of Mixtecs in Zapotec areas, and vice versa.

The major centers of Monte Alban V (or the Protohistoric period) were fortified or had fortified refuges. Mitla and Yagul are the best known. At Yagul, an extensive palace complex has been excavated, with six patios very similar in design to nearby Mitla. A formal fortress was built on the top of the mesa. A large and impressive ball court is located near the palaces. Several T shaped major tombs have been found at Yagul which are dissimilar in layout to the rectangular, formally planned tombs at Monte Alban. Similarities are to be noted to Mitla. For example, the door to the burial chamber of Yagul tomb 30 is closed by a stone slab which is carved with the same "running fret" motif so common in the Mitla palaces. Bernal points out some near identities in plan between palace groups at the two sites. Yagul apparently was occupied at the time of Spanish conquest, and its population was moved to Tlacolula, where their descendants still live.

Mitla's period V aspect is that of a town built near the river, with a nearby fortress on a defensible mesa. Recent work by Flannery's group indicates that the town was 1 to 2 square kilometers (.4 to .8 square miles), with a sustaining area of about 20 square kilometers (7.7 square miles). The latter includes dry land terracing of the hillside up to the 1800 meter line (5900 feet). The major civic construction known from period V is represented by the three large and famous palace groups so often visited today, as well as the "Adobe Group" of palaces. These palace groups consist of rectangular buildings arranged around the four sides of spacious patios. The buildings themselves emphasize the horizontal with their facades broken by mosaic decorated panels. The interior upper walls are dizzyingly covered with continuous and repetitious frets of various sorts: running, interlocking, and stepped. Bernal suggests that these decorative motifs and others indicate a fusion of cultural ideas between Zapotec and Mixtec. Huge monolithic columns supported the roof in the Hall of the Columns. Lintels are massive, and stones of the same size supported the roofs of tombs which lie beneath the fronts of two of the palace structures. Father Burgoa, a seventeenth-century priest of Zaachila, records that these were traditional burial places for the priests at Mitla and that they smelled abominably (Paddock, 1966c). A nearby hill two kilometers distant was fortified with massive walls that closed off the gaps in the naturally rugged terrain.

Mitla held a religious primacy over the other Zapotec communities and was apparently a center for the worship of a certain "Lord and Mistress of the Underworld" (Coqui Bezelao and Xonaxi Quecuya). Spores characterizes Valley Zapotec religion in the early sixteenth century as using stone and wooden idols, requiring a trained priesthood, with ritual sacrifices of dogs, birds, and human beings. Liturgical matters included blood offerings from body parts as well as fasting, penance, feasting, intoxication, and ritual cannibalism. This religious complex involved the underworld as the place of death and of the ancestors. In keeping with the religious focus of Mitla, a priest ruled the center rather than the usual local lord (Spores, 1965).

Zaachila or Teozapotlan is located at the entrance to the arm of the valley of the same name. Until recently the site was little known due to the incredible hostility of the inhabitants toward outsiders in general, and archaeologists in particular, whom they had run out of town twice in the past. The rather extraordinary finds of Mexican archaeologists Roberto Gallegos (1962) and Jorge Acosta (1972) have begun to fill this void, albeit under the unusual circumstances of military protection. The ancient site is evidently extensive, but is partly covered by the modern town as at Mitla. The major architecture is located on natural and man-made elevations and consists of patio groups of the usual sort. A ball court may be included in the site. All the visible material is evidently of period V date. Mound B is the largest at the site and is high enough to enable one to see Monte Alban 15 kilometers (9 miles) to the north-northeast. This complex structure consists of several terraces leading to at least four elevated patios. Elevation would give defensive advantage.

Mound A is the location of the two tombs which have been the focus of most of the work at the site. It is lower than adjacent mound B, but still elevated some 30 or 40 feet above ground level. A sunken patio on the top of mound A is surrounded by the usual set of stone and adobe rooms. Tombs 1 and 2 are located under the north building. Both tombs have antechambers. Tomb 1 contained one principal individual and nine others crumpled along the walls. Eighty pieces of some of the most magnificent pottery ever found in Mesoamerica were found in the antechamber. This is the famous Mixtec polychrome with its glossy lacquer-like finish in brilliant colors. The individual pieces are extraordinary. A small blue hummingbird perches on the edge of a gloriously colored drinking cup. A howling coyote's head forms the mouth of a pitcher with the spout being the animal's red tongue. Turquoise mosaic disks and masks, and gold

rings were included with the offerings. On the walls of the tomb are modeled stucco figures of humans with calendrical names attached to them by a line, codex-style: 5-Flower and 9-Flower. Before each of these figures marches the modeled figure of the death god, Mictlantecuhtli. It is possible that both of these individuals are mentioned in the *Mixtec* codices as rulers in the dynasty of Mixtec Yanhuitlan. By a complex and tortuous genealogical argument, Alfonso Caso thought that the person buried in tomb 1 was probably 8-Deer "Fire Serpent," a ruler known to have been born about A.D. 1400. 5-Flower and 9-Flower were ancestral figures to 8-Deer "Fire Serpent" (Caso, 1966a). However, the argument depends on the assumption of a recording mistake in one of the codices, which weakens it. Tomb 2 contained another sumptuous burial with twelve persons in the latest interment, the prior occupants' bones having been carefully stored in the niches of the tomb. Mixtec grey ware, a well-made plain pottery, was used for the ceramic offerings, but this was offset by the occurrence of some superb pieces of gold work and carved bones which are quite the equal of any found elsewhere.

Two other tombs have been found at Zaachila with less spectacular offerings, but which nonetheless give information. These were located in a small mound under the ruins of a colonial Catholic chapel. It is known that the early sixteenth-century chapels were often placed on the razed sites of former native shrines. The two tombs date from the Monte Alban V period and contained 124 pieces of pottery, some of it very fine indeed. Several nontomb burials were found, one with an exceptional combined gold and turquoise-jade disk. The gold was beaten thinner than tissue paper and is exquisitely decorated with Mixtec codical-style seated human figures. Relying on the documentary evidence which states that Zaachila was the Zapotec political capital, but fell late in the prehistoric period to the Mixtecs, it seems probable that the persons in these tombs were Mixtec. However, if they were Zapotec, marital connections to Mixtec elite families would explain the Mixtec luxury goods in the tombs and burials.

Monte Alban tomb 7 is famous as a great treasure house of Mixtec art. As interpreted here, the evidence is equally good for considering that the occupant was Zapotec as Mixtec. However, considering the documentary evidence that the Mixtecs controlled the nearby zones in the sixteenth century, the tilt now seems to be toward a Mixtec tomb.

The tomb is located in a small architectural group of the usual sort with stone buildings facing inward upon the courtyard. The tomb entrance is in the patio and the burial chamber is under one of the structures. The occupants of tomb 7 were literally mixed up, with the count of individuals seven to nine adult males with the remains of two women and one infant thrown in for good measure. The discrepancies and uncertainties in numbers can be explained by the possibility of body parts of various individuals having been included as part of the funerary offerings. The principal occupant was a human monster with a cerebral tumor. Caso suggests that he might thus have represented an incarnation of the god Xolotl, god of monsters. A skull was included which had been overlaid with turquoise mosaic with a flint knife in the nasal opening: a symbol of Tezcatlipoca. The offerings were extraordinary and comprehended 337 separate items of gold, silver, copper, carved bone, jade, and other materials. The quality of the jewelry work is notable. Ten gold pectorals were in the tomb, one with a calendrical date. Another is a composite example with sections showing a ball game in progress, a sun symbol, and other scenes, and hung with delicate golden rattles. Rings, brooches, fan handles (one of jade), a gold

diadem with a gold feather, earplugs, bracelets, and a copper axe were included in the inventory.

The carved human bones are extremely complex and rich in iconography. They are nearly identical to those found in Zaachila tomb 2. The gold objects also show great similarity to the Zaachila tomb 1 material. So complex is the tomb and its implications that Caso needed 400 pages in a sumptuous volume to completely describe and analyze it (1969). The implications of wealth, craftsmanship, and economic networks are all enormous. The legendary skills of the Mixtecs as artificers of the sixteenth century are confirmed. Brockington points out that Mixtecs were imported to Tenochtitlan in Aztec times to practice their skills in the great capital (personal communication).

The Zapotecs had spread and expanded into the coastal plain of Oaxaca and into the Isthmus of Tehuantepec during the late prehistoric period. In point of fact, they may have been refugees. The *Relacion de Cuilapa* says, ". . . finally these [Mixtecs] had a war with the people of Teoçapotlan, who, recognizing that they were at a disadvantage fled to Teguantepec" (after Paddock, 1965: 375). Spores goes so far as to say that the major center of Zapotec political power may have shifted completely away from Zaachila to the Tehuantepec center of Guiengola a few years before the Spanish conquest (1965).

Guiengola is little known, having only been incompletely explored by the great Eduard Seler in 1896 (Seler, 1960: Vol. 2, 184–199) and remapped lately by Peterson and MacDougall (1974). It is a large and imposing fortress located on a ridge. Paddock comments that the site has the typical Zapotec arrangement of major buildings around patios (1966b). David Potter points out that the style of the buildings at Guiengola is very different from Lambityeco (personal communication). There is also a ball court and a curious and complex palace area. The rugged hillside is ringed with two massive walls, evidently for defensive purposes. The pottery on the site is all late Postclassic. We know from historical accounts that in about 1497 Guiengola was the location of one of the most resounding defeats suffered by the Aztecs in their expansion of empire. For once, the Zapotecs and Mixtecs patched things up and joined together in resisting the common enemy. A ruler, "Cocijoeza," led the resistance during the four-year siege and then turned on the Mixtecs. Brockington notes that the name means simply "Rain God Worshipper" and therefore could be a title carried by any or many rulers (personal communication). Paddock notes that a real person, despite questions about his title, occupied the throne in the early sixteenth century (personal communication).

The suggested Zapotec comeback after Mixtec aggression may have been mainly accomplished after the Spanish conquest. The Zapotecs invited the Spaniards into Oaxaca to help them against the Mixtecs, seemingly an act of desperation. In any case, the Spaniards came and conquered both Mixtecs and Zapotecs in a one-month campaign in 1521.

The Zapotecs and Mixtecs survive today. They have suffered the trauma of the conquest, the worst blows of the colonial period, a steady erosion of their economic and biological base, and the continuing assaults of the modern world on their cultural traditions. In their fierce independence and cultural persistence, they are somewhat like the highland Maya and the Zuni of the southwestern United States.

THE MIXTECS.   Spores has commented on the diversity of cultural groups which constitute the Mixtec language family (1969, 1972). These regional variants are usually grouped into the Mixteca Alta (Highland), Mixteca Baja (Lowland), and Mixteca de la Costa (Coastal and Coastal Range). Brockington's work in the

cultural fracture zone which is the Oaxacan coast will be treated separately. It includes Mixtecan groups but probably also archaeological remains from other linguistic groups. The only regional variants of which we know anything of archaeological substance at present are those of Coixtlahuaca and the Nochixtlan Valley (Bernal, 1949). Spores' Nochixtlan sequence is as follows:

Phases	Dates
Convento	A.D. 1520–1535 to 1820
Natividad	A.D. 1000 to 1520–1535
Las Flores	A.D. 500 to 1000
Ramos	200 B.C. to A.D. 500
Cruz	1300 to 200 B.C.

In terms of many of the regional sequences of Mesoamerica, these are fairly long periods of time, but the sequence is continuous and shows considerable internal development. For these reasons and others that will become clear, we will review the sequence from beginning to end.

Preclassic or Formative: Cruz Phase.   Nochixtlan developed a fairly standard highland Preclassic culture during the *Cruz* phase, one which was mainly village-oriented but with contacts both inside and outside the region. Ceramics reflect ties with adjacent valleys and farther away as do the ubiquitous figurines. Housing within the small communities evolved from houses with packed-earth floors to some with plastered floors. Block adobe walls were favored from the earliest times. One probable elite residence was found at Inityu, and an immense platform from a nearby site indicates that the general Mesoamerican Preclassic trends toward social complexity and associated civic architecture were in train in the Nochixtlan Valley. Parallels with the central Valley of Oaxaca are striking.

Early Classic: Ramos Phase.   The first appearance of an urban center takes place about 200 B.C. at Yucuita. Several hundred structures, including ten major civic groups, are concentrated in an area of 1 to 1.5 square kilometers (.4 to 1.2 square miles). Spores thinks that Yucuita probably dominated the whole valley. There was considerably more to dominate than in the Preclassic period. Population had doubled (12,000 to 14,000 people) and communities had grown both in size and in complexity. Some ten towns and at least twenty hamlet-type sites were in the valley, most of them clustering about the developing urban center.

Yucuita seems to have been internally specialized with a number of different kinds of craft and social groups living together. Yucuita probably had only about 7000 people, but these were supplemented by people in the subordinate communities, themselves specialized. Spores feels that the consistency of pattern between the settlement complexes of historic times and of the *Ramos* phase allows him to infer that the pattern of the Mixtec petty state ruled by an aristocratic family was already in existence. This inference is reinforced by the fact that the sequence shows no significant breaks and indicates that the same cultural tradition is involved throughout at least 2000 years. The latter is reflected in the gradually changing grey wares which last from Cruz up to Convento times.

Late Classic: Las Flores Phase. Total valley population reached an estimated 30,000 during the *Las Flores* phase. Less desirable lands were developed, particularly those higher upslope, probably as a result of population pressures. Again the region was dominated by a single large center, this time located in a defensible position on one of the highest mountains in the valley. This capital, Yucuñudahui, covered about 2 square kilometers (.8 square miles) and was a planned urban area. Sculptured monuments have been found with a

system of writing similar to that in use at Monte Alban in period III. The center existed within a context of an increased number of communities. The larger centers were composed of a number of palace complexes surrounded by humble housing of the one- or two-room type. The smaller centers had one or two palaces surrounded by many small and inferior houses. Spores finds in this pattern great similarity to the settlement pattern which accompanied the distinctive Protohistoric social organization. Ruling families in the latter days occupied the main centers, while outlying settlements were administered by a network of loyal nobility. All nobility maintained two or more homes, one in the administered communities and one in the capital. There, the historically known social organization would fit the Las Flores settlement pattern quite well. Nobility would have been supported by the service and tribute system well known from the Protohistoric period. It is also noteworthy that the same late Classic shift from open to defensible locations which took place in the Guatemalan highlands also occurred here.

Postclassic-Protohistoric: Natividad Phase. The Nochixtlan Valley has relatively sparse shows of the famous Mixtec polychrome during the *Natividad*, a late prehistoric phase, although Coixtlahuaca has abundant polychrome. On the other hand, a very diagnostic red-on-cream type is exceedingly common. We must, therefore, look elsewhere for the origin of the Mixtec polychrome tradition, perhaps to another valley such as Coixtlahuaca or to the Mixteca de la Costa area. Paddock suggests that Maya polychrome tradition may be the ultimate origin. Gray pottery, of the kind that appeared in the Oaxacan central valley, continued its gentle but persistent modulation throughout the period.

The Nochixtlan Valley population reached its maximum during this long phase. One hundred and fifty-nine Natividad sites have been found thus far, and an estimated 50,000 people occupied them. An intensive form of agriculture based on terracing (lamabordo) of the upper slopes was developed. There was a shift from an even distribution of valley population during the preceding period to one in which it was concentrated in the northern end of the valley, around Yanhuitlan. Spores correlates this shift with the rise of the kingdom of Yanhuitlan, although it was only the largest of seven kingdoms in the valley. Most population was located in indefensible positions, and therefore it seems that this phase was a time of peace and tranquility. According to the codices and relaciones the Yanhuitlan petty state was fairly stable for the last 400 or 500 years before the Spanish conquest. However, there were outside pressures on the valley, among them aggressive moves by neighboring Mixtec states, especially the coastal kingdom-empire of Tututepec. Late in the period, the major aggressor was the Mexica-Culhua (or Aztec) empire, which rather easily overran the area in 1486 and in 1506. To the internally generated stresses of growing population and growing elite classes, then, were added the external stresses of tribute demands from outside political systems.

It is clear that the Nochixtlan Valley had less demographic potential than that of the Basin of Mexico, simply on account of lesser size. In addition, the subsistence base was poorer. The city-states of the basin averaged about 50,000 per unit, whereas that figure was shared among seven kingdoms in the Nochixtlan area. Spores thinks that eventually the stresses would have led to conflict within the valley in spite of the stability afforded by elite alliances and economic interdependence. For other parts of the Mixtec area, the main period of upset and conquest was in the eleventh and twelfth centuries. Perhaps these regions had still less demographic potential than Nochixtlan and reached their limits more rapidly, triggering predatory competition.

Ethnohistoric Yanhuitlan. Using documents from the sixteenth century, Spores has reconstructed late prehistoric Mixtec society in the specific region of Yanhuitlan (1967). Social organization was based on a four-class system. At the top was the ruling family with its privileged relatives. They were supported by a tribute system yielding goods and services. A second group was made up of supporting nobility who served as the civil servant group for the small kingdom. They were also entitled to support from the tribute system. Together with the ruling family, the nobility made up a caste. A third class was made up of commoners who carried a large part of the burden of the tribute system. A special status group may have been formed by merchants. Tribute included items not available in the valley, such as "Guatemala (quetzal) feathers," and these traders therefore ranged fairly far. The lowest class was made up of tenant farmers, servants, and slaves, and was smaller than the commoner class. Kinship ties were important at all levels of society although not beyond the community except in the case of the elite. The latter maintained their caste exclusiveness by careful recording of genealogies which appear in the preconquest codices and in the colonial documents as well. This system was in use all over the Mixteca of which the Valley of Nochixtlan was only a part and of which the kingdom of Yanhuitlan was only one among many. It is to these fascinating prehistoric picture books that we now turn.

The Mixtec Codices: Content, Decipherment, and Characteristics. There are two main topical groups of pre-Columbian manuscripts from the Mixteca-Puebla area. One is the "Borgia Group," named after the chief document, *Codex Borgia.* This cluster of six manuscripts is mainly ritual and calendrical in content. The gods are depicted, mythological events transpire, and the mysteries of the sacred almanac and yearly calendar are laid out. At least three are certainly from the Mixteca. These codices are discussed further in the concluding chapter.

The second major group is that which here interests us most and is genealogical-historical in content. It consists of eight surviving manuscripts. Bishop Burgoa tells us that the painted books of the Mixtecs give us the day and year signs, name and god-hieroglyphs, marriages, ceremonies, sacrifices, and military events (M. E. Smith, 1973). Some few codices combine information from both groups: the *Codex Vienna,* for example.

The major decipherment of the manuscripts was done over a period of 50 years. Zelia Nuttall in 1902 first suggested that the *Codex Nuttall* contained historical information. James Cooper Clark in 1912 put together from several manuscripts the story of the great Mixtec conqueror 8-Deer "Tiger Claw." Although inaccurate in many respects, this was a major step forward. Interest in the manuscripts then lapsed except for commentary by Long and Spinden. The latter set up the genealogical-historical category. The great breakthrough came with the publication of "El Mapa de Teozacoalco" in 1949, by Alfonso Caso. In this study, Caso dealt with a pictorial document which shows the genealogies of the Mixtec ruling families of Tilantongo and Teozacoalco. The record was carried back into the prehistoric past and overlapped with pre-Columbian manuscripts such as the Nuttall. Further, "El Mapa de Teozacoalco" carried European dates corresponding to the Mixtec hieroglyphs, as well as commentary in Roman script. Using these keys, Caso proceeded to a series of brilliant commentaries on the various codices of the genealogical-historical group. With this extraordinary work, and those of his colleagues, we now have available

elite-class histories for a great part of the Mixtec area running continuously from A.D. 692(?) to 1642. The colonial documents overlap, and we are thus able to carry the record up to modern times in some cases.

For our purposes, some of the major features of the information produced by Caso and others are as follows. We are able to construct (at times) amazingly detailed historical records for regions which are as yet archaeologically unknown. Our perspective, therefore, is more than that which is given us by the still small archaeological sample. It is still an incomplete perspective, but the basic outlines of historical events comprehend most of the Mixteca. Social structural features are contained in great detail in the colonial documents which supplement and continue the prehistoric records. Thus we can infer these same features onto the framework provided by the prehistoric manuscripts and archaeology.

Most of the codices are painted in bright colors on deer or other animal skin sized with plaster coating. The codices are screen-folds and usually are to be read in a zig-zag fashion. Reading is helped by the use of red lines which divide the codices into registers, and one usually reads until a break in the red line is found and then shifts up or down to the next register. Multiple colors are used and the superficial appearance is like that of our Sunday comics. However, the resemblance ends with the surface stylistic features. Several codices are extremely pleasing in an aesthetic sense, and indeed, Burgoa says that the nobility also used them as room decorations.

Walter Krickeberg said about the codices that "Gods and mythical figures continually intervene in human destiny and the beginning of a genealogy in particular always depicts a 'Prologue in Heaven,' and presents the primal ancestors emerging from the centre of the earth and out of the trees" (1956: 277). Burgoa favored the theory that the elite class had come from the northwest and over the mountains. He also mentions two other theories current in the seventeenth century. One story had the Mixtec settlers coming from the West. Another myth was that the Mixtecs came from trees on a river bank near the town of Apoala. In the *Bodley Codex,* there is an extraordinary scene early in the manuscript which seems to show the birth of an ancestress of the Tilantongo rulers from the Apoala trees. This origin myth, however, seems only to apply to the aristocracy. Commoners had come from the center of the earth.

All persons shown in the codices are named after their birthdays in the sacred almanac system. Thus the ancestral female shown in the *Bodley Codex* had the name 1-Death. However, to distinguish among all persons born on the same day, at the age of seven each was given a nickname. Thus we have the famous conqueror 8-Deer "Tiger Claw" to distinguish between him and later rulers, 8-Deer "Quetzal Cobweb," and 8-Deer "Fire Serpent."

Each small city-state kept such records, usually in the temple, or in the palace buildings. These constituted the validation of the right to rule, of the patrimony and the rights and privileges that went with the position, and a record of how things went during a reign. Only a few of the presumed many documents have survived to this day, most in European libraries and museums. Fortunately for us, the historical circumstances of the Mixteca were such that at one point most of the records overlapped through the activities of 8-Deer "Tiger Claw."

According to the amalgamated story pieced together by Caso, 8-Deer was born in A.D. 1011 to the ruler of Tilantongo, whose name was 5-Alligator "Rain-Sun" (1966b). Tilantongo dominated an area in the northern Mixteca Alta. There is a possibility that this 5-Alligator may have been involved in the military break-in to the Maya area in the tenth century. A certain 5-Alligator is prominent on the fine orange pottery found at Altar de Sacrificios. However, he may also have been another, previous 5-Alligator named in the codices or not a Mixtec at all. In any case, 5-Alligator was a fairly successful militarist as such things went. He died in 1030, leaving his son the throne at the age of nineteen. It may be that a regent acted for 8-Deer in the first few years of his reign. Relatively soon, however, 8-Deer "Tiger Claw" showed outstanding ability and began to put together a political-tribute-alliance system which was more than the standard Mixtec city-state. He may well have been helped by the possible additional inheritance of the throne of the most important south coast town, Tututepec. In that case, 8-Deer's story is a little less fabulous and more like that of the self-made millionaire who used to brag about having arrived in town with only the clothes on his back and a paper bag. Finally, when someone asked him what he had had in the paper bag, he admitted that it had contained $50,000.

Be that as it may, 8-Deer, with or without striking advantages, came the closest to establishing a Mixtec empire as any Mixtec ruler in prehistory. He conquered various places and allied himself to others by judicious and multiple marriages. As an example of the latter, 8-Deer is recorded in the *Bodley Codex* as having married 13-Serpent "Serpent of Flowers" in 1051, 6-Eagle in 1053, 11-Serpent in 1060, and two other women. One of the great events in 8-Deer's life was the incident in which he was requested by the ruler of Tula, 4-Tiger, to capture another ruler. With the help of his half-brother, 8-Deer did as requested in 1045 and drove the captive to Tula. He was rewarded by having his nose perforated and a jade nose plug inserted, signifying his elevation to the rank of *tecuhtli* (lord). At the age of sixty-two, 8-Deer finally went to war once too often and attacked the town of some of his in-laws, who resisted, took 8-Deer prisoner, and promptly sacrified him, sending him to join the gods. Still, he was a great man and was buried with proper ceremony eleven days after his death. He is shown in the *Bodley Codex* as seated in his mummy bundle in a stone chamber with incense pots smoking around him.

The last few pages of the *Vienna Codex* are lined off in red, but not filled in, the last entry occurring ca. 1397. This codex's records were cut short by the Aztec conquest of the area. Apparently the codex was taken back to Tenochtitlan as part of the loot. Many other interesting histories are set down in the codices; for example, that of the formidable woman ruler, 6-Monkey, who, having been insulted by two male rulers, promptly conquered and sacrificed them. Yanhuitlan no doubt had such pre-Columbian records, but they have not survived, except in colonial transcriptions.

A number of problems remain in the decipherment of the Mixtec pictorial books, one of the most crucial being that of identifying the places named in the codices with archaeological sites or present-day communities. Mary Elizabeth Smith has made great headway in this area. Another intriguing possibility is that lords of other ethnic groups (Zapotec, Chatino, Mixe, etc.) are mentioned in the Mixtec codices. Caso has identified some Tlaxcalan lords in the *Codex Nuttall*. Overlap of dynastic records between the Mixtec and Maya has already been mentioned as a possibility. Caso, unfortunately, is no longer with us, but his work goes on.

The Spaniards built one of their principal colonial churches at Yanhuitlan in the sixteenth century, a handsome example of a "fortress" church. They also retained much of the old Mixtec social order as an administrative and exploitative apparatus. It was not until the seventeenth century that the system began to break down under the twin assaults of a drastic population loss which, in turn, was linked to a severe economic depression. By 1600, population in the valley had been reduced by all causes to about 10,000, for an 80 percent loss. The tribute system sustaining the old nobility could no longer be supported along with that imposed by the Spanish colonial empire. The surviving members of the Yanhuitlan ruling family sold off the last of their inherited lands in the mid-nineteenth century (Caso, 1966a).

THE COAST OF OAXACA AND THE ISTHMUS OF TEHUANTEPEC. At the time of the Spanish conquest both the Coast of Oaxaca and the Isthmus of Tehuantepec were exceedingly complex areas ethnically, linguistically, and culturally. From Brockington's survey of the coast and Wallrath's work in the isthmus, it appears that this fractionation may have been the case since at least the end of the Preclassic period, and perhaps before (Brockington, Jorrin, and Long, 1974; Brockington and Long, 1974; Wallrath, 1967).

On the Oaxaca coast, Spores notes the presence in the sixteenth century of the Mixteca de la Costa, Chatino, Southern Zapotec, Nahuatl, and Chontal (Tequistlateco) groups (1965). Various origin myths, some recorded, and others of oral tradition, mention Nahuatl speakers coming down to the coast from Tula via Jalisco. Other traditions bring in Chontal from Tabasco.

Brockington's survey and excavations, especially at Sipolite near Puerto Angel, show a long and complex occupation of the coast from late Preclassic times to present. Late Preclassic ceramics are vaguely similar to those of Monte Alban I and II. A considerable body of stone sculpture may go with this period's development, with the stone stelae showing some resemblances to the material from the nearby south coast of Guatemala. Some small civic centers were found, consisting of platforms grouped around courtyards. This seems reminiscent of the west Mexican pattern. Long notes that the relatively undisturbed development of coastal ceramics is upset in the late Classic and early Postclassic with the appearance of various Fine Orange, Fine Gray, and Fine Black wares. These are linked to the ceramics of the Tabasco Coast across the isthmus, and Long suggests that it represents an intrusion of Maya people from that zone. Long also notes the variability of the local sequences from the several sites. In the late Postclassic period, some sites have Mixtec pottery, indicating Mixtec trade or presence. This correlates with the fact that Tututepec is known from documents to have made repeated attempts to dominate the coast, and was in perennial conflict with the coastal range Zapotec town of Coatlan. Thus, the shattered nature of the archaeological regions ties in with the documents, the linguistics, and the ethnographic picture in indicating a marginal, but complex area which was continually changing hands or being penetrated by new cultural groups.

The Oaxaca coast continues to the east and becomes part of the plains of the Isthmus of Tehuantepec. In the sixteenth century, Huave, Zapotec, Mixe, Zoque, and Nahuatl groups inhabited the Pacific side of the isthmus. The only major archaeological work so far has been done by Matthew Wallrath (1967), who established a sequence which runs from 850 B.C. to present. The earliest known settlements were centered on the lagoons and are about contemporary with Chiapa II (Dili) at Chiapa de Corzo. However, as with most of the rest of the sequence, the ceramics show remarkable regionality and do not closely relate to any other known cultural area. Platform building did not begin until about 100 B.C., appearing in small sites. Presumably we have a long period of village-centered society with small civic architecture, through most of the sequence. Four major Mixteca-Puebla horizon

sites are known. This includes the Guiengola fortress which has already been discussed in connection with the Zapotecs. Again, the reconstruction with the data at hand is one of a marginal area largely out of the major cultural-historical action for most of the time and pushed around by events beyond its control in the late prehistoric period.

THE MIXTECA-PUEBLA STYLE HORIZON. "One of the most noteworthy things in their market was the pottery, of a thousand different designs and colors" (Lopez de Gomara, 1964: 131). Thus Lopez de Gomara describes the famed Cholula polychrome ceramics which were distributed all over central Mexico through a trade and religious network. This style seems to have evolved principally in the Cholula (Puebla) area, beginning at least by A.D. 900, but also to have absorbed influences from, and exerted influence on, Mixteca pottery styles. The final result was the broadly connected set of similar style groups spread over Mesoamerica at the time of Spanish contact. Regional variants of the ceramic expression of the style include the Mixtec polychrome of Monte Alban V period, Isla de Sacrificios V polychrome, Cholulteca III with its "policroma firme," and in the Basin of Mexico, Chalco polychrome pottery. The Borgia group of codices are included in the style by Nicholson, and he argues that the *Borgia Codex* itself was painted in Cholula (1960). The Mitla palace murals show strong affinities to the ceramic and codical styles as do the Tizatlan mural from Tlaxcala, and the Santa Rita murals from Belize.

Nicholson has given the concept a definition which expresses Vaillant's original idea. The style is extraordinarily precise in delineation of motifs. Numerous vivid colors are used and are symbolic themselves. Highly characteristic symbols include solar and lunar disks, water, fire, hearts, war symbols, the 20 *tonalpohualli* signs, serpents, jaguars, deer, and many others. The style is distributed from the Huasteca to the Maya lowlands and possibly even into Central America.

Cholula's position as an exceedingly important pilgrimage center during the Protohistoric period would alone account for wide distribution. Cholula was the center for the worship of Quetzalcoatl. Robertson, as noted before, has characterized the mural style expressed at Santa Rita as a sort of international style of the late Postclassic period, and it is indeed, being a local variant of the Mixteca-Puebla horizon. The distribution is also a fairly nice indicator of the efficiency and vigor of the late prehistoric Mesoamerican trade network along which passed many things not so distinctive as Mixteca-Puebla pottery. The style has no connection with any single ethnic or linguistic group.

Evolution of pottery which seems ancestral to the style at Cholula can be detected around the end of the late Classic. However, the period of the developed style's spread outside its heartland of southern Puebla and the northern Mixteca was probably between A.D. 1400 and 1520. Most centers outside the main area acquired the style either as trade wares or as a localized variant and can be dated thereby.

POSTCLASSIC AND PROTOHISTORIC VERACRUZ

The great Gulf Coast plain of Veracruz was inhabited by at least four major ethnic-linguistic groups at the time of the Spanish conquest: historic Olmecs (their name meaning "Rubber People"), Totonacs, Huastecs, and Nahua groups. We have already seen the difficulties in attempting to equate archaeological cultures with such groups. However, if there is one grand trend in such matters in this area, it is that during the Postclassic period Totonac, Huastec, Uixtotin, and historic Ol-

mec found themselves being compressed into ever smaller territories by expansion of Nahua groups from the highlands. Caution is therefore necessary in dealing with claims of ethnicity projected back through 500, 1000, or 1500 years. Within all coastal areas there was great variability, and multi-ethnic and multi-lingual towns are mentioned in historical documents as well as being reported ethnographically.

Withal, this cultural variability can be organized by means of the two major horizons within the area. The first of these horizons is that of the Toltec, falling between A.D. 1200 and 1450, and physically marked by the appearance of Plumbate and the later styles of Fine Orange pottery as trade wares. The later horizon is that of the Culhua-Mexica empire (Aztec), beginning about 1450 with the first Triple Alliance conquests, and extending up to 1519, the date of arrival of Cortes at Cempoala on the central coast. The latest horizon is an areal variant of the Mixteca-Puebla horizon.

SOUTHERN VERACRUZ. Little is known from the historic Olmec area except from documents and ceramics. Needless to say, these Postclassic and Protohistoric people had no necessary connection with the "Olmecs" of early Preclassic times. Their territory occupied the northern entrance to the trade route across the Isthmus of Tehuantepec.

Early Postclassic pottery is found at Tres Zapotes which is highly regionalized: the Soncautla complex. This complex is different in almost every respect from anything earlier at the site and includes large, hollow, human effigy figures. The pottery is related to other early Postclassic pottery found at Isla de Sacrificios. However, the Fine Orange and Plumbate horizon markers are not found. Cremation burial appears as a new means of disposal of the dead. Taken all together (discontinuity of ceramic tradition, cremation burials, stylistic linkages of the large clay figures and other traits), the situation suggests that this is possibly the time that the historically known Nahua speakers of the area moved into it. Very little is known of architecture during the period, but apparently population was fairly dense judging by the high frequency of early Postclassic remains in the area.

To the east, in the Chontalpa plain of Tabasco, Sanders excavated a small site named Sigero which may be typical of this period for both areas (1963). The site is a small ceremonial center oriented around a central plaza. A main temple is located on the north edge of the plaza, a residential structure on the west, and a ball court to the east. Small housemounds are scattered over the surrounding countryside and probably represent the population served by the center. There is little evidence of larger centers, and the settlement pattern reminds Sanders greatly of the modern pattern of the area.

The Protohistoric period is marked by pottery styles that are related to the general Mixteca-Puebla groups of pottery, associated in this area with Aztec trade and conquest. Brilliant polychromes show up in some zones of the south, but Basin of Mexico black-on-orange pottery is unknown. Settlement patterns and population sizes were probably the same as for the preceding period.

Sixteenth-century documents indicate a high population of 150,000 to 200,000. Aztec control of the area was typically exercised through native leaders, tax collectors, and garrisons. However, there was no overall Aztec control of the Chontalpa and southern Veracruz. At least one "province" (Coatzalcoalcos) was independent. In other words, the political situation matched the linguistic-ethnic fragmentation. The zone was economically important and furnished rubber, cacao, cotton, and medicinal herbs to the surrounding area and to the central plateau. The people were famous as multilingual traders, and

Malinche, Cortes' Spanish translator, came from this zone. These zones rapidly became depopulated during the epidemics after the Spanish conquest.

CENTRAL VERACRUZ: EARLY AND MIDDLE POSTCLASSIC CENTERS. The late architectural tradition developed at Tajin was somewhat carried on in the middle Postclassic period (A.D. 1250 to 1450) of central Veracruz, in the continuing traits of jutting cornices, columns, friezes with high relief frets, and communication tunnels, according to Garcia Payon. During this period, the Toltecs possibly established themselves in the area. Alfonso Medellin-Zenil (1960) and Jose Garcia Payon (1971) attribute the well-preserved pyramid-temple at Teayo to the Toltecs and say that it was built in A.D. 815. Both the date and ethnic identification seem dubious on the evidence. There is no doubt whatsoever of the affiliation of Teayo's temple with central plateau architecture. Elsewhere, at the Tuzapan fortress, there are ceramics which are quite close to Toltec-affiliated Mazapan red-and-orange pottery. Other Tuzapan pottery is related to plateau ceramic groups such as Coyotlatelco and Culhuacan black-on-orange wares. Much of this alien pottery is associated with fortified centers. Although there is some doubt about the Toltec identification of Teayo and Tuzapan occupations, then, there is little doubt that central plateau peoples are involved, perhaps in a military way.

During the early Postclassic period several regional and native styles of pottery were developed, including a particularly lively type of polychrome called Tres Picos I which was decorated with dancing coyotes and monkeys. The Isla de Sacrificios site off the central coast apparently assumed its sacred burial ground function during this period, and a particular tradition of polychrome types found there are named after the site (Isla de Sacrificios I, II, III, IV).

The intrusion of central plateau pottery and formal architectural styles into the Veracruz plain may reflect the beginning of the intrusion of peoples from the overpopulated highlands. This trend certainly is historically known for the next period, when it intensified.

The Protohistoric period in central Veracruz begins about A.D. 1400 and represents the certain emergence of the land of the Totonacs or El Totonacapan. A major center of Totonacapan included Quauhtochco, which was conquered by the Aztecs between A.D. 1450 and A.D. 1472. The site has been excavated and is located in the Orizaba-Cordoba district. Although the ecological setting is semi-arid, the site is on a river as are all of the other major sites. Although Quauhtochco was founded in late Preclassic times, the major period is clearly the latest when it was under the domination of the Aztec empire. The major temple of the center is much like those found in the Basin of Mexico. For example, the panels on the upper facades of the temple itself are studded with "nailhead" stones which probably represent stars. Many of the associated ceramics are related to the Aztec III black-on-orange wares, and to the "lacquer-finish" polychromes of Cholula. It is interesting that the Mixteca-Puebla polychromes at Quauhtochco were made from local clays. There are large braziers of coarse, heavy ceramic material which served as temple incense burners. Gods represented in the associated clay figurines include many central plateau deities, according to Medellin-Zenil.

Another fifteenth century center in the same district is the fortress-cemetery of Comapan, built high on an escarpment. The fortifications, as in the case of Tepexi el Viejo in the Mixteca-Puebla area, consist of high stone-revetted terraces and free-standing walls. The site includes temples, residential palaces, tombs, shrines, and other architectonic complexities. Unfortunately, it has never been adequately explored or mapped. Historical documents indicate that the fortress goes back to the fourteenth century, and that it was occupied by the historic Olmecs. Mixteca-Puebla horizon polychrome pottery occurs at the site.

CEMPOALA AND QUIAHUIZTLAN. The most densely inhabited regions of Totonacapan were dry and warm zones along major rivers which were used as irrigation sources. I. T. Kelly and A. Palerm (1952) have estimated that about 250,000 people lived in the province of Cempoala alone, with between 80,000 and 120,000 in the city. Cempoala was near the coast, but the center of Jalapa, further inland, is estimated also to have had about 120,000 persons. Other, smaller centers had respectable populations: Colipa 24,000, and Papantla 60,000.

Based on these density estimates, the descriptions left us by the Spaniards, and the archaeological remains, there is no doubt that Cempoala was a true urban center. The city lies in the bend of the Rio Grande de Actopan which has an interlaced network of wandering channels at this point. Highly productive irrigation architecture supported the large populations. The site is laid out on the flat flood plain and arranged in at least nine major precincts. These zones are paved areas surrounded by walls which served both defense and flood control purposes. High platforms elevate the main structures above flood level.

The major group at Cempoala includes five separate temples arranged about three sides of an enclosed courtyard of substantial size. This courtyard was the scene of the crucial battle between Cortes' and Narvaez's troops during the conquest of Mexico. Dance platforms are located in front of some of the temples. A round temple base indicates the presence of a structure dedicated to Quetzalcoatl-Ehecatl. At least ten T-shaped tombs are known from the main group. There is a total area of 120,000 square meters (1,296,000 square feet) covered by the formal architecture at Cempoala with much more represented by domestic housing. It is known that a water system furnished fresh water to each house.

Ceramics associated with the latest period are closely related to late Cholula (Mixteca-Puebla) style pottery, and still other types continue the regional Isla de Sacrificios ceramic tradition.

Cempoala was the first major Mesoamerican city to be seen by the Spaniards. Cortes' expedition went there at the invitation of the Totonac leaders, and was warmly received by a ruler that they affectionately called "the Fat Cacique."

Quiahuiztlan is located a short march away from Cempoala and was a smaller contemporary site. Several major temples dominate the fortress center. Defensive works consist of location on a ridge which has been modified by high terrace walls. Quiahuiztlan also contains at least a dozen cemeteries of a special kind. These cemeteries consist of small mausoleums in the form of miniature temples. Secondary burials are found in chambers in the base platforms, and small conduits often lead up to the temple-shrine above. Presumably we have here something paralleling the Maya practice of making sure that the distinguished dead were kept apprised of the latest events and could be appealed to for supernatural aid. At any rate, only the important dead were buried in these small buildings along with their funerary offerings of ceramics and jewelry. Medellin-Zenil says that animal sculptures are frequently found by the mausoleums and suggests that these represent the "animal-souls" (*tonals*) of the individuals buried inside (1960). This belief in animal souls (tonalism) is ethnographically widespread in Mesoamerica, and presumably these cemeteries represent an origin of the belief in the archaeological past.

It was at Quiahuiztlan that Cortes first met representatives of the Aztec empire. These were some very haughty tax-collectors (*calpixque*) who demanded that the Spaniards be refused hospitality. Cortes arranged for their arrest, thereby initiating the first assault on the Aztec political system.

THE HUASTECA

The vast Huasteca area is one of extreme ecological complexity, even for Mesoamerica, and is united only loosely by certain cultural traits and by language. The Huasteca lies in northern Veracruz and southern Tamaulipas and includes both very mountainous and flood plain topography. The Huastec speak a form of Maya which may have split from the rest of Maya languages about 1500 B.C., according to lexico-statistics. However, aside from the linguistic affiliation, the Huastec followed their own cultural trajectory, which seems closer to that of the rest of Mexico than to their Maya relatives. One further handicap in understanding the Huastec area is that the area is poorly known, and the sample of data varies wildly in quality.

The earliest cultural development in the Huasteca has already been discussed in the section on the development of sedentary life and domestication of plants. The Tamaulipas caves and villages excavated by MacNeish also have yielded a series of phases which continue from where we left it, 1500 B.C., to about A.D. 1520 (MacNeish, 1958).

The major features of the archaeological record of this area are the increasing amounts of domesticated foods and the increasing numbers of people which accompany that. There is also the remarkable stabilization at the village level of cultural complexity. In other words, the Huasteca cultural development was somehow arrested at the late Preclassic level for most of its history. The major perturbations are in the direction of deevolution.

**Chronological Chart for the Huasteca,
1400 B.C. to A.D. 1750**

Time	Sierra de Tamaulipas	Southwest Sierra Madre
1750	Los Angeles	San Antonio
1300		
		San Lorenzo
900		
	La Salta	
500		
		Palmillas
AD 1	Eslabones	
BC 1	Laguna	La Florida
500		
		Mesa de Guaje
1400		
		Guerra

MacNeish, 1958

In more detail, the *Mesa de Guaje* phase represents a village-oriented society in which agricultural stability has been achieved with about 40 percent of the food produced by cultivated plants. The following *La Florida* phase shows about the same subsistence proportions of wild to domesticated plant foods, but the numbers of communities and their nature change significantly. MacNeish says that temple-oriented village groups are the normal pattern. During the *Palmillas* phase, shortly after the time of Christ, there is a further increase in the numbers of villages and people, and a maximum population is reached in the mountains of the Huasteca. Up to 1400 house platforms have been found around a single temple, each presumably representing a household. The villages reach their most complex development with the addition of ball courts and possible water storage facilities. At this time (about A.D. 500) the area has reached a degree of complexity equal to that used by other Mesoamerican peoples to launch themselves on the quantum jump to civilization. However, that did not happen, and the period after about A.D. 500 represents a drastic simplification of material culture and of the incipient civic centers. The villages of this time mainly lack the civic center features of the preceding period. The final period from A.D. 1300 to 1750 seems to represent a stabilized version of this impoverished culture, and was the situation encountered by the Spaniards during their incursions into the zone during the colonial period.

SOUTH AND WESTERN HUASTECA.   To the south and west of the Huasteca area in which Mac-Neish has worked were more sophisticated developments (1971). These sites lie in what are now the states of San Luis Potosi, Hidalgo, and Queretaro. The area is thinly known, and the sample is poor in quality.

Ceramics show that the area was occupied by at least the end of the late Preclassic period. Some Teotihuacan contact is indicated by certain forms of pottery. Presumably this part of the Huasteca was exploited by or was a trade area for the Teotihuacanos. Presumably also, the area had gone through much of the same cultural evolution as that which we have seen for the area to the east and north in Tamaulipas. However, it did not stabilize at the same level. By about A.D. 500, a number of small ceremonial centers had developed with at least a few larger ones. The pattern of site hierarchy is similar to that of the Etzatlan region in west Mexico.

Tamuin in San Luis Potosi is one of the largest of the sites of the late Classic and early Postclassic periods and is located on a river. Presumably the center was founded in the Preclassic period. However, the period best known at the site is the Toltec horizon. The site occupies about 17 hectares (42 acres) and has dozens of mounds, but no satisfactory map has ever been published. The largest platforms are arranged about the inevitable open courtyards. Excavations have been concentrated around the south platform. This structure seems to have supported a number of perishable buildings.

One small temple platform produced an interesting mural, painted in dark red on a stucco-covered altar. Associated pottery dates the mural to the ninth century A.D. Eleven resplendent personages appear in a line, all facing in the same direction. In this arrangement and theme the painting is similar to the carved Toltec altars noted before at Tula and Toltec Chichen. Five persons are seated and six stand. All hold diverse and ornamented items which appear to be fans, spear-throwers, and symbols of rank. One individual holds what seems to be a human head by the hair.

A small, nearby structure produced a magnificent piece of sculpture, the so-called Huastec Boy. The appealing naturalism of the piece is strongly modified by intricate low reliefs on various parts of the body, probably indicating tattoos. A child clings to the "boy's" lower back. The "tattoos" are stylistically related to the paintings. Other sculptures from the Huasteca seem to represent life images of a person on one side and a death image on the other.

Tombs were found on both sides of the main staircase of the south platform, all with men and women buried in the fetal position. Only the south line of tombs had offerings, including brand-new vases apparently acquired or made for the occasion.

The Aztecs did a great deal of trading with the Huastecs in Protohistoric times. Distinctive pottery was made then in the area and features intricate black-on-white designs painted on various forms of jars and vases. Some are effigy vessels and many have pouring spouts and strap-handles.

Other large centers such as Tancanhuitz, Tantoc, and Tamposoque are similar to Tamuin but much less known.

The Gulf Coast section of the Huasteca has a long ceramic sequence running back into the early Preclassic period. This tropical area is roughly centered around Tuxpan and Tampico. One site is better known than others in the area: La Florida. Only one structure was dug by Ekholm, principally because most of the site had already been destroyed. The clay platform and perishable temple atop it were both round. The temple had a wooden roof. The latest construction phase dates to the fifteenth century, probably about the time that the Aztecs, under Moteczoma I, conquered the zone (A.D. 1460–1461).

Ethnohistorical documents state that the Huastec, like the Totonac, had once occupied much more territory than they held in the sixteenth century. It seems clear that a principal reason for this territorial contraction was the fact that Nahua groups, including the later Aztecs, had pressed the Huastec northward.

THE VALLEY OF TOLUCA

Although the Valley of Toluca is an attractive place ecologically, the Matlazinca who occupied it during at least the Protohistoric period were in a truly unenviable position. To the west were located the formidable Tarascans, while the predatory and militaristic Aztecs were just over the mountain range to the east.

At the time of the Spanish conquest, a principal Matlazinca city was Tecaxic, located near Calixtlahuaca. Ixtlilxochitl mentions that the Matlazincas were conquered by the Toltecs and forced by them to pay tribute. According to several chronicles the Matlazincas later underwent great difficulties in dealing with their more powerful neighbors during the fifteenth century. Lack of political unity led to disorganization in the face of Aztec aggression during the reign of Axayacatl. A series of wars begun in 1473 led to eventual Aztec domination of the central valley of Toluca and later, in 1476, Malinalco. Tizoc, Axayacatl's successor, had trouble with the Matlazincas and destroyed Tecaxic's temples during his punitive campaign. Tecaxic also made the error of rebelling against Moteczoma II in 1510, who abolished the town. Nearby Calixtlahuaca, which had been favored by the Aztecs, assumed Tecaxic's place in the tribute lists.

Having inherited the tributaries in the Toluca Valley, Ahuitzotl, the ruling Aztec emperor, had construction begun in 1501 on the House of the Eagle and Tiger Knights that perched high on its cliff above Malinalco.

THE ARCHAEOLOGICAL RECORD: CALIXTLAHUACA AND MALINALCO. Calixtlahuaca is located on the steep hill called Tenismo, which was anciently terraced. Middle Preclassic material has been found in the Toluca Valley but not at Calixtlahuaca. Excavations at the site in the 1930s established a ceramic sequence running from Teotihuacan times to the Aztec conquest period. The ceramic record is supplemented by both architecture and the chronicle information summarized above.

Seventeen major buildings and complexes are scattered without much apparent plan over the terraced areas. One of these, Structure 3, has a round plan and went through four stages of construction. The first period dates from that of Teotihuacan, although the building shows no apparent relationship to the architecture of that greater city. The final building is the platform on which the temple to Quetzalcoatl-Ehecatl, the wind god, was located. Presumably this temple was one of those destroyed by Axayacatl or Moteczoma II. A well-done sculptured figure of a man equipped with not much more than the wind god's face mask was found in the ruins of this temple. Structure 17 is actually a complex of many rooms which may have been a true palace structure. It includes many small ". . . patios, living rooms, small shrines, and passageways at different levels . . ." (Marquina, 1964: 232).

Malinalco is located in a small valley just to the south of the main Toluca Valley. It is a zone of extraordinary fractured cliffs hung with greenery. High on one of these cliffs, 700 feet above the valley floor, the House of the Eagle and Tiger Knights was built on a shelf cut from the rock. Most extraordinarily, major portions of the buildings themselves are cut from the cliff rock forming an architectonic conception which is essentially that of a gigantic sculpture. The shelf was cut around a corner leaving an L-shaped space. The rock forms the lower parts of the temples, which were roofed with elaborate perishable materials. Channels cut into the cliff rock lead rainwater away from the buildings. Three of the temples are round in plan. Structure I has a bench within, upon which are carved eagles and an ocelot pelt. The building was evidently dedicated to the sun god in spite of the round plan. In Structure III, the front of which is built of masonry, were found the remains of a large mural. The fragments show a line of warriors advancing to the attack with their shields and spears at the ready. The theme harks back to Tula at least, but the style is definitely Aztec. The present town of Malinalco somehow preserved a magnificent carved wooden drum until the beginning of this century. It is now in the National Museum. Presumably it comes from the temple zone above, and in any case is appropriately carved with eagles, dancing ocelots, and solar signs.

Malinalco is only one of dozens of shrines and pilgrimage temples which once were scattered throughout Mesoamerica. Some drew pilgrims from all over, such as the great temple of Quetzalcoatl at Cholula. Some, like Malinalco, were dedicated to special activities and are somewhat analogous to the ritual buildings of such organizations as the Masonic order among us today. Still other temples probably were dedicated to gods of only local interest. For example, there is a small Protohistoric temple located above the present, anthropologically famous town of Tepoztlan. The temple is dedicated to the god of intoxication and pulque, Ome Tochtli (2-Rabbit). The building is presently known as the Temple of Tepozteco. Its pilgrims today are tourists.

TEPEXI EL VIEJO: A LATE FORTRESS SITE

The Tepexi el Viejo fortress is located in southern Puebla and is near to the Mixteca Baja. We will spend perhaps more space on it than seems warranted, but it represents one of the few small states about which we have both archaeological and documentary information, thanks to the work of Shirley Gorenstein (1973). In the vicissitudes of Tepexi we may see mirrored something of the typical dilemmas and resolutions of this type of traditional Mesoamerican community.

Tepexi (Rocky Place) is mentioned in chronicles as being part of a kingdom of southern Puebla ruled by the city of Quauhtinchan until that place was conquered by Tlatelolco (Tenochtitlan's twin city) in A.D. 1438. Tlatelolco made marriage alliances with various towns of southern Puebla, including a linkage with the ruling family of Tepexi. In the meantime, Tepexi pursued its traditional rivalries with other small city-states to the south and north, fighting with them over tributaries. The city apparently remained more or less independent until 1503 when the Mexica-Aztecs conquered the place and made it tributary to one of their regional garrison points, Tepeaca, located 70 kilometers (44 miles) to the north. The fortress remained in this network of the Aztec tribute system until 1520, when it was conquered by Cortes. Soon after this final disaster, the remaining population was congregated at a village site which replaced Tepexi el Viejo as the regional capital. This is the town of Tepexi de Rodriguez, also known as Tepexi de la Seda. The latter name comes from the fact that a strong silk (*seda*) industry was introduced by the Spaniards in the early colonial period in the same way as was done in the Mixteca Alta. The silk industry in both areas was successful for a while and then failed due to the population losses during the late sixteenth-century plagues and the competition of Chinese silk in the European markets.

THE ARCHAEOLOGICAL RECORD. Tepexi Fortress is located atop a steep ridge which is defined by three deep canyons. One canyon is the river bed of the Xamilpan River and most of the cultivable land around Tepexi is located there. *Lama-bordo,* a terrace-check dam system of soil conservation, was used on the steep hillsides.

The fortress itself is only the main precinct among five associated hilltop groups of formal architecture. The flattened top of the ridge was retained and expanded by the use of massive outer walls which were as high as 15 meters (50 feet). Formal gates and what may have been guard houses on the walls complete the inventory of fortifications. The height of the walls and the fact that they were plastered were the major functional features of military construction at Tepexi. Construction of the walls and other buildings is of the same nature. A mass of adobe mortar was combined with blocks of *caliche*. Shaped caliche blocks faced the walls, being laid in the same mortar, and were finished off with a thin plaster. Plazas, pyramidal platforms, and building complexes occupied the space inside the walls. The building complexes are agglomerations of rooms, of the sort we have seen repeatedly and which were probably used as elite-class housing. No burials have been recovered because most of these were looted in 1949. Counting all of the roofed-over space, Gorenstein estimates that the 62,000 square meters (203,360 square feet) could have accommodated between 6000 and 12,000 people. In a 1565 census, Tepexi is listed as having 10,000 to 11,000 people, lending weight to this estimate.

The ceramic sequence runs from A.D. 1300 to 1520, thereby falling entirely within the Protohistoric period. Ceramics for all three phases indicate heavy reliance on local manufactures for domestic pottery, but strong contacts with outside areas for fine pottery. Especially important are Mixteca-Puebla regional polychromes from the Mixteca and Cholula, as well as black-on-orange pottery from the Basin of Mexico. Ceramic linkages with Veracruz are confirmed by documentary evidence for two major trails leading from Tepexi to the Veracruz lowlands. One trail connects with Cempoala on the coast, and the other turns southward to the Tuxtlas Mountains area.

Gorenstein comments that the tributary system of a small city-state such as Tepexi was decentralized. Although subordinate communities owed economic tribute to the dominant community, they were left more or less alone in their sociopolitical affairs. According to Gorenstein, this decentralization also corre-lates with the nonspecialized militarism reflected at Tepexi el Viejo. The Aztecs had moved beyond the simple economic tribute system and toward the control of the sociopolitical affairs of their tributaries. This trend was part of a move to a greater degree of state centralization. In the more traditional characteristics, Tepexi represented a much older and more vulnerable order of society. Both Aztecs and Tepexijeños, however, fell before the Spaniards.

THE TEHUACAN VALLEY: THE LAST PHASES

The master chronology of the Tehuacan Valley includes a long Postclassic phase called Venta Salada, which runs from A.D. 700 or 800 to A.D. 1520. The Tehuacan Project members and Edward Sisson have been able to amass a remarkably detailed amount of data relating to the Tehuacan Valley in the Postclassic period, including details of ordinary life. (Sisson, 1973, 1974).

Valley population is estimated by MacNeish to have been between 60,000 and 120,000 just before the Spanish conquest (1962: 41). This population was supported by intensive agriculture based on a variety of irrigation techniques. The main technique used on the relatively flat valley floor was and is still the canal system type. These systems have a dendritic pattern as seen in Woodbury and Neely's maps and usually depended on springs (1972). Many of these systems have been fossilized by the travertine content of the water. Almost as important were combination terracing and check-dam systems used on hillsides. Large dam building was tried once in the Tilapa River area of Tehuacan, but finally given up. The Purron Dam was begun about 700 B.C. and the last phase of this immense structure was built about A.D. 300. It silted up and was abandoned. Early Postclassic population, therefore, also abandoned the area. Our own Corps of Army Engineers might do well to study this.

Of the 456 archaeological sites in the Tehuacan Valley, 357 have Classic and Postclassic remains. Coxcatlan is recorded as being one of the principal towns of the area in the sixteenth century, and the center of a tributary network. Before the Spanish conquest it had been a tributary of Teotitlan del Camino in the Mixteca area.

Salt production is mentioned in many colonial documents as being a principal resource of Coxcatlan both then and in pre-Hispanic times. The 1580 production figures are listed as being between 6400 and 8000 bushels per year, some of which was exported to the Basin of Mexico and to mining areas in the north and northwest. No preconquest tribute list notes salt as a tribute item for Coxcatlan, however. Salt was produced by solar evaporation of water from saline wells, and by leaching it from mineral-bearing earth. Salt-making sites in the valley are marked by special, coarse pottery salt molds, mounds of earth with pottery tubing probably used for brine filtering, and by the solar evaporation pans. The latter are still in use in the valley today and are nearly identical to the ancient examples.

Sisson has excavated in the vicinity of many of the small ward temples within Coxcatlan Viejo and other sites. At Coxcatlan Viejo houses were clustered around what are apparently calpulli temple plazas. The remains of looted tombs have been found near the tops of these temples, while dozens of cremation burials in coarse jars and pots are buried in front of them. In one case, ninety-seven cremation burials were found under a plastered apron extending out from the temple base.

Ceramics of the valley during the Venta Salada period are heavily regionalized for the major domestic wares. However, Mixteca-Puebla polychromes (Mixtec and Cholula), and Veracruz ceramics are also found, as at Tepexi el Viejo.

Perhaps the most fascinating part of Sisson's work has been in the common housing areas. These houses were not necessarily mean and humble. One house excavated at the site of San Mateo Tlacuchcalco (Tr 65) contained at least 500 square meters (1650 square feet) and perhaps double that. The pattern is one of several rooms or apartments clustered around an open patio, or even a series of patios. Stucco floors cover the patios, and the interiors of the rooms are plastered. Drains lead rain water away from open areas. Plastered water storage basins set in floors are nearly identical to those in use in modern Coxcatlan. Several houses have evidence of craft specialties: spinning and weaving and pottery-making. Perhaps the only example of a prehistoric kiln in Mesoamerica was found at Coxcatlan Viejo in a house. An amazing find of a carved greenstone Olmec figure is truly puzzling. No explanation can be readily suggested for the presence of a 2400-year-old antique being the property of a humble potter in whose house it was found.

Altogether, the housing and the artifacts of Venta Salada period indicate a fairly high standard of living for even common people in the Tehuacan Valley. Sisson makes the point well:

The patios, open to the sky, must have been the focus for most activities carried out within the residence. Here younger children could play while their mothers chatted and went about their daily activities. Men engaged in certain crafts may have worked on the patio floor. Probably on every clear day, a woman could be found seated on the patio floor weaving, one end of her backstrap loom attached to a circular column of one of the surrounding rooms. In the evening, men returning from the fields or from the hunt would gather in small groups in a neighbor's patio to relax after dinner and to discuss those things which men, and farmers, and hunters always discuss. Finally, each man would return to his wife and children and fall asleep in his family's room located along one side of a patio. Before dawn, the patio would echo with the sound of mano on metate and the patting of masa between bare hands, and the daily cycle would have begun anew" (1974: 15).

It was this life style which ultimately proved the most durable and which still survives today in Mexico, Guatemala, Belize, and El Salvador, the modern political inheritors of ancient Mesoamerica.

CHAPTER 10

GENERAL AND
SPECIAL FEATURES OF
MESOAMERICAN PREHISTORY

Father Roman [y Zamora] relates of the people of Tehuacan, Coscatlan, and Teotitlan del Camino that on the day when the morning star appeared for the first time a human offering was sacrificed, which the king of the land had to provide, and that on each day at the hour when this star rose it was the duty of the priests to burn incense and to draw their own blood, which they offered up to it.
—Seler, vol. 2, 1960: 184.

Of the moral effect of the monuments themselves, standing as they do in the depths of a tropical forest, silent and solemn, strange in design, excellent in sculpture, rich in ornament, different from the works of any other people, their uses and purposes and whole history so entirely unknown with hieroglyphics explaining all but being perfectly unintelligible, I shall not pretend to convey any idea. Often the imagination was pained in gazing at them.
—Stephens, 1949.

COPAN, Glyph Panel, Structure 11. At least 140 such glyph blocks, from which the building gets its name, flanked the doorway entrances to the Temple of Inscriptions. A dedication date of 6 Caban 10 Mol (736 A.D.) firmly places it in the late Classic period. The Temple of Inscriptions, rising 90 feet above the Hieroglyphic Stairway Court, is but one source of the thousands of glyphs so far recorded at Copan.

IF THE REGIONAL CHARACTER OF MESOAMERIcan civilizations has been emphasized in the preceding chapters, it is also worth noting that unifying features tied them together from very early times. It can be argued that much of what was regional about Mesoamerica was mainly on the "folk" level and that most of the unifying features were on the elite level. When the Spaniards came, they destroyed a great deal of elite-class culture and replaced it with another unifying but elite pattern. Our purpose in this final chapter is to examine some of the most important of the widespread native patterns. Another aim is to examine and attempt to explain some of the processes and transformations of whole cultures and culture groups. Finally, we will examine those parts of Mesoamerican culture that survived the conquest.

INTELLECTUAL ACHIEVEMENTS: PAN-MESOAMERICAN RELIGIOUS AND PHILOSOPHICAL PATTERNS

Our perceptions of the nature of Mesoamerican religions are faulty for several reasons. A major factor is the spottiness of the information from the various areas. The Spaniards concentrated on the Aztecs and their allied cultures because of their political and economic importance. Therefore, an overwhelming amount of information comes from the Basin of Mexico. No other Mesoamerican area is so well documented, with the possible exception of highland Guatemala. No Sahagun collected the same amounts of data for the Huasteca or the Totonac that he did for the Mexica. Even in areas with major chronicles, these rarely provide us with the wealth of detail that comes from the combination of chronicles, church documents, conquerors' memoirs, and judicial proceedings that pertain to central Mexico. In addition, there is the historical circumstance of Aztec imperi-

alism having spread central Mexican religious variations over Mesoamerica. Even though all this is true, there is still an amazing amount of cross-cultural information that indicates the unity of philosophical and religious conceptions as indicated above. These unifying elements can be organized into several themes.

Duality is apparently a very basic and lasting theme. The creator pair was a widespread concept throughout central Mexico, and in fact, most gods had consorts. The famous "Hero Twins" of the *Popol Vuh* also come to mind. The more general idea of fertility/life and barrenness/death is still more widespread, with expressions being found in Mexican and Maya religious belief. The malevolent and beneficent aspects of Mesoamerican gods are generally related. This complex of ideas seems traceable back to the Preclassic Olmecs and perhaps to Tlatilco in the highlands. Indeed, M. D. Coe believes that most of the fundamental religious ideas of Mesoamerica were developed by the Olmecs and passed on to most of the later civilizations (1968: 114 et passim). Some of the evidence for this hypothesis has been presented in the chapters on the Olmec and epi-Olmec.

The concept of the underworld and of death gods is another fundamental theme. Among the Aztecs, the ruling deities of the afterlife were Mictlantecuhtli and his wife, Mictlancihuatl, equivalent in function to Ah Puch among the Maya. Related to this concept of the underworld were the gods of caves and of the night sun, Tepeyolotl among the Aztecs, and Votan among the Maya. Cave worship and shrines were important over all of Mesoamerica for these reasons. A small cave shrine recently found under the Pyramid of the Sun at Teotihuacan has been interpreted by Doris Heyden as possibly being the legendary Chicomoztoc (Seven Caves) from which the Aztecs and allied tribes originated (1975). The Maya, both in ancient times and today, worship in caves, regarding the drip water found there as the most sacred and ritually pure. Caves and dark places were artificially created in the small and dark temple rooms of Mesoamerica, and the elite were occasionally buried in natural caverns under temple structures. Perhaps the formal tombs within the temples were conceived of as artificial caves, but there is no confirmation of this idea at the moment.

In addition to the concepts of duality and the importance of the underworld, personified deities also had aspects relating to the various world directions and their associated colors. Thus, one finds the four Tezcatlipocas corresponding to the four cardinal directions. More protean still, the gods melded into one another, the white Tezcatlipoca of the East being an aspect of Quetzalcoatl. Colors varied in their associations with the directions from area to area. For at least some groups, the zenith was considered another direction with its own color.

Sacrifice was an integral part of all Mesoamerican religions. This took the form of sacrifice that we are accustomed to; that is, allocation of time and resources to participate in rituals and in other support of formal religion. It also took more extreme forms such as animal and flower sacrifices, and human sacrifice. As has been outlined, the Aztecs argued that the human sacrifices helped to hold the universe together. Without human blood as sustenance, the sun would weaken and the forces of darkness would end the world. The Maya may have looked on human sacrifice in the same way because they had the same grounding in the basic myth of cyclical creations and destructions. However, they also emphasized the concept of man as the creation and therefore the slave of the gods, with the obligation to offer the gods tangible evidence of obeisance and obedience. Doubtless there were many such philosophical justifications for this practice, but there is also the suggestion that however it began, human sacrifice was ultimately transformed by the Aztecs into an instrument of political terror and social control. Padden's interpretations of Aztec culture have been criticized, but this seems a sound hypothesis and one which has considerable evidence behind it (1967: Chap. 3).

The argument has been made that in Greece, the failure of religious-ethical systems as expressed in plays took place simultaneously with the rise of formal rhetorical-rationalist philosophy. The latter could justify anything and the rhetoric was the persuasive instrument used to impart the message (D. Conley, personal communication). As an example of rhetoric using rationalist logic there are the formal speeches recorded in Thucydides' *Peloponnesian Wars*. Compare this oratory to the discourses of ethical instruction given to Aztec youth as recorded in Sahagun (Book 6). The underlying differences are that the formal religious systems of both the Greeks and Aztecs had fundamental premises from which all discourse flowed. In contrast, the rhetorical philosophers of later Greece had cut loose from the traditional premises and were pragmatists in the extreme. We in the modern world partake of both systems, often compartmentalizing them. We go to church on Sunday, and many of us who do so then do things not in accordance with church teachings on Monday through Saturday. Ancient Mesoamericans apparently never fully developed the formal rhetorical-rationalist mode of thought. Perhaps someone like Tlacaelel did think pragmatically and did manipulate the system, but such a case was a rarity.

The general effect on the Mesoamericans of such a prerationalist philosophical system of thought is illustrated in the game of patolli. This was a board game in which dice were used to advance the pieces. The gods were invoked and presumably determined the outcome. There was a certain fatalism in the outcome, but there was also the excitement of finding out what had been predetermined. The same attitude prevailed about the sacred ball game. Duran discusses the extraordinary incantations used by gamblers in attempts to nail down a fortunate outcome when they bet on the ball game (1971: 302–305).

Certainly, the Mesoamerica-wide concepts of repetitive historical and philosophical cycles were related to these practices. History was repetitious and foreordained. The most famous case is that of Moteczoma II, who lived during a cycle of time for which diviners had predicted that Quetzalcoatl would return to reclaim his patrimony. Moteczoma's startlingly passive behavior in the face of the Spanish can partially be explained by his training in this system. Similarly, the Itza at Lake Peten resisted the conversion efforts of sixteenth- and seventeenth-century Spanish priests, explaining to them that the coming of a new religion was predicted, but that the time had not yet arrived. Indeed, Morley points out that the year of the final conquest of the Itza-Maya was only five months before the return of the malevolent *katun* (twenty-year cycle), which was the one for which the event had been predicted (1964: 477). The larger cycles of history and cosmology have been somewhat further explained in the appropriate chapters.

It should be noted that the gods themselves were not immune to this sort of cyclical transformation and process. The myths indicate the changes in status and the worlds within which the gods lived and operated. In historical reality, it also happened repeatedly that many tribal and localized deities became important only when their adherents achieved notable political and military success. At that point the local gods usually began to assume qualities of the greater and more widely known deities. Again, the Aztecs furnish us with an example. Huitzilopochtli was a tribal deity who became important only during the time of Aztec rule. Formerly of concern only to the Aztecs, when other ethnic groups were brought under Mexica control, Huitzilopochtli began to assume some of the qualities of Quetzalcoatl and Tonatiuh. This was probably partly to widen his "appeal" to other people, but by enhancing the importance of their special god the Aztecs also raised their own social and religious status. There is little question but that there was fluctuation in the fortunes of various major deities throughout Mesoamerica according to what group espoused them and how that group fared in the sociopolitical arena.

MATHEMATICAL AND CALENDRICAL SYSTEMS

THE SACRED ALMANAC. Two major calendrical cycles governed the lives of the Mesoamericans. These are analogous in operation to our weeks and months, which are solar and lunar calendars we use simultaneously. One cycle seems to be more ancient than the other, and was a sacred almanac consisting of 260 days. Twenty named days were combined with thirteen numbers, with the various permutations of number-day name combinations rotating until they began to repeat after 260 days. Morley's analogy of two unequal gear wheels meshing with one another is probably the clearest picture of the operation of this cycle. The day names vary throughout Mesoamerica but there is a surprisingly great correspondence from group to group. Alfonso Caso's studies of the Mesoamerican calendrical systems make clear that no known group lacked this sacred almanac (1967: Table 9). It is called the *Tzolkin* among Maya scholars, although we don't know what the Maya called it. Among Nahua speakers it was called the *Tonalpohualli*. Each day was symbolized by some concept. For example, the second Nahua day of the cycle is *Ehecatl* or wind, corresponding to the Matlazinca day *In Ithaatin*

Comparison of the Day Names and Their Meanings from Various Parts of Mesoamerica

Mexica (Tenochtitlan)	Lowland Maya	Zapotec
1. Cipactli (crocodile)	Imix (earth monster)	Chilla (crocodile)
2. Ehecatl (wind)	Ik (wind)	Quij (wind)
3. Calli (house)	Akbal (darkness)	Guela (night)
4. Cuetzpallin (lizard)	Kan (ripe maize)	Ache (lizard)
5. Coatl (serpent)	Chicchan (serpent)	Zee (serpent)
6. Miquiztl (death)	Cimi (death)	Lana (black)
7. Mazatl (deer)	Manik (hand)	China (deer)
8. Tochtli (rabbit)	Lamat (Venus)	Lapa (rabbit)
9. Atl (water)	Muluc (water)	Niza (water)
10. Itzcuintli (dog)	Oc (dog)	Tella (dog)
11. Ozomatli (monkey)	Chuen (monkey)	Loo (monkey)
12. Malinalli (grass)	Eb (bad rain)	Pija (drought)
13. Acatl (reed)	Ben (growing maize)	Quij (reed)
14. Ocelotl (ocelot)	Ix (jaguar)	Geche (jaguar)
15. Cuauhtli (eagle)	Men (moon/eagle)	Naa (eagle)
16. Cozcaquauhtli (vulture)	Cib (wax)	Loo (crow)
17. Ollin (earthquake)	Caban (earth)	Xoo (earthquake)
18. Tecpatl (flint knife)	Etznab (knife)	Opa (cold)
19. Quiauitl (rain)	Cauac (storm)	Ape (cloudy)
20. Xochitl (flower)	Ahau (lord)	Lao (flower)

or winds. The second Maya day was *Ik* or wind. On the other hand, there are variations which are not always apparently related. The first day is named *Cipactli* (crocodile) among the Nahua speakers, *In Beori* (long) among the Matlazinca, and *Imix* (earth monster) among the Maya. A day in the sacred almanac was designated by its number and day name; thus *2 Cimi* (2 Death) in the Maya lowland system. As noted elsewhere, the sacred almanac had great ritual significance for all members of a Mesoamerican society. Divination was and still is carried out by means of the omens and gods associated with any particular one of the 260 possibilities, and a person's fate was more or less determined by the circumstance of birthday. Among the Mixtec and Zapotec, children were named from their birthday with a nickname to distinguish among all born on the same day. Thus, the rulers 8-Deer "Tiger Claw" and 8-Deer "Tlaloc-Sun" were linked ritually but historically discriminated. The days were conceived of as having lives of their own in the sense that they were divine. The Maya seem to have carried this conception of time to its utmost refinement, using the metaphor of the god of the day carrying the day as a load. Religious festivals falling according to days of the sacred almanac were called "movable feasts" by the early chroniclers who made the analogy between these native celebrations and the Christian Easter, which also shifts within the astronomical year. The sacred almanac proved to be the most durable of all calendrical systems in Mesoamerica and is still in use today in many parts. Around Nebaj, in northern Guatemala, for example, Lincoln and Colby have recorded the modern version of the almanac and its use in divination.

THE ASTRONOMICAL YEAR. The use of the 365-day year was equally widespread among

Mesoamericans at the time of the Spanish conquest. This calendar was an approximation of the "tropical" or astronomical year and was a sun calendar similar to our own. The mathematical arrangements were in the form of eighteen named months with twenty numbered days in each. $18 \times 20 = 360$, and therefore a short five-day period was added on to the end of each year to produce 365. Again, there are correspondences across Mesoamerica in the month names, although much more variance than with the day names of the sacred almanac. A day in the tropical year was designated by means of its number and month name.

The Fifty-Two-Year Cycle. Obviously, both the systems outlined above can be and were combined. Thus, a particular day among the Maya could be *4 Ahau* (sacred almanac) *8 Cumku* (astronomical year). Since these cycles are mathematically indivisible (260 will not divide into 365), then the repetition of any particular combination will only come after the multiplied sum of days: 260 almanac days $\times$ 365 astronomical days, or 18,980 days, or approximately 52 years. This fifty-two-year cycle was known among the Aztecs as the *xiuhmolpilli* or "year bundle." The present world would come to an end at the completion of one of these cycles and therefore there was always a certain amount of anxiety at this time. Children were watched that they not turn into ravening beasts, nor were they allowed to sleep on that night lest they turn into mice. In Tenochtitlan, houses were cleaned and old pots broken, and life begun anew when the gods had begun a new cycle by vouchsafing a new sunrise.

All of the above interrelated calendrical systems probably date back into the Preclassic period and all may be a legacy of the Olmec culture. However, when we proceed to more complex calendrical permutations, we apparently leave behind all but the lowland Maya.

MAYA MATHEMATICS, THE LONG COUNT, AND SUPPLEMENTARY ELABORATIONS. It seems likely that the Classic Maya and certain epi-Olmec groups were the only cultures to use this exceedingly accurate system of counting time. The day was the basic unit of the long count as it was of the sacred almanac. In fact, the latter was incorporated into the former. An infinite count of days is achieved by the long count. The structure of Maya mathematics is *vigesimal* or a progression by twenties, but modified to be able to handle natural cycles. At the third order of vigesimal progression, the Maya went by a multiplier of 18 instead of 20 in order to achieve a unit of 360 instead of 400. The 360 unit was desired because of the approximation to tropical year length and the correspondence to the astronomical life cycle. Positional notation is also a feature as well as a notation system which uses a bar for five and a dot for one. Finally, the concept of zero or completion was used as a necessary part of the system.

One day is expressed by the lowest dot (1×1). The Maya wrote their numbers vertically and thus the next dot represents 20 (1×20). The third and highest dot indicates one unit of 360 (1×360). Say that the figure desired was 1821. In that case it would be written similarly, except that the third and highest unit would be a bar representing 1800 (5×360).

An excellent book by a mathematics teacher, George Sanchez, deals with how the Maya probably handled numbers of all kinds, including fractions and uneven figures. Sanchez concludes that it was extremely flexible (Sanchez, 1961; see also Anderson, 1971).

The long count consists of a hierarchy of units which are progressively larger according to the vigesimal system with the modification noted above. Thus we have the following:

1 kin   = 1 day
1 uinal   = 20 days
1 tun   = 360 days
1 katun   = 7200 days (about 20 years)
1 baktun = 144,000 days (about 400 years)

Special glyphs were developed to designate the various units. As usual, there is a bewilderment of variation, the nature and reasons for which are beyond the scope of this essay. For these and other related matters, see J. E. S. Thompson's deceptively titled *Maya Hieroglyphs Without Tears* (1950). Higher orders of time units were probably in use, but most Maya inscriptions begin with the *baktun* number. The Maya began their count with a mythologically determined date of 3113 B.C., and most of their calculations fall within the ninth baktun although dates from both the eighth and tenth baktun exist. There are a few seventh baktun dates and these indicate that the bar and dot system was in use in the epi-Olmec cultures and may have been passed on to the lowland Maya by the Izapan cultural groups. Tres Zapotes stela C dated at 31 B.C. is one of the earliest of these seventh baktun monuments and it is in the heart of the old Olmec area. In fact, no baktun 7 texts come from the Maya lowlands.

The correlation of the Maya calendar has generated almost as much heat among epigraphers as transubstantiation once did among theologians. With the massive confirmation of radiocarbon dates from Tikal, it now appears that the Thompson correlation is correct (Satterthwaite and Ralph, 1960). This is the correlation that leads to the long count starting date noted above. Archaeologists have developed a convention in writing Maya dates. The notation 9.16.3.0.0 means 9 baktuns, 16 katuns, 3 tuns, 0 uinals, 0 kins.

A lunar calendar was also a widespread Mesoamerican feature and according to Caso's calculations ran fairly close to the actual astronomical length of the moon's cycle or 29.53059+ days. The Mesoamericans used a figure of about 29.50 achieved by judicious alternation of 29- and 30-day moon months.

A Venus count was kept, again with a remarkable approximation to the measurement by modern astronomical means, yielding a 583.920 value. Important sections of the *Codex Borgia* from the Mixteca-Puebla area and of the *Dresden Codex* from the northern Maya lowlands concern the movements of this planet and its astrological implications.

Mesoamerican astronomy had roots in astrological purposes, as does our own astronomical science. The stars and planets were the creation of the gods, in some cases gods themselves, and it behooved mankind to be as observant as possible in order to attempt to divine what the future might hold and the desires of the supernatural powers. Numbers themselves were magical and some of them, thirteen and nine especially, were combined, split, and recombined into various permutations (see Thompson, 1950, and Caso, 1967, for more on these matters).

WRITING SYSTEMS

There was a strong divergence between the elaborations of the basic Mesoamerican system of writing as used in the Central Plateau and the Maya areas. The Central Plateau system seems to have been a much more simplified one. If it ultimately derived from the Olmec and epi-Olmec, it apparently remained at the level of development at which it was received. The symbols involved in Central Plateau systems are, in the main, logographic. That is, as M. E. Smith points out (1973), they can be understood across language and cross-culturally. Good examples are the place signs in the Mixtec codices. Tututepec, the Mixtec kingdom and its capital, are identified by a symbol for a cultivated hill combined with an eagle's head, usually topped off with a temple. Tututepec is the Nahua rendition of the Mixtec name *Yucu dzaa,* both of which mean "Hill of the Bird." But it is understandable even to speakers of Spanish or English.

As noted before, Mixtec and Mixteca-Puebla codices fall into two subject-matter groups, one largely liturgical-religious, and the other historical-genealogical. In both cases, we know that scribes not only were trained to read and write the books, but were also drilled intensively in the oral traditions necessary to expand and fully explain the books. Thus, central Mexican written record tended to be mnemonic and presented only skeletonized versions of information. Burgoa mentions that the Mixtec younger sons of the nobility were trained in these arts. Recall that such schools as were set aside for the nobility in Tenochtitlan, the *calmecac,* gave instruction in writing, among other things. Much of what has been preserved by Sahagun and Duran and others is undoubtedly transcribed oral tradition passed on to them by their native informants. The oral tradition is also reconstructable through such meticulous and detailed studies as those made by Eduard Seler in his commentaries on the codices (1963). In many other parts of Mesoamerica, very little, if any, of the oral tradition was preserved and we have little chance of reconstructing it. The Maya case is different, but as will be seen, the difficulties are great in eliciting historical materials from Classic hieroglyphic texts.

It might also be noted that the central Mexican area varied in its system of numerical notation from that of the Maya. Although it is known that the bar and dot system was in use at places such as Monte Alban in the late Preclassic period and at Xochicalco in the early Postclassic period, somehow it was dropped and the convention adopted of writing numbers of up to twenty by dots alone. Be-

yond that there was a sequence of different symbols which advanced by twenties, but altogether, the system was less elegant and economical than the bar and dot scheme, especially as developed by the Maya (Caso, 1965).

The Maya lowlands developed the art of writing beyond anything achieved elsewhere in Mesoamerica. It became a true writing system in that it had the capacity to carry a message without the aid of oral explanation or exegesis. However, the system was, as Thompson says, the result of an "unsystematic hodge-podge of slow growth" (1965). It was also characterized by a high degree of similarity and derivation from the baroquely complex Maya art style. However, being so tied to the art style and being also a mixture of systems, part ideographic, part rebus and part syllabic, it was very language-specific. In other words, like Chinese ideographs, the Maya writing system could be related to other languages only with difficulty.

At the moment, only about 10 percent of Maya hieroglyphs can be even tentatively translated. The amount that is surely translated is even less. The numerically patterned calendrical and mathematical glyphs are long since fully understood. The subject matter itself is a consistent code even if the script which carries it is not. It is when one comes to the noncalendrical materials that difficulties become extreme. However, beginning in 1958 with Berlin's emblem glyph paper, there has been a series of breakthroughs and attacks which have given steady success.

An illustration of some of the principles of Maya writing may help an appreciation of the amount of knowledge gained so far against formidable difficulties. Thompson gives an example of rebus writing which is easily comprehended. The Maya word *U* means "moon" and also denotes the possessive. The use of a lunar glyph in a hieroglyphic text may therefore take either meaning, and a decision must be made according to context. It is somewhat analogous to our having to distinguish in our oral speech between "their" and "there." The ideographic principle may be illustrated by another of Thompson's discoveries. The mythological *xoc* fish was sometimes indirectly represented by the water in which it lived. Xoc, however, also means "to count." Therefore, by writing either the fish itself or its water synonym, one could also indicate "to count" within the proper context.

Most glyphs had both symbolic and head forms, as with the xoc fish. Along with these variances for single times and places, consider also that Maya writing was used for at least 1500 years and that it changed through time, as well as having regional variations.

Withal, Berlin and Proskouriakoff have made and led significant strides forward in decipherment. Proskouriakoff's breakthrough into dynastic and political histories as recorded in Classic texts continues to afford us new insights (1960 et passim). Conquests are noted, for example. Thomas Barthel has made a series of brilliant inferences of political organization from Maya cosmology. Joyce Marcus has built on the histories and emblem glyph distributions to suggest recently that ancient Maya political structure was organized according to cosmological principles (1973). She has proposed that four main capitals of the Maya headed four realms. These realms and their capitals shifted through time, but she asserts that this was the dominant pattern until at least the collapse, about A.D. 900. Although there are severe difficulties in reconciling this proposal with other evidence, it is a noteworthy difference that Maya archaeologists are able to wrangle now about political boundaries of specific Classic states, whereas only fifteen years ago there was great doubt about whether the Maya even had states or cities.

ILLNESS, MEDICINE, AND THE "PSYCHIATRIC" APPROACH

Epidemic diseases can be recognized from descriptions in both Aztec and Maya sources. The Aztec disease name, *matlazahuatl*, has been identified by Francisco Guerra as exanthematic typhus (1966). *Cocoliztli* seems likely to Guerra to have been yellow fever. Yellow fever is almost certainly referred to in the Maya books of Chilam Balam when bloody vomit is described as part of the evil coming in a certain katun 4-Ahau. Shimkin notes that the Amazon Basin primate populations serve as a reservoir for yellow fever between outbreaks and probably so served in the past. In addition to these afflictions, there were the usual individual traumas to be dealt with, such as broken bones, contusions, lacerations, and internal disorders.

Several great treatises and compilations of information were made by the Spaniards in the colonial period on the subject of healing. Many of the questionnaires made up by the Spanish bureaucracy had parts which specifically asked about medicinal plants, and curing practices. The *Badianus Herbal* and the plant inventory of Sahagun's *Florentine Codex* are examples of this information. Much of the material is well illustrated and is useful to modern pharmacognosy. The *Relaciones Geograficas* of 1580 contain information in response to question 26: "Note the herbs or aromatic plants with which the Indians cure themselves, and their medicinal properties" (Cline, 1972: 236).

There was much in Aztec, Maya, and other Mesoamerican medicine that we can recognize as empirically derived, tested procedure. Many of the herbal remedies fall into this category. An infected ear is to be treated with drops of tepid *coyoxochitl* sap three times daily, according to Sahagun's informants. Breast tumors were treated with poultices of herbs and infusions to drink. The *Badianus Herbal* lists some 251 plants, while 123 are noted in Sahagun's *Florentine Codex*. A sixteenth-century Spaniard (Hernandez) surveyed the botany of central Mexico and mentioned 1200 medicinal plants, and has 4043 separate items in his general plant index. Surgery was practiced or at least tried. Severed noses were to be sewn back on as soon as possible and bathed with salted bee honey. Sweatbathing was a widespread part of many cures, which also had purifying, ritual significance.

The good physician [is] a diagnostician, experienced — a knower of herbs, of stones, of trees, of roots. He has [results of] examinations, experiences, prudence. . . . He provides health, restores people, provides them splints, sets bones for them, purges them, gives emetics, gives them potions; he lances, he makes incisions in them, stitches them, revives them, envelops them in ashes" (Sahagun, *Florentine Codex:* Part XI, 30).

There is also a scathing condemnation of bad physicians who kill with medicines, are frauds, and seduce women.

On the other hand, there was much in Mesoamerican medicine which was aimed at curing the soul as well as curing the body. The belief in animal souls and the conception that illness could be caused by the escape of the animal soul was widespread. This diagnosis is still very common among Mesoamerican Indian groups, and the cure is as much ritual as medicinal. Religion is very much a part of the modern curer's professional resources and undoubtedly was so in pre-Hispanic times. There is a book of medical incantations from northern Yucatan called the *Ritual of the Bacabs* which throws great light on this matter. Although from the Maya area, this is the late preconquest northern zone which had been heavily influenced by Mexico and therefore which may also reflect practices in the Central Plateau area. R. Roys says that "Medi-

cine was closely associated with benevolent magic in pre-Spanish Yucatan" (1956: ix). Landa mentions "the priests, the physicians and sorcerers, who are all the same thing" (1941: 153). "There were also surgeons, or, to be more accurate, sorcerers, who cured with herbs and many superstitious rites" (1941: 94). Landa also mentions that these curers used books and had medicine bags which contained idols of the goddess of medicine (Ixchel) and "many little trifles." R. Roys says that a disease was considered to be a personified being and therefore vulnerable through its genealogy, which was recited by the curer. Animal and tree associations of the disease derived from the sacred almanac day of its birth are mentioned. Most incantations first banish the evil spirit, after which the curer ordered, admonished, and even cursed the deities, but, surprisingly, never supplicated them. Dr. William B. Cook, Jr., R. Roys' psychiatric consultant, said that the trust in the doctor was the source of curative powers. He also observed that the alliterative and repetitious incantations could produce a somnolent, hypnotic effect. It is interesting that nearly one-third of the incantations are for the treatment of some sort of seizure. Thus, with chemical medicine, mainly herbs, with physical procedures such as inducement of sweats and massaging, and with the psychological weapons at his command, the ancient doctor confronted and often overcame those ailments which universally affect mankind.

TECHNOLOGY AND USE OF PHYSICAL PRINCIPLES

Even though they possessed metals at the time of Spanish contact, the Mesoamericans were essentially in a state of stone tool technology for all of their prehistory.

LITHIC TECHNOLOGY. With the exception of predynastic Egypt and paleolithic Europe, probably nowhere else in the world were the potentialities of worked stone explored as fully and brought to as exquisite a pitch as in Mesoamerica. For practical purposes the raw materials narrowed down to two main categories, obsidian and flint. However, there are many varieties of each, varying in qualities which allow more or less virtuosity in manufacturing and therefore in form. Other stones were used, but these, such as jadeite, were generally used for luxury and high art productions. Jade had a ritual symbolism in that it represented water, and hearts of the nobility were represented by jade pieces placed in their mouths after death. In the end it was on the tools made from flint and obsidian that the utilitarian functions depended. The traditions of stone technology were so widespread that they must be regarded not as a Mesoamerican specific set of characteristics, but rather, a New World complex of traditions which Mesoamerica shared. It was in the development to perfection and the virtuosity of treatment of these traditional skills that Mesoamericans differed somewhat.

Most stone technology was already developed by the time Mesoamerican village life was established. Essentially, we are speaking of two main techniques of manufacture, flaking and blade striking. Flaking seems to have everywhere preceded blade manufacture. Clovis and other early lithic stage complexes include blade industries, however. It seems clear that in terms of lithic technology, Mesoamerica was almost stagnant after about 1500 B.C.

"But seeing that they were without metals, God provided them with a ridge of flint . . . from which they got stone from which they made the heads of their lances for war and the knives for the sacrifices" (Landa, 1941: 186). R. Roys translates an entry in the *Vienna Dictionary* (Maya-Spanish) to read: "To make lancets and knives of flints and points for arrows, getting them from some thick (piece of) flint, which is set upright: *bah tok*" (1972: 49). Roys points out that indirect rest percussion is inferred. However, the Maya had fallen to a low estate in their stone working by the Mayapan period and therefore we have relatively little in the way of information. Wooden tools evidently had taken over many of the functions formerly performed by stone tools. For the Aztecs we have somewhat more data, thanks as usual to the ethnographic approach of Sahagun. "The obsidian seller is one who, [with] a staff with a crosspiece, forces off obsidian blades. He sells . . . obsidian razors, blades, single-edged knives, double-edged knives, unworked obsidian. . . . He sells white obsidian, clear blue obsidian, yellow obsidian" (Sahagun, *Florentine Codex:* Part IX, 85). Sellers of the more precious stones were separate individuals in the great market in Tenochtitlan, as jewelers and hardware merchants are separated in our own commercial districts.

Rather extraordinary stone art productions are known, and many have been noted in their proper places. The Olmec jade pieces still excite our admiration 3000 years later, as do late Classic flint knives of exquisite form from the Maya lowlands. In the end, however, the major tools were the humble instruments of agriculture and manufacture. Flint hoes, chisels, spearblades (for hunting and war), animal skin scrapers, and a multitude of other general and special purpose tools were made. Obsidian blades were prized for their sharpness and undoubtedly were used for woodcarving, among other things.

When used in ritual, flint knives were thought to be endowed with a divine spirit. In certain codices, especially the Borgia, one sees a face on the descending sacrificial knife.

Trade in these resources was early, widespread, and continuous. Most of the highlands had obsidian sources, but lacked flint. The

Maya lowlands had a great deal of high quality flint, but little obsidian. These were primary commodities in early exchange systems. Obsidian seems to have been shipped in the form of roughly shaped bulk pieces to reduce weight. Finishing was done by local artisans.

Metallurgy was a late introduction to Mesoamerica, probably directly from South America or by way of Central America. Metalworking was introduced perhaps as early as A.D. 800, and chiefly was used for ornamental and ritual objects, although some copper axes have been found. These last are of two types, one lightweight and of doubtful utility. This form may have been used as a standardizing means much as copper and bronze in the ancient Mediterranean were cast into the form of cattle hides as a standardized unit of weight and measure. The other type is heavier, fully functional, and is widespread in distribution.

Metallurgical skill was developed most highly in the Central Plateau area. We have seen how the productions of the Mixteca-Puebla zone were traded around. The Tarascans also seem to have been within this metalworking area. Sahagun mentions the seller of metals in the Tenochtitlan market as being chiefly a dealer in cast gold objects. "He sells shield-shaped necklaces, shrimp necklaces, golden bracelets" (*Florentine Codex:* Part XI, 61). Metallurgy never seems to have taken hold in Mesoamerican technology, however, and metal seems to have been treated only as a superior form of stone.

Basic physical principles were well known and used extensively in the massive construction projects. Everything indicates that there were groups of architects and engineers who planned and supervised such projects. The great dike across Lake Texcoco was evidently devised by engineers from Texcoco, although the credit is given to the ruler Nezahualcoyotl. The immense numbers of large structures erected during the Maya Classic period could have been essentially built by foremen under

general direction of an aristocrat, according to Potter's architectural studies. Lawrence Roys' studies of Maya engineering have been mentioned as concluding that the major strength of Maya structures was in their concrete interiors rather than in their masonry veneers (1934). The use of the lever, ramps, pulleys, rollers, and infinite amounts of rope and manpower accomplished the major tasks in Mesoamerican construction. Organization of manpower made up in large part for the lack of more sophisticated technology, as Armillas has commented.

CULTURAL-HISTORICAL AND PROCESSUAL CONSIDERATIONS

It has been argued that the essence of science is to explain a phenomenon by selection of the most crucial factors from the dozens or hundreds which may be involved. Thus, one winds up with an explanation which, although not complete, does explain, for example, 80 to 90 percent of the phenomenon by the use of two or three factors. W. T. Sanders has forcefully advanced this point of view, and to a great degree it has been followed in this book. However, any complex of factors do not and did not remain constant in the cultural past. When considering historical or processual events we are talking of change by definition and therefore our explanations must change as the phenomenon changes. To bring it down to the case at hand, during the development of complex societies, the same factors were not always all important. Thresholds were constantly being reached beyond which other matters came into play.

In the section that follows, we will examine certain detailed and broad-scale phenomena in the cultural history of Mesoamerica. We will also examine certain crucial factors that seem to explain these phenomena when combined into certain theoretical patterns. We will briefly review the major theoretical stances that utilize these factors. Finally, we will, with some trepidation, try to reconcile some of these theories and to synthesize them into an acceptable form.

SPECIAL FEATURES. Most of the particular but widespread features of Mesoamerican civilizations are included in the definition of Mesoamerica as given in the first chapter. Others are mentioned throughout the book. However, there are some special features that deserve further discussion.

Royal cults, or the practice of regarding the elite of a society as semi-divine and as surviving physical death to continue to influence this world from the afterlife, were especially strong. Many of the great monuments of Mesoamerica such as Maya temples seem to have been built with the purpose in mind of providing a place of contact between the dead elite and their survivors. The Mixtecs and Zapotecs and certain other Central Plateau groups seem to have shared this attitude. On the other hand, ancestor worship is a fairly restricted practice. West Mexico, with what are clearly family crypts, seem to have most intensively developed the practice, but the highland Maya also were very concerned with the matter. It seems that the areas which developed complex sociopolitical structures, the Mixtec city-states, and the Classic Maya regional states, emphasized the elite or royal cult aspect of this practice. Areas that were less politically developed, such as far west Mexico and the north Maya highlands, perhaps depended more on widespread ancestor worship as an integrative social mechanism than they did on more formal political structures. The larger and more sophisticated states, such as the Aztec, seem to have completely lacked the practice, except in the sense of casual memorialization as evidenced in Sisson's calpulli temple cremations at Coxcatlan Viejo. It seems possible that a progression from ancestor worship through royal cults through abandonment of these for more formal and standardized religious memorialization might be correlated with progressively more formal and sophisticated sociopolitical organization. Kin-oriented societies are generally viewed in anthropological theory as archaic forms compared to relatively impersonal and institutionalized forms.

Royal cults seem to go along with royal castes. It is no accident that two of the most genealogically oriented societies in Mesoamerica were the Mixtec and the Maya. Great efforts were made in both societies to record royal genealogies. Origin myths augmented the superior social statuses of the elite. It has been noted that the Mixtec rulers were so set apart that they were regarded as even being the result of a separate creation. These royal caste–oriented societies depended greatly for their relative strengths on elite marital alliances. Although we have more data at present on the Mixtec, the Maya texts are giving us ever-increasing quantities of evidence indicating the importance of ascribed status to rulers.

Another way in which the matter can be approached is through the order of magnitude of the ruling elites. For the Maya we have already seen that we are probably dealing with small numbers of people at the top. For Uaxactun, the elite was probably less than 1 percent of the total population, and the active elite much less than that. No figures have been estimated on the sizes of the highland state elites as yet and so we cannot compare directly to them, but the order of magnitude may not be much different, although the absolute numbers were undoubtedly higher. For sixteenth-century England, already moving toward some industrialization, the total elite population, including rural gentry, was about 1 percent, according to Slavin (1973: 27). This was in 1520, and later in the century the numbers of aristocrats had risen to a proportion of about 2 percent. Considering that England already had developed a considerable degree of mercantilism and outside trade, these figures may indicate the approximate correctness of the figures for the more restricted Maya societies.

Spores comments on the loose organization of the political units dominated by this kind of elite (1967). Due to the dependence on kin alliances among elites, political arrangements were continually in flux, and much attention had to be paid to these matters, to the detriment of issues of total societal organization. In this view, then, marital alliance patterns as practiced by the Classic Maya, by the Mixtec, and probably by many other regional Mesoamerican societies, are the political expression of a rigid caste system. The latter is characteristic of a state which has not reached the threshold of urbanism so complex and high in population that it cannot be supported by the immediate region. The stable unit is the small regional city-state. This is a definition of the petty state as we used it in the introductory chapter, but from a different point of view. In evolutionary terms, these petty states with their elite castes are probably developed forms of the initial pristine states. We shall return to these matters of sociopolitical magnitude and their evolutionary implications.

Varieties of urbanism are another phenomenon that probably set Mesoamerica apart from other early civilizations. Julian Steward's functional definition of urban centers as being those foci which perform special services for a regional society has been adopted here (1961). Urban centers were those communities which had most of the famous criteria listed by V. G. Childe (1950): relatively higher density population than the surrounding countryside; a stratified society; nonfarming occupational specializations; formalized religions; market systems; a bureaucracy or civil service supported by a social surplus; and finally, writing or accounting systems. This is a near-universal

definition of cities and their functional characteristics which comprehends the varieties of urban centers in Mesoamerica. However, it is essentially a qualitative definition. In order to better understand the variations noted we must also deal with quantitative differences.

Ignoring temporal differences for the moment, there are calculations of density and total populations for various centers now available which are enlightening. Turning to the Maya lowlands where we have some of our best data, Tikal is estimated to have had population densities of 600 to 700 per square kilometer and a total population of about 49,000 at its height, around A.D. 750. This population was spread over a space of about 123 square kilometers. By the same date, the Becan-Chiccana-Xpujil area to the north had reached a density of about 168 persons per square kilometer based on intensive agriculture, and a total population of about 25,200 in a 150-square-kilometer zone. In other words, the Maya centers were serving as the foci of interaction of about the same number of people as many Central Plateau high-density cities of the sixteenth century, but at the low end of the scale. The primary difference is that the Maya city-state populations, although of the same order of magnitude, were spread over more land.

Using a middle range estimate of total Teotihuacan population (125,000), one arrives at a population density of about 6250 per square kilometer within the city. Another 30,000 lived outside the city. Using the total area of the basin as its support zone (6658 square kilometers), this population (155,638) could be supported with a theoretical density of only 74.1 per arable square kilometer. However, the concentration at Teotihuacan was far beyond anything ever achieved in Mesoamerica outside the Basin of Mexico. The order of magnitude of Teotihuacan is clearly beyond that of the city-state level, either highland or lowland, and falls within what we may call a megacenter category. Those centers needed extraregional support. That this was necessary at Teotihuacan can be demonstrated by the fact that a maximum of 5000 hectares of spring-fed, irrigated land was available in the vicinity of the city. Using the 10 to 18 persons per hectare support capacity figure based on sixteenth-century production figures, a maximum of 50,000 to 90,000 people could have been supported by this zone. Clearly, Teotihuacan needed the whole Basin of Mexico, and probably something beyond, to support its population. If the elite and a supporting bureaucracy were greater than the usual 1 percent, as seems likely, then the need for resources beyond those of the basin is clearly demonstrated.

Later, Tenochtitlan was such a megacenter. On present evidence, the Basin of Mexico seems to have been unique in providing the base for such high density megacenters. Population units of these sizes, organized into integrated sociopolitical-economic systems, were agglomerations of city-states, usually with one center larger than the others.

As a contrast, Tikal in the Maya lowlands and its support area had a theoretical capacity for about 9000 persons, if one uses swidden farming figures. Using even the new figures derived from Turner's Rio Bec study (1974), and assuming that Tikal practiced intensive agriculture, we still only reach a capacity of about 20,500 (at 168 per square kilometer). Tikal with its total of 49,000 people, therefore, had to have support from a tribute or alliance system which comprehended much more than its own immediate territory. The relatively greater fragility of such low-density systems compared to the more stable and secure population support base of the highland states is clear.

Sanders has made the point that state politics may require the organization of a certain minimum number of people (personal communication). We can, with some confidence, say that 13,000 or the lower end of the population range of the sixteenth-century highland city-states is probably the minimum number of people that interacted in most Mesoamerican petty regional states. Thirty thousand seems to have been about the upper end of this sort of political unit. Beyond that, there is a jump into the high-density megacenter category which seems to be from 80,000 up to about 200,000. There is the theoretical possibility of low-density megacenters, and this is what Tikal may indeed represent. In this case, the numbers of people again may approach that of the highland urban areas, but with significant differences. The total populations are on the low end of the range, the centers themselves are smaller in population, and the overall density of the major urban centers is lower.

Part of the difference between the low- and high-density megacenters is the size of the social fraction representing nonelite, nonfarmer craft specialists. At Maya lowland sites like Uaxactun (low-density city) the evidence is that such artisans made up much less than 1 percent of the population, or virtually a handful. At the megacenter of Tikal there were more such craftsmen but still fewer than 1 percent. In contrast, the high-density megacenter of Teotihuacan had at least 500 workshops which have been detected. No quantitative data are available yet on this matter at Teotihuacan, but an "eyeball" estimate would put such full-time artisans at perhaps 10 to 20 percent of the population.

Given these criteria and examples, we can classify other, less well-documented areas of Mesoamerica in terms of the comparative scheme outlined above. West Mexico seems to have achieved only a city-state or lesser level of society for the most part. The population figures, either order of magnitude or absolute, are lacking for this area, but generally, low-density city-states scattered rather widely apart seem to have been the rule. The

Tarascan kingdom was a late phenomenon and seems to have been a low-density unit which was city-state oriented. It is difficult to decide which category the Toltecs fit into without more information on the size and density of Tula. At the moment it seems likely that Tula was a city-state of high density, but with an empire built around it. It was not anything on the order of Teotihuacan or Tenochtitlan, however. Other representative cities and their supporting areas are classified on the table on this page. Its categories obviously can have some evolutionary implications for sociopolitical systems.

Mesoamerican Cities by Population Density

	Low-density	High-density
Cities	Yaxchilan, Palenque, Uaxactun, Tajin, Tututepec, Kaminal-juyu, etc.	Tula, Cempoala, Texcoco, Yanhuitlan, Tzintzuntzan (?), etc.
Mega-centers	Tikal, Uxmal (?), etc.	Teotihuacan, Tenochtitlan, Cholula (?), etc.

There are chronological-historical progressions in the arrangements of these centers along evolutionary lines. In terms of centralization of political control, the trend would run from the low-density to the high-density cities, and then to the megacenters and from low- to high-density types within that category. There are also interesting differences within the Basin of Mexico. Teotihuacan and Cuicuilco are contemporary high-density cities near the beginning of the Christian era, and then Cuicuilco is destroyed and Teotihuacan is the only community of that size and organization left. At that time, Teotihuacan is rapidly converted into a megacenter, the first in Mesoamerica, by a concentration of virtually 80 percent of the basin's population

within it. During the 600 years or so of Teotihuacan's growth and development, most population growth in the basin is absorbed by the city, with the rural population apparently remaining more or less at the same levels (J. R. Parsons, 1974: 98). When Tenochtitlan began its conversion from a high-density city 600 years afterward, it was one among many such cities both in and out of the valley. The nature of the structure of Teotihuacan with its unique apartment complexes must owe something to the fact that it was the first large high-density city and the first megacenter. Tenochtitlan's structural options must have been somewhat constrained by the competitive atmosphere within which it grew and in which it had to survive.

Some of the above points and many of the ideas have been set out by Sanders and Price (1968), Palerm and Wolf (1960), but certainly are not in a form necessarily recognizable or acceptable to them. There is a vast literature on hierarchies of settlement types and how they are and were organized into varying systems. At this moment the explanatory benefits of this literature are perhaps more technical than enlightening, although it will lead to much greater understanding in the future.

All of these distinctions and contrasts are really concerned with the fundamental issue of definition of the sizes and the qualities of various interaction units within Mesoamerica. These factors interacted with one another through several kinds of mechanisms. Formal religious pilgrimage patterns are an example of these mechanisms, as are the various kinds of markets and economic networks. Another point to be made about these mechanisms is that they are generally the factors that explain the remaining 15 to 20 percent of the phenomena of civilization. Now we must turn to the factors that constitute the 80 to 85 percent explanations.

ELEMENTS AND THEORIES
OF PROCESSUAL IMPORTANCE

POPULATION GROWTH: BOSERUP AND CARNEIRO. Population fluctuations have been mentioned frequently in this book as having significantly affected cultural evolution. Archaeologists have generally dropped their neo-Malthusian views and converted to Esther Boserup's theory of the relationship between population growth and agricultural intensification (1965). The followers of a modified Malthusian theory have sometimes viewed population growth as being largely a matter of the populations expanding to fit the food supply available. Boserup has argued that on the contrary, agricultural production is intensified in response to population growth. Population grows in response to all sorts of factors, ideological and sociopolitical among them. Intensification may take several forms which include the shortening of fallow periods, the bringing of marginal lands into cultivation, and in nearly every case, the increased investment of man-hours of labor. Thus a man may wind up spending ten hours to produce the same unit that his grandfather produced in one hour.

Anthropologists have modified and somewhat expanded Boserup's theory. It is clear that there are lower and upper thresholds beyond which the process does not operate. Below the lower threshold, populations expand through space as they expand absolutely. Beyond the upper threshold of high density, another turn of the intensification screw produces no perceptible improvement. In addition, one may expand Boserup's definition of agricultural production to simply read subsistence activities. This includes such activities as fishing, gathering of wild foods, hunting, herding (although not in the New World), and other intensification techniques. All of these activities were carried on in conjunction with the most intense sorts of cultivation

techniques in pre-Hispanic times. We have cited several examples of intensification of food production in response to population growth. The chinampa system and its expansion were responses in the Basin of Mexico, especially from the thirteenth century on. The terracing of hillsides, drainage of swamps and building of drained fields, and use of orchard crops in the seventh-century Maya lowlands is another example. Indeed, it was only when intensive agricultural techniques had been developed under the stress of population pressures that these could be transferred into marginal land areas. The latter could only be brought into cultivation in the first place by the use of such techniques.

According to Shimkin (1973), there is a historically attested relationship to be seen between various forms of political systems and population growth. He argues that village-level societies tend to stabilize in population largely because their primary orientation is toward survival. On the other hand, Shimkin continues, traditional elite-ruled states the world over tend to encourage population growth in order to have masses to manipulate. These arguments have been presented at greater length in connection with the Maya collapse, but they have more general application in that they may indicate the sorts of conditions that led to population growth in certain cases, such as at Teotihuacan. Once a certain level of population was reached at Teotihuacan, however, even it stabilized, probably due to the transportation and productivity limits outlined by Parsons (1974: 105).

There is also the viewpoint that humans should be studied in their reproductive capacities and population growth aspects in the same light as animal populations, and subject only to the same sorts of limiting stress factors. Although this may be so on a fairly primitive level of social organization, I would argue that cultural and social factors become more important at about the same time that the village stage of social organization is reached.

Carneiro's theory of the origin of the state has a complementary relationship to Boserup's ideas. Carneiro has developed the view that, given natural ecological boundaries, a human population is likely not to spread beyond it, but rather to involute or intensify its cultivation processes and, more crucial to his argument, to develop more highly organized systems to take care of the problems of high density living (1970). In areas where circumstances of resource circumscription were extant, the state developed in response to the buildup of social and population units. Social circumscription, in the sense of a society being surrounded and bounded by other like societies, could produce the same political result, Carneiro argues. In the Maya case, we have seen that artificial dry season water storage facilities might have been the resource circumscription factor involved.

ECOLOGICAL CONSIDERATIONS: THE INTERPLAY OF BIOLOGICAL AND CULTURAL WORLDS. The geographical characteristics of Mesoamerica already outlined in Chapter 1 have been noted as probably being permissive in their effect on cultural evolution. In other words, the special circumstances of high diversity at least permitted, if they did not actually stimulate, the interaction of human groups in Mesoamerica. Sanders and Price, Willey, Wolf and Palerm, and others have noted these circumstances and their effects on the intensity and quality of cultural interaction.

Sanders and Price together (1968), and Sanders alone (1970), have argued that the ecological diversity and differential resource distribution within Mesoamerica led to the formation of symbiotic regions. These regions were formed through the mechanisms of trade networks, at first primitive, later sophisticated. The development of formal markets was simply a more evolved stage of this process of symbiotic integration, but carried on something that had started with the first trading of obsidian by 1500 B.C. and the trading around of plant varieties as far back as 7000 B.C. In this view of things, the formation of these symbiotic regions led to corollary social mechanisms and ultimately to the development of the state. The stimulus to development of symbiotic regions, however, is argued to have been immanent within the nature of the opportunity. Phrased another way, the potentialities of such market systems and also of intensive agriculture were grasped, and human groups moved in that direction by a means of stochastic realization even if not by long-range planning. Lately, however, Sanders has shifted his ground to view population as the prime mover of these shifts toward more complex economic and social arrangements. Essentially, the shift has been from an opportunity model of events to a stress model, stresses being created by population growth. However, Sanders also emphasizes the transformational effect of different kinds and different volumes of trade passing through the market nexuses. These nodes in the networks would be differentially changed by the degree and nature of the trade in which they were engaged. Trade may have been a necessity by virtue of population pressure, but it was also an evolutionary mechanism in itself.

Palerm and Wolf have taken more of a macro-view of matters in their synthetic theory (1960). In their scheme, the areas of Mesoamerica with the highest potentials for population and economic growth were prima facie those with the longest florescences. Early civilizations such as the Olmec did not reformulate themselves in an unending and self-generating cyclical manner for lack of further growth potential in the tropical lowland ecological zones in which they were located. These early cultures "peaked out" early, having reached their demographic and economic limits. Such areas as the Basin of Mexico and the Central Valley of Oaxaca were able to continue their growth by continually adding to and never discarding agricultural and other food production means. Further, hydraulic systems being the most intensive forms, all of these regions ultimately added some type of irrigation to their repertories. The cumulative effect of these heterogeneous subsistence systems was that of high-density populations and greater security against crop disasters through diversity. Late florescences on the Mesoamerican scene were those cultures located in areas for which sophisticated and laborious cultivation systems had to be worked out before their limited agricultural potential could be exploited. In such areas, population buildups would have been slower. Such an area was that of the Mixteca Alta which really did not begin to reach a cultural climax until the early Postclassic period.

As can be seen, this synthetic theory is complementary to others discussed above. Implicit in it, or at least adaptable to it, is the Boserup concept of population growth as fueling subsistence development and cultural evolution. Sanders and Price's concepts of symbiotic areas define the practical details of Palerm and Wolf's zones of "massed economic and demographic power." The theory was put forth some twenty years ago and is only now having the effect that it deserves, but at the same time needs some adjustment to take account of new data.

Willey has used the concept of symbiotic regions to explain the rise of the early great styles of Peru and Mesoamerica: Chavin and Olmec. This interpretation is concentrated on mechanisms of development rather than on the prime movers themselves. In Willey's view, the Olmec early stylistic spread throughout Mesoamerica represents a proselytizing religious movement with a powerful symbolism of specific order (1962). It was through this religious movement with something like the fervor of early Islam or Christianity that

cultural ideas were also spread. Through the integrative device of pilgrimages, the religious movement was sustained and spread to peoples of diverse cultural and ethnic backgrounds. Willey points out the possibilities of intensified interaction in such a situation. Again, this theory refers to the compressed diversity of Mesoamerican ecology and cultures with its potential for interaction and stimulation. The Olmec furnished the means for intensified interaction, and thus interstimulation, of many forms of regional cultural evolution.

Differential resource distribution is an important factor lying back of all of the above theories, and William Rathje has developed this specific aspect in his explanation of the rise of Maya lowland civilization (1971). Rathje argues that the Maya lowlands lack three necessities for settled life: basalt for grinding stones to process maize, obsidian for cutting tools, and salt, which is a biological necessity. He argues that the lack of easily obtainable supplies of these necessities led to the development of trade networks designed to obtain them. In his view, the zone most lacking in these resources and many others was the central northeastern Peten of Guatemala, precisely that zone where the earliest and most sophisticated variant of Maya civilization grew up. Rathje's theory is that the lack of these items stimulated this region to take the most innovative steps in social and economic organization to remedy it. In other words, the greater deprivation of natural resources in this zone led to a greater stimulus to correct economic lacks through sociopolitical development.

There are certain objections to Rathje's stance, centering on the question of whether or not those items designated as necessities were really necessary. Salt is unquestionably so, but the grinding stones and obsidian trade are less obvious. Nonetheless, it is a fact that one of the earliest and most developed forms of Maya lowland culture did arise in one of the poorest of natural regions. However, it may also be that equally sophisticated contemporary variants were located in northern British Honduras and along the Pasion River.

Flannery, in a typically stimulating and lucid paper, has come forth with an expansion of ecological theory. He argues that, "In the ecosystem approach to analysis of human societies, everything which transmits information is within the province of ecology" (1972b: 400). He elaborates this argument to make ecological theory a comprehensive one which can explain the various and more strictly cultural features: writing, ritual, sociopolitical characteristics, ancestor worship, and so forth as information processing and transmitting mechanisms. The usual definition of cultural ecology is that it is the study of the interaction and interrelationships between cultural and natural systems. Flannery proposes to broaden this by including information exchange as well as matter and energy exchange. Informational exchange no doubt occurs, but I contend that past a certain point of complexity information is exchanged between different *cultural* systems and subsystems. Further, much of the information so passed has little to do with system interaction between nature and culture. All of which is not to say that Flannery is wrong. I would simply say that he has applied modified systems and ecological approaches to general anthropological theory to produce a new synthesis. This is a valuable achievement and all the more so for being broader than the ecological rubric that it carries. It utilizes many of the fragmented and somewhat ineffective theoretical concepts which before were always so unconvincing when applied to complex cultures. For these reasons we retain the traditional definition of cultural ecology here while welcoming the new synthesis and awaiting a more appropriate label for it, such as "cultural systems theory."

Competition. Sanders and Price have elaborately dealt with this concept and pointed out that cooperation and competition are often alternative approaches to the same sets of problems (1968). Competition often precedes and gives way to cooperation. Warfare is an extreme form of competition and was practiced widely in Mesoamerica. However, it is not the only form, and Webb has cogently pointed out the consequences of economic competition and of exclusion from trade. Webb argues that much of the success of Maya elite culture was based on its long-distance, prestige trade connections, especially those reaching outside the Maya area. Exclusion from these trade networks by reason of their shifting or being disrupted weakened the Maya Classic elite and made them vulnerable to other pressures. Webb also argues that the lack of recovery from the Classic collapse might be explained by the lack of success of the surviving elite in reestablishing such trade connections.

David Webster has approached the matter from the other end of the evolutionary continuum, the beginning of Maya civilization, to argue that warfare was endemic in the Maya lowlands, especially in the late Preclassic period (1976). Webster finds evidence to indicate high competition between the regional variants of Maya lowland culture, often taking the form of warfare. Following Sanders' and Price's arguments, he says that ultimately this warfare led to amalgamation of these regional variants, not necessarily in a political sense but in a cultural sense. Much of early Classic homogeneity in the central Maya lowlands would be explained by the competitive success of the Tikal-Uaxactun cultural and organizational variant. Webster's argument is again largely concerned with mechanisms of interaction and change and assumes the fueling thrust of population growth and the modifying effects of resource or social circumscription.

Intensification Factors and Theories. Boserup's theory could also fall into this category, but we refer here to explanatory schema such as that propounded by Wittfogel (extracted and summarized in Sanders and Price, 1968). Such theories tend to be universal and nonspecific. The Palerm-Wolf theory is, in a way, an attempt to introduce and apply Wittfogel's concepts to Mesoamerica. Wittfogel's main points are that, where extensive irrigation agriculture is introduced, for whatever reasons, sophisticated organizations are needed to develop and maintain it. Further, such organizational needs tend to lead to the development of the state, with a strong tendency for such states to be centralized and despotic. Flannery has opted for the Palerm-Wolf theory as being an alternative to Wittfogel, specifically rejecting the premise that centralized and despotic sociopolitical systems are the inevitable result of irrigation agriculture. Work on Preclassic cultures in the Oaxaca Central Valley have shown that these village-oriented societies developed extensive irrigation systems without an overarching authority, at least for a long period of time. It might be observed, however, that in such zones as the Maya lowlands where irrigation and swamp reclamation projects did develop, they did not appear until such an authority was present. All of which is to say that the Palerm-Wolf theory is adequate to the explanatory task, but needs modification to take account of the insights of Boserup and the recently demonstrated greater demographic potential of tropical forest agriculture as shown by the work of William Denevan and Bill Turner.

Let us now turn to a review of some examples of cultural evolution in Mesoamerican prehistory and then to an attempt at a comprehensive explanation of the general and special features of Mesoamerican civilizations.

PATTERNS OF FLORESCENCE AND COLLAPSE. Selecting four major areas of Mesoamerica

and contrasting them in their patterns of florescence and collapse seems instructive. Two of these areas, the Basins of Mexico and Oaxaca, are highland, one is tropical forest (the Maya lowlands), and west Mexico is variable and drier than the other three.

Florescence is defined here as being the intensive development of areally characteristic and interrelated cultural patterns, both systemic and stylistic. For example, the development of the Maya temple is a stylistic feature of the late Classic which is tied to the systemic pattern of royal castes. Chinampa development would be a systemic feature of Mexica culture linked to the stylistic characteristics of the rain god cult of Tlaloc and the tlaloques.

The Basin of Mexico shows a pattern of at least two major florescences (J. Parsons, 1974: Fig. 11). The first is one which begins about 100 B.C. with the two major centers of Cuicuilco and Teotihuacan and then continues transformed at Teotihuacan until about A.D. 650, for a duration of about 750 years. The period from A.D. 750 to about 1200 is one of population decline and relative unimportance in terms of sociopolitical development. It is only when the Azcapotzalco city-state and then the succeeding Triple Alliance appear that another round of cultural buildup begins (A.D. 1200–1520). Anton Kovar has traced the rise and fall of the lake levels, which fluctuations closely reflect those in rainfall (1970). It is noteworthy that the two major rises in lake level and rainfall were those which coincided with the rise in population in the basin and the development of the Teotihuacan and Mexica megacenters and empires. It is equally noteworthy that a precipitous drop in lake level from about A.D. 700 to 1200 coincides with a drop in population and the relative unimportance of basin political units. J. Parsons cites data that indicate that the basin was a buffer zone at this time between the city-state polities of Cholula in the Puebla valley and Xochicalco in the Morelos valley (1974); or, as Cowgill suggests, between Tula and Cholula (personal communication). The growth of Tula to the northwest also possibly constrained the basin's recovery of political importance.

In the case of the Central Valley of Oaxaca, there are also two florescences. The first begins about 100 B.C. and lasts until about A.D. 600, being roughly simultaneous with that of the first cultural peak in the basin, and of about the same length. A less well defined florescence is that of the immediate Protohistoric period, in which cultural vigor is obvious but political expression is more fragmented than in the basin. The buildup begins about A.D. 1400 in Oaxaca's Central Valley, some 200 years after the start of the final peak in the basin. This delay may account for the lack of political unification. It may be that the situation in the Valley of Oaxaca represents a transitional processual stage achieved by the Basin of Mexico earlier. It is interesting to project such a trend, if such it was, toward unification of the valley under the Mixteca. However, this trend was truncated by Spanish intervention.

The Maya lowlands are interesting in that there are at least four periods of florescence. The first is that of the early Classic and measures about 350 years in length. The hiatus marks the end of this period and possibly a collapse from which there was a recovery. The transformed Maya culture began a new and stronger surge in the late Classic terminated by a collapse in about A.D. 900. A delayed late Classic peak is represented by the Puuc centers which began to peak about A.D. 750 and did not collapse until about A.D. 1000. The Toltec period at Chichen represents reformulation, but under outside stimulus. This period lasted about 250 years, as did the late Classic. The final cultural flowering is the Mayapan period, which is a far weaker expression than the preceding three, although it

lasted about the same length of time, 250 years (A.D. 1200–1450).

West Mexico is altogether a different case. It is interesting that this area had only one climactic period of cultural growth and that was the latest or Protohistoric period. The Tarascan phenomenon represents the only comparable kind of development to those other periods in the other areas.

PROCESSUAL SYNTHESIS. Having at this point reviewed a somewhat heterogeneous number of ideas and theories, it behooves us to set forth a framework within which to coherently examine the larger processual events of Mesoamerican prehistory. In the following schema, there is surely something to offend everyone. However, the synthetic attempt outlined below has the virtue of some consistency, based on the following premises.

First of all, it is clear that in dealing with various historical and processual events, we are dealing with differences of order and quality even when we approach macromatters such as cycles of florescence and collapse. Therefore, analytical and theoretical intensity should be graded to meet the demands of the subject. Secondly, for the most part I accept Sanders' ideas on the nature of scientific explanation as set out above. That is, I think that prime movers can be isolated in specific instances of process. However, in dealing with larger and longer-term processes, I believe that the systemic paradigm of nonlinear causality is most appropriate. In this kind of explanation, there is no single cause, but a system of interacting factors connected by mechanisms which vary in importance at various stages of development. These interrelationships and processes are best expressed through models which are graphic and symbolic explanations. Barbara Price has eloquently discussed this and related matters at length (1971). Finally, I believe that no single model can explain any major processual event of any complexity, for example, the rise of Maya lowland civilization. For this sort of explication, a series of models is necessary in order to retain clarity and control of the explanatory process. Such a conception of cultural evolution might be likened to a Rube Goldberg–style machine in which there are several motors and several ways to hook them up to the machine of developing culture. Thus, population growth is probably a continually operating motor in the model, but ideational factors, as well as economic and ecological ones, may be hooked in with higher or lower gear ratios in order to have larger or smaller influences on cultural and sociopolitical development. These operant factors are those listed under the label "circumstances" in the section below, with the results and feedback mechanisms listed together. These factors and mechanisms and results could obviously be elaborated and the stages broken down almost indefinitely, but the fairly gross divisions used here are sufficient to indicate the explanatory powers of such an analytical and systemic approach.

Maya prehistory can be divided into at least six major processual episodes.

STAGE 1.

Circumstances: Population growth began in an essentially empty landscape.

Results: Emigration and spread through space took place. In the Maya case, this happened during the middle and late Preclassic periods. The technological basis was slash-and-burn agriculture.

STAGE 2.

Circumstances: Population growth continued during the late Preclassic and early Classic periods in a landscape increasingly occupied by maximum numbers of people subsisting on slash-and-burn and garden agri-

culture. Dry season water sources became scarce or inadequate. Necessities, such as salt, obsidian, and other items were largely lacking locally. Teotihuacan made intrusions into selected Maya zones.

Results: Conflict broke out among Maya communities and social organizational feedbacks began to transform the nature of these communities. Development proceeded in several respects. One direction was the emergence of Classic warfare patterns and of formal leadership in reaction to the atmosphere of intensive competition, as Webster suggests. Economic systems and a trend toward formal market systems were fostered by economic competition. Teotihuacan made a connection with several Maya centers, especially Tikal, for mutual economic and social advantages. Various ideologies were elaborated as social integration mechanisms. Development of large water storage facilities led to social circumscription circumstances which, Carneiro theorizes, gave the developing elite another lever for social control. Rathje suggests that the elite functioned as the information processing units of Maya societies, thus becoming institutionalized feedback mechanisms. The pristine state developed within the Maya lowlands by the end of the Preclassic period in a few zones and by the end of the early Classic period overall. This was partly stimulated by Teotihuacan presence and its role as a prestigious model.

STAGE 3.

Circumstances: Population growth in a landscape overcrowded for slash-and-burn subsistence, even supplemented with imports, gardening, and orchards. Declining soil fertility may have begun to affect crop yields.

Results: Involution of cultural systems in the following ways:

1. Development of intensive agriculture with formal and massive works such as

hillside terracing and bajo reclamation.

2. Development of and expansion of a managerial elite immediately below the aristocratic elite. A corollary development of the apparatuses of more highly urbanized forms of state thereby followed.

3. The possibility of a systemic overspecialization, or hypercoherence, has been suggested by Flannery. Such a situation would be one in which specialized functions had been parceled out among the various Maya lowland centers to such a degree that they became highly interdependent. We are defining here a certain kind of centralization in which any disaster in any part of the system would automatically involve the other parts. Evidence for this kind of over-development would be in the form of filling up of the landscape with settlements to the extent that boundaries of their domains effectively formed a *closely packed* polygon pattern. In fact, as Flannery (1972b) himself and Hammond (1974b) have demonstrated, this seems to have been the case, at least in the northeast Peten, during the late Classic period.

These events took place during the late Classic period of the southern lowlands and the Rio Bec–Chenes areas. The Puuc late Classic florescence was delayed, but followed much the same pattern, and outlasted the other variants of Classic civilization.

STAGE 4.

Circumstances: High population levels led to lower nutrition intake, overbalanced fractions of food producers versus nonproducers in Maya society, renewed military competition and disrupted crop production, and outside military intervention due to increased vulnerability. Deteriorating climatic conditions may have increased the stresses beyond bearing.

Results: Collapse of socioeconomic structures, abandonment of overworked lands, weakening of biological resistance, epidemic diseases, drastic increase in mortality rates, declining food production, and eventual disintegration of the social fabric and abandonment of the patterns and physical centers of social integration.

STAGE 5.

Circumstances: Military intrusion of foreign cultural forms into a fairly homogeneous cultural area and establishment of a permanent colonial capital controlling a large part of that area.

Results: A reworking of previously established forms and reorganization of the social fabric into less aristocratic patterns. The period being generalized on is the Toltec-Maya episode, and the colonial capital was at Chichen. The delayed late Classic florescence in the Puuc may have been partially the result of stimulation by Mexican Postclassic culture as well as its own predatory exploitation of the weakening southern Maya centers. Puuc florescence possibly came to an end as a result of losing out in competition with the even more successful Mexican Toltec militarists based at Chichen.

STAGE 6.

Circumstances: Withdrawal and absorption of the foreign influences from Yucatan and of the political and military apparatuses supporting them.

Result: The revival of more nativistic forms of culture at Mayapan, albeit in a new hybrid form.

The qualitative differences among the various florescences are underlined by framing them in the processual stages outlined above. Admittedly interpretative, the stages are also synthetic of data at hand. Turning to the specific problem of the initial rise of Maya civilization as an example, one can see that the first stages had several characteristics that set them apart from the later florescences. One feature is that of thinner population density than those found in stages 3, 5, and 6. However, relative to what went before, population reached something of a threshold, leading, if one accepts Webster's ideas, to military conflict and consequent development of greater sociopolitical complexity (1976). It is also possible that the last ninety years of Maya prehistory, from the fall of Mayapan to the arrival of the Spaniards, may have been a reversion to about the population density of the late Preclassic period and to conflict of about the same order.

Another distinction of the late Preclassic cultural buildup is the probable lack of intensive forms of agriculture of the kind that developed later, about A.D. 600. On the other hand, relatively speaking, more intensive forms of gardening and orchard tending may have been practiced than earlier.

To attempt to summarize the differences between the first and last pairs of florescences even more succinctly, we might take a slightly different stance. If the first two climaxes established the systemic nature of Maya civilization, then the last two were products of a striking characteristic of complex cultures. In my opinion, that characteristic is self-perpetuation through reformulation.

Turning to the less well understood Mexican highlands, we can arrange the prehistory of the Basin of Mexico and Central Valley of Oaxaca into several stages.

STAGE 1.
Circumstances: Buildup of agricultural populations in a thinly populated landscape of diverse ecology.

Results: Development of diverse cultivation systems geared to local ecological conditions, including irrigation farming. Symbiotic systems of economic exchange through incipient market systems, and development of merchants — itinerant, full-time, and part-time. The early Preclassic is the period under consideration. Village-level polities seem to have been the most developed form present.

STAGE 2.
Circumstances: Population growth in a landscape filling up with villages and in which the choice lands were already occupied. Intrusion of culturally sophisticated and foreign religious ideas and perhaps the establishment of Olmec trading colonies and religious centers in various highland regions.

Results: The development of canals and other forms of irrigation in response to burgeoning numbers of people, as well as the emergence of leadership on the village and village-alliance level. The appearance of formal market systems linked to long-distance trade in obsidian, jade, and other minerals was reciprocated by the Olmec with manufactured goods iconographically transformed into precious objects. Formal religious centers appeared with stratified societies and religious elites at their heads. Special architectural forms began to assume socioreligious meanings. By the end of the period, effects of religious-ideational mechanisms on population growth and organization had produced at least two major towns in the Basin of Mexico and perhaps two in the Central Valley of Oaxaca.

STAGE 3.
Circumstances: Elimination of Cuicuilco by natural catastrophe gave Teotihuacan an enormous edge over any other possible rivals. Population buildup and subsistence-

pattern development continued. Ideational factors began to intervene at this point on a significant scale, through the agency of a politico-religious elite.

Results: Concentration of 80 percent of the Basin of Mexico's population at the urban center of Teotihuacan. Concentration of an undetermined, but significant, fraction of the population of the Central Valley of Oaxaca in an urban zone at Monte Alban. Development of long-distance trade in earnest for purposes of basic commodity import. Expansion of trade routes and trading colonies throughout Mesoamerica, especially into symbiotically compatible regions, by Teotihuacan. Involutional development in the Valley of Oaxaca and surrounding zones, combined with limited expansion into such areas as the south coast of Oaxaca. Pan-Mesoamerican religious-commercial pilgrimages accelerated interstimulation among the regional cultures. During the final phases of Teotihuacan's development, population growth and sociopolitical evolution led to the fully evolved city-state and its proliferation as a political form outside the Basin of Mexico. Some of these outside city-states eventually became large enough to challenge the megacenter of Teotihuacan by forming an alliance against it.

STAGE 4.

Circumstances: Receding lake levels and possible rain failures in the Basin of Mexico. Rival city-states, possibly allied against Teotihuacan. Loss of contact with external regions and consequent loss of external resources weakened Teotihuacan.

Results: Teotihuacan lost its primacy, and its urban population was dispersed throughout the basin and possibly beyond. Elite and urban craft specialists apparently spread over Mesoamerica. In the Central Valley of Oaxaca, increasing population and ethnic divisions led to the historically attested

Zapotec-Mixtec rivalry and the eventual abandonment of Monte Alban by the Zapotec elite. This process was less of a collapse, however, than a shifting of power to other centers and continued, uninterrupted development of Oaxacan cultural traditions.

STAGE 5.

Circumstances: Recovery of population loss in the Basin of Mexico. Recovery of rainfall and rising lake levels beginning about A.D. 1200. In the Oaxacan Central Valley, competition continued and intensified between Zapotec and Mixtec.

Results: Extensive areas of chinampa agriculture developed in response to population growth in a competitive atmosphere. There was an eventual accretion of city-states into larger tributary and political systems headed first by Azcapotzalco and then by the Triple Alliance. Tenochtitlan achieved megacenter status on expansion of a tributary network and trading colonies outside the Basin of Mexico. The Valley of Oaxaca cultures achieved a new synthesis of elite class culture as expressed in Monte Alban V. Multi-ethnic towns and states in the Oaxacan area became the norm.

Again there is a significant difference between the stages. The first three stages are those of establishment of new orders of affairs with the achievement of true urbanism, and the first and greatest megacenter in Mesoamerica's prehistory, Teotihuacan. The fourth stage is a collapse, with a recovery in the fifth stage. These later stages again seem different in that they seem to be functions of the repetitive patterns of formulation and reformulation mentioned before as typical of mature, complex societies.

West Mexico shows an interesting contrast in its processual stages.

STAGE 1.

Circumstances: Slowly expanding population in an area of ecological diversity and drastically varying potential. The prolonged Preclassic period is the time frame. Ecological zones of large areal extent, and conversely, general lack of the "compressed" nature of ecological diversity as found in the central highlands. Spread of a specific religious complex involving subterranean tombs and ceramic figurine offerings.

Results: Establishment of isolated and allied village societies, loosely linked by trade in obsidian and other materials. A larger and more unifying type of phenomenon was that of the funerary ritual complex which became more elaborated and regionalized in expression through the Preclassic period. Limited and individualized warfare was characteristic. Some limited interaction with the Olmec-related cultures left no perceptible developmental results.

STAGE 2.

Circumstances: Expanding populations based on combined limited-intensive agriculture and extensive cultivation. Intrusion of Teotihuacan into the northwestern zones and the establishment of trading and mining colonies. Pochteca groups probably penetrated most of the area.

Results: Derivative states based on the developed models furnished by the Teotihuacan-linked colonies were begun. There was limited development and relatively little competition. An elite was established, but its nature was probably of weakened transitional forms.

STAGE 3.

Circumstances: Teotihuacan presence was withdrawn and Tula Toltecs intruded into some zones. Some areas were exploited for mining, and linkages were established with more native forms of Mesoamerican centers. The pochteca penetrated nearly all west Mexico. Introduction of metallurgy from Central and South America.

Results: Native western variants of the Mesoamerican small city-oriented states were elaborated. Metallurgy gave the west a technological attraction, and through the pochteca network of the Toltecs the west exercised some influence on the central highlands.

STAGE 4.

Circumstances: Population buildup in certain restricted zones, including the Patzcuaro area. Withdrawal of Toltec control and influence. Pochteca penetration and linkages with the central highlands continued more or less intermittently up until the Spanish conquest. Continued extension of native ideological forms took place.

Results: The emergence of a new elite was based on the Toltec models of the past, and greater populations were organized into a conquest state based on Tzintzuntzan. The unification of a great deal of west Mexico into a single polity for the first time took place under the ideologically reinforced leadership of a Tarascan royal caste.

The west Mexican stages are quite different in that they represent only one major florescence of the magnitude found in other areas examined. Further, it is a delayed florescence somewhat like that of the Puuc delayed late Classic period. Both areas were less ecologically and demographically favorable compared to the areas where the cultural traditions had initially been formulated. The lack of the compressed ecological diversity may account for part of the delay, as well as the lack of early population growth.

DISCUSSION. If a single characteristic is to be abstracted from these larger cycles of prehistory, it may be that there is a crucial threshold beyond which a complex cultural system becomes more or less self-perpetuating, so that in spite of disasters and catastrophes the system is reformulated and carried on. In all three cases, the first stages are characterized by rapid population growth, establishment of religious and market centers, and the growth of an elite leadership, in a competitive atmosphere. At this point the systems seem to take off on trajectories which stylistically may be quite distinct, but which have many functional similarities. The first florescences are spectacularly diverse, perhaps because in each case there was lack of serious competition from competing cultural paradigms. The later climaxes became stylistically more similar, as well as functionally nearly identical. Throughout the survey and discussion of various regional Mesoamerican cultures, it has been noted that there perhaps was an adaptive advantage to the construction of an empire from many city-states rather than trying to centralize the system and thereby transform the capital of it into a megacenter. The Mixtec built agglomerations of city-states, and their cultural and social forms seem to have fared better after the Spanish conquest than did those of the Aztec. In other words, segmentary larger polities may have been more adaptive and flexible. In contrast, if Flannery is right in his hypercoherence interpretation, over-organization and over-specialization may have had something to do with the collapse of Maya Classic culture. However, it may also have been the case that the Maya had responded in this organizational manner to the peculiar ecological circumstances in which they found themselves. In any case, their recovery from collapse was weaker and less stable.

Simplified to its most reductionist form, the processual sequence to be gleaned from these cycles might be as follows. In the first stages population growth was the major factor with a number of feedback mechanisms eventually leading to more intensive food production and more complex social organizations. At about the point that the landscape filled up with communities of about the same order of magnitude, economic and military competition seems to have led to the burgeoning of one or more communities and to have produced a hierarchy of settlements. Ideational factors also served as feedback mechanisms, with directing elites both serving and being served by such ideological systems. At the shift point where the larger centers were established, ideational factors may have taken over and led to unique developments which stylistically distinguished regional cultures one from another. Another characteristic of this sequence is that it was accretive. Population growth continued while economic systems were being elaborated, and likewise both were increasing in complexity while ideational factors were becoming directive, all interacting on one another through various linkages. The achieving of the political structure known as the "pristine state" was another shift point leading toward cyclical reformulation. In strictly Mesoamerican terms we are probably safe in equating a simplified form of the city-state with the pristine state. All of the above is highly abstract and considers (not surprisingly) only those factors that an archaeologist can control as given by the nature of the data. However, it also apparently nearly omits any consideration of the influences of personality and historical circumstance. The answer to this objection is that personality and historical circumstance were and are largely formed by the cultural and ecological factors under control, and in any case were usually individual fractions of feedback mechanisms; for example, political systems, in the case of a ruler. None of which is to say that cultural systems run themselves; they are composed of people and created by them, and it is hoped that the reader can fill in the roles with real humans from the information given in previous chapters.

ANALOGIES WITH OLD WORLD CULTURE HISTORY AND THE POSSIBILITIES OF CONTACT. References have been made from time to time to evolutionary processes and events in the Old World similar to those in Mesoamerica. These have mainly been specific, although many have processual implications. The most systemic and systematic analogies between Old and New World complex cultures have been made by Julian Steward (1955: Chap. 11) and Robert M. Adams (1966). These theorists speak best for themselves. However, neither concerns himself with the specific fluctuation patterns of florescence and collapse as outlined previously. I feel that it is useful to continue on our own to draw analogic parallels which may give some insights into two specific phenomena. One of these phenomena is that of the durations of florescence of Maya climaxes. It has been noted that these lasted from 250 to 350 years and occurred with some regularity throughout the prehistory of the lowlands. Shimkin has brought it to my attention that Old World dynastic cycles in both Europe and Asia roughly parallel the Maya cycles in length. This raises the interesting question as to whether or not the Maya cycles are political failures rather than total systemic failures as we have presented them. I would argue that the ends of most, if not all, florescences are indeed systemically caused, and I believe that the Old World dynastic cycles were likely of the same nature. The Chinese projected a moralistic, ex post facto judgment on the failure of a dynasty. That is, there was obvious favor in heaven manifested toward a new dynasty by the fact of its establishment, and the eventual failure was explained as the result of a moral decline and a consequent divine displeasure. A cycle of rectitude and hubris framed Chinese cycles in their own thinking and constituted a tautology. However, if one examines the record closely enough, one can outline both internal and external stresses for Asian states just as we have done for the Classic Maya. Another analogy, more specific this time, can be drawn between the Classic Maya collapse and the collapse of medieval western European civilization. Woodruff Smith has pointed out to me the population factor similarities in the explanations advanced for both disasters. According to A. J. Slavin, between 1086 and about 1337, population in medieval England took an enormous jump (1973). There is some dispute about the exact numbers of people involved, but the following table gives the principal estimates.

Population Estimates for Medieval England

Date	According to Russell	According to Postan-Hallan
1086	1.1 million	1.6 million
1279–1337	3.7 million (+336%)	6.25 million (+406%)
1377	2.25 million (−40%)	3.75 million (−40%)

Adapted from Slavin, 1973, with permission.

Clearly, there was an increase in population prior to the great plagues of 1348–1349 (the Black Death) on the order of three to four times. Postan says that population growth led to a bare subsistence level of existence for most people by 1300. A lower standard of living and a high carbohydrate diet made people more vulnerable to disease. Most land was in the hands of the lords and unavailable to the peasantry. The severe famine of 1315–1317 and epidemics among the herds in 1320 increased the stresses. When the Black Death did strike, there was about a 40 percent population loss. There also followed some thirty plague years over a period from 1348 to 1485. Cultural and social reorganization and recovery did not really come about in England until the beginning of the sixteenth century. The syndrome of overpopulation, overexpansion, and poor land management combined with no less severe secondary consequences such as lowered nutrition and lower biological resistance to diseases. Clearly the parallels deserve more detailed exploration. They might produce more testable insights which can be applied to New World materials.

Analogies, however, cannot prove anything. They merely suggest explanations, or interrelationships among factors, or other pertinent matters that must be independently tested on the data generated about the case being attacked. Other people have used analogies and similarities to suggest that New World civilizations were derived from the Old World.

It has been theorized that native Americans were derived from Egypt, from the lost seven tribes of Israel, from Polynesia, as well as from the lost continents of Atlantis and Mu. European and American writers have conjectured that the high culture variants were introduced from Scandinavia, the Mediterranean, and from outer space. During the eighteenth and early nineteenth centuries, this eagerness to attribute the origins of New World civilization to an outside source stemmed partly from an unwillingness to credit American Indians with the capacity for civilized life. In a sense, it was and is a form of intellectual racism with the implication being that American Indians lacked the inherent ability to develop complex cultures. Be that as it may, it is a fact that there are striking Old World and Asian parallels to stylistic and systemic fragments of Mesoamerican civilizations. Serious scholars such as David Kelley have pointed out the similarities between the animal and deity patrons of days in Southeast Asia calendars and those of Mesoamerica (1974). Specific religious iconography such as the use of water lily motif in Southeast Asia and among the Classic Maya in hieratic art has been cited as proof of historical linkage.

The arguments against these alleged linkages are based on systemic integrity of New World cultures and the phenomenon of convergence. It is exactly because the parallels are between fragments of cultural subsystems and not between whole systems that they are finally unconvincing. Convergence, or accidental reinvention of similar cultural forms, can be documented historically between unconnected cultures. Especially in the case of complex societies and formal qualities of great intricacy, there are nearly bound to be reinvented forms. Thus, the water lily is present in ecological zones of both the Maya lowlands and Southeast Asia, where tropical forest civilizations developed. Since it is a common and attractive plant, it is not surprising that it was independently picked as a religiously and aesthetically important symbol in both areas.

Even more striking similarities, such as those between Chinese Shang dynasty bronzes and Teotihuacan lidded, slab-footed tripods, are paradoxically even more difficult to explain. Storm-driven ships from Asia have made it to the New World in historic times with survivors. However, there is no evidence that a boatload of Asians should have had any great cultural effect on the Mesoamericans among whom they landed. Even if they introduced a ceramic form to the New World, it was in the context of already developed native culture. European and Asian castaways on the mainland of America during the period of exploration had little effect on native cultures, and in fact the foreigners usually adapted themselves, if they survived at all.

A few lines of summary discussion are not going to convert any who truly believe in derivation of New World civilizations from the Old World. However, the burden of proof is on them to reinterpret the vast body of data produced by archaeologists in some convincing manner that will explain the enormous divergence of New World cultures and Mesoamerican civilization specifically.

One final set of processual questions concerns us. These revolve around the explanation for the stylistic peculiarities of Mesoamerican civilization both as a whole and in its regional variants.

Let us use the lowland Maya again as an example. Maya centers are composed of combinations of a few building types: mainly temples, palaces, paved courtyards, ball courts, and causeways. The Maya temple can be explained as a memorial, at least commemorative and often funerary. As noted, Mesoamerican civilizations were elite-oriented, and the elite in most regions reinforced their social status by exaltation of lineage. Royal castes were functionally related to this effort.

Prestige-conferring systems of symbols are invariably conservative. The reason is, of course, that the more the symbols become reified and elaborated, the more communicative function they perform. The Maya may have begun with a system of meritoriously selected leaders in a middle Preclassic village context. However, it is well known that in traditional, village-centered societies, the leaders' kin have an edge in succeeding to leadership roles. That is, leadership becomes almost invariably kin–unit associated. Prestige of lineage aids in competition for office. The "big man" phenomenon of Oceania is an example of this process. Many may aspire to be "big men" in Melanesia, but only a few actually make it, and those who do tend to be those who had former "big men" among their older kin. Such a situation can explain the later Maya royal caste emphasis. However, it does not explain the formal qualities that Maya civilization assumed. The explanation of that question, I believe, lies in the interplay between the nature of Preclassic leadership and the changing role of Maya leadership in the late Preclassic and early Classic. If Webster's and my own schema are correct, then the leadership during the late Preclassic and early Classic periods was under pressure to become

military leadership, at least in part. Under such pressures, the old symbols are usually not discarded, but are often reinforced. For example, the mainline Philadelphians are still very much oriented toward traditional family mansions and many activities which are more consonant with rural estates than urban living. Many still engage in fox hunting and the social activities surrounding it, although relatively few actually cultivate lands over which the hunt is run. Most of the mainliners are business-engaged, but the traditional symbolism of social prestige has survived and even become more important to social status. Another, perhaps closer analogy can be derived from the behavior of present-day Latin American elites. These groups tend to invest money made in commerce or government in landed estates, the prestige symbol of the old aristocracies. Such landed estates, especially where agrarian reform has taken place, are often financial losers. This is remarkable because those investing in them have made their money by astute financial means. As Thomas Greaves points out, "Clearly the estates are symbols" (personal communication).

Maya leadership in the Preclassic period almost certainly was kinship-oriented with certain units monoplizing the positions. Worship of selected ancestors was a part of the reinforcement of this prestige-conferring activity. Proper and increasingly elaborate burial was traditional through the late Preclassic period with small thatched-roof temples being erected over burial platforms. Eventually these became stone and mortar temples and the burial chambers became tombs (for example, Tikal burial 85). In regard to the shift point into the early Classic period, the argument is that the leadership roles were changing, becoming more military and managerial in addition to dealing with such matters as conflict resolution. Large-scale water storage was probably begun during this period of transition. Management of such created resources would have been a new role. Leadership either had to adopt the new functions or relinquish the offices. Reinforcement of traditional forms of prestige activities, in this case royal caste ancestor worship, also meant elaboration of the burial monuments. This is offered as an explanation of one of many of the formal qualities of Maya civilization. If one accepts this argument, then it may also be postulated that the elite desired to live in close proximity to their ancestors and their monuments. Sumptuous housing for the exalted social class is a functionally related step. Accounting for these two classes of buildings, temples and palaces, one accounts for probably 95 percent of Maya monumental architecture. The stela cult is seen as an elaboration of the ancestor and lineage glorification idea. It may well have been adapted and adopted from the Izapan cultures, but it was functionally very appropriate to the Classic Maya, who carried it and much else of their cultural inheritance to new levels of complexity.

CONTINUITIES INTO THE COLONIAL AND MODERN ERAS. Four hundred and fifty years of cultural change separate us from the Protohistoric cultures of Mesoamerica. We can only sketch here some of the major features of events occurring after the Spanish conquest. After the brutal disasters of the 1520s a new reformulation of culture began taking place. Gibson points out that the first fifty years of Spanish colonial rule had many creative and positive features to them (1964). However, he and McLeod also make clear the fundamentally exploitative nature of the relationship of the Spaniards, Mestizos, and Negros to the Indians (McLeod, 1973). This was partially responsible for the cultural failure. The three major forms of Spanish exploitation were through their control over tribute, labor, and land. Control of land was most important, and its eventual near-monopolization by non-

Indian populations of Mexico and Central America led to the degradation of the native ruling classes, as well as to the compression of all Indians into a single social stratum and condition. Before the great plagues of the sixteenth century, when there were yet substantial numbers of Indians, and little land was unoccupied, the principal means of exploitation was by assignment of towns and populations to the private benefit of individual Spaniards under a system called *encomienda*. Theft of title, robbery, and other abuses were flagrant even though the Indians were in theory in the care of the *encomenderos*. Usurpation of titles to lands became easier after depopulation due to disease and later, when native populations began to recover, the institution of the *hacienda* absorbed them as it had absorbed their ancestral lands. There is a major controversy among historians over Borah's interpretation of the seventeenth century as one of economic depression leading to the establishment of the hacienda (self-sufficient landed estate) as a response (1951). Whatever the case, there is little doubt that the hacienda did become the major landholding unit aside from church and state during the late colonial and early republican periods of Mexico.

Institutional parallels between preconquest and postconquest political units are interesting. The city-state system essentially was based on the tributary relationship between a dominant town (*cabecera*) and a subordinate community (*sujeto*). This system was retained for tribute-gathering and other administrative conveniences during most of the sixteenth century. It later broke down for various reasons, among them the upwards of 90 to 95 percent population loss and its social consequences. It might be noted, however, that the modern *municipio* with its politically subject communities is not unlike the *cabecera-sujeto* system.

Land-holding institutions likewise carry

some parallels. It will be recalled that the Aztec nobility had the privilege of private estates to which serfs were attached. These obviously have a functional if not direct historical relationship to the later haciendas. In fact, the hacienda still exists in Mexico and Central America, although the workers are no longer serfs tied to the land.

Although much native communal land was lost through the predatory nature of the haciendas and of individual mestizo land owners, the remote areas of Mesoamerica still shelter communities in which the system is strong. The Maya highland communities of Chiapas and Guatemala are examples of this ancient style of land tenure, though it is breaking down. A modern attempt at revival of communal landholding has been the *ejido* program in Mexico, but this has distributed relatively little land proportionate to the amount tied up in large estates.

The gradual degradation of the native ruling classes in the Valley of Mexico is documented by Charles Gibson (1964). The Spaniards made many new demands on the *tlatoques* or rulers and interfered with succession. Native leaders of all kinds became known as *caciques,* an imported Caribbean word. The Spaniards naturally favored those native leaders who collaborated and confirmed their titles and tribute support. Status symbols were granted them, such as the right to ride horses, carry firearms, and live in a European lifestyle. Some of these families remained vigorous into the nineteenth century, but only indirectly because of inherited status. Gibson notes that by 1800 "neither the urban economy of Mexico City or the hacienda economy favored the preservation of cacique status" (1964: 165). Zapata, in his 1911 Plan de Ayala, classified caciques with *hacendados* and *científicos* (advisors to Diaz) as enemies of reform.

The above features are all systemically interrelated and perhaps more subject to pressures than those cultural features which depended on individual behavior and values. Ritual and religious behavior especially fall into this last category. The measure of intractability in these areas can be inferred to some extent from the fact that the major Spanish documentation on Aztec and other native religions was specifically justified as guides to pagan liturgy and philosophy hiding behind Christian masks. The sacred almanac still survives in a few remote zones, such as around Nebaj, in Guatemala, and is used for one of its ancient primary purposes, divination. Curing ceremonies are an integral part of life in most native communities. These ceremonies are more or less acculturated by European folk medicine, dependent on the community. An apparently unchanged ceremony involves the sacred hills and shrines around the highland Chiapas ceremonial center and town of Zinacantan. E. Z. Vogt and his colleagues have examined these ceremonies in detail and have pointed out the massive survivals in them from the native past (Vogt, 1971). Folk medicine in general has heavy doses of Indian medicinal lore, although in Mexico there is a substantial influence from Mediterranean cultures.

It has been pointed out so often as to become a truism in anthropology that many fortuitous parallels in Mesoamerican and Roman Catholic religious systems made it at the same time harder and easier to carry out the massive conversions of the sixteenth century. Religious pilgrimages, for example, were and are parts of both patterns. At present, native religious pilgrimages tend to be to shrines outside of the main urban centers. However, this is perhaps a function of the lesser status of Indian cultures. Indian pilgrims also make trips to such widely recognized shrines as that of the Virgin of Guadalupe. These congruences and their subsequent changes are reflected in the sixteenth-century open-atrium churches. John McAndrew has defined the habitual open-air worship patterns inherent in the pre-Hispanic religious architecture with its open plazas and restricted temple space (1965). To handle the massive conversions of the sixteenth century the first friars adapted religious architecture of Europe to the circumstances and native background, producing churches in which the altar was half-covered and the congregation stood or knelt in the walled open space around it. It is probably not chance that these churches date from the early colonial period with its still massive native populations and that the architectonic form fell into disuse after the plagues and the loss of vast numbers. The reduced congregations could easily fit into the interior of more restricted and covered churches afterwards.

Market systems, begun deep in the past, continue today in the age-old manner on weekly schedules. The market at Chichicastenango, for example, operates on Thursdays and Sundays with the latter as the most important day. Itinerant merchants from all over the Guatemalan highlands come to the market to exchange tropical and highland goods. McBryde's great study of the Atitlan zone with its market systems shows that symbiotic regions and their economic integration are still working in the traditional manner (1947).

For all of their variation and richness, Mesoamerican civilizations were unable to successfully confront the pragmatic soldiery of the European Renaissance. The promising start made at a cultural amalgam during the early colonial days was ultimately a failure. Modern Mexico and Guatemala owe as much to the industrialized West as to their own traditions. However, all over Mesoamerica people eat foods developed by their predecessors, cooked in much the same way, in houses built in the same manner, and speaking many of the same languages. And, in the remote and not so remote regions of Mesoamerica, the 260-day calendar is still used, the ball game is still played, divination and curing ceremonies are performed, and other fragments of native cultures confront the modern traveler either subtly or outright.

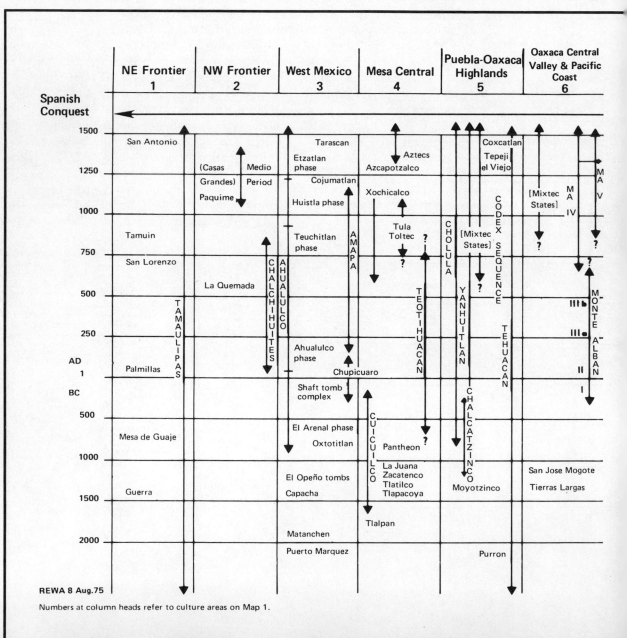

	NE Frontier 1	NW Frontier 2	West Mexico 3	Mesa Central 4	Puebla-Oaxaca Highlands 5	Oaxaca Central Valley & Pacific Coast 6

Spanish Conquest

1500 — San Antonio / Tarascan / Etzatlan phase / Aztecs Azcapotzalco / Coxcatlan Tepeji el Viejo

1250 — (Casas Grandes) Paquime / Medio Period / Cojumatlan / Xochicalco / [Mixtec States]

Huistla phase

1000 —

Tamuin / La Quemada / Teuchitlan phase / Tula Toltec / CHOLULA / [Mixtec States] / [Mixtec States]

750 — San Lorenzo

CHALCHIHUITES / AHUALULCO / AMAPA

500 —

Ahualulco phase / TEOTIHUACAN / YANHUITLAN / CODEX SEQUENCE / MONTE ALBAN IIIb IIIa

250 — TAMAULIPAS

AD 1 — Palmillas / Chupicuaro / TEHUACAN

BC — Shaft tomb complex

500 — Mesa de Guaje / El Arenal phase / Oxtotitlan / CUICUILCO / Pantheon ? / CHALCATZINCO

1000 — Guerra / El Opeño tombs / Capacha / La Juana Zacatenco Tlatilco Tlapacoya / Moyotzinco / San Jose Mogote Tierras Largas

1500 —

Tlalpan

2000 — Matanchen / Puerto Marquez / Purron

Numbers at column heads refer to culture areas on Map 1.

CHRONOLOGY CHART

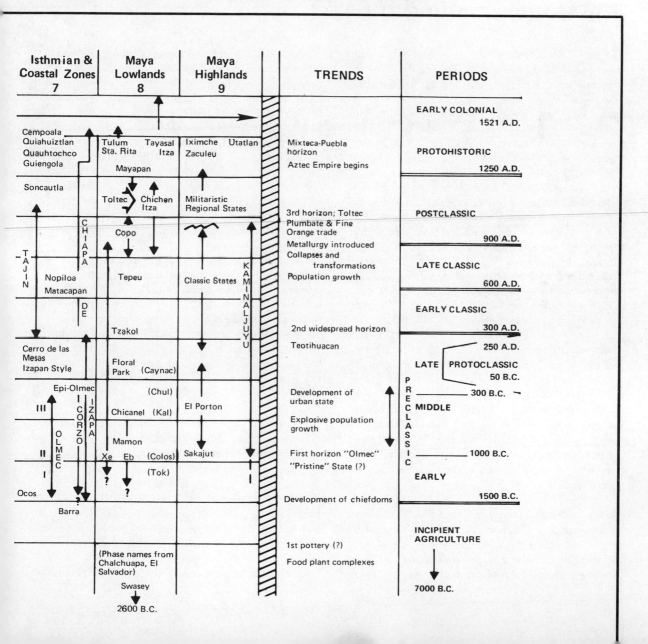

Isthmian & Coastal Zones 7	Maya Lowlands 8	Maya Highlands 9	TRENDS	PERIODS
				EARLY COLONIAL 1521 A.D.
Cempoala Quiahuiztlan Quauhtochco Guiengola	Tulum Tayasal Sta. Rita Itza Mayapan	Iximche Utatlan Zaculeu	Mixteca-Puebla horizon Aztec Empire begins	PROTOHISTORIC 1250 A.D.
Soncautla	Toltec Chichen Itza	Militaristic Regional States	3rd horizon; Toltec Plumbate & Fine Orange trade	POSTCLASSIC 900 A.D.
Nopiloa Matacapan	Copo Tepeu	Classic States	Metallurgy introduced Collapses and transformations Population growth	LATE CLASSIC 600 A.D.
				EARLY CLASSIC 300 A.D.
Cerro de las Mesas Izapan Style	Tzakol Floral Park (Caynac)		2nd widespread horizon Teotihuacan	250 A.D. LATE PROTOCLASSIC 50 B.C.
Epi-Olmec III	(Chul) Chicanel (Kal)	El Porton	Development of urban state Explosive population growth	300 B.C. MIDDLE
II	Mamon Xe Eb (Colos) (Tok)	Sakajut	First horizon "Olmec" "Pristine" State (?)	1000 B.C. EARLY
I Ocos Barra	? ?		Development of chiefdoms	1500 B.C.
			1st pottery (?) Food plant complexes	INCIPIENT AGRICULTURE
	(Phase names from Chalchuapa, El Salvador) Swasey 2600 B.C.			7000 B.C.

Appendix A
Explanatory and Analytical Tools for Understanding the Past

There is no intention of being original in this section. Indeed, the aim is just the opposite: to be unoriginal. That is, I mean to outline the commonly accepted theoretical and analytical tools with which archaeologists organize their data into coherent patterns. Therefore, most of the material presented here is standard, used by most archaeologists in part or as a whole. This statement applies to both the "new" archaeologists and to the "pragmatists." The distinction made above is one which is most often insisted upon by the "new" archaeologists who consider themselves explicitly committed to the "scientific" method or the hypothetico-deductive system of research. The rest of the profession which is not so specifically committed, and which is willing to use anything that comes to hand, I have grouped into a loose category under the label "pragmatists." Wishing to avoid the polemics which has often characterized the debate between the two groups, I shall only refer to the distinctions at appropriate points (Binford and Binford, 1968; Fritz and Plog, 1970; Watson et al., 1970; R. E. W. Adams, 1969).

Archaeologists deal with three elements: time, space, and content. There are a multitude of structures for each of these qualities. These give us some control over the materials, and with them many inferences are possible and testable. Without such control, nothing is certain. We will consider time first.

TIME. Relative and absolute time distinctions are important. The former can be determined by the most useful field technique ever developed: *stratigraphy*. This is a principle borrowed from geology; simply stated, it means that physical deposits and the cultural materials that they contain can be ordered by the sequence in which they are found in excavation. This means that the latest deposits are on top and the earliest on the bottom of a pit. There are many permutations to the technique, but that is the essence of it, and with it one can establish relative time. The lowest material in a pit thus is usually the oldest and the highest is the youngest, and the order of the rest of the materials, say pottery, falls in between in the order indicated by the deposits. By this, then, we can determine that pottery type 3-R is more recent than type 7-X and that both come before type 2-A.

Absolute time can be inserted into the relative time sequence by the use of several sources of information. History may aid us, as do native calendars, such as the Maya calendar. However, physical science has provided us with the majority of independent checks on the absolute dating of archaeological materials. Carbon 14, thermoluminescence, obsidian hydration, tree-ring analysis, and other wonderful and arcane techniques lead to absolute dating.

CONTENT. This term comprehends all of the items and kinds of information that an archaeologist digs up. At the most basic, it means artifacts and their contexts. Artifacts are usually separated by raw material categories and then classified further according to style. Thus, there are stone, bone, antler, pottery, textiles, basketry, wood, and so on. Within these classes, there are taxonomically or descriptively organized units. For example, red-slipped pottery makes up a large amount of the ceramics in the Maya lowlands.

This is distinguished by the forms, color variants, surface decoration (punctation, incision, etc.), wall thickness, tempering (grog) qualities, and others. Thus a type such as Sierra Red is defined, which has a certain range of forms and associated qualities that distinguish it from all other red pottery specifically and all other pottery generally. By stratigraphic means, it is known that Sierra Red occurs before polychrome pottery decoration is developed, and after the height of white-slipped pottery's popularity. This constitutes the establishment of relative dating. Similarly, other kinds of artifacts and associated information are classified, such as house types, art styles, and estimated population sizes. By these means an organized inventory of the entire material content of a particular place at a particular time is developed.

SPACE.   It is obvious that all of the above types are specifically located in space. The distribution of Sierra Red pottery and associated materials at a site or a series of sites, together with the data from colleagues or predecessors, allows rough boundaries to be drawn on a map. Thus we know that Sierra Red is most common in the Maya lowlands, but also occurs in the Chiapas lowlands. Further, stratigraphy has repeatedly shown that these samples of the type occur at about the same time.

SYNTHETIC UNITS.   It is obvious that ancient peoples did not use just one type of pottery at any one time. Usually there were up to twenty types of pottery in use simultaneously. Once the contemporaneity of a group of pottery or lithic or wooden artifact types has been established, a ceramic, lithic, or wooden artifact *complex* has been determined. Putting all of the contemporary complexes together defines the entire known artifact inventory of a particular place at a particular time. At this point we have the necessary information for the establishment of that most useful of all archaeological units, the *phase*. The phase is the unit in which all three elemental qualities (time, space, and content) are combined. A phase is defined as a distinctive body of content located in a specific place (or region) and with a specified duration in time. It follows that all phases are not the same length. Depending on circumstance, the archaeologist makes the phases

as short as possible, but they may range from 1000 years to 20. A series of such phases constitutes a *sequence*. Sequences are often referred to in this book and they usually mean *site sequences,* but they can be region-wide, as the Tehuacan phases are. The problem is obviously one of sampling, and indeed, as I have said in another context, archaeology can be viewed as a kind of grand sampling game. Usually, the archaeologist is dealing with only a 1 to 2 percent sample at the best, and often the excavated material from a site is far less than that proportion. Archaeological reconnaissance over large zones can extend our knowledge. Surface collecting of pottery and other artifacts and test pits at other sites may greatly expand the site or regional sequence.

Cross-tying of regional sequences into larger sequences is accomplished by use of *horizons*. Horizon styles are widely spread in space but fairly short-lived in time. The Mixteca-Puebla style is a Protohistoric example from Mesoamerica, as is the widespread use of slab-footed, tripod, cylindrical vases with lids for the Teotihuacan period. By these means and absolute dating, the large *stages* are established which are developmental epochs, with roughly contemporary events from all over the Mesoamerican area. The specific meanings of these stages and *periods* are discussed in the introductory chapter. However, it bears repeating here that periods are regarded as simply large blocks of time applicable to all of Mesoamerica and which have no specific evolutionary or cultural historical implications.

LEVELS OF ORGANIZATIONAL DEVELOPMENT.   Certain terms are used in the body of the book to refer to levels of complexity in social, political, and economic organization. Most of these are derived from the general body of ethnological theory. There are several problems with these labels, however. One is that there is no stable agreement as to what constitutes a tribe, say, across all world culture areas. Therefore, it cannot be assumed, for example, that a tribal level of organization in the Tehuacan valley at a specific time had all of the characteristics that have been cross-culturally defined for us by such scholars as George P. Murdock (1949) and Elman Service (1962). Further, there is a problem of the differences between the nature of archaeological evidence and the character of definitions based on ethnological data. Sanders and Price have ably discussed this matter (1968). Ethnologists tend to deal with nonmaterial evidence derived from observation of living societies. Archaeologists are constrained to deal with a fragment of the material remains of extinct societies. Therefore, any statements about social organization of archaeological cultures are usually and mainly inferential. There is an obvious incongruity in the nature of the two sets of organizational labels. A partial solution to the problem would be to pay more attention to the material correlates of organizational levels of living societies. However, there is another problem, and one more fundamental. The ethnological record is small and somewhat uneven in quality. Further, it is largely, although not entirely, confined to the past 100 years of anthropological work. For these and other reasons, the resultant cross-cultural and universal categories of social organization may well be inappropriate to apply to the archaeological cultures of the past. The early cultures must have gone through many stages that were only relatively fleeting and unstable. However, the peculiarities of these transitional stages may have had lasting effects on the later stylistic and functional characteristics of developed cultures. For example, the Olmec culture arose in a world largely free of the intense competition that the later Mixtec states faced. The Olmec may be regarded as a form of "pristine state" and one which was by nature transitory. However, as we now see it, certain crucial features of Olmec social organization may have been perpetuated in Classic Maya civilization, lasting until the collapse at about A.D. 900. For these reasons then, it is proposed here that archaeologists must eventually work out their own typologies and sequences of social organizations which will be largely independent of ethnological categories. The matching of archaeological and ethnological categories, then, would be a still further and comparative step toward understanding of both conceptual frameworks.

In the meantime, however, we are stuck, at least for the purposes of this book, with a terminology derived from ethnology and which carries a load of possible misinformation. In the Service terminology the evolutionary scale runs from *band* (simplest), to *tribe,* to *chiefdom,* to *primitive state.* In a sense, the definitions of these levels are too detailed with the kind of evidence extremely unlikely to show up in the archaeological record. On the other hand, they are not refined enough to take account of the apparent variation in the crucial transition stages of passage from the chiefdom to the state or from the tribe to the chiefdom. In practice, it is exceedingly difficult to distinguish between villages inhabited by people organized into tribes, and those organized into chiefdoms or even states. Therefore, the reader will often encounter the term "village-oriented society" as a euphemism which leaves open the social organizational possibilities.

One distinction I have introduced is the concept of a "high chiefdom," or of a transitional stage between the fully developed urban state, and that of the village-oriented chiefdom. The "high chiefdom" would fit the case of the Olmec and would probably also take in the early Classic Maya. The distinction is based on the possession of ceremonial centers by "high chiefdoms" versus the lack of such centers in an otherwise fairly sophisticated village-oriented society such as Pre-classic west Mexico. The criterion of a ceremonial center is satisfactory in that it is archaeologically detectable, and carries the implication of a full time specialization of leadership and of minimal occupational specialists, but not of urbanism. The elite class would have been less than 2 percent of the total population, and its active part less than 1 percent. Obviously, high chiefdoms could coexist with the urban states. The latter would be distinguished by permanent high-density populations, and larger and complex leadership and specialist classes. Tikal, in the Maya lowlands, achieved this status in the late Classic period. The concept of the pristine state is appropriate here either in the context of the high chiefdom or the urban state. The latter apparently arose directly from an unmodified chiefdom level in the highlands. But enough commentary. The distinction is made and I believe that it is useful for the heuristic and presentational purposes of this book. The theoretical implications and difficulties will have to be threshed out elsewhere.

Appendix B
Guide to Pronunciation

The reader who is confronted with the names of Mixtec (MEESH-tek) or Aztec deities is liable to be dismayed at first sight. This guide is intended to allay that sinking feeling. However, there is no substitute for buckling down and slowly taking apart some words and getting something of the verbal rhythm of those rich languages. If this book is used in a classroom the student will, at the least, be able to make a connection between the written word and the word as it is spoken by his instructor.

The reader may find some solace in the fact that the first Spaniards had equally as difficult a time with Nahuatl, the Aztec language. Indeed, most of them never did master it, judging by the book written by that old conqueror, Bernal Diaz. *Huitzilopochtli*, the principal Aztec deity, became *Huichilobos* in many 16th century Spanish accounts.

Sixteenth century Spanish was different from modern Spanish and had an *x* used to represent a "*sh*" sound. Thus, Tlaxcala is *Tlash-KAH-lah*, and Texcoco is *Tesh-KOH-koh*. Xaltocan is *Hal-TOH-kahn* today, but in preconquest times was *Shal-TOH-kahn*. *A's* are nearly always long as in "*ah*," and all other vowels are long, as with *i* being pronounced "*ee*" and in Huitzilopochtli, *Weet-see-low-POCH-tlee*. The accents have been dropped in this book, but nearly all Aztec and Spanish words are accented on the next to the last syllable. Thus, Xochimilco is *Shoh-chee-MEEL-koh*, and Tenochtitlan is *Tay-noch-TEET-lahn*.

In Maya the accent is often on the last syllable, as in Chichen Itza (*Chee-CHEN Eet-ZAH*), or Becan (*Bay-KAHN*). The *x* in Maya words is nearly always pronounced "*sh*", as in Iximche (*Eesh-eem-CHAY*). *U* on the beginning of words takes the place of *w* in English, as in Uaxactun (*Wah-shock-Toon*).

Mixtec words are complicated by the use of the Spanish tilde, or ~, indicating a *y* sound; thus Yucuñudahui is *Yoo-koon-yoo-dah-WHEE*, and Nuiñe is *NYOO-een-yea*. The reader may take some small comfort from knowing that at least he is not required to pronounce Parangaricutirimicuaro.

Examples of many of the most commonly encountered deity and place names follow.

MAYA DEITIES

Written	Pronounced
Ah Kin	Ah Keen
Ah Puch	Ah Pooch
Bacabs	Bah-KAHBS
Chac	Chahk
Ek Chuah	Eck Choo-AH
Hunab Ku	Hoo-NAHB Koo
Itzamna	Eet-zahm-NAH
Ixchel	Eesh-CHEL
Kinich Ahau	Kee-NEECH Ah-HOW
Kukulkan	Koo-kool-KAHN
Xamen Ek	Sha-MEN Eck
Yum Cimil	Yoom Kee-MEEL

NAHUATL DEITIES

Coatlicue	Kwat-LEE-kway
Huitzilopochtli	Weet-see-low-POCH-tlee

Mixcoatl	Meesh-KOH-ahtl
Quetzalcoatl	Kayt-zahl-KOH-ahtl
Tezcatlipoca	Tez-caht-lee-POH-kah
Tlaloc	TLAH-lohk
Xipe Totec	SHEE-pay TOH-teck
Xochipilli	Shoh-chee-PEEL-yee
Xolotl	SHOH-lohtl

WESTERN MESOAMERICAN PLACE NAMES

Aztlan	Ahz-TLAHN
Azcapotzalco	Ahz-kah-poht-ZAHL-koh
Cempoala	Sem-poh-AH-lah
Cholula	Choh-LOO-lah
Chupicuaro	Choo-PEE-kwar-oh
Coxatlan	Kosh-KAHT-lahn
Cuicuilco	Kwee-KWEEL-koh
Tajin	Tah-HEEN
Malinalco	Mah-leen-AHL-koh
Popocatepetl	Poh-poh-kah-TAY-petl
Santa Isabel Iztapan	Eez-TAH-pahn
Tamuin	Tah-MOO-een
Tehuacan	Tay-wah-KAHN
Tehuantepec	Tay-WAHN-tay-peck
Tenayuca	Tay-nah-YOO-kah
Tenochtitlan	Tay-noch-TEET-lahn
Teotihuacan	Tay-oh-TEE-wah-kahn
Teotitlan del Rio	Tay-oh-TEET-lahn
Tepexpan	Tay-PESH-pahn
Tequixquiac	Tay-KEESH-kee-ahk
Tilantongo	Tee-lahn-TOHN-goh
Tlatelolco	Tlah-tay-LOHL-koh
Tlatilco	Tlah-TEEL-koh
Tula	TOO-lah
Tzintzuntzan	Tzeen-tzoon-TZAHN
Valsequillo	Vahl-say-KEEL-yoh
Xochicalco	Shoh-chee-KAHL-koh

Xochimilco	Shoh-chee-MEEL-koh
Zacatenco	Zah-kah-TEN-koh

EASTERN MESOAMERICAN PLACE NAMES

Acanceh	Ah-kahn-KAY
Chiapa de Corzo	Chee-AH-pah day KOHR-zoh
Chichen Itza	Chee-CHEN Eet-ZAH
Chixoy River	Chee-SHOY
Dzibilchaltun	Dzee-beel-chahl-TOON
Holmul	Hohl-MOOL
Iximche	Eesh-eem-CHAY
Jaina	High-NAH
Kaminaljuyu	Kah-mee-nahl-hoo-YOO
Kohunlich	Koh-hoon-LEECH
Nebaj	Nay-BAH
Oxkintok	Osh-keen-TOHK
Palenque	Pah-LEN-kay
Quirigua	Kee-ree-GWAH
Seibal	Sigh-BALL
Uaxactun	Wah-shock-TOON
T'ho	Tuh'HOH
Usumacinta	Oo-soo-mah-SEEN-tah
Uxmal	Oosh-MAHL
Xunantunich	Shoo-nahn-too-NEECH
Yaxchilan	Yash-chee-LAHN
Zaculeu	Zah-koo-LAY-oo

MAYA MANUSCRIPTS

Chilam Balam of Chumayel	Chee-LAHM Bah-LAHM Choo-mah-YELL
Popol Vuh	Poh-POL Vooh

Glossary

AGUADA a waterhole, most often in the Maya lowlands. A shallow, weedy rain catchment which may dry up during the dry season. Often was improved in ancient times by deepening and lining with clay and stone.

ALTARS stone monuments that may be sculptured, found commonly in nearly all regions of Mesoamerica within urban or ceremonial centers. An inaccurate name for what probably were thrones.

AMARANTH a small seeded bushy plant now considered a weed in most of the United States, but prehistorically harvested by New World groups, including many Mesoamerican societies.

ATLANTEAN FIGURES carved human figures in the form of a large or small column. These may hold up roofs (as at Tula) or low table-altars (as at Chichen Itza). Toltec period mainly.

ATLATL a spearthrower device. Very ancient and spread throughout the New World. Operates by acting as an extension of the arm and as a lever pushing the butt of the spear's shaft, thus increasing accuracy, length of throw, and striking power.

ATOLE a corn gruel, nourishing and palatable, used widely in ancient and modern Mesoamerica. Used for infants and the elderly especially because of easy digestibility.

BACKFRAME a wooden frame strapped to the back of a person to which were attached feathers and other symbolic and ornamental items. Usually part of elaborate elite class costuming.

BAJO a periodic swamp in the Maya lowlands. Up to 42% of the lowlands in the south are covered with such low areas which fill with water during the rainy seasons. Possibly were once shallow lakes which silted in due to erosion during the Maya Classic period.

BAKTUN a period of 144,000 days, or about 400 years, in the Maya long count calendar. The original Maya term for this period is unknown.

BALL GAME a game, played throughout Mesoamerica, that was played with a solid rubber ball in a formal court. Rules and courts varied, but generally the game was used for divination, with the future indicated by the outcome. It was also recreational. Earliest ball courts date from Chiapas ca. 1200 B.C. Game was most popular among the Classic Maya, to judge from the number of courts.

BIOME broadly defined as total communities of plants and animals; for example, temperate deciduous forest, or tropical rain forest. Each biome is made up of many specifically adapted biotic communities. Usually, these communities contain the variation at the level discussed in the section on development of agriculture.

CACAO beans of the cacao tree (*Theobroma cacao*) are used to produce chocolate. Native to Mesoamerica.

CALDERA a volcanic crater.

CALENDAR ROUND a shortened form of date which gives the day within the 260 day almanac and within the current 365 day calendar. However, these dates repeat themselves each 52 years. The Maya developed the long count in order to specify time more exactly.

CALICHE secondary calcium carbonate deposit usually found in lower soil zones and precipitated out of ground water or irrigation waters.

CALMECAC Aztec school for young men and women of the nobility. These schools were attached to specific temples.

CALPULE the head of a *calpulli*. A principal duty was as custodian of the land maps of the *calpulli*. Reported to the city-state ruler.

CALPULLI the Aztec social-residential unit which had land-holding, military, labor, religious, and political functions. Equivalent to George P. Murdock's *deme* (1949).

CANDELERO small, usually crudely made incense burner found in quantity at Teotihuacan. Associated with the apartment compounds and therefore assumed to have been part of "home" worship.

CAUSEWAY raised road of stone. In the Aztec case, these were dikes and roads through the lakes. In the Maya case causeways, or *sacbes,* were elevated roads across land.

CELT a form of small stone axe. Common as a manufactured item from Olmec times on. Usually highly polished.

CENOTE the Maya term for a sinkhole; cavity in the limestone area of Yucatan where the bedrock has collapsed and exposed the water table.

CEREMONIAL BAR OR STAFF bars or staffs which are usually richly ornamented and which apparently served as symbols of authority among Mesoamerican rulers. Equivalent in function to scepters of European rulers.

CEREMONIAL CENTER a collection of temple, administrative, and elite residence structures that serves as the focus of a dispersed urban center. Most population lived out in the country and congregated in the ceremonial center for markets and religious and political events. Mainly found in Olmec and Maya cultures.

CHACMUL (CHACMOOL, CHACMOL) literally, "red tiger." Actually, a stone sculpture of a reclining human figure with an offering plate on the stomach. These figures are characteristic of Toltec period culture and sat in front of temple doorways to receive initial offerings.

CHAPALOTE a primitive type of popcorn still grown in Mexico. The early wild corn found in the Tehuacan caves is chapalote.

CHIAN a bushy plant of the *Salvia* family which produces seeds. Used by the ancient Mesoamericans for oil and as a drink.

CHICHIMECA (GRAN CHICHIMECA) the northern mountain and desert lands beyond the limits of Mesoamerican civilization and inhabited by so-called barbarians. In reality, the inhabitants were a mixture of nomadic hunting-gathering groups, intermittent and marginal farmers, and farming communities. Interspersed among them were Mesoamerican trading and mining colonies. The Aztecs and other Mesoamericans may have been originally Chichimec immigrants from the north and west.

CHICLE sap from the zapote tree in the Maya lowlands is boiled down to make chicle, the ingredient in chewing gum that gives it "bounce."

CHINAMPA an agricultural field developed by swamp drainage, extensive irrigation, or filling operations along the edges of lakes. Especially characteristic of the Basin of Mexico, but also found elsewhere in the central highlands. The most productive of all intensive agricultural techniques developed in ancient Mesoamerica.

CHULTUN underground bell-shaped chambers dug in ancient times in the Maya lowlands. Through experimentation, the multiple chambered types have been shown to have been storage pits for ramon (breadnut tree) nuts. Some in northern Yucatan are immense and are lined with stucco to make them watertight and usable as cisterns.

CLOISONNE decorative technique by which a surface zone of a clay pot is scraped away while the pot is still soft. The zone is then filled with colored paint, and with differing zones and differing colors complex designs are created. Especially characteristic of Western Mexico and the Toltec period.

COA a wooden, spade-like instrument used in the Valley of Mexico and the central highlands generally for cultivation of fields.

COATEPANTLI literally, "serpent wall." Both Tula and Aztec Tenochtitlan had such walls which set apart the ceremonial precinct from the rest of the civic structures. In both cases, the wall was decorated with serpents.

CODEX a hand-drawn manuscript. In Mesoamerica, a screen-fold illustrated book of indefinite length. Made of either native paper (amate bark) or animal skin, lightly coated with plaster. Used for historical, religious, and tribute information. Codices were made both prehistorically and for a short time after the Spanish conquest. See also *lienzo*.

COMAL flat griddle made of pottery for the express purpose of cooking tortillas or flat, thin cakes of corn flour.

CONVERGENCE a phenomenon wherein two unrelated complex cultures independently developed similar features. These features are usually stylistically similar but functionally different; for example, wheels used on toys in Mesoamerica and wheels used on carts in the Old World.

COPAL Maya word for incense made from pine resin. Used extensively in ceremonies throughout Mesoamerica and still in use in the Maya highlands in religious affairs.

COPROLITE dried-out human feces. Often found in cave sites and useful for laboratory analysis of prehistoric diet.

CORBEL VAULT vault made without the use of keystone principle. Constructed by erecting two parallel stone walls and then gradually edging parallel courses of stone out towards one another until the space can be closed by a single capstone. In general, confined to the Classic Maya.

CORD MARKING pottery decoration technique achieved by wrapping a paddle with string. The still soft clay of the unfired pot is patted with the paddle and the string leaves the twisted marks of itself.

DANZANTES bas-relief sculptures from Monte Alban, Oaxaca, dating from the period of about 100 B.C. to 100 A.D.

DIFFUSION anthropological concept in which it is assumed that complex inventions or ideas are only likely to be invented once. The diffusion or spread of such ideas and inventions can be traced archaeologically.

EARSPOOLS OR EARPLUGS both terms refer to jewelry or decorative items commonly worn by both male and female Mesoamericans in pierced ears. Jade, feathers, gold, copper, and other materials were used.

EMBLEM GLYPHS glyphs in Maya writing which identify ceremonial centers or the ruling lineages of those centers. Deciphered by Heinrich Berlin in 1958.

FORMATIVE synonym for Preclassic, usually used for highland Mesoamerican cultures.

FRESCO used synonymously with mural (wall painting) and synonymously with the European technique of painting on a plastered surface while the plaster is still wet. Maya murals may have been painted this way or by other methods.

GLYPH a drawn symbol in a writing system. In Mesoamerican systems, a glyph may stand for a syllable, a sound, an idea, a word, or a combination of these qualities.

GRAPHEME a minimum unit of written meaning.

HACHA (Spanish: axe) An axe-like small stone sculpture which is usually carved into a human or animal likeness. Found most commonly in the Veracruz lowlands and Guatemalan highlands in Classic times.

HIEROGLYPH a term derived from Egyptology meaning literally, "priestly writing." Adopted in Mesoamerican archaeology to mean the depictive, art-related systems of writing developed there. Hieroglyphs are the units themselves. See *glyph*.

INCENSARIO an incense burner. Mesoamerican ceremonies, both religious and political, involved incense burning in special vessels made of pottery and sometimes of stone. These incensarios are often decorated with elaborate religious symbolism.

INITIAL SERIES Maya inscriptions of the Classic period often open with the complete designation of a point in time, using the "long count." This statement is the initial series.

KATUN a period of 7,200 days (about 20 years) in the Maya long count calendar. Used in the period 1250 A.D.–1520 A.D. as an abbreviated notation system for the longer dates used in the Classic period.

KIN (Maya: sun) The single day unit in the Maya calendar.

LIENZO a large, map-like document made of cloth or animal skin, similar to a codex. Often a map showing the traditional land holdings of a native community or family. The famous *Lienzo de Tlaxcala,* however, shows the Spanish Conquest and the important part played in it by the Tlaxcalans, traditional enemies of the Aztecs. Differs from a codex only in physical characteristics, being rectangular or irregular in shape instead of a long screen-fold of indefinite length.

LINTEL a beam of wood or stone supporting the wall above a doorway. In many Mesoamerican areas, these beams were carved with scenes and written texts.

LONG COUNT the Classic period Maya system of dating which could specify a point in time in infinity. Such a date is usually noted as being in a specific *baktun* (cycle of ca. 400 years), *katun* (cycle of ca. 20 years), *tun* (cycle of 360 days), *uinal* (cycle of 20 days), and on a specific day (*kin*). In addition, the day was specified in the cycles of 18 months of 20 days each, 20 named days, and 13 numbers.

"LOST WAX" PROCESS a metal casting technique much used by Mesoamericans of Protohistoric times. A wax sculpture is made and then a pottery casing formed around it, leaving several vents. Metal is poured in one of the vents and melted wax and heat leave by the other vents. The cooling metal assumes the shape of the wax sculpture by filling the inside form of the pottery casing.

LUNAR SERIES the part of the text following the date specification (initial series) part of a Classic Maya inscription. The subject is dating of the moon phase and notation of associated god(s).

MACEHUAL (PL. MACEHUATIN) a member of the Aztec commoner class and invariably a member of a *calpulli.* Theoretically a free man, but with obligations as a *calpulli* member and also through it to the city-state.

MANIKIN SCEPTER badge of office often held by Maya rulers depicted in Classic sculpture. The "manikin scepter deity" may be a corn god.

MAYEQUE a member of the Aztec serf class. Attached to the private estates of the aristocratic class (*pipiltin*) and therefore landless peasants. Apparently did not belong to a *calpulli.*

MAZAPAN WARE Toltec (Postclassic) period horizon marker in Central Mexico. Pottery of orange color was decorated with multiple, parallel, wavy red lines. Most often on *molcajete* forms.

MEGAFAUNA giant forms of animal species characteristic of the Pleistocene. At least three kinds of elephant and a giant species of bison (buffalo) existed in North America and either died out or were replaced by smaller species toward the end of the Ice Age.

METATE AND MANO food grinding apparatus of all Mesoamericans. *Metates* were slab or trough shaped stones and *manos* were loaf shaped stones used to grind the substance (e.g., corn) against the *metate.* Still in wide use in Mexico and Guatemala, although being replaced by village mills.

MEXICA literally, the followers of Meci, a legendary leader of the Aztecs or Mexica on their way from Aztlan or Chicomoztoc to the Basin of Mexico.

MOLCAJETE open bowl form with feet, and a roughened bottom. Usually interpreted as a chili grinder.

MUSHROOM STONE OR POT effigies of mushrooms in either clay or stone. Most common in late Preclassic period in the Maya area. May be associated with hallucinogenic mushrooms used to induce visions as a part of a religious experience.

NAHUA (NAHUAT, NAHUATL) Nahua are the speakers of an important language family. Nahuat is a group within that family and seems to be more ancient than the Nahuatl group. The Aztecs spoke Nahuatl.

OBSIDIAN DATING a means of absolute dating by which the hydration layers (patina) of a piece of obsidian are measured. The thickness of the hydration layers indicates how long it has been since the obsidian artifact was manufactured.

OLLA (Spanish: pot) Usually refers to pottery vessels used for cooking.

PALMA a specific kind of thin, portable sculpture designed to be worn in the belt as an ornament. Found in lowland Veracruz.

PATOLLI board game widespread in Postclassic Mesoamerica. The board and rules are somewhat like the South Asian game of pachisi, but there is apparently no historical connection between the games.

PERCUSSION technique by which stone flakes are removed from a block usually of flint or obsidian. A blow is struck with a stone at the edge of the block of stone (direct percussion), or a hammer stone is used to tap a chisel against the edge of the stone block (indirect percussion).

PETATE mat woven of reeds or grass and usually used for floor covering and sleeping mat. Still in use today.

PILLI (PL. PIPILTIN) a member of a current or former ruling lineage of the Aztec upper class.

PISOTE coatimundi; a medium to large rodent common in the tropical forests of Mesoamerica. There are two sizes: the smaller, which runs in packs; and the larger, which goes in pairs. One of many animals the Maya used as models for their glyphs.

PLEISTOCENE the last major stage of the Wisconsin glaciation. Generally dated as beginning about 100,000 years ago and having lasted until about 7,000 years ago.

PLUMBATE pottery type, decorated with a lead colored glaze. Manufactured in the Izapa-Tajumulco zone and widely traded throughout Mesoamerica in Postclassic times.

POCHTECA the long-distance merchants of Tlatelolco, the twin city of Aztec Tenochtitlan. Used also as a generic term for all long-distance merchants in Mesoamerica. Privileged and often aristocratic class sponsored by the state. Often acted as military and intelligence units.

POSOLE a drink in which maize dough is dissolved in water. The difference between *atole* and *posole* is one of degree, the latter being more diluted and the former often having additional sweetening and spices added.

POT IRRIGATION a simple irrigation method by which a pot of water is poured upon each plant in a narrow field around which are dug wells to the water table.

"POX" POTTERY pottery whose surface is dimpled with pockmarks created by poorly controlled firing. Expansion of the clay in the pottery caused bits of the surface to flake away leaving the dimples.

PUNCTATION pottery decoration technique by which the surface of a pot is indented by use of a sharply pointed instrument or even by fingernails.

PUTUN (MAYA) Chontal speaking Maya from the Tabasco zone of the Gulf coast. Natives from Poton-chan, a capital of the Chontal in the 16th century. May have invaded the Classic Maya lowlands at the end of the Classic period.

QUIDS chewed up and spat out mouthfuls of vegetable matter. Early corn was chewed for its juices, being such a small plant. Residue was discarded as a quid and these are often found in the dry caves of Mesoamerica.

REPOUSEE technique by which thin sheets of metal, usually gold or copper, are decorated. Cold hammering of the metal from the back raises the front of the piece into a design.

RESIST PAINTING pottery decoration technique in which the vessel is painted with the design in wax or grease. A slip or thin paint is then applied to the pot. Upon firing, the paint resting on the waxed areas is burnt away, leaving the design subtly shown in the unslipped areas.

ROCKER STAMPING technique of pottery decoration especially in vogue in Early and Middle Preclassic times. The rounded edge of a shell or sherd was rocked back and forth over the wet surface of a pot to form a continuous in-and-out line.

ROOF COMB a free-standing wall built atop Maya temples with the function of providing broad areas for modeling in stucco of human figures and hieroglyphs. Apparently fulfilled the same purpose as the stelae.

RUBBER native American plant (*Parthenium argentatum*) used for several purposes, including as an incense, for making dolls, effigies, and rubber balls for the ball game.

SACBE (Maya: white way) Raised causeway type roads which connect many groups of Maya ceremonial centers, internally and externally.

SETTLEMENT PATTERN STUDIES the study of the

disposition of houses and communities over the landscape. These patterns reveal relationships and hierarchical structures from which archaeologists deduce information such as social and political arrangements.

Shell midden middens are discard heaps. Shell middens resulted when the principal food used at a prehistoric site was shellfish.

Short count the same as the calendar round; an abbreviated Maya date.

Slate ware pottery tradition in the northern and intermediate lowlands of the Maya lowlands. Handsome, greenish-white pottery fabric which may or may not be decorated.

Slip a solution of clay and pigment either painted on a pot or into which a pot is dipped to give it a color other than that of its natural clay.

Stela erect stone monument, often sculptured. Olmec and Izapan cultures and the Maya used such monuments most often.

Stirrup jar jars with spouts so shaped that they form a stirrup from which a single orifice allows a flow of liquid.

Swidden synonym for slash-and-burn system of agriculture in which forest is cut down and the land cultivated for a time, abandoned, allowed to recover, and then the cycle repeated.

Talpetate a soil level in the Guatemalan highlands which is made up of compacted volcanic ash, yellowish and clay-like in characteristics.

Talud-tablero architectural feature characteristic of Teotihuacan Classic period. Used on terraced platforms in which each terrace slopes upward (the *talud*) toward a recessed vertical panel (the *tablero*).

Tamale a delicious dish in which a preparation of chopped meat is wrapped in a corn meal dough and then wrapped again in a corn shuck and steamed until done. Eaten piping hot after discarding the shuck.

Teccalli lower judicial court for Aztec commoners.

Tecomate literally, a gourd vessel, or a pottery vessel which looks like a gourd with the neck cut off. One of the earliest forms of pottery.

Tecuhtli (Nahuatl: lord) An honorific title given to various kinds of Aztec nobility, usu-

ally in combination with a modifying title; e.g., *amiztlato-Tecuhtli*, lord of the hunt.

Temple mound/pyramid Mesoamerican "pyramids" are actually platforms which are usually terraced and are never pyramidal in shape as are Egyptian pyramids. The platforms almost invariably supported temples of wood or stone, and are sometimes known as temple mounds. Archaeologists prefer to call them "temple structures."

Teosinte a grass and closest relative of maize or corn. There is argument over its relationship to corn and whether it is an ancestor or an offspring.

Tlachtli the Aztec word for the ball court in which the Mesoamerican ball game was played. Each town had at least one, it seems.

Tlacxitlan Aztec higher judicial court used for appeals from the *teccalli*. Also the principal law court for aristocrats.

Tlaloque the Aztec rain gods. Usually refers to the multitude of smaller helpers to the great rain god *Tlaloc*.

Tlatoque (pl. tlatoani) a city-state ruler of the Basin of Mexico, and member of the aristocratic *pipiltin* class. Usually from a hereditary leadership lineage within the class.

Tonalpohualli the Nahuatl name for the 260 day sacred almanac.

Tortillas flat, thin corn dough cakes cooked on a griddle (*comal*). Perhaps a relatively late and regional development in the use of corn flour in Mesoamerica. Substituted for wheat bread in ancient Mexico and Guatemala.

Trait a distinctive and notable cultural characteristic, such as a pottery decorative motif. Often used in old fashioned diffusion studies of archaeological cultures. The preference is now to study functionally related groups of traits.

Tripsacum member of the grass family and a relative of corn and *teosinte*.

Tumpline a band of leather or woven grass which can be attached to a heavy load. The load is lifted onto the lower back of the human porter and the band is placed around the forehead. At a dog trot, a Mesoamerican merchant could travel considerable distances with respectable loads. Still used today by itinerant merchants in the Maya highlands.

Tun a 360 day period in the Maya long count dating system.

Tzolkin the 260 day calendar among the Maya (who may not have used this word) made up of 20 named days and 13 numbers (20 × 13 = 260 combinations).

Tzompantli Nahuatl word for skull rack. The Aztecs displayed the skulls of their sacrificial victims on wooden frames in their town squares.

Uayeb the last, unlucky five days of the year in the Maya calendar.

Uinal a 20 day period in the Maya long count system of dating.

Volador ceremony a ritual still practiced today in Mexico. Dancers dressed as birds ascend to the top of a tall pole from which they launch themselves into the air upside down attached to the top of the pole by ropes. The ropes have been wound intricately around the pole and gradually unwind, bringing the dancers to the ground once more. In ancient times, there was much calendrical symbolism in the number of dancers, the number of revolutions in their descent, and other variables.

Were-jaguar (as in were-wolf) The major deity cluster of the Preclassic Olmec culture, characterized by combined jaguar and human figures.

Yoke-palma-hacha small stone sculpture complex from Classic period lowland Veracruz cultures. Yokes all may be associated with important dress used by ball players in ritual associated with the ball game.

Zoned dentate stamping technique of pottery decoration by which a zone was marked off by incised lines on the surface of a pot. The zone was then filled with marks that resemble those that would be left by a modern hair comb if the teeth were repeatedly jabbed into the wet clay. Especially favored in Early and Middle Preclassic.

Bibliography

ABBREVIATIONS

AMN   *Anales del Museo Nacional de Mexico,* Mexico City.

BAE   Bureau of American Ethnology, Smithsonian Institution, Washington, D.C.

CIW   Carnegie Institute of Washington, Washington, D.C.

HMAI   *Handbook of Middle American Indians.* Universiy of Texas Press, Austin.

ICA   International Congress of Americanists (meets every two years and alternates between New World and Old World)

INAH   Instituto Nacional de Antropologia e Historia, Mexico City.

MARI   Middle American Research Institute, Tulane University of Louisiana, New Orleans.

NWAF   New World Archaeological Foundation, Provo, Utah.

PMP   *Papers of the Peabody Museum,* Harvard University, Cambridge, Mass.

VUPA   Vanderbilt University Publications in Anthropology, Nashville, Tennessee.

Abascal, R., P. Davila, P. J. Schmidt, and D. Z. de Davila
   1976   La Arqueologia del Sur-Oeste de Tlaxcala (Primera Parte). Suplemento, *Comunicaciones, Fundacion Alemana para la Investigacion Cientifica,* No. 11. Puebla, Mexico.

Acosta, J. R.
   1956   "Resumen de los Informes de las Exploraciones Arqueologicas en Tula, Hidalgo, durante las VI, VII, VIII Temporadas, 1946–1950." INAH *Anales* 8:37–115.

   1964a   "El Palacio del Quetzalpapalotl." INAH, *Memoria,* No. 10.

   1964b   "La Decimotercera Temporada de Exploraciones en Tula, Hgo." INAH *Anales* 16:45–76.

   1972   "Exploraciones en Zaachila, Oaxaca." INAH *Boletin,* Epoca II, No. 3.

   1974   "La Piramide de El Corral de Tula, Hgo." In Matos Moctezuma, 1974: 27–50.

Adams, R. E. W.
   1969   "Maya Archaeology 1958–1968: A Review." *Latin American Research Review* 4:3–45.

   1970   "Suggested Classic Period Occupation Specialization in the Southern Maya Lowlands." In Bullard, 1970a:487–498.

   1971   "The Ceramics of Altar de Sacrificios." *PMP* 63, No. 1.

   1973   "Maya Collapse: Transformation and Termination in the Ceramic Sequence at Altar de Sacrificios. In Culbert, 1973:133–163.

   1974a   "A Trial Estimation of Classic Maya Palace Populations at Uaxactun." In Hammond, 1974:285–296.

   1974b   (Ed.) "Preliminary Reports on Archaeological Investigations in the Rio Bec Area, Campeche, Mexico." MARI Pub. 31:103–146.

1977a (Ed.) *The Origins of Maya Civilization.* Albuquerque: University of New Mexico Press.

1977b "Rio Bec Archaeology and the Rise of Maya Civilization." In R. E. W. Adams, 1977a.

Adams, R. E. W. and T. P. Culbert
1977 "The Origins of Civilization in the Maya Lowlands: Background for a Conference." In R. E. W. Adams, 1977a.

Adams, R. E. W. and J. L. Gatling
1964 "Noreste del Peten: Un Nuevo Sitio y un Mapa Arqueologico Regional." *Estudios de Cultura Maya* 4:99–118.

Adams, R. E. W. and A. Trik
1961 "Temple I (Str. 5D-1): Post-Constructional Activities." *Tikal Reports*, No. 7.

Adams, R. M.
1961 "Changing Patterns of Territorial Organization in the Central Highlands of Chiapas." *American Antiquity* 26:341–360.

1966 *The Evolution of Urban Society.* Chicago: Aldine.

Agrinier, P.
1960 "The Carved Human Femurs from Tomb 1. Chiapa de Corzo, Chiapas, Mexico." NWAF Paper No. 6.

Anales de Cuauhtitlan
1945 In *Codice Chimalpopoca.* Translated from Nahuatl to Spanish by Primo Feliciano Velazquez. Mexico: Imprenta Universitaria.

Anderson, W.
1971 "Arithmetic in Maya Numerals." *American Antiquity* 36:54–63.

Andrews, E. W., IV
1965 "Archaeology and Prehistory in the Northern Maya Lowlands." *HMAI*, Vol. 2:288–330.

1967 "Progress report on the 1960–64 field seasons." National Geographic Society–Tulane University Dzibil-

chaltun Program. MARI Pub. 31: 23–67.

1970 "Balankanche, Throne of the Tiger Priest." MARI Pub. 32.

Anonymous
1917 *Narrative of Some Things of New Spain and the Great City of Temestitan, Mexico.* New York: Cortes Society.

Armillas, P.
1971 "Gardens on Swamps." *Science* 174:653–661.

Aufdermauer, J.
1970 "Excavaciones en Dos Sitios Preclasicos de Moyotzingo, Puebla." In *Comunicaciones* 1. Fundacion Alemana para la Investigacion Cientifica.

1973 "Aspectos de la Cronologia del Preclasico en la Cuenca de Puebla-Tlaxcala." *Comunicaciones* 9:11–24. Fundacion Alemana para la Investigacion Cientifica.

Aveleyra Arroyo de Anda, L.
1964 "The Primitive Hunters." *HMAI*, Vol. 1:384–412. Austin: University of Texas Press.

Ball, J. W.
1974a "A Teotihuacan-Style Cache from the Maya Lowlands." *Archaeology* 27:2–9.

1974b "A Coordinate Approach to Northern Maya Prehistory." *American Antiquity* 39:85–93.

1977 "The Rise of the Northern Maya Chiefdoms: A Socioprocessual Analysis." In R. E. W. Adams, 1977a.

Ball, J. W. and J. D. Eaton
1972 "Marine Resources and the Prehistoric Lowland Maya: A Comment." *American Anthropologist* 74:772–776.

Barlow, R. H.
1949 *The Extent of the Empire of the Culhua Mexica.* Berkeley and Los Angeles: University of California Press, Ibero-Americana 28.

Beadle, G. W.
1972   "The Mystery of Maize." *Field Museum of Natural History Bulletin* 43, No. 10:2–11.

Becquelin, P.
1969   *Archeologie de la Region de Nebaj.* Paris: Université de Paris.

Bell, B.
1971   "Archaeology of Nayarit, Jalisco, and Colima." *HMAI*, Vol. 11:694–753.

1974a   *The Archaeology of West Mexico.* Ajijic: Sociedad de Estudios Avanzados del Occidente de Mexico, A.C.

1974b   "Excavations at El Cerro Encantado, Jalisco." In B. Bell, 1974a: 147–167.

Benson, E. P. (Ed.)
1968   *Dumbarton Oaks Conference on the Olmec.* Dumbarton Oaks Research Library and Collection, Washington, D.C.

Berlin, H.
1958   "El Glifo "Emblema" en las Inscripciones Mayas." *Jour. Societe des Americanistes de Paris* 47:111–119.

Bernal, I.
1949   "Exploraciones en Coixtlahuaca, Oax." *Revista Mexicana de Estudios Antropologicos* 10:5–76.

1964   "Introduction" to Duran, *The Aztecs: The History of the Indies of New Spain.* New York: Orion Press.

1965a   "Archaeological Synthesis of Oaxaca." *HMAI*, Vol. 3:788–813.

1965b   "Architecture in Oaxaca after the End of Monte Alban." *HMAI*, Vol. 3:837–848.

1966a   "Teotihuacan. Capital de Imperio?" *Revista Mexicana de Estudios Antropologicos* 20:111–146.

1966b   "The Mixtecs in the Archaeology of the Valley of Oaxaca." In Paddock, 1966a: 351–356.

1967   "Excavaciones en Dainzu." INAH *Boletin*, No. 27:7–13.

1969   *The Olmec World.* Berkeley and Los Angeles: University of California Press.

Binford, L. R. and S. R. Binford
1968   *New Perspectives in Archaeology.* Chicago: Aldine.

Blom, F.
1932   "The Maya Ball-Game *Pok-ta-pok* (Called *Tlachtli* by the Aztec)." MARI Pub. 4:485–530.

Borah, W.
1951   "New Spain's Century of Depression." *Ibero-Americana* Vol. 35.

Boserup, E.
1965   *The Conditions of Agricultural Growth.* Chicago: Aldine.

Brockington, D. L.
1973   "Archaeological Investigations at Miahuatlan, Oaxaca." VUPA Pub. No. 7.

1974   "Spatial and Temporal Variations of the Mixtec-Style Ceramics in Southern Oaxaca." Paper prepared for the 41st ICA, Mexico.

Brockington, D. L., M. Jorrin, and J. R. Long
1974   "The Oaxaca Coast Project Reports: Part I." VUPA Pub. No. 8.

Brockington, D. L. and J. R. Long
1974   "The Oaxaca Coast Project Reports: Part II." VUPA Pub. No. 9.

Bronson, B.
1966   "Roots and the Subsistence of the Ancient Maya." *Southwestern Journal of Anthropology* 22:251–279.

Brunhouse, R. L.
1973   *In Search of the Maya: The First Archaeologists.* Albuquerque: University of New Mexico Press.

Brush, C.
1965   "Pox Pottery: Earliest Identified Mexican Ceramic." *Science* 149: 194–195.

Bullard, W. R., Jr.
1960   "The Maya Settlement Pattern in Northeastern Peten, Guatemala." *American Antiquity* 25:355–372.

1970a   (Ed.) "Monographs and Papers in Maya Archaeology." *PMP*, Vol. 61.

1970b   "Topoxte: A Postclassic Maya Site

in Peten, Guatemala." In Bullard, 1970a:245–307.

1973   "Postclassic Culture in Central Peten and Adjacent British Honduras." In Culbert, 1973:221–241.

Byers D. S. (Gen. Ed.)

1967a   *The Prehistory of the Tehuacan Valley: Environment and Subsistence,* Vol. 1. Austin: University of Texas Press.

1967b   *The Prehistory of the Tehuacan Valley: The Nonceramic Artifacts,* Vol. 2. Austin: University of Texas Press.

Calnek, E. E.

1971   "Settlement Pattern and Chinampa Agriculture at Tenochtitlan." *American Antiquity* 37:104–115.

Carmack, R. M.

1973   *Quichean Civilization.* Berkeley: University of California Press.

Carneiro, R.

1970   "A Theory of the Origin of the State." *Science* 169:733–738.

Carr, R. F. and J. E. Hazard

1961   "Map of the Ruins of Tikal, El Peten, Guatemala." *Tikal Reports,* No. 11.

Carrasco, P.

1971a   "Social Organization of Ancient Mexico." *HMAI,* Vol. 10:349–375.

1971b   "The Peoples of Central Mexico and Their Historical Traditions." *HMAI,* Vol. 11:459–473.

Caso, A.

1942   "El Paraiso Terrenal en Teotihuacan." *Cuadernos Americanos* 1, No. 6:127–136.

1949   "El Mapa de Teozacoalco." *Cuadernos Americanos* 8:145–181. Mexico.

1960   *Interpretation of the Codex Bodley 2858.* Mexico City: Sociedad Mexicana de Antropologia.

1963   "Land Tenure among the Ancient Mexicans." *American Anthropologist* 65:863–878.

1965   "Zapotec Writing and Calendar." *HMAI,* Vol. 3:931–947.

1966a   "The Lords of Yanhuitlan." In Paddock, 1966a:313–335.

1966b   *Interpretacion del Codice Colombino* (includes English version). Mexico City: Sociedad Mexicana de Antropologia.

1967   "Los Calendarios Prehispanicos." Universidad Nacional Autónoma de México, *Inst. de Invest. Hist., Serie de Cultura Nahuatl, Monografias* No. 6.

1969   "El Tesoro de Monte Alban." INAH *Memoria,* No. 3.

Caso, A. and I. Bernal

1952   "Urnas de Oaxaca." INAH *Memoria,* No. 2.

Chadwick, R.

1971   "Archaeological Synthesis of Michoacan and Adjacent Regions." *HMAI,* Vol. 11:657–693.

Chamberlin, R. S.

1948   "The Conquest and Colonization of Yucatan." CIW Pub. 582.

Chilam Balam of Chumayel

1967   *The Book of Chilam Balam of Chumayel.* Translated by Ralph L. Roys. Norman: University of Oklahoma Press.

Childe, V. G.

1950   "The Urban Revolution." *Town Planning Review* 21:3–17.

Chimalpahin Quauhtlehuanitzin, D. F.

1965   *Relaciones Originales de Chalco Amaquemecan.* Mexico City: Fondo de Cultura Economica.

Cline, H.

1972   "The Relaciones Geograficas of the Spanish Indies, 1577–1648." *HMAI,* Vol. 12:183–242.

1973   "Selected Nineteenth-Century Mexican Writers on Ethnohistory." *HMAI,* Vol. 13:370–427.

Cobean, R. H.

1974   "The ceramics of Tula." In Diehl, 1974:32–41.

Cobean, R. H., et al.

1972   "Obsidian Trade at San Lorenzo, Tenochtitlan, Mexico." *Science* 174:666–671.

Coe, M. D.

1956   "The Funerary Temple among the Classic Maya." *Southwestern Journal of Anthropology* 12:387–493.

1960   "Archaeological Linkages with North and South America at La Victoria, Guatemala." *American Anthropologist* 62:363–393.

1964   "The Chinampas of Mexico." *Scientific American* 211:90–98.

1965a   "Archaeological Synthesis of Southern Veracruz and Tabasco." *HMAI*, Vol. 3:679–715.

1965b   "The Olmec Style and its Distributions." *HMAI*, Vol. 3:739–775.

1965c   *The Jaguar's Children: Pre-Classic Central Mexico.* New York: The Museum of Primitive Art.

1968a   *America's First Civilization.* New York: D. Van Nostrand Company.

1968b   "Map of San Lorenzo: an Olmec Site in Veracruz, Mexico." Department of Anthropology, Yale University.

1968c   "San Lorenzo and the Olmec Civilization." In Benson, 1968: 41–71 (incl. map).

1970   "The Archaeological Sequence at San Lorenzo, Tenochtitlan." University of California Archaeological Research Facility Contributions, No. 8:21–34.

1977   "Olmec and Maya: a Study in Relationships." In R. E. W. Adams, 1977a.

Coe, M. D., R. A. Diehl, and M. Stuiver

1967   "Olmec Civilization, Veracruz, Mexico: Dating of the San Lorenzo Phase." *Science* 155:1399–1401.

Coe, W. R., III

1959   "Piedras Negras Archaeology: Artifacts, Caches, and Burials." University of Pennsylvania, *University Museum Monographs.*

1965a   "Tikal, Guatemala, and Emergent Maya Civilization." *Science* 147:1401–1419.

1965b   "Tikal: Ten Years of Study of a Maya Ruin in the Lowlands of Guatemala." *Expedition* 8:5–56.

Colby, B. N. and P. L. van den Berghe

1969   *Ixil Country.* Berkeley: University of California Press.

Cook, O. F.

1921   "Milpa Agriculture, a Primitive Tropical System." Annual Report of the Smithsonian Institution, 1919.

Cook, S. F.

1949   "The Historical Demography and Ecology of the Teotlalpan." *Ibero-Americana* Vol. 33.

Cook, S. F. and W. Borah

1960   "The Indian Population of Central Mexico, 1531–1610." *Ibero-Americana* Vol. 44.

Cortes, H.

1963   *Cartas y Documentos.* Mexico City: Editorial Porrua.

Covarrubias, M.

1946   *Mexico South.* New York: Knopf.

1957   *Indian Art of Mexico and Central America.* New York: Knopf.

Cowgill, G. L.

1963   "Postclassic Period Culture in the Vicinity of Flores, Peten, Guatemala." Ph.D. dissertation, Department of Anthropology, Harvard University.

Cowgill, U. M.

1961   "Soil Fertility and the Ancient Maya." *Transactions of the Connecticut Academy of Arts and Sciences* 42:1–56.

1962   "An Agricultural Study of the Southern Maya Lowlands." *American Anthropologist* 64:273–286.

1971   "Some Comments on Manihot Subsistence and the Ancient Maya." *Southwestern Journal of Anthropology* 27:51–63.

Culbert, T. P.

1965   "The Ceramic History of the Central Highlands of Chiapas, Mexico." NWAF Paper, No. 19.

1973   (Ed.) *The Classic Maya Collapse.* Albuquerque: University of New Mexico Press.

1977   "Early Maya Development at Tikal, Guatemala." In R. E. W. Adams, 1977a.

Davies, C. N. B.
1968   *Los Senorios Independientes del Imperio Azteca.* Mexico City: INAH.

Davies, N.
1973   *The Aztecs.* London: Macmillan.

Denevan, W. M.
1970   "Aboriginal Drained-Field Cultivation in the Americas." *Science* 169: 647–654.

Denevan, W. M. and B. L. Turner, II
1974   "Forms, Functions and Associations of Raised Fields in the Old World Tropics. *The Journal of Tropical Geography* 39:24–33.

Diaz del Castillo, B.
1968   *Historia Verdadera de la Conquista de la Nueva Espana.* 2 volumes, 6th ed. Mexico City: Editorial Porrua, Nos. 6 and 7. Translated to English by A. P. Maudslay in 1908; of which there are various abridged editions, including *The Discovery and Conquest of Mexico.* New York: Farrar, Straus, and Giroux (1972).

Diehl, R. A. (Ed.)
1974   *Studies of Ancient Tollan: A Report of the University of Missouri Tula Archaeological Project.* Department of Anthropology, University of Missouri-Columbia.

Diehl, R. A., R. Lomas and J. T. Wynn
1974   "Toltec Trade with Central America: New Light and Evidence." *Archaeology* 27:182–187.

DiPeso, C. C.
1968   "Casas Grandes and the Gran Chichimeca." *El Palacio* 75:47–61.
1974   *Casas Grandes: A Fallen Trading Center of the Gran Chichimeca.* Amerind Foundation Publication, Flagstaff, Ariz.: Northland Press.

Drucker, P.
1943a   "Ceramic Stratigraphy at Cerro de las Mesas, Veracruz, Mexico." BAE Bulletin 141.
1943b   "Ceramic Sequences at Tres Zapotes, Veracruz, Mexico." BAE Bulletin 140.
1955   "The Cerro de las Mesas Offering of Jade and Other Materials." BAE Bulletin 157:25–68.

Drucker, P., R. Heizer, and R. J. Squier
1959   "Excavations at La Venta, Tabasco, 1955." BAE Bulletin 170.

Duran, D.
1964   *The Aztecs: The History of the Indies of New Spain.* Translated with notes by Doris Heyden and Fernando Horcasitas. New York: Orion Press.
1967   *Historia de Las Indias de Nueva Espana e Islas de la Tierra Firme.* Edited and annotated by Angel Ma. Garibay K. in 2 vols. Mexico City: Biblioteca Porrua, Vols. 36 and 37. (Includes the *History,* the *Book of the Gods and Rites,* and *The Ancient Calendar.*)
1971   *Book of the Gods and Rites* and *The Ancient Calendar.* Translated by Fernando Horcasitas and Doris Heyden. Norman: University of Oklahoma Press.

Eaton, J.
1975   "Prehistoric Maya Farmsteads in the Rio Bec Area." In *Contributions.* Berkeley; University of California Archaeological Research Facility.

Ekholm, G.
1944   "Excavations at Tampico and Panuco in the Huasteca, Mexico." *Anthropological Papers of the American Museum of Natural History* 38, No. 5.

Ekholm, G. F.
1964   "Transpacific contacts." In Jennings and Norbeck, 1964: 489–510. Chicago: University of Chicago Press.

Erasmus, C. J.
1965   "Monument Building: Some Field Experiments." *Southwestern Journal of Anthropology* 21:277–301.

Flannery, K. V.
1968   "The Olmec and the Valley of Oaxaca: A Model for Interregional Interaction in Formative Times." In Benson, 1968:79–110.

1972a   The Origins of the Village as a Settlement Type in Mesoamerica and the Near East: A Comparative Study. In P. Ucko, R. Tringham, and G. W. Dimbleby, 1972:25–53.

1972b   "The Cultural Evolution of Civilizations." *Annual Review of Ecology and Systematics* 3:399–426.

1973   "The Origins of Agriculture." *Annual Reviews of Anthropology* 2:271–310.

Flannery, K. V., A. V. Kirkby, and A. W. Williams, Jr.

1967   "Farming Systems and Political Growth in Ancient Oaxaca." *Science* 158:445–454.

Ford, J. A.

1969   *A Comparison of Formative Cultures in the Americas,* Vol. 11 of Smithsonian Contributions to Anthropology. Washington, D.C.: Smithsonian Institution.

Fritz, J. M. and F. Plog

1970   The Nature of Archaeological Exploration. *American Antiquity* 35:405–412.

Furst, P. T.

1974   "Ethnographic Analogy in the Interpretation of West Mexican Art." In B. Bell, 1974:132–146.

Gallegos, R.

1962   "Zaachila: The First Season's Work." *Archaeology* 16:226–233.

Gann, T.

1900   "Mounds in Northern Honduras." BAE 19th Annual Report, Part II: 665–692.

Garcia Payon, J.

1957   *El Tajin: Guia Oficial.* Mexico City: INAH.

1971   "Archaeology of Central Veracruz." *HMAI,* Vol. 11:505–542.

Gibson, C.

1964   *The Aztecs Under Spanish Rule: A History of the Indians of the Valley of Mexico, 1519–1810.* Stanford: Stanford University Press.

1971   "Structure of the Aztec Empire." *HMAI,* Vol. 10:376–394.

Gillmor, F.

1949   *Flute of the Smoking Mirror: A Portrait of Nezahualcoyotl, Poet-King of the Aztecs.* Tucson: University of Arizona Press.

1964   *The King Danced in the Market Place.* Tucson: University of Arizona Press.

Gomara, F.

1964   *Cortes: The Life of the Conqueror by His Secretary.* Translated and edited by Lesley Bird Simpson from *Istoria de la Conquista de Mexico.* Berkeley and Los Angeles: University of California Press.

Gorenstein, S.

1973   "Tepexi el Viejo: A Postclassic Fortified Site in the Mixteca-Puebla Region of Mexico." *American Philosophical Society Transactions* 63, Part 1.

Graham, J. (Ed.)

1966   *Ancient Mesoamerica: Selected Readings.* Palo Alto, Calif.: Peek Press.

Green, D. F. and G. W. Lowe

1967   "Altamira and Padre Piedra, Early Preclassic Sites in Chiapas, Mexico." NWAF Paper No. 20.

Grosscup, G. L.

1961   "A Sequence of Figurines from West Mexico." *American Antiquity* 26:390–406.

Grove, D. C.

1968   "The Pre-Classic Olmec in Central Mexico: Site Distribution and Inferences." In Benson, 1968.

1969   "Olmec Cave Paintings: Discovery from Guerrero, Mexico (Juxtlahuaca)." *Science* 164:421–423.

1970a   "The San Pablo Pantheon Mound: a Middle Preclassic Site in Morelos, Mexico." *American Antiquity* 35:62–73.

1970b   "The Olmec Paintings of Oxtotitlan Cave, Guerrero, Mexico." *Studies in*

Pre-Columbia Art and Archaeology, No. 6.

1973   "Olmec Altars and Myths." *Archaeology* 26:128–135.

1974a   "San Pablo, Nexpa, and the Early Formative Archaeology of Morelos, Mexico." VUPA Pub. No. 12.

1974b   *Chalcatzingo Symposium.* 42nd International Congress of Americanists, Mexico.

1974c   "The Highland Olmec Manifestation: A Consideration of What It Is and Isn't." In N. Hammond, 1974.

Guerra, F.
1964   "Maya medicine." *Medical History* 8:31–43.

1966   "Aztec medicine." *Medical History* 10:315–338.

Guillemin, J. F.
1966   "Iximche: Capital del Antiguo Reino Cakchiquel." Guatemala City: INAH de Guatemala.

Hammond, N.
1974a   (Ed.) *Mesoamerican Archaeology: New Approaches.* Austin: University of Texas Press.

1974b   "The Distribution of Late Classic Maya Major Ceremonial Centres in the Central Area." In N. Hammond, 1974a:313–334.

1977   "The Rise of Maya Civilization: A Position Paper." In R. E. W. Adams, 1977a.

Hammond, N., D. Pring, R. Berger, V. B. Switsur, and A. Ward
in press   "Radiocarbon Chronology for Early Maya Occupation at Cuello, Belize." *Nature,* London.

Harrison, P. D.
1974   "Archaeology in Southwestern Quintana Roo: Interim Report of the Uaymil Survey Project." Department of Anthropology, Trent University, Peterborough, Canada.

Haviland, W.
1968   "Ancient Lowland Maya Social Organization." MARI Pub. 26:93–117.

Hay, C. L., S. K. Lothrop, R. L. Linton, H. L.

Shapiro and G. C. Vaillant (Eds.)
1962   *The Maya and Their Neighbors,* 2nd ed. (1st ed., 1940). Provo: University of Utah Press.

Healan, D. M.
1974   "Residential Architecture at Tula." In R. A. Diehl, 1974.

Healey, P. F.
1974   "The Cuyamel Caves: Preclassic Sites in Northeast Honduras." *American Antiquity* 39:435–447.

Heizer, R. F.
1968   "New observations on La Venta." In E. Benson, 1968:9–36.

Heizer, R. F. and J. A. Bennyhoff
1972   "Archaeological excavations at Cuicuilco, Mexico, 1957." *National Geographic Society, Research Reports,* 1955–60 Projects:93–104.

Hester, T. R., R. F. Heizer, and J. A. Graham
1975   *Field Methods in Archaeology.* Palo Alto, Calif.: Mayfield Press.

Heyden, D.
1975   "An Interpretation of the Cave Underneath the Pyramid of the Sun in Teotihuacan, Mexico." *American Antiquity* 40, No. 2:131–147.

Hole, F. and R. F. Heizer
1973   *An Introduction to Prehistoric Archaeology,* 3rd Ed. New York: Holt, Rinehart and Winston.

Holland, W. R.
1964   "Contemporary Totzil Cosmological Concepts as a Basis for Interpreting Prehistoric Maya Civilization." *American Antiquity* 29:301–306.

Holmes, W. H.
1895–97   "Archaeological Studies Among the Ancient Cities of Mexico." *Field Museum, Anthropological Series* 1, No. 1.

Hooton, A. E.
1940   "Skeletons from the Cenote of Sacrifice at Chichen Itza." In Hay et al., New York: Appleton-Century, 1940.

Ixtlilxochitl, F.
1952   *Obras Historicas.* Mexico City: Editora Nacional.

Jennings, J. D. and E. Norbeck (Eds.)
1964   *Prehistoric Man in the New World.* Chicago: University of Chicago Press.

Jimenez-Moreno, W.
1941   "Tula y los Toltecas segun las Fuentes Historicas." *Sociedad Mexicana de Antropologia Revista* 5:79–83.
1966a   "Mesoamerica before the Toltecs." In J. Paddock, 1966a.
1966b   "Los Imperios Prehispanicas de Mesoamerica." *Sociedad Mexicana de Antropologia Revista* 20:179–195.

Johnson, F. (Ed.)
1972   *The Prehistory of the Tehuacan Valley,* Vol. 4. Austin: University of Texas Press.

Joralemon, P. D.
1971   "A Study of Olmec Iconography." *Studies in Pre-Columbia Art and Archaeology,* No. 7.

Kampen, M. E.
1972   *The Sculptures of El Tajin, Veracruz, Mexico.* Gainesville: University of Florida Press.

Kelley, D. H.
1974   "Eurasian Evidence and the Mayan Calendar Correlation Problem." In N. Hammond, 1974a:135–143.

Kelley, J. C.
1971   "Archaeology of the Northern Frontier: Zacatecas and Durango." *HMAI,* Vol. 11:768–801.

Kelly, I.
1943   "Notes on a West Coast Survival of the Ancient Mexican Ball Game." CIW *Notes on Middle American Archaeology and Ethnology,* No. 26.
1974   "Stirrup Pots from Colima: Some Implications." In B. Bell, 1974a:206.

Kelly, I. and A. Palerm
1952   *The Tajin Totonac.* Part 1: *History, Subsistence, Shelter and Technology.* Washington, D.C.: Smithsonian Institute, Institute of Social Anthropology Pub. No. 13.

Kidder, A. V., J. Jennings, and E. M. Shook
1946   "Excavations at Kaminaljuyu, Guatemala." CIW Pub. 561.

Kirchhoff, P.
1943   "Mesoamerica, Sus Limites Geograficos, Composicion Etnica y Caracteres Culturales." *Acta Americana* 1:92–107. Republished 1974 by Students Association, Escuela Nacional de Antropologia e Historia, Mexico. English translation in J. Graham, 1966.
1961   "Der Beitrag Chimalphains zur Geschichte der Tolteken." In *Beiträge zur Volkerforschung: . . . .* Berlin: Akademie-Verlag.

Kovar, A.
1970   "The Physical and Biological Environment of the Basin of Mexico." In W. T. Sanders et al., 1970:13–101.

Krickeberg, W.
1956   *Las Antiguas Culturas Mexicana.* Mexico City: Fondo de Cultura Economica.

Krieger, A. D.
1964   "Early Man in the New World." In J. D. Jennings and E. Norbeck, 1964.

Kroeber, A. L.
1963   *Configurations of Culture Growth.* Berkeley: University of California Press.

Krotser, P. and G. R. Krotser
1973   "The Life Style of El Tajin." *American Antiquity* 38:199–205.

Kubler, G.
1967   "The Iconography of the Art of Teotihuacan." *Studies in Pre-Columbian Art and Archaeology,* No. 4.

Landa, D.
1941   *Relacion de las Cosas de Yucatan.* English translation and notes by A. M. Tozzer. PMP, No. 18. Spanish edition by Garibay, 1966, Mexico City: Editorial Porrua.

Lange, F. W.
1971   "Marine Resources: A Viable Subsistence Alternative for the Prehistoric Lowland Maya." *American Antiquity* 73:619–639.

Leon-Portilla, M.
1961   *Los Antiguos Mexicanos, a Traves de sus Cronicas y Cantares.* Mexico City: Fondo de Cultura Economica.

Litvak-King, J.
1970   "Xochicalco en la Caida del Clasico: Una Hipotesis." *Anales de Antropologia*:101–124.

Lorenzo, J. L.
1965   "Tlatilco: Los Artefactos." INAH *Investigaciones* 7.

Lothrop, S. K.
1952   "Metals from the Cenote of Sacrifice, Chichen Itza, Yucatan." *Peabody Museum Memoirs* 10, No. 2.

1961   (Ed.) *Essays in Precolumbian Art and Archaeology.* Cambridge: Harvard University Press.

1964   *Treasures of Ancient America.* Skira Editions d'Art. New York: Crown Publishers.

Lowe, G.
1962   "Mound 5 and Minor Excavations, Chiapa de Corzo, Chiapas, Mexico." NWAF Paper No. 12.

1971   "The Civilizational Consequences of Varying Degrees of Agricultural and Ceramic Dependence within the Basic Ecosystems of Mesoamerica." University of California Archaeological Research Facility Contributions, No. 11:212–248.

1977   "Priority and Persistence of the Mixe-Zoquean Ceremonial Center in Prehispanic Southern Chiapas. In R. E. W. Adams, 1977a.

Mace, C. E.
1973   "Charles Etienne Brasseur de Bourbourg, 1814–1874." *HMAI,* Vol. 13: 298–325.

MacNeish, R. S.
1954   "An Early Archaeological Site Near Panuco, Veracruz." *American Philosophical Society Transactions* 44, Part 5.

1958   "Preliminary Archaeological Investigations in the Sierra de Tamaulipas, Mexico." *American Philosophical Society* 48, Part 6.

1962   *Second Annual Report of the Tehuacan Archaeological Botanical Project.* Andover, Mass.: R. S. Peabody Foundation for Archaeology.

1964   "Ancient Mesoamerican Civilization." *Science* 143:531–537.

1966   "Speculations about the Beginnings of Village Agriculture in Meso-America." *Actas y Memorias del 35a Congreso Internacional de Americanistas* 1:181–185.

1970   (Gen. Ed.) *The Prehistory of the Tehuacan Valley: Ceramics,* Vol. 3. Austin: University of Texas Press.

1971   "Early Man in the Andes." *Scientific American* 224:36–46.

1972   (Gen. Ed.) *The Prehistory of the Tehuacan Valley: Chronology and Irrigation,* Vol. 4. Austin: University of Texas Press.

Mangelsdorf, P. C.
1974   *Corn: Its Origin, Evolution, and Improvement.* Cambridge: Belknap Press, Harvard University Press.

Mangelsdorf, P. C., R. S. McNeish, and W. C. Galinat
1967   "Prehistoric Wild and Cultivated Maize." In D. S. Byers, 1967a.

Marcus, J.
1973   "Territorial Organization of the Lowland Maya." *Science* 180:911–916.

Margain, C. R.
1971   "Pre-Columbian Architecture of Central Mexico." *HMAI,* Vol. 10: 45–91.

Marquina, I.
1960   "El Templo Mayor de Mexico." Mexico City: INAH.

1964   *Arquitectura Prehispanica,* 2nd Ed. INAH *Memoria* I.

1970   (Ed.) "Proyecto Cholula." INAH *Investigaciones* Vol. 19.

1971   "The Paintings at Cholula." *Artes de Mexico,* No. 140:32–40.

Martin, P. S. and P. J. Mehringer, Jr.
1965   "Pleistocene Pollen Analysis and

Biography of the Southwest." In H. E. Wright, Jr. and D. G. Frey (Eds.) *The Quaternary of the United States, Biogeography: Phytogeography and Palynology,* Part II: 433–451. Princeton: Princeton University Press.

Matos Moctezuma, E.
1974   "Proyecto Tula (la Parte)." INAH *Coll. Cientifica* Vol. 15.

McAndrew, J.
1965   *The Open-Air Churches of Sixteenth-Century Mexico.* Cambridge: Harvard University Press.

McBryde, F. W.
1947   *Cultural and Historical Geography of Southwest Guatemala.* Smithsonian Institution Institute of Social Anthropology Publication No. 4.

McLeod, M. J.
1973   *Spanish Central America: A Socioeconomic History: 1520–1720.* Berkeley: University of California Press.

Medellin-Zenil, A.
1960   *Ceramicas del Totonacapan.* Xalapa: Universidad de Veracruz.

Meggers, B. J. and C. Evans
1962   "The Machalilla Culture: An Early Formative Complex on the Ecuadorian Coast. *American Antiquity* 18:186–192.

Meighan, C.
1972   "Matanchen Complex: New Radiocarbon Dates on Early Coastal Adaptation in West Mexico." *Science* 175:1242–1243.

1974   "Prehistory of West Mexico." *Science* 184:1254–1261.

Melgar, J. M.
1869   "Antiguedades Mexicanas, notable escultura antigua." Boletin de la Sociedad Mexicans de Geografica y Estadistica, Epoca 2, Vol. 1, pp. 292–297. Mexico City: Mexico.

Merwin, R. E. and G. C. Vaillant
1932   "The Ruins of Holmul, Guatemala." *Peabody Museum Memoirs* 3, No. 2.

Miles, S. W.
1965   "Sculpture of the Guatemala-Chiapas Highlands and Pacific Slopes, and Associated Hieroglyphs." *HMAI,* Vol. 2:237–275.

Miller, A. G.
1973   *The Mural Painting of Teotihuacan.* Washington, D.C.: Dumbarton Oaks.

Millon, C.
1972   "The History of Mural Art at Teotihuacan." In *Teotihuacan, XI Mesa Redonda,* Vol. 2:1–16. Mexico City: Sociedad Mexicana de Antropologia.

1973   "Painting, Writing, and Polity at Teotihuacan, Mexico." *American Antiquity* 38:294–314.

Millon, R.
1967   "Teotihuacan." *Scientific American* 216:38–49.

1970   "Teotihuacan: Completion of Map of Giant Ancient City in the Valley of Mexico." *Science* 170:1077–1082.

1973   *"The Teotihuacan Map,* Vol. 1, Part 1 (text). Austin: University of Texas Press.

Millon, R., B. Drewitt, and G. Cowgill
1973   *The Teotihuacan Map,* Vol. 1, Part 2 (maps). Austin: University of Texas Press.

Morley, S. G.
1937–38 *The Inscriptions of Peten.* CIW Pub. 437 in 5 vols.

1946   *The Ancient Maya.* Stanford: Stanford University Press.

Morris, A. A.
1931   "Murals from the Temple of the Warriors and Adjacent Structures." In E. H. Morris, J. Charlot and A. A. Morris, 1931.

Morris, E. H., J. Charlot, and A. A. Morris
1931   "The Temple of the Warriors at Chichen Itza." CIW Pub. 406. 2 vols.

Murdock, G. P.
1949   *Social Structure.* New York: Macmillan.

National Geographic Society
1968   *Archaeological Map of Middle*

America, researched and compiled by George E. Stuart. Washington, D.C.: National Geographic Society.

Nicholson, H. B.

1960 "The Mixteca-Puebla Concept in Mesoamerican Archaeology." In J. Graham, 1966.

1971a "The Religious-Ritual System of Late Prehispanic Central Mexico." *Verhandlungen des 38th Internationalen Amerikanisten-kongresses* 3:223–238.

1971b "Religion in Prehispanic Central Mexico." *HMAI,* Vol. 10:395–446.

1973 "Eduard Georg Seler, 1849–1922." *HMAI,* Vol. 13:348–369.

Noguera, E.

1954 *La Ceramica Arqueologica de Cholula.* Mexico City: Editorial Guarania-Mexico.

Norman, G.

1973 "Izapa Sculpture. Part 1: Album." NWAF Paper, No. 30.

Oliveros, Jose Arturo

1974 "Nuevas exploraciones en El Openo, Michoacan." In B. Bell, 1974a:182–201.

Padden, R. C.

1967 *The Hummingbird and the Hawk: Conquest and Sovereignty in the Valley of Mexico, 1503–1541.* Columbus: Ohio State University Press.

Paddock, J.

1966a (Ed.) *Ancient Oaxaca.* Stanford: Stanford University Press.

1966b "Oaxaca in Ancient Mesoamerica." In J. Paddock, 1966a.

1966c "Mixtec Ethnohistory and Monte Alban V." In J. Paddock, 1966a.

1974a "Mesoamerica No Es el Valle de Mexico." Paper prepared for the 41st ICA, Mexico.

1974b "Mixtec-Puebla Culture in the Valley of Oaxaca." Paper prepared for the 41st ICA, Mexico.

Palerm, A. and E. Wolf

1960 "Ecological Potential and Cultural Development in Mesoamerica." *Social Science Monographs* 3:1–38.

Parsons, J. R.

1968 "Teotihuacan, Mexico, and its Impact on Regional Demography." *Science* 162:872–877.

1974 "The Devolopment of a Prehistoric Complex Society: A Regional Perspective from the Valley of Mexico." *Journal of Field Archaeology* 1:81–108.

Parsons, L. A.

1967–69 "Bilbao, Guatemala: An Archaeological Study of Pacific Coast Cotzumalhuapa Region." *Milwaukee Public Museum Publications in Anthropology,* Nos. 11 and 12.

Pasztory, E.

1974 *The Iconography of the Teotihuacan Tlaloc.* Washington, D.C.: Dumbarton Oaks.

Pendergast, D. M.

1962 "Metal Artifacts from Amapa, Nayarit, Mexico." *American Antiquity* 27:370–379.

Peterson, D. A. and T. B. MacDougall

1974 "Guingola: A Fortified Site in the Isthmus of Tehuantepec." VUPA Pub. No. 10.

Piggott, S.

1965 *Ancient Europe.* Chicago: Aldine.

Pina Chan, R.

1958 "Tlatilco: 1 and 2." INAH *Investigaciones,* Nos. 1 and 2.

1962a "Las Pinturas de Mul-Chic, Yucatan." INAH *Boletin* 8:1–3.

1962b "Informe Preliminar Sobre Mul-Chic, Yucatan." INAH *Anales* 15:99–118.

Pollock, H. E. D.

1965 "Architecture of the Maya lowlands." *HMAI,* Vol. 3:378–440.

Pollock, H. E. D., R. L. Roys, T. Proskouriakoff, and A. L. Smith

1962 "Mayapan, Yucatan, Mexico." CIW Pub. 619.

Popol Vuh

1971 "The Book of Counsel: The *Popol Vuh* of the Quiche Maya of Guatemala." Translated by Munro Edmonson. MARI Pub. 35.

Porter, M. N.
1953   "Tlatilco and the Preclassic Cultures of the New World." *Viking Fund Publications in Anthropology*, No. 19.

Potter, D. F.
1973   "Maya Architectural Style in Central Yucatan." Ph.D. dissertation Department of Anthropology, Tulane University.

Price, B. J.
1971   "Prehispanic Irrigation Agriculture." *Latin American Research Review* 6:3–60.

Proskouriakoff, T.
1960   "Historical Implications of a Pattern of Dates at Piedras Negras, Guatemala." *American Antiquity* 25:454–475.
1961   "The Lords of the Maya Realm." *Expedition* 4:14–21.
1962   "Civic and Religious Structures of Mayapan." In H. E. D. Pollock et al., 87–163.
1963   "Historical Data in the Inscriptions of Yaxchilan, I." *Estudios de Cultural Maya* 3:149–167.
1964   "Historical data in the inscriptions of Yaxchilan, II." *Estudios de Cultura Maya* 4:177–201.
1974   "Jades from the Cenote of Sacrifice, Chichen Itza, Yucatan." *Peabody Museum Memoirs* 10, No. 1.

Puleston, D. E.
1968   "Brosimum Alicastrum as a Subsistence Alternative for the Classic Maya of the Central Southern Lowlands." M.A. thesis, University of Pennsylvania.
1971   "An Experimental Approach to the Function of Maya Chultuns." *American Antiquity* 36:322–335.

Quirarte, J.
1972   "El Juego de Pelota en Mesoamerica: Su Desarrollo Arquitectonico." *Estudios de Cultura Maya* 8:83–96.
1973   "Izapan-Style Art: A study of Its Form and Meaning." *Studies in Pre-Columbian Art and Archaeology*, No. 10.
1975   "Wall Paintings at Santa Rita, Corozal." Belize *National Studies* 3, No. 4:5–29.
1977   "Early Art Styles of Mesoamerica and Early Classic Maya Art." In R. E. W. Adams, 1977a.

Rands, R. L.
1955   "Some Manifestations of Water in Mesoamerican Art." BAE Bulletin 157:265–394.
1973   "The Classic Maya Collapse: Usumacinta Zone and the Northwestern Periphery." In T. P. Culbert, 1973: 165–206.
1977   "The Rise of Classic Maya Civilization in the Northwestern Zone: Isolation and Diffusion." In R. E. W. Adams, 1977a.

Rathje, W. L.
1971   "The Origin and Development of Lowland Classic Maya Civilization." *American Antiquity* 36:275–285.
1973   "Classic Maya Development and Denouement: A Research Design." In T. P. Culbert, 1973:405–456.

Reichel-Dolmatoff, G.
1965   *Columbia*. New York: Praeger (Ancient Peoples and Places series, No. 44).

Reina, R.
1967   "Milpas and Milperos: Implications for Prehistoric Times." *American Anthropologist* 69:1–20.

Religion en Mesoamerica.
1972   Mexico City: Revista Mexicana de Estudios Antropologicos.

Robertson, D.
1970   "The Tulum Murals: The International Style of the Late Post-Classic." *Verhandlungen des 38th Internationalen Amerikanistenkongresses* 2:77–88.

Romero Quiroz, J.
1963   *Teotenanco y Matlatzinco (Calixtla-*

huaca). Mexico City: Ediciones del Gobierno del Estado de Mexico.

Roys, L.
1934   "The engineering knowledge of the Maya." CIW Pub. 436, Contrib. No. 6.

Roys, R.
1957   "The Political Geography of the Yucatan Maya." CIW Pub. 613.

1962   "Literary Sources for the History of Mayapan." In H. E. D. Pollock et al, 1962:25–86.

1965a   "Lowland Maya Native Society at Spanish Contact." *HMAI*, Vol. 3: 659–678.

1965b   *Ritual of the Bacabs*. Norman: University of Oklahoma Press.

1966   "Native Empires in Yucatan: the Maya-Toltec Empire." *Sociedad Mexicana de Antropologia Revista* 20:153–177.

1972   *The Indian Background of Colonial Yucatan*. Norman: University of Oklahoma Press.

Ruppert, K., J. E. S. Thompson, and T. Proskouriakoff
1955   "Bonampak, Chiapas, Mexico." CIW Pub. 602.

de Sahagun, B.
1950–69   *General History of the Things of New Spain. Florentine Codex*. English translation by Charles E. Dibble and Arthur J. O. Anderson. 12 volumes. Provo: The School of American Research and the University of Utah.

Sanchez, G. I.
1961   *Arithmetic in Maya*. Privately printed, 2201 Scenic Drive, Austin, Texas.

Sanders, W. T.
1956   "The Central Mexican Symbiotic Region." In G. R. Willey, 1956.

1963   "Cultural Ecology of the Maya Lowlands, Part II." *Estudios de Cultura Maya* 30:203–241.

1965   *Cultural Ecology of the Teotihuacan Valley*. Department of Sociology and Anthropology, Pennsylvania State University.

1970   "The Population of the Teotihuacan Valley, the Basin of Mexico and the Central Mexican Symbiotic Region in the Sixteenth Century." In W. T. Sanders et al., 1970:385–487.

1973   "The Cultural Ecology of the Lowland Maya: A Reevaluation." In T. P. Culbert, 1973:325–365.

Sanders, W. T., A. Kovar, T. Charlton, and R. A. Diehl
1970   "The Natural Environment, Contemporary Occupation and 16th Century Population of the Valley." The Teotihuacan Valley Project, Final Report, Vol. 1. *Occasional Papers in Anthropology*, No. 3, Department of Anthropology, Pennsylvania State University.

Sanders, W. T. and J. W. Michels
1969   "Kaminaljuyu Project — 1968 Season: Part 1, The Excavations." *Occasional Papers in Anthropology*, No. 2. Department of Anthropology, Pennsylvania State University.

Sanders, W. T. and B. J. Price
1968   *Mesoamerica: The Evolution of a Civilization*. New York: Random House.

Satterthwaite, L., Jr. and E. K. Ralph
1960   "Radiocarbon Dates and the Maya Correlation Problem." *American Antiquity* 26:165–184.

Saul, F. P.
1972   "Human Skeletal Remains of Altar de Sacrificios." *PMP* 63, No. 2.

1973   "Disease in the Maya Area: The Pre-Columbian Evidence." In T. P. Culbert, 1973:301–324.

Schilling, E.
1939   "Die 'schwimmenden Gärten' von Xochimilco." *Schriften d. Geogr. Inst. d. Univ. Kiel, Bd.* 9, Heft. 3.

Scholes, F. V. and R. L. Roys
1948   "The Maya Chontal Indians of Acalan-Tixchel." CIW Pub. 560.

Sejourne, L.
1966   *Arquitectura y Pintura en Teotihua-*

can. Mexico City: Siglo Vientiuno, Editores, S. A.

Seler, E.
1960 "Die Ruinen auf dem Quie-ngola." *Gesammelte Abhandlungen . . . ,* Vol. 2:184–199. Graz, Austria: Akademische druck und-Verlags Anstat.

1963 *Commentaries al Codice Borgia.* 3 vols. Traduccion de Mariana Frenk. Mexico City: Fondo de Cultura Economica.

Service, E. R.
1962 *Primitive Social Organization: An Evolutionary Perspective.* New York: Random House.

Sharer, R.
1974 "The Prehistory of the Southeastern Maya Periphery." *Current Anthropology* 15:165–187.

Sharer, R. J. and J. C. Clifford
1970 "Preclassic Ceramics from Chalchuapa, El Salvador, and Their Relationships with the Maya Lowlands." *American Antiquity* 35:441–462.

Sheets, P. D.
1971 "An Ancient Natural Disaster." *Expedition* 14:24–31. University of Pennsylvania.

Shimkin, D.
1973 "Models for the Downfall: Some Ecological and Culture-Historical Considerations." In T. P. Culbert, 1973:269–300.

Siemens, A. H. and D. E. Puleston
1972 "Ridged Fields and Associated Features in Southern Campeche: New Perspectives on the Lowland Maya." *American Antiquity* 37:228–239.

Sisson, E. B.
1973 *First Annual Report of the Coxcatlan Project.* Andover, Mass: R. S. Peabody Foundation for Archaeology.

1974 *Second Annual Report of the Coxcatlan Project.* Andover, Mass.: R. S. Peabody Foundation for Archaeology.

Slavin, A. J.
1973 *The Precarious Balance: English Government and Society.* Vol. 3 of the *Borzoi History of England.* New York: Knopf.

Smith, A. L.
1950 "Uaxactun, Guatemala: Excavations of 1931–1937." CIW Pub. 568.

1955 "Archaeological Reconnaissance in Central Guatemala." CIW Pub. 608.

1961 "Types of Ball Courts in the Highlands of Guatemala." In S. K. Lothrop, 1961:100–125.

Smith, M. E.
1973 *Picture Writing from Ancient Southern Mexico.* Norman: University of Oklahoma Press.

Smith, R. E.
1955 Ceramic Sequence at Uaxactun, Guatemala. MARI Pub. 20.

Spooner, B. (Ed.)
1972 *Population Growth: Anthropological Implications.* Cambridge: MIT Press.

Spores, R.
1965 "The Zapotec and Mixtec at Spanish Contact." *HMAI,* Vol. 3:962–987.

1967 *The Mixtec Kings and Their People.* Norman: University of Oklahoma Press.

1969 "Settlement, Farming Technology, and Environment in the Nochixtlan Valley." *Science* 166:557–569.

1972 "An Archaeological Settlement Survey of the Nochixtlan Valley, Oaxaca." VUPA No. 1.

Stephens, J. L.
1949 *Incidents of Travel in Central America, Chiapas, and Yucatan.* New Brunswick, N.J.: Rutgers University Press.

1963 *Incidents of Travel in Yucatan.* New York: Dover.

Steward, J. H.
1955 *Theory of Culture Change.* Urbana: University of Illinois Press.

1961 "The Urban Focus: Is There a Common Problem and Method in Studies of City Development—a

Science of Urbanology?" *Science* 134:1354–1356.

Stirling, M. W.
1943 "Stone Monuments of Southern Mexico." BAE Bulletin 138.
1965 "Monumental Sculpture of Southern Veracruz and Tabasco." *HMAI*, Vol. 3:716–738.

Thompson, E. H.
1938 "The High Priest's Grave, Chichen Itza, Yucatan, Mexico." Ed. with notes by J. E. S. Thompson. Chicago: Field Museum of Natural History, Anthropological Series 27, No. 1.

Thompson, J. S.
1950 *Maya Hieroglyphic Writing: An Introduction.* CIW Pub. 589; reprinted, Norman: University of Oklahoma Press.
1965 "Maya hieroglyphic writing." *HMAI*, Vol. 3:632–658.
1966 *The Rise and Fall of Maya Civilization,* 2nd ed. Norman: University of Oklahoma Press.
1970 *Maya History and Religion.* Norman: University of Oklahoma Press.
1972 "Maya Hieroglyphs without Tears." London: British Museum.
1974 " 'Canals' of the Rio Candelaria Basin, Campeche, Mexico." In N. Hammond, 1974a:297–302.

Tolstoy, P.
1969 "Review of Sanders and Price 1968." *American Anthropologist* 71:544–558.

Tolstoy, P. and L. I. Paradis
1970 "Early and Middle Preclassic Culture in the Basin of Mexico." *Science* 167:344–351.

Torres Guzman, M.
1972 "Hallazgos en El Zapotal, Ver." INAH *Boletin,* Epoca II, No. 2.

Tozzer, A. M.
1957 *Chichen Itza and Its Cenote of Sacrifice: A Comparative Study of Contemporaneous Maya and Toltec.*

Peabody Museum Memoirs, Vols. 11 and 12.

Turner, B. L., II
1974 "Prehistoric Intensive Agriculture in the Mayan Lowlands." *Science* 185:118–124.

Ucko, P., R. Tringham, and G. W. Dimbleby
1972 *Man, Settlement and Urbanism.* London: Gerald Duckworth and Co., Ltd.

Vaillant, G. C.
1941 *The Aztecs of Mexico.* Second edition revised by Suzannah B. Vaillant, 1962. Garden City, N.Y.: Doubleday.

Villagra Caleti, A.
1971 "Mural painting in central Mexico." *HMAI,* Vol. 10:135–156.

Vogt, E. Z.
1971 "The Genetic Model and Maya Cultural Development." In E. Z. Vogt and A. Ruz, 1971:9–48.

Vogt, E. Z. and A. Ruz
1971 *Desarrollo Cultural de Los Mayas,* 2nd ed. Mexico City: Universidad Nacional Autonoma de Mexico, Centro de Estudios Mayas.

Wallrath, M.
1967 "Excavations in the Tehuantepec Region, Mexico." *American Philosophical Society Transactions,* 57, Part 2.

Watson, P., S. A. LeBlanc, and C. L. Redman
1971 *Explanation in Archaeology: An Explicitly Scientific Approach.* New York: Columbia University Press.

Wauchope, R.
1965 *They Found the Buried Cities.* Chicago: University of Chicago Press.

Webb, M. C.
1973 "The Peten Maya Decline Viewed in the Perspective of State Formation." In T. P. Culbert, 1973:367–404.

Webster, D.
1974 "The Fortifications of Becan, Cam-

peche, Mexico." In R. E. W. Adams, 1974b:123–128.

1977   "Warfare and the Evolution of Maya Civilization." In R. E. W. Adams, 1977a.

West, R.
1964   "Surface Configuration and Associated Geology of Middle America." *HMAI*, Vol. 1:33–83.

West, R. and P. Armillas
1950   "Las Chinampas de Mexico." *Cuadernos Americanos* 50:165–182.

Weiant, C. W.
1943   "An Introduction to the Ceramics of Tres Zapotes, Veracruz, Mexico." BAE Bulletin 139.

Weigand, P.
1968   "The Mines and Mining Techniques of the Chalchihuites Culture." *American Antiquity* 33:45–61.

1974   "The Ahualulco Site and the Shaft-Tomb Complex of the Etzatlan Area." In B. Bell, 1974a.

Wicke, C. R.
1971   "Olmec: An Early Art Style of Pre-Columbian Mexico." Tucson: University of Arizona Press.

Willey, G. R.
1956   Settlement Patterns in the New World (Ed.). New York: Viking Fund Publication in Anthropology, No. 23.

1962   "The Early Great Styles and the Rise of the Pre-Columbian Civilizations." *American Anthropologist* 64: 1–14.

1967   *Alfred Vincent Kidder, 1885–1963. A Biographical Memoir.* Washington, D.C.: National Academy of Sciences.

1972   "The Artifacts of Altar de Sacrificios." *PMP* 64, No. 1.

1973   "The Altar de Sacrificios Excavations: General Summary and Conclusions." *PMP* 64, No. 3.

1974   "The Classic Maya Hiatus: A Rehearsal for the Collapse?" In N. Hammond, 1974a:313–334.

1977a   "The Rise of Classic Maya Civiliza-

tion: A Pasion Valley Perspective." In R. E. W. Adams, 1977a.

1977b   "A Synthetic Model for the Origins of Maya Civilization." In R. E. W. Adams, 1977a.

Willey, G. R., W. R. Bullard Jr., J. B. Glass, and J. C. Gifford
1965   "Prehistoric Maya Settlements in the Belize Valley." *PMP* No. 54.

Willey, G. R. and J. C. Gifford
1961   "Pottery of the Holmul I style from Barton Ramie, British Honduras." In S. K. Lothrop, 1961.

Willey, G. R., R. Millon, and G. Ekholm
1964   "The Patterns of Farming Life and Civilization." *HMAI*, Vol. 1: 446–498.

Willey, G. R. and P. Phillips
1958   *Method and Theory in American Archaeology.* Chicago: University of Chicago Press.

von Winning, H.
1961   "Teotihuacan Symbols: The Reptile's Eye Glyph." *Ethnos* 26: 121–166.

1974   "The Shaft Tomb Figures of West Mexico." Southwest Museum Papers, No. 24.

von Winning, H. and O. Hammer
1972   *Anecdotal Sculpture of Ancient West Mexico.* Los Angeles: Ethnic Arts Council of Los Angeles.

Winter, M. C.
1974   "Residential Patterns at Monte Alban, Oaxaca, Mexico." *Science* 186: 981–987.

Woodbury, R. B. and J. A. Neely
1972   "Water Control Systems of the Tehuacan Valley." In F. Johnson 1972.

Woodbury, R. B. and A. S. Trik
1953   *The Ruins of Zaculeu, Guatemala.* Richmond, Va.: William Byrd Press.

Zorita, A.
1963   *Life and Labor in Ancient Mexico: The Brief and Summary Relation of the Lords of New Spain.* Translation and introduction by B. Keen. New Brunswick, N.J.: Rutgers University Press.

Index